Noel 'Razor' Smith was born in London in 1960. He has fifty-eight criminal convictions and has spent the greater portion of his adult life in prison. Whilst in prison he taught himself to read and write, gaining an Honours Diploma from the London School of Journalism and an A Level in Law. He has received a number of Koestler awards for his writing and has contributed articles to the *Independent*, the *Guardian*, *Punch*, the *Big Issue*, the *New Statesman* and the *New Law Journal*. Smith is currently serving a life sentence for armed robbery. *A Few Kind Words and a Loaded Gun* is his first book.

A Few Kind Words and a Loaded Gun

The Autobiography of a Career Criminal

RAZOR SMITH

PENGUIN BOOKS

Published by the Penguin Group
Penguin Books Ltd, 80 Strand, London WC2R ORL, England
Penguin Group (USA) Inc., 375 Hudson Street, New York, New York 10014, USA
Penguin Group (Canada), 90 Eglinton Avenue East, Suite 700, Toronto, Ontario, Canada M4P 2Y3
(a division of Pearson Penguin Canada Inc.)
Penguin Ireland, 25 St Stephen's Green, Dublin 2, Ireland (a division of Penguin Books Ltd)
Penguin Group (Australia), 250 Camberwell Road,
Camberwell, Victoria 3124, Australia (a division of Pearson Australia Group Pty Ltd)
Penguin Books India Pvt Ltd, 11 Community Centre,
Panchsheel Park, New Delhi – 110 017, India
Penguin Group (NZ), cnr Airborne and Rosedale Roads, Albany,
Auckland 1310, New Zealand (a division of Pearson New Zealand Ltd)
Penguin Books (South Africa) (Pty) Ltd, 24 Sturdee Avenue,
Rosebank, Johannesburg 2196, South Africa

Penguin Books Ltd, Registered Offices: 80 Strand, London WC2R ORL, England

www.penguin.com

First published by Viking 2004
Published in Penguin Books 2005

011

Copyright © Noel Smith, 2004
All rights reserved

The moral right of the author has been asserted

Printed in England by Clays Ltd, St Ives plc

ISBN-13: 978–0–141–01579–8

www.greenpenguin.co.uk

Dedicated to my son, Joseph Stephen Smith
1982–2001
See you at the crossroads, kid

'Sometimes you can get more with a few kind words and a loaded gun than you can with just a few kind words'

– Alphonse 'Scarface' Capone, 1929

Acknowledgements

Writing this book has sometimes been a very dark journey for me, and I would like to thank some of the people who helped to light the way. Firstly my family, for putting up with me and always being there when I needed them. Will Self, for all his hard work on my behalf, for always having something positive to say, and for his invaluable supply of pipe-lore. Tony Lacey and all at Penguin, without whom you would not be reading this. Julian Broadhead, for all his help and encouragement over many years. John Bowers and the team at *Inside-Time*, James Morton and the *New Law Journal*, John McVicar and *Punch*, Duncan Campbell and the *Guardian*, and the *New Statesman*, who all allowed my writing to take up space on their pages. Joe, Sharon and Parris Regan, for the regular Red Cross parcels. Liam and 'Ginge' McClean, of the Essex branch of the family. Dave C., John Simmons, Steve Bunker, 'Big Beat' Kris, and Nicky 'Ugly Mates' Wood. All the members of the Balham Wildkatz, the Battersea Katz and those who were 'rockin'. All the chaps on Red Spur, A-wing, HMP Whitemoor, and all the good and loyal friends I have made, both inside and out, over the years.

And most of all, those who have been the most constant light in my life – Denise, Dean, Joe and Lianne.

Contents

1. Quo Vadis?

6 January 1998
London Road, west Croydon

I didn't feel at all conspicuous in my bulky leather coat and woollen hat. The wind was whistling around my ears, chill with the promise of snow. My hands, thrust deep into my pockets, were sweating inside the surgical gloves. My right hand gripped the butt of the Walther 9mm pistol, and I kept flicking the safety-catch on and off. It was a sign of nerves. I hated the waiting, I always had. To the casual glance of a passer-by, I hoped I looked like a normal man, just waiting for a bus. But I wasn't normal. And I wasn't waiting for a bus.

Andy caught my eye from the public phone-box across the street and grinned nervously. His voice crackled loudly in my earpiece.

'Just unloading now,' he said. We were using hands-free mobile phones, and we kept communications to the minimum.

I nodded slightly, and turned my gaze toward the plate-glass windows of the Midland bank, which was situated to the left of the phone-box. I could see the blue crash helmets of the two security guards as they handed over the money-box to the chief cashier. Despite the cold, my back felt clammy under the layers of clothing, and my mouth was drier than a witch's tit.

I turned slightly and nodded to Danny. He was pretending to be engrossed in the small-ad cards in the window of a newsagents, but he had one eye on me. He shrugged and slapped his gloved hands together against the cold. He was ready. I hunched my head into my upturned collar and spoke into the hands-free mike without moving my lips: 'T? It's a "go". Start her up.' Tommy was parked around a corner in the getaway car, monitoring the airwaves.

My heart rate kicked up a gear as the adrenaline began to flood my body. I was itching to be on the move, and it took all of my willpower to keep standing still and outwardly calm. This was the moment that every adrenaline junkie lives for; the intoxicating rush that comes from knowing that you are about to step into a dangerous unknown. Professional robbers call this 'the buzz', and it can be just as addictive and destructive as any Class A drug habit.

The two guards came out of the bank and climbed back into their security van. The driver indicated and pulled out into traffic. I was vibrating like a tuning fork. I took a deep breath which seemed to shudder into me. My limbs were starting to feel leaden, as though I was rooted to the spot. I suddenly felt very tired and knew it was the effect of an adrenaline overload. It was flight or fight time. I swallowed, hard, and my mind let out a massive roar – 'GO!'

As soon as I stepped off the pavement it was like the world had just come into sharp focus. My senses switched to maximum input; I could taste acrid exhaust-fumes on my tongue, I could hear the click-click-click of a car indicating at the traffic lights and the tension-heavy breathing of Danny as he fell into step beside me. We crossed the road at a brisk pace, our eyes seeking and checking every parked vehicle and shop doorway one final time. As a team we were top of the Flying Squad's 'most wanted' list, and they loved nothing more than a 'ready-eye' ambush. Their propensity to shoot first and shout warnings only when the gunsmoke had cleared was legendary.

Andy stepped from the phone-box and fell into step behind our march across the wide pavement. As I reached for the door of the bank a strange and unfamiliar thought fleetingly crossed my mind: 'You can stop now. It's not too late to walk away.' My hand hesitated six inches from the door handle, and Danny bumped into me. I immediately forced the treacherous notion from my consciousness and pushed the door open.

As I stepped into the bank I was instantly aware of a rush of warm air on my chilled face and the hum of quiet conversation coming from the banking hall. We slid through the familiar motions like a well-oiled robbery machine. Woollen hats were pulled down over features to reveal only eyes and mouth. Danny produced a fearsome-looking fireman's axe, Andy shook out a folded plastic bag and I got a good grip on the gun.

We had honed our performance over many such bank robberies. We each had a part to play and we knew those parts intimately. I was always the gunman, the 'heavy', the 'frightener'; it was my job to put the fear of God into bank staff and civilians and make sure everything ran smoothly and quickly. Any 'have-a-go heroes' would be dealt with by me. I was first man in and last man out. Danny was the 'doorman'; his job was to make sure nobody left the premises before the job was done. He also had to make sure that anyone who came in while the robbery was in progress stayed in. Andy was the 'bagman'. He would collect and bag up the cash.

There were two customers in the banking hall, both males in their mid-thirties. Four cashiers, including the chief cashier, were busying themselves behind the counter along with several clerical staff. I came into the hall like a whirlwind. Before anyone knew what was happening I had my pistol pointed at a customer's head.

'Down! Get the fuck down!' I roared menacingly.

He dropped like a stone, and the other customer quickly followed. I stepped up to the counter and pointed the gun at the bullet-proof screen so the staff could get a good look at it.

'You all know the drill,' I shouted. 'We're here for the reserve. No fucking about, just hand it over and no one gets shot.'

Andy was already up at the counter, bag at the ready, but the staff were still in shock. I was used to this, and I knew how to get them moving. I stood over one of the downed customers and pointed the gun at his head. I pointed my free hand at the chief cashier.

'Move!' I screamed. 'Or I'll put his brains all over the carpet!'

One of the women cashiers gave a little groan and then fainted. The chief cashier, an Asian man with a pencil moustache, hurried forward and began to unlock his safe. I kept the gun pointed at the customer. He had both his hands crossed over his head and he was sobbing in terror. The second customer looked up at me, anger on his face. I switched the gun to him. 'Who you fucking looking at? You even attempt to get off that fucking floor and I'll put one in you,' I growled at him.

He put his head back down.

Andy was loading the packets of money into the bag as fast as they came across the counter. We had been told that there would be £100,000 in cash in the reserve. For a moment the only sounds in the banking hall were the sobbing of the customer and the swish of the packets hitting the bag. I looked over at Danny. He had his back to us, keeping his eyes on the street outside. A movement behind the jump caught my eye and I saw one of the clerical staff duck into a back office. Probably gone to press the silent alarm. It didn't matter, we were just about finished.

'How we doing, Number Two?' I called to Andy.

He brushed the last packets into the bag with his arm, then gave me a thumbs-up. 'That's the lot,' he said. 'Unless you want me to get the cash drawers as well?'

There might be another five grand in the cash drawers, and so far we were ahead of schedule. 'Fuck it, get the lot,' I said.

I knew I was pushing it, but the buzz was on me strong and I was reluctant to end it, the comedown was a bitch. I knew that even if the silent alarm had been activated it would take a good eight minutes before the police would be on their way. The alarm would sound at the bank's security HQ; they would try to confirm that it had not been pushed by accident, then notify the nearest police station and Flying Squad office, who would then have to radio whoever was close and mobile. The chances of being caught in the commission of a robbery, unless the police knew in advance, were very low.

Only one of the cash drawers was unlocked, so the cashiers had to come forward and unlock their own drawers. After the third one, even I was getting itchy. I looked up at the security cameras that dotted the banking hall; they had been getting some cracking smudges from the moment we burst in. It was time to go.

'How many left, Number Two?' I asked.

'Three more,' said Andy.

'Leave them,' I said. 'We're off.'

Andy came past me, clutching the bag in both arms, and headed for the door. I heard Danny in my earpiece, checking with Tommy and letting him know we were on our way out. I stepped over to the customer who had given me the angry look. I crouched down by his head and kept the gun pointed at him. He looked up at me and still looked pissed off.

'It ain't your money, pal,' I said. 'Now, it's all over and nobody's been hurt. So just fucking chill out. 'Cos if you try to come after us, I won't hesitate to kill you. Understand?'

He nodded.

I joined the rest of the team at the door. This was the most dangerous moment for us. If anyone had noticed anything suspicious we could be walking out into an ambush. We had only been inside the bank for a few minutes, but the street outside was once again unchecked territory. I held open the door and let Andy and Danny slip out. I glanced back into the banking hall to make sure the customers were still prone. I stepped out, pocketed the gun and rolled my mask up into a hat. The boys were waiting for me, and they had rolled their masks up too. We walked briskly away.

My scalp was crawling and my back felt like one huge target as we hurried across London Road. I kept expecting to hear the sounds of shouting or gunfire, but nothing happened. We reached a sidestreet and ducked into the alley where Tommy was waiting behind the wheel of a four-door Vauxhall with the engine running. We piled into the car and drove sedately away without attracting any attention.

By the time we reached the flop, I was really feeling the comedown. My hands were shaking, my guts were churning, and I had the makings of a blinding headache. For every high there is a low. Normally, the fact that we had got away with the prize would be enough to buoy me up, but all I felt was sick, and slightly depressed. I remembered how I had hesitated on reaching the bank door. That was a first for me. I had always been supremely confident when committing crime: it was my element. I craved the feeling of power from taking over a strip of pavement or a banking hall and imposing my version of reality on it, for even a short time. It was a rush that no amount of cocaine or Ecstasy could imitate. But now I just felt guilty.

The boys were laughing and joking as they emptied the money on to the floor. Cruising on post-job euphoria and relief, they seemed like children let loose in a chocolate factory. Big, ugly kids, mind you. Andy held up two sealed packets of £50 notes and kissed each one in turn. Tommy and Danny were singing a chorus of 'We're in the Money'. I flopped into an armchair and peeled off my surgical gloves. The gun was digging into my ribs, so I pulled it from my pocket, checking that the safety-catch was on. I had always liked guns, and I had a particular liking for the weight and feel of the Walther. Guns were the tools of my trade, and without them I would not be able to make such a good living. A good gun is to be prized and taken care of, and the Walther was a good gun. I had paid £500 for it, which was about average for a handgun in London. It had been nicked off a burglary out in the sticks by a couple of junkies. I had only fired it twice, but the Walther had served me well. Now, looking at it, I felt an irrational loathing for it. For the first time, I saw how ugly and evil it must look to someone who has it pointed in their face. It felt too smooth and oily, too black and deadly. I dropped it on the floor and wiped my hand on my T-shirt.

I lit a cigarette and leant back in the chair. Images from the bank flooded my mind: the shocked faces of the cashiers, the woman who fainted, the sobbing customer who thought he was going to die and the anger and, yes, contempt on the face of the second customer. What were they doing now, right at this moment? Telling their story to the police? Struggling to recover from their ordeal? I had never given a second thought to my victims before. When you do what I do for a living you can't afford to think of the target as having any human dimension. It's them or me. They've got it and I want it, and if anything gets in my way, tough.

I had always had this strange notion that armed robbery was an honourable profession. I didn't go around coshing pensioners for their bingo money, or burgling people's homes or raping women and children; I was the cream of the criminal classes, a 'blagger', one of the heavy mob, a modern-day highwayman. I didn't steal from poor people's pockets, I robbed the rich, the banking and insurance institutions. People who could afford it. The only 'victims' of my crimes were the faceless money-shufflers who had to tally up what was nicked. I was almost a Robin Hood figure, for fuck's sake! Or was I?

Not once in my life had I questioned my criminality. I just accepted it as my lot. I embraced the life of crime and punishment as though it was my only friend. I loved the excitement and danger of living life on the edge, the vagaries of fate deciding whether I would be shot, stabbed or nicked. I craved the recognition of being a 'face' in, and out of, prison, and I loved the respect I got from others in my world. I relished the courtroom battles in which I could pit my wits against the top people in the educated straight world, and sometimes beat them at their own game. What else could someone like me hope for? It was odds on I was never going to play midfield for Chelsea and marry a popstar.

Why was I feeling like this? Is this how it happens? Can you suddenly just have enough of something, get so sated that it begins to make you sick? I could imagine eating so many cream cakes or crabsticks or watching so many Chuck Norris videos that they would make me ill; but this was my life I was thinking about. I tried to analyse what might be different about today that would make me think like this. Maybe I was losing my bottle. I was thirty-seven years old and I had been committing armed robberies since I was fifteen. Most of my life had been spent either in prison or on the run. What a waste. And here I was, fast approaching middle age, doing the same old self-destructive shit I had always done. I felt uncomfortable with these thoughts.

I watched the boys as they counted the money. No one noticed that I didn't join in. Andy and Danny were experienced robbers; they had both already served long prison sentences in some of the toughest jails in the country for it. Tommy, the wheel-man, had a background in cannabis cultivation, for which he had served time in the same prisons as the rest of us, and had only joined the team originally to get the cash to bankroll a huge skunk-growing operation. But, like the rest of us, once he got a taste for the money and excitement, everything else took second place.

We were a good team – staunch, loyal and totally committed to our profession and each other. I would trust these men with my life and I knew they felt the same about me. When not 'working', we socialized with each other and each other's families. One phone-call in times of trouble, from any of us, would be enough to get the other three to drop everything and come running.

On the surface we had our lives sorted. We made decent money and had plenty of leisure time in which to spend it. But deep inside, we all knew that one day – maybe tomorrow, maybe next week – we could be brought to book and forced to pay for what we were doing. Our payment might involve a bullet in the head from a Flying Squad ambush or a long stay in a top-security prison via the Old Bailey. We were professional career criminals and we knew the score. The best we could hope for was a good long run before the hammer dropped. We would cram as much 'good living' as we could into whatever time we had, storing up experiences as memories to sustain us during the bad decades. Every single moment was lived to the full and then carefully packed away; we were like bears gorging themselves before hibernation.

Nobody spoke about going back to prison. That kind of thing

was a bok, a bad omen, and I have never met a robber who was not superstitious. We all had our little good-luck moves. Andy, though not religious, would cross himself before stepping into a bank. Danny always had to wear the same Reebok jacket on a bit of work and walk the getaway route the day before the job. Tommy had his lucky driving-gloves. And me? I always removed one bullet from the gun and put it in my pocket. The rituals of armed robbery.

We would hit two or three targets per month, mainly banks, working on snippets of information given, or bought, from our vast network of criminal associates, or sometimes from unsuspecting members of the 'straight-going' public. Mini-cab drivers are the best, they just cannot keep their mouths shut for five minutes. When the first Ikea superstore opened in Croydon, they had an account with local mini-cab firms to ferry their management to and from work. I learned that they had taken a quarter of a million pounds on their first weekend and that they were worried about their 'sub-standard security' just by talking to a mini-cab driver who drove Ikea's accounts manager and his secretary to work. The driver had no idea that I was a robber, but I gave him a £10 tip at the end of my journey and took his personal card for future reference. Coming a close second to mini-cab drivers in the information stakes are disgruntled employees who think that what they blurt out in their local pub at the weekend is covered by the rules of the confessional. The information is out there, floating around all the time, and there are people who make a good living from catching it and selling it on.

In reality, by the final decade of the twentieth century, bank-robbery had become a dying game. Gone were the halcyon days of the 1960s and 70s, when an enterprising young blagger could vault the counter of his local NatWest and put a bit of cosh about before scarpering with one hundred large. The days of sawn-off shotguns on the highstreet at lunchtime, sawn-off jeans on the beach in Marbella at teatime, were nothing more than a warm, fuzzy memory for most of the heavy mob. During the

Thatcher era, the sensible blagger invested his ill-gotten in the drugs boom and then retired to the Costa del crime to count his profits.

Robbing banks became passé, a mug's game, fit only for desperate junkies who wielded fake guns and didn't have enough sense to wear a mask. At best, all they could get was the till money – enough to keep them in skag heaven for a couple of weeks; and also enough to get them twelve years in jail. The real money came from robbing money in transit or from kidnapping supermarket managers and making them hand over the takings. You could still stick up security guards walking across the pavement, but the insurance limit had dropped to fifteen grand a bag, and they were only allowed to carry one bag at a time. And security had come a long way from the days when the guard was equipped with a police whistle. Now there was CCTV everywhere, and there were bank screens that shot up to the ceiling, screamer-alarms, exploding dye-packs, automatic-locking bankdoors, bullet-proof glass, tracking devices in the money-packs and security vans that emitted a loud electronic warning when a robbery was in progress.

The police had also upped their game and were now more willing to shoot first and shout warnings later. The names of the men who had been shot dead by the police in ambush were well known to all of us. Some of them had been friends and associates. The Flying Squad (Special Operations 8) dealt only with armed robbery in London, and they cherished their reputation as hard, violent coppers. Trojan Units also cruised the streets of London twenty-four hours a day, armed 'gunships' just waiting for a radio-call that would allow them to unleash their awesome weaponry on the unsuspecting robber.

But the professional robber is nothing if not resourceful, and in the last years of the 1990s bank robbery, against all odds, was going through something of a renaissance. This was due to one small piece of information, known only to a handful of blagging teams in the capital. It became known that there was one small window of opportunity in the routine of certain banks when large amounts of cash were vulnerable. This was known to us as 'The Reserve Game'. The reserve is the cash that every bank will need in order to carry out its business over the month. This cash has to be delivered by a security firm, and as most bank vaults work on a time-lock and the delivery van could be held up in traffic, the exact time of this delivery cannot be known in advance. The day is known, and whether the delivery will be in the morning or the afternoon, but the rest is just an estimate. So when the reserve arrives, instead of going straight into the vault, it is locked into a small safe under the chief cashier's counter.

For us the hard work was in finding out which day the reserve was expected, and this was mainly done by picking a good-sized bank and putting it under observation for a while. If six cash-bags were delivered on a Thursday afternoon, it was odds on that this was the reserve. Then it was just a matter of being ready to go in as soon as the van left after its next delivery. We didn't have to call attention to ourselves by pulling guns and rolling about on the pavement with the guards, we could just take it from the chief cashier. It did not always work out. Sometimes we got the timing wrong and had to be content with robbing the till money, but we chalked that up to experience and moved on to the next target.

We knew we were on the Flying Squad's 'most wanted' list by now, but what we didn't know was that we were the subject of regular briefings by three of the four London squads. Tower Bridge squad had nicknamed us 'The Laughing Bank-Robbers' because while robbing the Midland Bank in Clapham on Christmas Eve we had worn Santa hats over our ski-masks and wished staff and customers a 'merry Christmas and a happy New Year' before making our getaway with a few timely 'ho, ho, ho's. We gave the expression 'laughing all the way to the bank' a new meaning. When you cop for thirty large the day before Christmas it does tend to lighten your mood, no matter what line of work you're in.

The team had finished counting the cash, and the notes were

stacked up nicely, most of it still in plastic packets. Andy worked out the total on a pocket calculator.

'Not as much as we expected,' he said, 'but still a nice little earner.'

I nodded. 'How much?' I asked.

'Forty-two thousand, three hundred and seventy. That's forty G from the reserve, and the rest is till-money. About a ton and a half of the till-money is scrag-ends.'

Scrag-ends are the odd and damaged notes that find their way into every bank-till eventually. Scottish banknotes, ripped notes, burned notes and notes damaged by exploding dye-packs. 'OK,' I said. 'Burn the scrag. The odd two hundred goes into the kitty for exes. That leaves ten and a half grand each. Do the share-out, Andy, and make sure the fifties and the brand-new notes are shared out evenly.'

As we all came from different parts of London, an even share of any notes that might be traceable would save them all turning up in the same area and giving Old Bill a clue.

As Andy sorted the cash into even shares, the rest of us gathered up the robbery kit: coats, masks, gloves and weapons were bagged up ready for depositing in our hired lock-up. The slaughter was paid for in cash and hired under a false name that could not be traced back to any of us, and the robbery kit would be stored there until the morning of our next job. One of the things we had learned from previous nickings was never to keep evidence around where it could be tied in to us. Though we knew from experience that the Squad would not hesitate to plant evidence to get a conviction, it was not the done thing to make it too easy for them.

Tommy got busy putting a joint together, some of his own-grown skunk. He used a dye-stained £10 note from the small pile of scrag to light it. I dutifully took a couple of puffs when it was passed to me, but I didn't feel much like getting stoned. I went over to the window and cracked the curtains. It was getting dark outside and, apart from the usual late-afternoon traffic, everything seemed quiet and normal. We had got away with it again, and though I should have been filled with happy relief, I just felt strange and empty.

Danny volunteered to deposit the happy-bag in the slaughter, as he would be passing it on his way back to North London. He had his own legal motor parked up a couple of streets away from the flop, but the rest of us had to phone for cabs. We had reached the flop in the getaway car, which was now well ablaze in an underground car park half a mile away. Our 'changeover car' was parked across the road from the flop, and if it was still there on Monday it would be used as the getaway car on our next bit of work.

I was responsible for buying all the cars we used on our jobs. I sometimes spent a Saturday afternoon cruising the used-car forecourts looking for suitable rides. They had to be respectable-looking, four-doored and have at least a month's worth of tax on the windscreen. We could ill afford a tug for no tax when we were tooled up and plotted on a bit of work. I paid cash for the cars and claimed it back from the exes off the job. The normal price range I dealt in was between £150 and £400. The cars never had to go far.

Danny gathered his cash and the happy-bag, and made his goodbyes before heading off. We would all be meeting up the next day for a drink and a few lines of charlie in a safe boozer we knew over in Camden Town, just four middle-aged, obviously affluent blokes who sometimes talked in whispers and played pool for £50 a game. The governor of the pub called us 'the Four Yuppies' in his jocular Irish manner, but he always invited us to stay for the lock-in.

Tommy went next. We had all phoned different cab firms and requested cabs at half-hourly intervals so we weren't seen walking out of the flop like a gang. Tommy had changed into a suit and tie and, with his money in a cheap briefcase, he looked like a slightly stoned tax inspector. When he was gone I had a chance to talk to Andy.

Andy was my best pal on the team. We had been through a lot together, fought and plotted our way through the hardest jails in the country and partied like lunatics when times were good. Once, during an escape attempt from a prison in Dorset, Andy had managed to scramble up our home-made rope to the top of the prison wall, but when I tried, the rope snapped about half-way up the wall and left me stranded inside the prison grounds. Andy could have dropped to freedom, and he was serving a ten-year sentence, but he didn't hesitate, he dropped back into the prison. 'If you don't go, then I don't go,' was his explanation.

'I think I might be losing my bottle,' I blurted out.

Andy broke up laughing and told me to leave the skunk alone because it was making me paranoid. I explained about my hesitation at the door of the bank, and how I kept thinking about the way the geezer in the banking hall had looked at me.

'Fuck him,' Andy replied. 'He's just some nine-to-five mug, a straight-goer. Who gives a fuck what them people think?'

I was silent for a moment, trying to collect my thoughts, and then I said, 'Let me ask you this, do you ever think about the people we rob? Do you ever feel that we shouldn't be doing this? Does it ever feel wrong to you?'

Andy looked serious and shook his head. 'Nope. I don't think about it at all, and neither should you. All we do is put the frighteners on them so we can claim the prize. Nobody gets killed, and nobody gets seriously hurt unless they go begging for it. Now forget this shit. This is what we do, and we do it well.'

His explanation might easily have been my own, and there was some relief for me in his confirmation. I shrugged and smiled. 'Yeah. Fuck 'em!' I said.

Later, as I sat in the back of the cab heading home, I felt slightly better about the day's events. My headache had faded, and the sick, hollow feeling in my stomach was gone. Andy was right, I would be a mug to think too closely about the rights and wrongs of what we were doing. I had made my choices a long time ago and now was not the time to start getting a conscience – if that's what it was. And even supposing that I did want to get out of

the life, what else would I do? I was thirty-seven, with no qualifications, a record of fifty-eight previous convictions and an
employment history with more gaps than the London Underground. By law I had to declare my previous to any prospective
employer: I might as well have turned up at every job interview
dressed as the grim reaper and sucking on a crack-pipe. No one
in their right mind was going to employ me.

All the talk about people who have 'paid their debt to society',
and how the Criminal Justice System will do everything to 're-
integrate the ex-offender', it's all bullshit. If you break the law
and go to prison for it, you're an outcast from then on, and no
matter what you do with the rest of your life, there will always
be someone to remind you that you don't really belong. Employment is the prime example, but there are other things, such as
when you try to enter another country for a holiday and get
treated as an 'undesirable' or when you get stopped for a routine
check by traffic police and find that after they have run your
details through the PNC (Police National Computer), you are
no longer 'sir' but 'sunshine'. Society does not want criminals
reintegrated, it wants them where it can see them, out on the
fringes.

Many ex-prisoners reoffend precisely *because* they are made to
feel like outsiders. It is a never-ending cycle: the more you break
the law, the less you fit in; and the less you fit in, the more you
have to break the law. They should tattoo every criminal on the
forehead and fit revolving doors on every prison and drop all
this self-serving bollocks about 'rehabilitation' and 'reintegration'.
The sad truth is that it becomes clear to the lawbreaker pretty
early on in his career that he is marked for life. If by the age of
eighteen you already have a stay in youth custody under your
belt, the chances are you're heading for adult prison. Of course,
there are those few who manage successfully to put their youthful
indiscretions behind them and make a decent and honest life
for themselves. It does happen – if you get out early enough,
get a bit of luck and don't ever want to emigrate or stand for
Parliament.

I had tried a bit of the straight world. I found myself sweeping roads on council estates for a take-home wage of £109 per week. I had served eleven years. paying my debt to society, and as an incentive to leave the exciting and lucrative business of crime, I was offered a broom and a grotty bed-sit, which was no more than a cell that I could lock *myself* in. I only got the job because I had a friend on the council who convinced them it would not be worth my while to nick the broom, and the wages were so bad I was forced to live on Cup-a-Soup and toasted carpet for three days a week. It wasn't as bad as being in prison, but it ran a close fucking second.

I don't blame anyone for my situation. You can't spend all your life fucking things up and then cry foul on someone else for what you've done, I know that. And knowing that you have only yourself to blame doesn't make it any easier to swallow. My family gave me what support they could, both moral and financial, but there was only so much I would allow them to do. Being on the streets from a young age and making my own way in the world, I developed a fierce pride in my independence. I would rather steal than beg, and though accepting help from my family could never be construed as begging, it still did not sit right with me. The way I saw it. they were doing their best to get by, and they didn't need the added burden of me. The life I had chosen had already made them the victims of my actions for too long. I've lost count of the times that gangs of armed police have kicked in the doors of homes of members of my family in the early hours of the morning, looking for me. My family have travelled the length and breadth of the country to visit me in prison, and have been there for me in my moments of direst need. My thinking has always been that if I stand alone, then I won't take anyone with me if I fall.

I stuck at the straight life for four months before accepting the inevitable. I dumped my broom and shovel back at the council yard and made the phone-call that got me straight back into crime. Within a week I had a studio flat in Croydon, a nice car and money in my pocket. In the criminal world employment was never a problem, and my previous convictions were viewed as a major asset rather than a badge of untrustworthiness and cause for suspicion.

But I was getting old, and leaping bank-counters and jumping into getaway motors is a young man's game. I was lucky I had survived so long; many of the lads who started out at the same time as me were not. Those not shot to death in a police ambush or murdered by fellow criminals were doing endless prison sentences or nursing murderous drug habits that turned them into drooling husks. When I set out on my life of crime, 'going on the pavement and having a parcel of rocks' meant robbing a jeweller in transit; now it means living in a cardboard box and scoring a bit of crack. Today's breed of robbers is liable to shoot you for the fun of it, and it may sound strange coming from someone who has made a living from violence, but that was never my way. I followed the unwritten criminal code of honour that used to exist among thieves and blaggers.

Freddy Foreman, south London gangland legend and friend of the Krays, dedicated his book, *Respect*, to '. . . that almost mythical group of criminals known simply as the Chaps'. The Chaps belong to an era that is now past, and my generation of robbers was the last of the Chaps. We conducted our business according to a code that was handed down to us from former generations of infamous criminals, both real and fictional. The code was rarely spoken about; it was something you learned from observing others in the life and watching westerns and old gangster films. The code meant you did not have to be ashamed of being a criminal, as long as you were the right criminal. It gave us a sense of honour and righteousness in the face of society's condemnation. We absorbed the code by osmosis and did our best to live within it.

Rule one was Never grass. You learn early on that informing or giving evidence against others is unacceptable among the criminal fraternity and the punishment for it can be very harsh. At worst you can be killed for breaching this rule, and many have been. The average punishment for a grass is a severe beating and a striping. Striping is cutting someone across the face, usually in a curving line that stretches from the corner of the mouth to the earlobe. This kind of scar is also called a 'telephone' and indicates that the recipient has been talking to someone who is definitely *non grata* in criminal circles. Even if not physically marked, a grass will still be branded for life if a whisper of his activities gets out. Though rumours are usually not enough evidence to earn a striping, they are enough to get you ostracized, and that can be worse. In order to 'work' as a criminal, you need the cooperation and trust of other criminals, which is why face and reputation are so important in that world. Access to information, bent documentation, firearms and getaway drivers are just some of the things you can usually get only through the criminal network, and if you are not trusted by the fraternity, then you might as well give up crime and get a job on a building site.

The world of the professional career criminal is a small one. Of the 72,000 prisoners who presently inhabit UK jails, less than 5,000 of them could be classed as professional career criminals, that is, people who make a living from crime through choice and not necessity. And these men (for they are predominantly men) class themselves as the elite of the criminal world. They do not cosh OAPs for their pension money or burgle council houses for the video and the contents of the gas-meter or sexually abuse women and children, and they are just as disgusted and angry as you are when they read of such things in the newspapers. For the professional, crime is not personal, it is just a job, and they do not set out to deliberately harm or injure innocent members of the public. But if a security guard has to take one in the leg, or a bank cashier has to have the shit scared out of her in order to claim the prize, then that is unfortunate but all part of the game. The professional criminal is normally a lot less brutal than the amateur and will only use violence as a last resort, because he has worked out beforehand just how far he is willing to go. And he knows that if he gets caught, it will be a jury of straight-goers who decides his fate. Whereas the average straight-goer might have a bit of sympathy or even a sneaking admiration for the criminal who takes on a bank and uses minimal violence, they will almost certainly not be so predisposed towards a toe-rag who coshes everyone in sight to nick a bit of pension money. When the public confesses to a 'fear of crime', it is not bank robbers and underworld heavies who are high on their fright-list, but the petty little violent and mindless amateurs who intrude on their everyday lives.

So, yes, there is a class-system of sorts even in the criminal world, and the criminal code is part of what divides us. Our code allows us the luxury of elevating our lives and deeds above those of the 'common' criminal and invests us with a special status. In reality, the criminal code is no more than an eclectic mix of moral etiquette borrowed from such diverse sources as the Knights of the Round Table, the Japanese code of Bushido, Hollywood westerns and the British stiff-upper-lip set, among many others. Never leave a friend in dire straits, nor show cowardice when confronted by the enemy, nor persist in violence against those weaker than yourself; and comport yourself with honour and dignity at all times. It's as simple, and as complicated, as that.

Of course, the Criminal Justice System acknowledges our elite status in not so subtle ways; they set up special squads like the NCS (National Crime Squad), the RCS (Regional Crime Squad) and the Flying Squad to dedicate their working lives to our activities. And when we are captured, they set us apart in special units and prisons and class us as Category A prisoners. We are given armed-police escorts every time we go to trial and the Home Office has a department that deals only in our every word and move. All of this – the criminal code, the special treatment – only serves to reinforce our high opinion of ourselves.

But today's young criminals are not interested in concepts like honour, staunchness and reputation. They think nothing of shooting a young girl in the face for a £50 mobile phone or of beating a disabled pensioner half to death for the contents of her purse. Where my generation of criminals took as our role models men like Robin Hood, Dick Turpin and Jesse James (or rather the Hollywood interpretation of them), the latest crop of career criminals tries to emulate the unthinking violence of Jamaican Yardies, Colombian drug-barons and American street-gangs. A short and brutal life is the 'in' thing, and it's not what you nick any more, it's how many people you can kill or maim while you're doing it. I don't understand the mentality of it because, to me, logic dictates that if you have a loaded gun and are ruthless and determined enough to use it to get money, then why not hold up a security van and walk away with a bag of cash rather than shooting a middle-aged woman in the back for a five-grand watch that you'll only be able to sell for a couple of hundred quid? It doesn't make any sense. I can only conclude that today's criminals have no morals, no honour and are as thick as shit. And why they are like that is anyone's theory. Too much violence in films and television? Single-parent families? Growing up in a consumer-oriented society under successive governments which advocate greedy capitalism as the norm? Too much fluoride in the water or too little seratonin in the brain? The abundance of hard drugs? Natural progression? Take your pick.

I'm glad I'm getting out while I can. In criminal parlance, I am what is known as a 'rusty gun'; the criminal life and the endless pursuit of the prize have lost their tawdry lustre for me. I have been thoroughly disabused of the notion that armed robbery is a victimless and noble occupation, and I sometimes wonder how I ever arrived at that preposterous supposition in the first place.

In the aftermath of that robbery on London Road, the seeds of doubt were sown. There was no miracle overnight conversion; I carried on committing robberies and frightening the life out of innocent people – but the enthusiasm was no longer there. Things ran their course and I found myself facing the hibernation years once again. And now I sit here in my 'special' top-security cell, and I cannot help but wonder what I might have done with my life if I had not donated it to crime and punishment. I am not a monster, but I have done some monstrous things along the way. I've made some terrible choices and some plain-stupid decisions. I did what I felt I had to do at the time and not in a shy way.

I realize that writing my story will probably not discourage anybody who is already hell-bent on a life of crime, but it will help me to see exactly where I went wrong and not repeat my mistakes. And, when you consider that in thirty years the entire might of the British Criminal Justice System has failed to do that, you might say that writing has been an exercise in rehabilitation. I want people to know what goes into making a criminal like me: we are not assembled overnight but forged over many years in the unhallowed halls of juvenile jails and adult prisons. We do not emerge from the womb looking for something to nick and someone to slash; we are not born into crime, we learn it. And once we do learn it, we become court- and jail-fodder, the fuel that keeps the vast Criminal Justice machine grinding on and on. Let's not con ourselves here: if society and the Criminal Justice System were really interested in rehabilitating people like me, then they would find a way. They know that incarcerating children at a young age will make them more likely to grow up as criminals, and yet they rush to build more prisons and jail more children. If there was no crime in this country, then tens of thousands of people would be out of a job, and you can only have so many traffic wardens.

I have found my own rehabilitation, and writing this book is part of it. I do not seek to glorify crime; it is a dirty and brutal business, and there is nothing glorious about being coshed, stabbed or shot at. Nor is there any glamour in rotting away in a prison cell, missing out on your children's lives and not being there for them when they desperately need you. There is little kudos in having to go on the dole or sweep roads because you are an ex-con with no work record. And when you are lying in a strip cell, covered in your own shit and vomit and nursing a couple of broken ribs with a decade left to serve, you finally begin to realize how pointless and self-destructive it all is. Imprisonment in this country is not all *Porridge*-style jolly japes between wily cons and dim-witted warders, or lobster and steak dinners in front of Sky TV, as some of the tabloids would have you believe. People die in prison, an average of 115 per year, and still more are wounded and maimed or so psychologically damaged that they can never be released again. Our mental institutions are full of patients who started out as prisoners. Prison is hard, brutal and dangerous. This is a fact. I hope you won't be fooled into thinking otherwise just because I tell some of my story in a flippant and humorous manner. Humour is my way of dealing with certain memories that, even after many years, still have the power to wound. Without a sense of humour, no matter how off-key you may think it is, I would probably now be taking tea with the Yorkshire Ripper in Broadmoor and discussing the relative merits of screwdrivers over razors. See? I can't help it.

So, there you have it. I do not claim to be 'The Guv'nor', 'The Godfather' or 'The Colonel' of some mythical underworld where OAPs are always safe on the streets and where criminals only kill and torture 'our own'. I am quite sure you've heard all that before, and there are only so many ways you can say, '. . . and then I shot George Cornell right in the 'ead', before it all starts wearing a bit thin. I was not some crime 'kingpin' who spent my time hobnobbing with B-list celebrities and getting my photograph taken while waiting for my underlings to bring me the loot. I was out there, at the sharp end, nicking the loot myself. I took the rewards, and I took the punishments, and I ain't crying about none of it. I'm just telling it how it was.

I'm not 'one of the ones that got away' from the Train Job. Nor was I one of the Krays' numerous and varied 'right-hand men'. I have no inkling as to who killed Freddie Mills or the whereabouts of the mortal remains of Jack 'The Hat' McVitie, Frank 'The Mad Axe-Man' Mitchell or 'Ginger' Marks. As far as I know, they could all be running a jellied-eel stall down the Old Kent Road with 'Lucky' Lucan supplying the winkles and Shergar pulling the cart. But I do have a story to tell.

To read my story you do not need to have fought, robbed and swaggered your way through the mean streets of London and into courtrooms and top-security prison cells; I've done all that for you. So, welcome to my world. Come in and stay a while. And when the gunsmoke clears and the last gate is slammed, you'll be glad you can just walk away.

2. No Blacks, No Dogs, No Irish

I came into this world on Christmas Eve 1960, at the old Charing Cross Hospital in London. My mother and father had been enjoying a night out together at the cinema when I began to make my appearance. The film they were watching was Alfred Hitchcock's *Psycho*, and I sometimes wonder if that was some kind of portent to my life. Although I have stabbed more people than Norman Bates, I've never felt the compulsion to dress up in my mother's clothes while doing it, so I guess it was one of those mixed omens.

Though I was born in the heart of London, both my parents are Irish emigrants who came to England in the late 1950s for economic reasons. My father, Noel Stephen Smith, hailed from the rough-and-ready North Side of Dublin, where drinking and fighting are reputed to be the main pastimes, and throughout his life he has done his fair share of both. A doctor once asked him if he drank more than two pints of beer a day, to which my father matter-of-factly replied, 'Are you kidding me? I fucking spill more than two pints a day!' And he wasn't joking. My mother, Bernadette Mary Smith, *née* Merlehan, came from the far more genteel suburbs of south Dublin, which was all lace curtains and work ethic.

Six months after I was born my mother became ill, with bronchitis, and as my dad was out of work things were very sticky on the financial front. We were living in one room in north London, in a house that was too dilapidated to be described as a slum. So my mum got in touch with her family in Dublin, and it was decided that I would be taken to live with my maternal grandparents until things got better for my parents. My auntie Dolores, who was only fifteen at the time, came over to London in order to take me back to Ireland. In those days, in Catholic

Ireland, unmarried mothers were more than frowned upon, and somehow the story got around that the young Dolores had gone to England to have an illegitimate child – me. Whenever my auntie took me through the streets of south Dublin in my pram, there would be whispers and withering looks in our direction. It must have been a terrible time for Dolores, but she still remains my favourite auntie on my mother's side. I stayed in Dublin until I was two years old.

With two Irish parents, I am an Irish citizen under Section 2 of the Irish Constitution. But, having lived in London for most of my life, I would describe myself as London-Irish. I have always been very proud of my Irish roots, and though many English people spat on the Irish and their children during that dark period of the 1970s when the IRA brought their bombing campaign to Albion, I never once hid behind a declaration of Englishness like some of the children of Irish parents.

My father had been a promising boxer in the Irish Army, and there were few things he liked more than a good fight. He was never a criminal in the conventional sense of the word but tended to fall foul of the law through drunken violence. But there was also another side to him; he harboured a secret, or maybe not so secret, desire to write. He would collect scraps of paper that held words and phrases he had heard and jotted down during his day and put them away, saying, 'Those are for when I get around to writing my book.' And when he told us stories of his impoverished childhood on the streets and lanes of Dublin, us children would be captivated and beg for more. He is a great story-teller with a sense of humour that shines through, but he also has a powerful right hook and a terrible unpredictability when drunk. My father was the first and greatest influence on my life, but he was never around much when I was a kid.

My mother is also a strong character, though she possesses more of an inner fortitude. When I was born, my mother was nineteen years old and my father was twenty, and in those days it was the norm for Irish husbands to just leave the wives to it. My father would be out working all day and then out drinking and fighting all night, so my mother had it all to do, with little help. We lived in 'rooms', rented from landlords, in crumbling buildings, usually without a kitchen. So my mother, still in her teens and in a foreign country, had few friends and no one to turn to if anything went wrong. But she held it all together, and us kids were always well turned out and there was always a meal on the table when my father rolled in after the pub.

I was their firstborn, and they named me Noel Stephen Smith, after my father, and in honour of my Christmas birth. My brother, Michael, was born in 1962, and my sister, Samantha, followed in 1966. That might seem a bit on the small side for an Irish Catholic family, but my mother also had six miscarriages.

While my father would have loved to find the time in his busy schedule to write, my mother would have loved time to read. She always had a small stack of books awaiting her attention, but she rarely had the time to read them. Her favourite author is Charles Dickens. I once spent a weekend in the punishment block at HMP Wandsworth immersed in *Oliver Twist*, in order to see what it might be about Dickens that fascinated her. What I found was an interesting story that was very well written, and that's probably all my mum wanted from a book.

My father is also a reader, but he is a lot more complicated than my mother. When he first came to England, he had the misfortune to spend a short while in HMP Wormwood Scrubs after a bout of drunken fisticuffs and, to pass the time, he read. Unfortunately, someone had followed the age-old prison practice of ripping out pages from the centre of every book on the wing. Some prisoners do this out of boredom and spite, mainly the ones who can't read. My father was so incensed by this that he made a vow never to read again. It was twenty years before he read another book, but in those twenty years he collected a lot of books, in case he should want to start again. He refused to read fiction on principle – he hates liars and classes fiction-writers as just liars who earn a living from it – so it was surprising that the book that got him back into reading again was *The Carpetbaggers*, by Harold Robbins. It came highly recommended from a good friend who, in my father's words, 'drove me fucking mad until I had read it.' *The Carpetbaggers* was the last work of fiction he read, but he still has a voracious appetite for works of non-fiction.

I suppose that, by rights, having two parents from 'the land of poets and scholars', both with a love of the written word, I should have taken to reading and writing from an early age, but I was never a good pupil, and I was only interested in books when someone was reading them to me. I was into football and fighting, and junior school, to me, was playground time sandwiched between long, boring sessions of restraint in the classroom. I was a dreamer with a stubborn streak, and I found the rigid parameters of lessons stifling. When I grew bored I would disrupt the class or start a fight, and I lost count of the number of times I was caned. I would take three on each hand, doing my best not to flinch or cry out. Even getting caned was better than being bored.

From my father I inherited a sense of humour, a hatred of bullies and the love of a good fist-fight, and from my mother I gained a quiet strength and endurance in the face of the unchangeable, and the patience of a saint. I don't think I did too badly out of the deal. The bad habits and worse character traits are all my own.

Until I was nine years old we lived in north London in a succession of hovels and rented rooms, each one more dilapidated than the last. The earliest one I can remember was a couple of rooms above a hairdressers, at 502a Holloway Road. It was opposite the Odeon cinema, where my aunt Phyllis, my mum's younger sister, worked as an usherette. While my mum was working elsewhere, Michael and I would be babysat in the back-row of the cinema and given choc-ices and popcorn as my aunt worked the sparse matinee crowd. The only film I really remember seeing was *Help*, and that was because of the music. I couldn't say what the film was about, but the tunes stuck in my head.

We also lived in Blackstock Road, another two-room affair memorable only for its proximity to the delights of Finsbury Park. There was a miniature village at the top end of the park which fascinated me, and I would spend hours walking among the knee-high houses and playing with my Matchbox cars.

After Samantha was born we moved into the basement of a three-storey house on Hollingsworth Street, Islington. Two other Irish families occupied the upper storeys, and we all shared the toilet, which was located at the end of the back yard. Though this was the mid-60s in swinging London, our living conditions were what you might expect to find in a 1920s northern mining village. We had a tin bath that had to be filled by heating pots of water on a coal-fire, on which the cooking was also done, and when going to the toilet at night we had to keep an eye out for rats.

Every third house on Hollingsworth Street had been destroyed in the Blitz, and by 1967 the council had only just got around to putting corrugated fencing around the bombsites. These fenced-off areas were then used as handy dumping grounds for all and sundry. As a result, the rat population thrived. The rats became bigger and bolder. Facing our house was the printing works where the popular comics *Dandy* and *Beano*, among others, were printed and sent out for distribution. The yard and warehouse of the print works were always full of waste paper and were home to some of the biggest rats I have ever seen. I remember playing out in the street one summer's evening and seeing four huge ones come strolling out of a gap in the print-works fence as though they owned the street. I kicked my ball at them, but instead of running off they just turned malevolent stares on me until *I* ran off.

I loved living in Hollingsworth Street. There was always plenty for a kid to do. There were 'adventure playgrounds' set up on some of the bombsites where we could build 'camps' and roast potatoes on open fires. There was a bakery at the bottom of the street, and if you nipped around the back there was always a sack of day-old cakes and buns for the taking. There was also a coal yard which had, to us kids, a huge mountain of coal perfect for climbing and playing 'king of the castle'.

Hollingsworth Street came to an end in 1969 when the press finally discovered it. The beatnik couple who lived next door to

us had left their baby daughter in her pram out in the back yard
to get a bit of sun when a rat jumped into the pram and bit the
baby's face. The *Islington Gazette* got hold of the story and a
reporter and photographer descended on the street that time
forgot. My mother gave them a proper mouthful about the conditions we were forced to endure and our photo ended up on the
front page under the headline 'Rats as Big as Cats!' – though
that was obviously referring to the rodent problem and not a
description of my family.

It must have been a slow week for news, because the national
papers soon picked up on the story and gave it a splash. Islington
council, who, pre-publicity, had yawned when Hollingsworth
Street was mentioned, now began to sweat and bluster. The final
straw came when the mothers of the street were invited to appear
on a topical news programme on ITV to say what they thought
of the council. The council spokesman was ripped to shreds on
live TV, and my dear mother was in the forefront, doing most
of the ripping. The council had no explanation as to why all the
families housed in their slums were Irish, so they just had to
swallow and do the right thing.

A week after the programme was aired, Islington council
announced that it was going to demolish Hollingsworth and the
surrounding streets, and all the residents were to be rehoused in
modern council accommodation. My family was offered a three-
bedroom flat in Balham, south London, as far away from Islington
as they could put us. My mother accepted gracefully, while I was
gutted to be leaving the old place. All of my friends from the
street were staying in North London, but I would have to start
again in what to me was a foreign land.

Our new home was on the top floor of a three-storey block
called Sinclair House, just off Kings Avenue on the borders of
Balham and Brixton. The flat was heated by coal fire, but we had
hot and cold running water and a fixed bath, which was a novelty
for us. We were still poor, but at least we didn't have to go outside
to use the toilet.

Sinclair Estate consisted of three blocks set in a triangle, with a patch of grass between them. It would have been a lovely setting for old-age pensioners, but for kids like me and Mick, who were used to rat-hunts and bombsite exploration, it was far too tame and clean. There were 'No Ball Games' signs everywhere, strictly enforced by a couple of sour-faced caretakers who seemed to spend every waking hour waiting to jump out on any kid who had the audacity to organize a game of football, and all the other kids on the estate seemed a bit too 'posh' for my liking. They seemed happy to stay on the estate and didn't want to do anything that might get their clothes dirty. Mick and I were made of sterner stuff and couldn't stay within the confines of the estate; it was too limited. As soon as we were out of sight of our mother we were off roaming. In a very short time we had the surrounding areas mapped out in our heads and knew every garden with a fruit tree ripe for scrumping.

On one of our forays to Streatham Hill we met up with a group of scruffy brothers called the Brookers. The Brooker brothers – Tony, who was my age, the twins Michael and Martin, who were Mick's age, and a younger brother, David – were more like the kids we were used to mixing with. They had a bit of street-savvy about them and were not afraid to take chances. We also met up with Adrian and Vincent Street, whose father was a famous TV wrestler well known for his flowing blond locks, pink tights, lipstick and devastating forearm smash. With the Brookers and the Streets we discovered many uncharted territories and put our lives in danger on a regular basis. We found a way on to the roof of the *South London Press* building, via a fire escape. On the front of the building was a huge clock hanging out over the busy Leigham Court Road. We would nip up the fire escape to the roof and then play a game of 'dare', which involved one of us jumping out on to the clock and then swinging back on to the roof. It was an eighty-foot drop to the street below. We laughed our heads off one day when Mick missed his hold and had to grab on to the huge minute-hand in order to save himself. It was bent out of shape, and from that day the clock has never worked.

We would climb over the short fence around the railway lines and enter the tunnels. At regular intervals along them there were shallow recesses big enough to allow one railway worker to step off the line and take refuge should a train enter the tunnel. We would wait for a train to come through the far end of the tunnel and then have a mad scramble to try and get safely into a recess before it reached us. If you got into one that was already occupied you would be pushed out and have to find another one in time. Forget all your Big Dippers and other amusement-park rides, they all pale into insignificance when you are crouching in a pitch-black, shallow recess hearing the thunder of an approaching train. The noise builds in a crescendo so loud you can't hear your own screams, and I defy anybody not to jump in pure fear when the train finally makes its appearance in your short field of vision and goes rushing by screeching like a banshee.

No building site was safe from our invasions. At the weekend or when the work on it had been finished for the day we would creep in and swing on anything that looked like a rope and climb anything that looked unsafe. Buses were another favourite form of entertainment, the old double-deckers with the open platform at the back. We would jump on to the platform when the bus stopped at traffic lights and then wait for it to speed up before jumping off. The faster the bus was going, the more kudos you gained. We did not always escape unscathed, and between us we notched up quite a collection of broken bones and other injuries. It's a wonder that none of us was ever killed. But we just accepted the injuries as part of the game. A good injury was something to be admired.

We sometimes came across other gangs of kids on our travels, and when we did, it would always end in a punch-up. Fighting was normal to us, and a good way of settling any dispute, no matter how trivial. There were never any weapons involved, just straight, old-fashioned fisticuffs. We fought the 'posh' kids from our estate and kids from other estates and kids in the playground at school and each other. It was no drama.

My father, who had a fearsome reputation as a fighter around the drinkers of south London, taught me some boxing moves, including most of the illegal stuff, like standing on your opponent's foot before launching the haymaker, jabbing your thumb in his eye and headbutting when in close. I had a good right-hand, but my left was less than useless, so I would make up for it with a headbutt. I broke a few noses with my headbutt, and it was my most formidable weapon until I discovered the cut-throat razor a bit later in life.

I hated school and would do anything to avoid it – I just couldn't concentrate; my mind would be off roaming free – but I enjoyed a bit of history, when our teacher read us stories of the old days. My favourite was the tale of the highwayman Dick Turpin. I listened, spellbound, to the exploits of dashing Dick and his trusty steed, Black Bess. A cry of 'Stand and deliver!', a kiss on the hand for the ladies, a merry quip for the gentlemen, cop the prize and make a swift but dignified getaway. When I was eleven, I so wanted to be Dick Turpin, the hero on a stolen horse, the romantic outlaw, the robber. After my father, the hard-drinking fighter, Turpin was my role model.

Of course, if I had been told the truth about Dick Turpin, instead of the romanticized Hollywood version, I may have had second thoughts. I found out many years later that Turpin was a horse-thief and a burglar and a thoroughly nasty piece of work. On one occasion he and his gang forced their way into the home of a sixty-eight-year-old widow and sat her on a burning coal fire in order to find out where she had hidden her savings. Turpin was eventually hanged for cattle-rustling, and it seems that even Black Bess and the infamous ride to York were the figment of someone's imagination. Feet of clay indeed.

Around this time television also had a big influence on my life. The TV show I liked best was *The Adventures of Robin Hood*. I would tune in religiously to catch the exploits of this blagger in tights and cheer as he and his merry men made mugs out of the forces of law and order every week. Here we go again, an armed robber being presented as a folk hero. The message was getting through, loud and clear. Crime was good, as long as it was the right kind of crime; robbing rich people was acceptable, and even using violence to do it was OK, as long as you weren't overly cruel to them.

I began to seek out further criminal heroes, and I was not disappointed. Television and cinema kept me supplied with a steady diet of westerns and gangster films in which the 'baddies' did not seem that bad to me, films about Jesse James and his gang, Billy the Kid, John Dillinger, Machine-Gun Kelly, Pretty-Boy Floyd, Baby-Face Nelson, et al. These men were American folk heroes, and every one of them was a robber.

I loved fighting, and though I lost more fights than I ever won, I was always willing to have a go. For a short while I enrolled in a boxing club in Tooting, and did quite well in four amateur bouts. But I couldn't stand the discipline of training on a regular basis. I was also hampered by poor eyesight. I have a weak right eye, which is hereditary and known in the family as 'the Smith eye'. As in, 'Jaysus, he's a grand-looking youn' fella, and he's got the Smith eye, God love him.' When I was a child I had to regularly attend Moorfield Eye Hospital, and my mother was told there was a good chance I would lose the sight in my eye by the time I reached my teens. My mother, being a staunch Catholic, arranged for the church to take me on a pilgrimage to Lourdes. I haven't gone blind yet, and to this day my mother swears that Lourdes worked a miracle on me. Sometimes I wonder if it's true, but being the ungrateful bastard that I am I have never been particularly interested in religion and, when asked, I declare myself a born-again atheist. I tend to agree with Karl Marx: religion is the opium of the masses.

My father is also a lapsed Catholic, not interested in religion. Nor is he interested in politics. If he can drink it, fight it or bet on it, then it's worth a look; if not, then forget it. I never once heard him talk about the political situation in Ireland, and the only time he showed an interest in politics was in the 1980s, when he had a good job with Lambeth Council. He knew that if the Tories took over the council, the maintenance work would be tendered to agencies and he and his mates would have to reapply for their jobs, at a third less wages, so he urged Mick and me to vote Labour in the local elections.

Despite being the bare-knuckle champion of Clapham Junction, my father only ever gave me one good hiding when I was a kid. He beat both me and Mick with a belt, for telling lies. Like I said, the one thing he can't bear is a liar. His favourite expression for when we had done something outrageous was, 'Where do you think you are? In America?', as though America was famed for letting children go to extremes. His shoulders are huge, and his face is scarred and battered from countless street- and pub-fights in which the only weapons he relied on were his head, hands and feet. Unfortunately, his opponents were not always as game, and he has been glassed a few times. Even today pieces of glass still occasionally work their way to the surface of his face and head, relics of long-forgotten battles to be plucked from the skin and stared at in wonder.

A few years back, on a holiday to his hometown of Dublin, I spoke to one of my father's best friends from his younger days. 'Your da was a wild man in his day!' he told me. 'We used to go down to the pubs on the docks where all the foreign sailors drank, and your oul fella would pick the biggest Swede or Russian in the pub and call on the scrap. It was pitch black in the alley, but your oul fella had been out there so many times, he would just take off his jacket and hang it on the one small nail there, he did it without even looking. His opponents couldn't even see the wall, let alone the nail!'

But when I was caned in junior school for fighting and came home with thick red welts across my legs, it was my mother who rolled up her sleeves and marched down to the school to throw a few digs at the deputy headmaster, Mr Mathias. She chased him around the playground and threatened to knock him out if he ever laid a hand on me again.

I did my fair share of petty thieving in those days. Shoplifting pencils and Mars Bars, nicking milk from doorsteps and scrumping apples and pears. And in the winter, when there was no money for coal, Mick and I would take Samantha's old pushchair and scavenge wood for the fire. We discovered that it was easy to break down the garden fences in the residential area just up the road from the estate. We often got chased by irate homeowners, but we were nothing if not fast.

Along with the Brookers and the Street brothers we also had various scams with which to prise the odd shilling or two out of unsuspecting householders. The best one was the raffle-ticket game, which involved shoplifting a couple of books of numbered cloakroom tickets from the local stationery shop. We would then take our angelic faces around the doors of the posh houses, selling our fake raffle-tickets for ten pence each in aid of a new hut for the Boy Scouts. Another good scam was the sponsored swim. There was often a real one going on by one of the schools who used the local swimming-baths, so we would simply ask for a handful of the forms. Then we would go knocking on doors asking people to sponsor us for ten pence a length. We would then forge the signature of the official adjudicator, stating that we had done twenty lengths, and go back around the doors collecting our unjust deserts. Most people would hand over the cash without a murmur, and if anyone argued or questioned us we would just walk away.

Bob-a-job was another of our moves, although most times this one did actually involve doing something for our money. We would once again purport to be Boy Scouts in mufti and offer to work for money. We spent many a hot Saturday afternoon clearing rubbish-filled cellars, washing fleets of cars or digging acres of garden. We would spend the money on sweets and chips, but Mick and I would always bring some of the money home for our mum. She must have thought we were the luckiest kids in the world the way we were always finding the odd half-crown in the street.

I never tortured stray cats or pulled the wings off flies, but while other kids wanted to be train-drivers when they grew up, I would have preferred to be a train-robber. I wasn't particularly anti-police, I cried when Dirk Bogarde shot PC Dixon at the end of *The Blue Lamp*, and I was happy to see him alive again and promoted to sergeant on the weekly repeats of *Dixon of Dock Green*. To me, the police were interesting, just not as interesting as the villains.

My feelings towards the police were soon to change, though. My first experience of them taught me that what I had seen on *Z Cars* and *Dixon of Dock Green* was a load of old bollocks and would colour my attitude towards the police for many years to come.

When I was eleven years old I was transferred from Henry Cavendish junior school, where, due to my propensity for playground fights and rebellious attitude towards learning, I was a big fish in a little puddle, to Tulse Hill secondary modern, where I was just another target for the big boys.

Tulse Hill school was someone's rabid nightmare made reality. Situated just off Brixton Hill, it was an eight-storey block of concrete and glass that could have easily won an award for the most frighteningly ugly school ever built. It catered for 1,800 boys from the poorest and most crime-ridden catchment area in London. The school had a fearsome reputation for violence, both pupil-on-pupil and pupil-on-teacher, and at one stage they hired security guards to escort the teachers off the premises at the end of each day for fear they would be attacked by the kids.

I hated Tulse Hill from day one, when I was mugged by three sixth-formers who looked like extras from a *Shaft* film. I think the act of mugging may actually have been invented at Tulse Hill, because it was such a frequent occurrence in the darkened corridors; some kids just used to walk around with their dinner-money in their hands to save any hassle. Imagine a cross between Dante's *Inferno* and Ducky-Boy territory from the film of *The Wanderers*, and you have Tulse Hill secondary modern. I hated it, with a vengeance.

After my first week there I just didn't bother going any more. I would set off for school in the morning and end up bunking it with my pal Micky. We would go up to Kensington and spend the day in the science and history museums chatting up girls on school-trips and generally making a nuisance of ourselves. When we didn't have the bus fare to reach the museums we would just roam around south London. It was nearly three years before the school realized we were missing and sent letters to our parents, but by then we were never going back.

One school day, when we had no money and were bored out of our heads, Micky and I decided to make the five-mile walk to Crystal Palace, just have a mooch about. As we were passing through Gipsy Hill, we nicked a couple of pints of milk from the doorstep of a house on a residential street. Nicking milk from doorsteps was natural to us, like bunking on the tube or scrumping apples. We had drunk the milk and were strolling on our merry way when suddenly an old Commer van pulled up to the kerb just in front of us. Before we had time to protest, we were bundled into the back by a bunch of geezers who smelled strongly of booze and acted as though they wanted to kill us. I was fucking terrified. One of them had his arm around my neck and was putting so much pressure on that I thought I was going to die. Two more had Micky face-down on the floor with a knee on his neck. One of the men put his face up close to mine. 'You're nicked, toe-rag!' he said, gleefully, and then punched me hard in the stomach. I had just met some of the Metropolitan CID's finest.

The beating I received from the police in the back of that van and later at the police station amounted to nothing less than torture. I can only assume that their 'stake-out' duties had bored them so much that they had gone for a few drinks and then decided to nick the first likely-looking suspects they came across – which happened to be me and Micky.

After the initial punch to the stomach, which made me vomit up a pint of milk, my neck was released by the copper behind me and the blows came hard and fast. I tried to curl up in a ball, but it didn't help much, as they kept stamping on me. I could hear someone screaming, and I'm still not sure if it was me or Micky. After what seemed like hours but must only have been a couple of minutes, they stopped throwing punches and kicks at us. They sat us up, and then the 'interrogation' and the real torture began.

There were five plainclothes men in the back of the van with us, and two up front, including the driver. The one I remember most vividly had a 'Mexican' moustache and a Ziggy Stardust haircut. He was the one who interrogated me. He started by grabbing a handful of my hair so I couldn't look away from him.

'Stop your fucking snivelling or you'll get some more,' was his opening gambit. 'Now, don't even think about lying to me, because we've watched your every move today. You and your oppo there are at it, ain't you?'

I didn't have a clue what he was talking about, and in a moment of panic I thought he was saying that me and Micky were homosexuals, and that was why we were getting beaten up. I shook my head.

My denial brought a slap to the face.

'I told you not to fucking lie! You're out drumming. We've watched you knocking on doors to see if people are in and trying to get round the backs of houses. Now you better fucking well shape up and start telling the truth, boy.'

I couldn't believe it. I shook my head again and was rewarded with another hard slap in the face.

'DON'T FUCKING LIE TO ME!' he shouted in my face. 'You're going to tell us how many drums you've tried today, and how many nice people's homes you've screwed in the past. Got it?'

I was absolutely terrified. But we hadn't done anything and a part of my brain was still telling me this was all a mistake, the police didn't do this sort of thing. I began to wonder if they were police at all. We hadn't seen any uniforms or badges. I decided to try and explain.

'I swear, mister, we ain't done nothing! Honest!'

The copper shook his head, almost sadly. 'All right,' he said reasonably. 'If you want to try and take me for a cunt, it's up to you. Hold his hand out.' This to the copper who was behind me.

My wrist was grabbed in a vice-like grip and my hand proffered to the interrogator. He took hold of the middle finger of my left hand and smiled at me. 'Last chance,' he said. 'How many drums have you screwed?'

I looked pleadingly into his face, hoping to find a spark of pity, but there was only glee. 'I never done nothing . . .' I said.

He began to twist my finger, and the pain was so excruciating I had to scream. The copper who was holding my wrist out now clamped a hand over my mouth. I heard something snap in my hand and I fainted.

When I came to, the van was on the move and my hand was throbbing terribly. The coppers were all looking at me with smiles on their faces. I looked down at my hand and saw it had swollen up to twice its size. I couldn't move my fingers. I began to cry.

'Shut it, you fucking sissy,' said the interrogator. 'You're not dying. Yet. You're lucky your mate is a lot smarter than you.'

I looked over at Micky. He had been crying too, and he had a lump coming up under his eye where he'd been punched.

'I told them we did it, Noel. I had to.' There was a horrible whine in his voice that would have made me cringe under other circumstances.

I couldn't really blame him for caving in, but I was determined now not to admit to something I hadn't done. I was in pain and still in fear, but as I looked at the coppers I felt something else as well – pure hatred.

As the van pulled into the yard behind the police station, my interrogator leant into my face once again. 'You better liven your ideas up, cunty. Your pal is going to make a statement, and you'll do the same if you know what's good for you.'

I thought that now we were about to enter the station where there would be witnesses, he wouldn't dare to hit me again, and a bit of my confidence returned. 'I ain't done nothing,' I said firmly.

He reached over and grabbed my injured hand and squeezed it. I screamed again.

I was dragged from the van and hustled into the station. A uniformed sergeant stood behind a desk. The squad stood me and Micky in front of him.

'What we got here then, boys?' he asked.

The interrogator smiled at him. 'Couple of naughty little

drummers,' he said. 'Probably responsible for most of the screwings on the division by all accounts.'

I shook my head and went to speak. 'I ain't done . . .'

The uniform pointed a meaty finger at me. 'Shut your fucking
mouth.'

My heart sank. There would be no help from this quarter.

The interrogator continued. 'We watched them trying to force
a few dwellings and then moved in to make the arrest. We identified ourselves as police officers and they immediately tried to
make good their escape. This one,' here he pointed at me, 'tried
to climb over a wall, and fell off the top of it when I tried to
grab him. He's got an injury to his hand, and probably a few
bruises as well. This one,' and here he indicated Micky, 'put up
a bit of a struggle whilst resisting arrest and had to be subdued.'

The uniform nodded like there was nothing implausible about
this story at all. He wrote something in a ledger.

They put me and Micky in the same cell to await the interview, probably so that Micky could convince me to make a statement. As soon as the door was locked I gave him an earful about
how he was dropping us in it by admitting to things we had not
done. He told me that when he heard my finger snap he was
willing to admit to anything, just so they wouldn't do the same
to him. How could I blame him? The pain from my hand was
killing me.

The only way out of our predicament without further beatings was to admit to burglaries that we knew nothing about and
drop ourselves deeper in the shit. At this stage in my life I knew
nothing about burglary, but I was an old hand at exploring
derelict buildings and I knew every empty building on my manor.
The plan was to admit to burgling these buildings in the hope
that the police wouldn't know they were empty. That way, we
could keep the police happy, save ourselves from any more violence
and prove our innocence when we got out of the police station.

I was the first into the interview room, and they were prepared
for my denials. The small room was crowded with squad members,
all grim faces and rolled-up sleeves. I was shoved into a chair,

and they gathered around me the better to intimidate me. The interrogator from the back of the van was in charge, and he spoke first.

'Now. You've had time to think and reconsider your options, and you know we're not fucking about. So you better cough to all the screwings you've done, OK?'

I nodded, and the tension seemed to leak out of the small room. I couldn't believe the change that came over them as soon as I agreed to confess to the non-existent burglaries. In less than five minutes I was starting to wonder if these were even the same men who had tortured me in the van.

They put a call out for a doctor to treat my hand, gave me a cigarette and a cup of tea and had the brass neck to joke about my falling off a wall while trying to escape! They were relaxed and couldn't do enough for me, tutting, over the state of my injured hand and telling me how the court would be lenient with me because I was a first offender. I made a long statement detailing the jobs I had carried out and making up details of the stuff I had stolen and the characters I had sold it to. They swallowed it all and wrote it down, and as I made up more and more detail, they grew ever more friendly and helpful. By the time my statement was signed, I had become 'Noel' to them instead of toe-rag and cunty.

The police doctor turned up and examined my hand. He said my middle finger was fractured and two of my knuckles were dislocated and that I should go to a casualty department when I was released. He gave me two painkillers and a sling. Micky played along with the plan and also made a statement. Because we were both only thirteen years old our parents had to be called up to the police station for us to be released.

My mother, when she arrived, was not in the best of moods, and she got worse when she saw my injuries. She demanded an explanation from me, and I told her the truth – I had done nothing and the police had beaten me up. She immediately demanded to see whoever was in charge and made an official complaint against the officers who had arrested me.

When the case got to Balham juvenile court a couple of weeks later, me and Micky had already given full statements about what had happened to a solicitor. The magistrates listened intently to our story and then remanded the case for a week in order for the police to come up with proof that the burglaries we were charged with had actually occurred. They couldn't, of course, and this fact gave further credence to our statements about being tortured.

The magistrates dismissed the charges against us and called for an inquiry into the interrogation methods of the squad. For the next three years we were subject to unannounced visits from the police officers who were investigating our case, and it seems their brief was to discourage us from carrying on. It worked. We couldn't get legal aid and eventually dropped the case. To this day I wish we hadn't.

So, by the age of fourteen, I had a deep hatred and mistrust of the police, and I was more than enamoured with those who had chosen a life of daring villainy. After the incident, I became a target for police harassment. I could barely walk the streets without being stopped and searched. The court cases came thick and fast: loitering with intent, being a suspected person, acting suspiciously on enclosed premises, obstruction of a police officer – I was nicked for them all, more than once. I gained celebrity status among the black kids on my manor as the only person who got stopped by the police more than they did.

Whenever I was stopped or nicked the coppers would goad me about making 'false allegations' against their colleagues and warn me I had better drop the case. I came to accept their slaps and sly digs as just part of the game. They knew my parents were Irish, and when the IRA bombing campaign was at its height in England, they gave me stick about that as well, calling my family 'IRA paddies' and telling me that we better pack up and 'Fuck off back to the bogs.' This was nothing new; there was a real anti-Irish climate in the mid-1970s, and it was common for my mum to be verbally abused in the streets and shops whenever anyone heard her accent. Kids who had Irish parents had to either

try to hide their Irishness by becoming more English than the
abusers or fight. I chose the latter.

I remember one time, a kid from the estate who should have
known better because his father hailed from County Clare called
me a 'bog-trotting Fenian bastard' to impress his mates. I didn't
have a clue what a 'Fenian' was and, I suspect, neither did he.
But the fight was on.

By this time I had learned that rules counted for fuck all in
a street fight, and I fought by my father's motto: do unto others,
only do it first. While the kid was still making a show of taking
his jacket off, I stuck the nut on him and broke his nose. He ran
off, leaking blood and snot and crying like a girl. Five minutes
later he was back, with his father in tow. The old man was a
craggy-faced individual who looked as though he was no stranger
to a punch-up himself. He waved me over, and pointed at his son.

'Did you do this?' he asked.

I nodded.

'He called me a bog-trotting Fenian bastard,' I said in explanation.

He grabbed his still-snivelling son by the scruff of the neck
and shook him. 'Is that right?' he asked.

The boy nodded.

The old man cuffed him around the head. 'When I get you
in I'll give you the hiding of your life.' He reached into his pocket
and tossed me two bob. 'Sorry, son,' he said. 'Get yerself an ice-
cream.' And he dragged the boy off home.

That one incident made me proud to be Irish, and for the rest
of my life on Sinclair estate I was on nodding terms with the
old man.

One of the advantages of being openly declared Irish was that
I was welcomed by the black kids around Brixton. There has
always been a certain affinity between the Irish and Afro-
Caribbeans that has never existed between either group and their
English 'hosts'. Being black or Irish in this country has always
been a ticket for the back of the bus. We share the feeling that,
at best, we are being tolerated by the 'superior' English, and that

has brought us closer together. The black kids in Brixton were also regularly harassed by the police, so that was something else we had in common. So, while most of my white contemporaries were afraid to venture into Brixton after dark for fear they would be mugged, I could go anywhere I pleased.

At the age of fourteen I was a criminal in the making. I had very little fear of anything, I was willing to take dangerous gambles on little more than a whim, and I hated the police. I also had a string of criminal convictions for the most petty of offences and very little education. My father was rarely at home; he was always out drinking and fighting and didn't have a job. I would see him in the morning, before the pubs opened, and sometimes late at night when the pubs had closed. My mother was holding down two cleaning jobs and trying to keep my brother and sister from heading in the same direction I was going. I completely blanked school and began to knock around with the kids who had the same attitude as me.

A life of crime is like a raging river at flood time; once you get into it you find it hard to get out again without a bit of help. Up until now I had merely dipped my toe into the flow, but now I made a conscious decision to dive in and immerse myself completely. Within months I would be out in the middle where the waters raged most furiously, where struggling only makes you drown all the quicker. When you reach that stage it is best to just relax and go with the flow.

And that is exactly what I did.

3. A Small Corner of Hell

There are many pockets of loneliness in the life of the unsuccessful career criminal – the dock at Crown Court at the moment before sentence is pronounced; the punishment cell after a beating by the screws; the small hours of the morning with only the shadow of the bars for company – but none is as torturously poignant as being conveyed through familiar streets in a prison van heading for incarceration. It is at these moments that every criminal has his doubts and regrets. I have a theory that if you were to stop every prison transport on the roads tomorrow and release the occupants, instead of a crime wave you would find the reconviction rates dropping dramatically.

Through the tiny and darkened prison-transport window, you witness the mundane but comfortable life you can no longer be a part of. Everyday scenes that you don't even notice when you're free, such as a man walking from a newsagents with a pack of cigarettes and a can of drink, or kids laughing at a bus stop, or a nice-looking girl waiting to cross the road, strike up a wistful longing in your heart that is almost excruciatingly painful. The very ordinariness of life beyond that Perspex square seems infinitely more attractive than the world you are heading into. Career criminals class the ordinary, law-abiding citizens as mugs and targets, too stupid, weak and cowardly to break out of the mould that society has set for them. The criminal is the hungry wolf, and straight-goers are the sheep providing a veritable smorgasbord of criminal opportunities. But contempt turns to envy when punishment for our rebelliousness is imminent. Suddenly we long to be part of straight society, wrapped in the cosy conventionality that straight-goers take for granted. The moment passes the second you enter the prison gates and realize that you are not going to be given a second chance. All prison transports smell

of loneliness, dashed hopes and lost chances, but prisons themselves just smell like resentment and spite.

On 10 October 1975, I sat in one such prison transport, hands
shackled with four pounds of steel handcuffs, nursing a thick
lip and flanked by two grim-looking screws. I was on my way
to Her Majesty's Juvenile Detention Centre, Send, to serve a
sentence of three months. The handcuffs were tight on my
wrists, but my throat was even tighter. HMDC Send was the
flagship of the Short Sharp Shock regime, and it had a reputation for brutality that could shrivel the heart of the most hardened juvenile recalcitrant. If someone had stopped that van and
offered me freedom on the proviso that I turn my back on
crime from that moment, I honestly think I would not be sitting
in a prison cell today. A friend of mine, a prolific burglar and
car thief, was sentenced to three months at HMDC Send but
was released on appeal after ten days and never committed
another crime in his life. The regime was such that it frightened
the desire for criminality right out of him. But if he had served
his full sentence, he would have got past the initial fear after
the first couple of weeks, just as the rest of us did, and it would
no longer have had a deterrent impact on him. The reason the
Short Sharp Shock treatment didn't work was because it lasted
too long. Humans have a great capacity for getting used to even
the most horrific inflictions, and the younger we are, the quicker
we get used to it.

The prison van left the familiar streets of south London and
headed into the wilds of Surrey. To me, anywhere past the end
of the Northern Line was countryside and full of unknown dangers.
I felt uncomfortable going into this green and neatly affluent alien
landscape. I longed for the graffiti-covered walls, burnt-out cars
and piss-soaked lifts of south London council estates. One of the
escort screws nudged me in the ribs. 'Not long now,' he said, and
chuckled.

I tried to swallow but my throat was too dry. I closed my eyes
and wished I was back home with my mum. Fear of the unknown
was turning my limbs to lead, but I had made my own decisions

concerning crime, and now I would have to accept the consequences. The van pulled into a long driveway, and I said a silent prayer.

I had spent the summer of 1975 waging a one-kid war against the police. I hot-wired motorbikes and deliberately went looking for patrol cars hoping to instigate a chase. It was all a great game to me, but with an underlying barb of spite. They had fitted me up and branded me a criminal and had hurt and terrified me while doing it, so I craved revenge. The unfairness of it rankled and festered in my psyche until I had to show them that I was not to be fucked with. I had always been the sort of kid who would stand up for myself and fight and I hated bullies; my dad had taught me that. So after my run-in with the burglary squad, who I considered snides and bullies of the first order, I made it my mission to try and inflict some of the same kind of feelings of shame and humiliation on the police that they had inflicted on me.

I burgled the Grafton Lawn Tennis Club, the bar of which was a favourite after-hours haunt of the local police, and escaped with most of the wine and spirits, as well as the money from the fruit machines. With the proceeds I held a party for all the local tearaways on a bit of wasteground across the road from the estate where I lived. We lit a huge bonfire, got roaring drunk and caroused well into the night. A neighbour complained about the noise, and the police arrived, mob-handed, to be greeted by a barrage of empty wine- and vodka-bottles. There was a terrible tear-up, but once again I managed to get away. By now I was one of the most wanted kids in south London. I no longer lived at home, where it would be easy for the police to find me; instead I slept rough, sometimes on friends' floors, other times in abandoned cars or garden sheds. I did what I wanted when I wanted, and there was no one to stop me. I had complete freedom, and I loved it.

The police were going around in circles trying to find me. Whenever they stopped any of the other estate kids, which was often in those days of Stop and Search, they would always question them as to my whereabouts, and reports would get back to me. But I moved about too much for anyone ever to be sure where I was. Though I was no longer living at home, and the police knew that, it did not stop them from raiding my family's flat periodically. One night, at the height of my madness, I rode a stolen motorbike up to Streatham police station and launched a brick through the window because they had been rude to my mum during one of their searches. On another occasion I stole a copper's personal motorbike from his parking space inside the yard of Union Grove police station and rode it into the ground before dumping it in the pond on Clapham Common. The copper who owned the bike took to hanging around my known haunts when he was off duty in the hope of laying his truncheon across my head. He caught a mate of mine, Harry Mayne, on a stolen motorbike and gave him a terrible beating, all the while shouting, 'Where's Smith?'

My war on the police was temporarily halted in October 1975, when I was caught bang-to-rights trying to hot-wire a Honda 90, of all things. I fancied a joyride, and the Honda was the first bike I came across. I was crouched next to it, fiddling with the wires, when two patrol cars skidded up and boxed me in. I was well and truly nicked.

At the police station I was given a 'mattress job'. Every police cell has a two-inch-thick foam mattress for prisoners to sleep on, and a favoured trick of the police is to knock their victim to the floor, throw the mattress over him and then jump and stamp all over it. It is a way of giving out a painful beating without leaving any visible marks on the victim's body. The beating hurt, but I had already had a lot worse, and it only served to reinforce my hatred of the police.

By this time I hated them so much that if someone had given me a machine-gun and a bag of grenades I would happily have stormed any police station on a murder spree. I refused to make a statement other than to warn that I would be back to burn their station to the ground. I was charged with the theft of a Suzuki 550 from Union Grove police station, theft of a Honda CB250, attempted theft of a Honda 90, burglary of the Grafton

Lawn Tennis Club and assaulting three police officers during my arrest. The assaults on the police were a complete fiction and standard police procedure in those days, designed to cover the officers if I were to press charges for them assaulting me and also to make sure that even a liberal magistrate would consider nothing other than a custodial sentence.

The next day, I appeared before Balham juvenile court to answer the charges. The three worthy magistrates made it plain that they were not interested in my protestations of innocence on the assault charges. As far as they were concerned, they would neither see, hear nor speak of the police doing any evil. In fact, they commended the arresting officers for risking life and limb in bringing me to justice. The police officers preened and smarmed for the court, chuckling at the weakest jokes the magistrates made and feigning hurt and shock at my suggestion that they had trumped up the assault charges. Just standing there watching this performance between police and magistrates made me realize that I had no chance. The odds were severely stacked in the system's favour; they all understood each other, like one big club from which I had been excluded. I remembered hearing that IRA men turned their backs on British courts to show their contempt for a justice system that was biased against them from the start, and I decided to do the same. I turned my back on the magistrates, which only served to confirm their opinion of me as an arrogant young thug. I can't remember the exact words the magistrate used but it was something along those lines. After five minutes of deliberations by the three wise monkeys on the bench, I was sentenced to three months' detention at HMDC Send.

From the outside Send looked like a German prisoner-of-war camp, not Colditz Castle but one of the down-market ones they used for holding enlisted men rather than upper-class officers. It was all high fences, razor-wire and spotlights. As the van rolled through the huge gates and into the first compound, I spotted ranks of shaven-headed youths in blue overalls and hobnail boots giving it plenty of army-style dance steps, marching, marking time, doubling and dressing-off like a bunch of demented squaddies.

All around them, dog-headed screws in long black raincoats were barking orders at full volume. I was about to get my first taste of the Short Sharp Shock.

In the 1970s the Short Sharp Shock was all the rage for dealing with petty juvenile offenders. By some strange logic it was believed that criminality could be beaten out of children, rather as ignorant people in the seventeenth century believed they could drive 'the devil' out of lonely old women by burning them as witches. Boys between the ages of fourteen and seventeen were herded together in prison camps like Send, had their heads shaved and were subjected to extremes of bullying and violence by the kind of men who should never have been allowed access to society as a whole, let alone young boys. The Short Sharp Shock became an abuser's charter and attracted the hang-'em-and-flog-'em merchants like dead meat attracts flies.

In order to lend a veneer of respectability to the Short Sharp Shock regimes, the people who thought them up put forward the concept that what they were doing was 'training' their charges to lead a 'good and useful life'. In actuality, the 'training' consisted of menial, pointless tasks, like breaking up reject cassette-tapes with a toffee-hammer, or hard labour, like digging holes in a field and then filling them back in again. It was thought that the best way to a young thug's conscience was through his arse with a size-twelve boot. Violence was meted out on a daily basis and delivered so casually it became the norm, and if a screw raised his hand to scratch his nose, every boy in the vicinity would instinctively duck.

The whole concept of trying to rehabilitate young offenders by locking them up together and subjecting them to violence is a flawed one. By banding them together in adversity and giving them a system of authority as a common enemy, you can only give them more of an outlaw status and mentality. Kids like me who had been outsiders in their own communities because of their offending behaviour suddenly realized they were not alone. Places like Send gave us an identity and the sense of belonging to an elite brotherhood. The regime made us fit and mean and full of contempt for straight society. The screws, magistrates and police forced us into a pigeon-hole where we had to meld together, and we became stronger for it. They treated us as though we were rabid dogs, so in some ways that is what we became, biting the affluent buttocks of society whenever we got the chance.

But, most damaging of all, the Short Sharp Shock gave us the two essentials that were needed to consolidate our lives of crime – information and contacts. Without either, it's difficult to progress as a career criminal. I find it hard to credit that all the so-called experts on juvenile crime have repeatedly failed to grasp the fact that locking children up is not the solution but a major part of the problem. If criminals can be created, then it is surely places like Send, Rochester, Feltham, Aylesbury and Portland that create them. Today I can look around the yard of almost any prison in the country and see someone I did time with in the juvenile system. None of us was rehabilitated by it; in fact, just the opposite. We all went on to bigger crimes. The car thief became the getaway driver; the burglar became the robber; the kid serving time for assault became the murderer. So who's to say that the juvenile-prison regimes had no hand in our criminal development? I sincerely believe they did, maybe through ignorance, but the end result was the exact opposite of their professed aim.

I was dragged from the van by the two escort screws and pushed, roughly, into the reception building. The escort screws had already given me a few slaps in the court cell when they picked me up. Nothing spectacular, but enough to let me know who was in charge. And the first thing I was given at HMDC Send was a good hiding. Two screws, with their shirtsleeves rolled up and bored expressions on their faces, began to work me over before I was even through the door. I felt like a copper at a Millwall home game. I found out later that the reception beating was standard for everyone. The screws wanted all young tearaways to know who was in charge right from the start. It was supposed to instil fear and unquestioning obedience. And it worked, for a short while.

I was used to getting slaps and punches from grown men in uniform, due to my previous experience of the police, but even I was somewhat disconcerted by the zombie-like fashion in which the beating was delivered. I suppose even sadists can have too much of a good thing.

After the screws had finished punching the living daylights out of me, I was locked into a cell the size of a dog kennel and left to marinate in my fear and pain. I could hear the screws chatting and having the occasional chuckle somewhere beyond the steel door, and I wasn't sure if this made them more human or less. Every now and then the spy-hole would click open and I would be inspected by a glaringly malevolent eye. Eventually the door flew open and my tormentors were ready to dish out phase two of the Send initiation.

It started with a punch to the side of my head that for a moment made me stagger about like a drunken sailor until the screw grabbed my arm and made me stand still. My eyes were just beginning to come into focus when he barked in my ear. 'Whenever you see an officer, you fucking well stand to attention and shout, "Excuse me sir!", understand?'

My ears were ringing but I managed to nod. 'Yeah,' I said. Slap in the face.

'Yeah, what, you little toe-rag?'

I tried to think. 'Yeah, I stand to attention and . . .'

Kick to the shin.

'Yeah, what, you maggot?'

I caught the drift. 'Yeah, sir.' It was a slow and painful process, but I was learning the rules.

The screw nodded. 'Now, you fucking poor excuse for an afterbirth, when I say "go", you will double your stinking little body over to that desk and give your name and number to that nice officer sitting there. GO!'

As I ran to the desk my amazing powers of perception told me that I was in for another dig, because I didn't have a clue what number he was talking about. I jumped to attention in front of the desk and took a chance. 'Excuse me, sir,' I squealed. 'Noel

Stephen Smith. Er . . . 14.' It was my age, the only number I could think of apart from the 137 bus which stopped outside my estate.

Sure enough I got a hard kick in the arse from the screw who followed me to the desk.

'We don't want to know what your mummy calls you, you plank. You're not out robbing old ladies' gas-meters now, boy. In here, your name is Smith, and your number is K00064. What is it?'

I swallowed blood and whatever shreds of pride I had left.

'Smith, K00064, sir,' I shouted.

The screw behind the desk looked at a sheaf of paperwork. 'You were sentenced to three months' detention by Balham juvenile court, is this correct?' he asked.

'Yeah, sir,' I answered.

He slammed his fist down on the desk. 'Yeah? Yeah? Who are you then, one of the fucking Beatles? The word is "yes", understand?'

'Yes, sir,' I shouted.

And so it went. No humiliation was too small for them to miss. I was made to strip naked and stand in a corner as screws came and went through the reception area. And of course none of them could pass by without making a disparaging comment or giving me a slap. After thirty minutes of this I was ordered to bathe in three inches of cold water, given a set of overalls and taken to have my head shaved. The barber at Send was just any screw who happened to be standing nearest to the clippers. He shaved my head like he was shearing a flea-infested sheep. By now I had learned to answer every inquiry with 'Yes, sir' and run everywhere I was directed. By the time I left the reception area I had been at Send for about four hours but I felt like I had been there all my life.

I was given my kit wrapped in a large canvas raincoat and ordered to double from the reception area up to A-wing. The induction wing was the only one with single cells; the rest of the wings, B to Dx, were dormitories containing twenty beds in each. I doubled down the corridor to an open cell which contained an iron-frame bed, a plastic piss-pot and a small, barred window.

'You've got five minutes to get that fucking bed made up before lights out,' barked the escort screw.

With those kind parting words he slammed the door shut.

I was still straightening the green army blanket when the light was switched off from outside the cell, plunging me into an unfamiliar darkness. I finished making the bed as best I could and climbed into it. After a little while the spotlights around the grounds were switched on and shafts of light penetrated the dark cell. I lay in bed watching the moving shadows on the wall and listening to the noises of the prison bedding down for the night. I heard the occasional squeak from the night-patrolman's shoes and the click as he looked through the spy-hole on the door at regular intervals. I was battered, bruised and emotionally drained. I hated this place and I wanted my mum. Despite my outward shows of bravado I was still only a scared kid. I worried that I might not be able to get through this sentence and fretted at what else might be in store for me in the weeks to come. I cried for a short while, and eventually I fell into sleep.

I was awakened later in the night by a truncheon banging on the door and a torch-beam shining on to my face through the spy-hole.

'Keep your hands outside of the bedclothes,' said the voice from outside the door.

Even in sleep there was no escape.

The first week at Send was the worst. I was double-timed everywhere, harried by barking screws, poked and prodded by a doctor who declared me 'fit for training' and interviewed by various sour-faced officials who looked at me like I was a turd in a trifle. When I wasn't doubling, I was standing on the spot marking time, as pointless an exercise as walking the treadmill, a device employed by the Victorian prison system to make sure that prisoners were not left idle. It was a huge wheel with steps on every spoke which prisoners were required to constantly climb, thus keeping the wheel turning but the prisoner in exactly the same place he started. Sometimes this was done for fourteen hours a day. I had to mark time for an hour at one go. Apparently, marking time is very big in the army, and as far as I'm concerned, they can keep it.

Every morning at six we were woken by a screw marching up and down the wings banging a truncheon on a dustbin lid and screaming obscenities. We then had ten minutes to fold our bedclothes into a square pack about half the size of a pillow and lay out every piece of kit on the mattress in a specified order for morning inspection. The piss-pot had to be scrubbed clean and left in the designated corner of the cell with the lid off. Morning inspections were a nightmare as the screws usually had hangovers and would show their displeasure by scattering carefully laid-out kit and shouting at us to do it again.

After kit-inspection we had to line up outside the recess in our pyjama bottoms carrying towel, toothbrush and powder, and White Windsor soap. White Windsor is the soap that is supplied by the prison system. It has no smell to it and quickly becomes jellified if kept in water for too long. The 'recess' is what they call the communal bathroom in prison, and it usually consists of a line of metal sinks with a polished plastic mirror above each one and three toilet cubicles with half-doors. There is no such thing as privacy in a prison toilet; you might as well be having a shit in Oxford Street on a Saturday afternoon. Every boy was issued with a safety razor and expected to scrape their cheeks whether they had anything to shave or not. If the razor was handed back dry, you could expect to be placed on report for refusing an order. My first morning in Send I was shocked by the scene that greeted me in the recess. It looked like a slaughterhouse. The only way to avoid being placed on report was to leave the recess with a cut on your chin, thus proving the job had been done. The smell of blood in the mornings is an abiding memory of HMDC Send.

The tortures inflicted on us at Send were many and varied. Most were of the unsophisticated physical type but others had a psychological edge. For example, all meals were eaten in a large dining-hall while standing and maintaining complete silence. We were allowed to send out one letter a week, to parents only, and the words were dictated by a screw. If anyone dared to deviate from the officially sanctioned script about how well we were being treated, it would soon be brought to our attention by the censor. The offending boy would be made to stand at the front of the dining-hall as his letter was read out by a screw. The result was humiliation. Another form of humiliation was 'Skid of the Week'. Each item of our kit was marked with our DC number and had to be handed in for laundry every Friday night. The laundry workers, for a reward of one bag of Murray Mints, would pull out the most disgracefully skid-mark-laden Y-fronts and match the number with the name of the owner. The offending pants would then be pinned on a notice board outside the dining-hall for everyone to see.

Another dreaded torture was the 'bunny-hop', which was normally given as a block punishment. If one person was caught talking in a dorm after lights out, we would all be awakened at 5 a.m. and be forced on to the patch of concrete outside each wing. Barefoot and wearing only pyjama bottoms, with our bed-packs balanced on our shoulders we would be lined up and ordered to crouch in the squat position. Then for the next hour we would have to hop around in circles. The pain this produces in the body, and especially the legs, is excruciating. Any boy who dropped his bed-pack or lagged behind would have to do twenty press-ups before carrying on. The misery and pain was increased tenfold on winter mornings when the frost was thick on the concrete and would burn our feet with cold. Of course the screws would make sure we knew the name of the boy who was the cause of our punishment, and he would get a beating from all of us later in the day.

The regime at Send taught me to hate all kinds of authority. It was during this time that I found out exactly how tough I was, and this gave me a lot of confidence in myself. In my own mind my sentence became a contest between me and 'the system', and I was determined to win. In the first two weeks they had kept me off balance, but now I was coming through the pain barrier and shaking off my confusion. I refused to be beaten, either mentally or physically. I found the secret weapon that has helped many prisoners to get through their time and survive – hate. The more they prodded, poked and ordered me around, the more I grew to hate the bastards. I could feel my hate roiling and rumbling within me, like thick molten lava seeking the smallest crack to erupt out of, but I clamped down on it, set my face on neutral and used hate as the fuel that drove me. When I felt myself falling behind on one of their pointless punishments, I could summon up my hate in a second, grit my teeth to contain it and carry on. 'You can't have me!', became my personal mantra, running through my mind from the moment I woke up till the moment I fell asleep, and sometimes in my dreams.

By the end of the second week I had learned to roll with the blows. I progressed to B-wing, which was a dormitory wing, and the screws had new fish to give their attention to. I was still assaulted on a daily basis, as we all were, but it had lost its shock-value. I had never heard of Nietzsche, but I would have understood his philosophy that what doesn't kill us only makes us stronger; I was growing stronger by the day. Soon I was an old hand, a veteran who knew all the dodges and shortcuts that made the regime bearable. I had learned to crave the thrice-daily PE sessions, where I could vent some of my hate in physical exercise.

Mixing with the other boys was an education. I learned that most of them had suffered beatings and fittings at the hands of the police, and some of them hated the police almost as much as I did. We pooled a lot of criminal information, such as how to hot-wire cars, how to bypass a burglar alarm, and also specific information like the fact that Marks & Spencer stores did not alarm their skylights and kept a £20 float in each till overnight. There was a great sense of camaraderie, and we would help each other out whenever possible. Before the inspections we would all pull together and get the dorm shining like a guardsman's button. Those who had the knack of squaring off bed-packs and kit would help those who didn't.

We kept ourselves fortified with tales of daring crimes we had pulled off or were going to pull off when we got out. There was a lot of talk about how we might 'fuck the system' and, in a way, we thought of ourselves as partisans caught behind enemy lines whose job it was to sabotage the system in any small way we could. In our minds, we were the 'goodies' here and the screws were the 'baddies'. It was as simple as that. And when our talk turned to crime, which was often, it was universally agreed that the elite of the criminal world was the Heavy Mob, the big boys who committed armed robberies. As a breed, they seemed to be men of honour and humour, the swashbucklers of the crime world. They were our heroes and what most of us aspired to be. To us, the height of achievement was getting your picture in the papers. We all wanted glamour, respect, riches and notoriety, and most of us had figured out that the only way to get them was through crime, a profession in which we were already serving apprenticeships. We had all seen the films and television programmes that glorified and glamourized crime: the heroic Butch and Sundance wisecracking their way into a hail of Bolivian bullets; Cagney spitting in a screw's eye; De Niro as Johnny Boy in *Mean Streets*. Death was an abstract concept to us; it was how you got there that was important, and how much fame you picked up along the way.

On the other side, our prime examples of straight society were the bully-boy screws and cops and the snidey magistrates who had looked down their noses and passed judgement on us. Should we long to be just like our jailers, uniformed lackeys whose small moments of excitement and joy came from trying to break the body and crush the spirit of anyone who dared to deviate from society's rules, or should we crave the glamour and excitement of mythical heroes and rebels? We were kids, for fuck's sake – it was no contest.

A lot of the kids also admired the protection gangs of the 1960s, the Krays in east London and the Richardsons in south London. Personally, I was never that enamoured of them. To me, they were nothing more than bullies and ponces. You never heard of the Krays pulling off a decent blag; they waited for the real thieves to do the work and then demanded a share. My heroes were people like the Great Train-Robbers, John McVicar, the Wembley Bank-Robbers, John Dillinger and Willie Sutton, men with the bottle and panache to do their own thieving. They were violent robbers who controlled their violence and used just enough of it to get the prize. They didn't slash innocent people for looking at them 'funny' or eat Chinese take-aways while watching their henchmen cut off people's toes for some imagined slight.

There was one notable incident at Send which was to become typical of my character. I was on a party of 'trainees' whose job it was to dig holes in a field and then fill them back in again. It was back-breaking work and we all hated it. The screw in charge was a huge, beefy farmer-type with a red face who wasn't shy about throwing a few digs at us. One day we were all having a moan about the job when someone half-heartedly suggested that we should just refuse to do it. I liked this idea, so that night I told the lads that I was going to refuse to work the next morning. They were in awe, but delighted, and agreed that if I made the first move they would all back me up. Great, I thought, no more digging holes. We would be a real force of resistance.

The next morning we were marched to the large shed on the edge of our work field to change into wellington boots and get our shovels. Once inside the shed, everyone looked expectantly at me. By now I was shitting myself and wishing I had never opened my big mouth, but my pride would not allow me to back out now. I would rather suffer a thousand beatings than the embarrassment of bottling out in front of my peers. Beatings heal, but a reputation as a wanker can follow you all your life. The farmer screw came to the door of the shed to see what the hold-up was. I swallowed my fear and got ready to give him the bad news.

'Come on, you fucking toe-rags, get your boots on and get to work,' he shouted.

Nobody moved. He stared hard at us, waiting.

'I said, get your fucking boots on. Now.'

I stood up and faced him. 'We ain't working no more,' I said clearly, and I was pleased that my voice came out so steady.

He did a double-take that would have been comical under other circumstances. He screwed up his face and stared at me in silence for a moment, then nodded his big head as though coming to a decision. He walked up to me.

'You the leader of this little mutiny then, are you?' he asked.

I squared my shoulders and nodded.

'Well, that should have been, "We ain't working no more, *sir*."' And with that he hit me a tremendous punch to the side of the head.

I didn't see it coming but I certainly felt it landing. I was lifted off my feet by the force of the blow and cartwheeled on to my back into a pile of shovels. I tried to get up but felt sick and dizzy.

Through my pain and confusion I was aware of the farmer screw roaring and throwing digs at everyone. He sounded like a wounded bull, bellowing and thrashing about. All of my pals and confederates who had promised to be 'right behind' me were, in fact, right in front of me, grabbing their shovels like there was a cash-prize for the first one ready for work. They scampered out of the shed without a backward glance. So much for solidarity.

I managed to climb unsteadily to my feet and shook my head to clear the buzz. The farmer screw was talking into his radio. 'One for the block,' he was saying. 'Trying to incite a mutiny . . .'

I stared at his face as he spoke into the radio. He looked smug and happy. And suddenly all the black, bilious hate I had kept tamped down inside me for so long rushed to the surface. Something in my head seemed to snap; I heard it clearly, it sounded like a pencil being broken in two. A tidal wave of rage washed over me, filling me with strength and purpose. I grabbed a shovel from the floor and advanced on the farmer screw fully intending to cave his head in and wipe the smugness from his face. I was sick of being used as a punchbag by these fucking people, and if I was going to the block anyway, it might as well be for something as nothing. I was not blinded by my rage, I was fully aware of what I was doing. I was colder than a magistrate's smile and completely *compos*. I wanted to hurt this bastard, for making me look a mug more than for the punch itself.

Just as I started my swing with the shovel, the farmer screw caught my movement from the corner of his eye and took a huge step backwards. I missed him by the thickness of a Rizla and hit the concrete lintel of the doorway with enough force to send vibrations up to my shoulders. If the shovel had made contact with his head, he would now be dead, and he knew it. The look of fear and panic on his face was like petrol on a fire to me. I got a better grip on my weapon and went for him again. He was screaming into his radio now as he scrambled from the shed, and I chased him out into the field, swinging the shovel around my head like a tomahawk. The work party watched in astonishment as the farmer screw bounded into the field, babbling into his radio and throwing fearful glances over his shoulder.

The looks of amused contempt and amazement on the faces of the work party as this fat bully got his comeuppance were enough to slow me down and allow me to start dampening down my hate once again. My honour had been satisfied and my pride restored. I ran on after him for a moment, but then I stopped and dropped the shovel to the ground. The farmer screw didn't stop until he reached the razor-wire fencing that surrounded the work field. He leant against the fence, bent double and wheezing like an asthmatic. His face had reached a shade of red only usually found on the breasts of Christmas-card robins, and the look in his eyes was pure terror. I looked towards the gate on to the field and saw a posse of screws running towards me, batons drawn and bloodlust in their eyes. I pointed a finger at the farmer screw cowering by the fence and my heart swelled with pride and a residue of rage.

'You ever touch me again, and I'll fucking kill you!' I roared. And I meant it.

The screws piled into me, batons swinging, and knocked me to the ground. I knew the rules instinctively: for every victory over the system, there is a price to pay. I was prepared to accept my beating; there was no shame in taking a hiding when you are outnumbered and it isn't personal. But the screws did not strong it at all. I now realize that they were frightened. They had never been challenged before, let alone by a skinny little kid who weighed only eight stone wringing wet. And the rest of the work party, now emboldened by my display of rebellion, were approaching the screws, faces set and shovels gripped tightly. A senior officer shouted at the work party to get into the shed, but for a moment no one moved. 'Get him to the block, quickly,' muttered the same SO, indicating me. I was hustled off between two screws, and the deadlock was broken.

I was dragged down the short corridor that led to the punishment block and launched head first into a cell. Before I had bounced off the back wall, the cell door was slammed shut, leaving me alone in the silence. It had been touch and go on the work field, and I found out afterwards that when I was gone, the farmer screw began to bluster about the beating I was going to get in the block and the lads almost kicked off again, but in the end sanity prevailed and the work party was given the rest of the morning off. They were sent back to the wing for an extra kit-inspection, and the farmer screw was sent off duty, probably for a stiff drink.

I was brought in front of a worried-looking governor the next morning for adjudication. I was expecting a big show, but the event was very low-key. I was sentenced to five days' loss of remission for 'refusing a direct order to work'. There was no mention of my attempt to decapitate the farmer screw or inciting an incident of indiscipline. I was proud of myself for having stood up to the might of the system and for proving, to myself and others, that I was game.

When I was released from the block, the other kids were in awe of me and treated me like a hero. I lapped it up like a mangey cat with a saucer of cream. I was now a 'face' and deserved respect from my fellow prisoners. As a bonus, I was relocated to one of the workshops, where the work was repetitive but easier than digging holes. And though the screws would still shout in my direction, not one of them raised a hand to me again.

The field incident and its aftermath taught me a few lessons, the main one being that I could use violence and hate to get what I wanted. The system was not as unbeatable as it would have us believe, and fighting it was a way of getting respect and recognition. These beliefs were to stick with me and blight my life for years to come.

I was released from HMDC Send on a cold November morning. My head was shaved, my body bruised and my clothes wrinkled, but my spirit was stronger than ever. I had passed through a small corner of hell and survived to tell the tale. I had learned to harness my hate and use it to drive my body whenever my endurance was flagging. I had learned that I was not alone but that ultimately I could rely only on myself when things got tough, and I had learned to hate the system. I was now an ex-con, not yet sixteen years old but already firmly branded a criminal for the rest of my life. In my pocket I had the details of a kid from north London who had been released the week before me. He had promised me a shooter as soon as I could come up with £25, and I intended to take him up on that offer. Straight society had nothing to offer me other than contempt and discrimination but, as a criminal, the world was there for my taking. And I intended taking as much as I could carry.

4. Young Guns

After being released from HMDC Send, I really felt as though I had achieved something. I was fit and strong, and I had taken the worst the authorities could dish out and found something inside myself that had enabled me to survive. A lot of kids did not survive Send intact. There were five attempted suicides while I was there and at least two kids left in ambulances, never to be seen again. A few months after I left there was a lot of publicity about a fifteen-year-old who died when the gym screws pushed him too hard in a PE session. HMDC Send was a make-or-break deal, and no one gave a shit for the kids who got broken. For kids like me it was a rite of passage, the criminal's version of going out into the bush to kill a lion. It was the worst of the juvenile jails and once I had been through it I knew there was little left in the armoury of the authorities that could scare me – except borstal. And I had no intention of ever being caught again, so I never thought about that.

By rights I was still under school-leaving age but on leaving Send I had been asked to sign a document that allowed me to leave school early. I don't know whose idea that was, but it suited me fine. Maybe the school authorities knew that I would never willingly go back to school and gave up on me. I had been decreed 'unruly' by the courts and what was known as an 'unruly certificate' had been issued on me. This meant I was fit for jailing but not for educating. Perhaps they thought that if I was forced back into school my obvious criminality might rub off on the other kids and turn them all into juvenile delinquents. I didn't care, school to me was just a lesser form of prison.

In theory, I had served my time and I should now settle down, get a job on a building site and live happily ever after. But in

reality I was marked more indelibly than Cain. If any skulduggery went off on my manor the police would be at my door
a close second behind the accusing fingers. I was the local tearaway and, to be honest, I loved it. I felt I had found my niche
in life and I was determined to be good at it. I had learned a lot
about crime in Send and how much money could be earned
from it. Until I went to Send, my crimes had been of the
amateurish, spur-of-the-moment variety, committed out of petty
revenge and spite, but now I was looking at crime as a career
opportunity, something I could make a decent living out of. The
more I thought about it, the more attractive it seemed. Ironically,
it was the freedom of such a life that attracted me: I could have
whatever I wanted just by taking it. The opportunities were
boundless.

My family welcomed me back, as they always do. Mum cooked
me a big breakfast and fussed over me. Dad took me to one side
and gave me a serious talk about staying out of trouble, then he
slipped me a tenner as a welcome-home present. Mick and
Samantha just took my return in their stride. It was almost as
though I had never been away. I love my family, and I know they
love me, but I've always felt like a bit of an outsider, due mainly
to the amount of time I've spent away from them, either in prison
or on the run. One of the sad things about choosing a life of
crime is that I put an unbreachable distance between myself and
my family. I could never tell them a fraction of the things that
happened to me in prison; it would be like trying to explain
colour to a blind person.

I was soon back on the wrong side of the law. The afternoon
after I left Send, my old pal Micky, who was now also a confirmed
tearaway, turned up at the estate on a stolen Honda 500. I didn't
need much persuading to hop on the back. We went looking for
a police car to chase us. Getting chased by the police was our
idea of fun, just so long as we had the advantage of surprise and
manoeuvrability. With our reckless ability to drive on pavements
and through tight spaces, the police could rarely catch us. We
would find a patrol car and draw up alongside it, pulling faces

and flipping them the two-fingered salute, and then accelerate away to bring on the chase. Our favourite escape route was under the railway bridge at the Telford Avenue end of Tooting Bec Common and away across the open grassland.

I loved the speed and freedom of a motorbike, and when I was on the run from the police before my time in Send, I always had one handy, stolen and hot-wired. Sometimes I would take a stolen bike out at three in the morning and ride it at full speed, with no crash helmet, up and down the length of Kings Avenue. The long straight road that leads from Streatham to Brixton was perfect for building up plenty of speed, and though it's dissected by two sets of traffic lights, I never stopped at either during my early hours runs. A couple of times I did the run drunk and in the pouring rain, at speeds of 90 to 100 miles per hour, my open shirt flapping in the slipstream, my mouth wide open catching rain. If I had met a car coming the other way at either set of lights I would've been dead before what was left of my body hit the ground, but I didn't give a shit. It was a rush, and I loved doing it.

Looking back now, I can see that I was an adrenaline junkie. Everything I did was taken to the extreme, from taunting the police into chasing me to being an armed robber by the age of sixteen. I needed my fix of danger and excitement. I had to go right up to the crumbling edge of every abyss and stare in for longer than was necessary. Even in prison I could never just get my head down and do my time, I felt compelled to push my luck, fighting an all-out war against the might of a system that, in reality, could never be beaten. I am always the one willing to throw the first punch, to sit down first on the yard, to throw the first meal over the screws, to be first through the door on a robbery, to fire the first shot in a gunfight. I now realize that adrenaline was my drug of choice; that's why I've never been interested in heroin or crack and why I didn't even try cannabis till I was twenty-seven or coke till I was thirty-eight. My fix was being produced inside my own body, and my brain knew how to find it every time.

Now I have accepted the fact that I was an adrenaline junkie, I can theorize that what I really needed in order for my life to take a different direction was a war. My generation had no war in which to vent our violence and aggression, which I would guess is why there have been so many battles on the football terraces, in pubs and clubs and on the streets in the last thirty years. Certainly I believe a war would have been my chance to shine or die trying. I craved danger, and when none was forthcoming I created my own.

That afternoon, Micky and I spotted a patrol car sitting at traffic lights at Clapham South. We pulled alongside and I gave the passenger the wanker sign and kicked his door, and we shot the lights and screamed off down Balham Hill. The patrol car followed, blue lights flashing and siren wailing. We were both laughing as we blew through twisting side-streets at 70 mph. The patrol car had no chance, so a couple of times we slowed down to let it catch up. We were soon joined by a second patrol car, so we decided to end the chase by heading for the common. But as we came off the common at the other side, there was a motorbike copper waiting for us.

It's one thing to outrun a patrol car or two but motorbike coppers are different gravy, they can follow where a car can't go. We tried to shake him off, but every time I looked back he was on our tail, hanging around just behind us like a bad smell. And to make it worse, he was in radio contact with the patrol cars. Everywhere we turned there were flashing lights and sirens. Micky decided to take us back towards the estate so we could dump the bike and try to escape on foot through familiar territory, but as we came around the bend at the bottom of Streatham Hill, closely followed by a posse of police vehicles, the Honda went into an uncontrollable skid and we both came off.

I must have rolled about fifteen times before coming to rest against a garden wall. Luckily I was wearing a crash helmet that day, because my head bounced off every hard surface in the area. I didn't bother looking around, as soon as I hit the wall I was up and running. But I had no chance. A patrol car sped alongside me, and the copper in the passenger seat opened his door suddenly. I went straight over and landed on my head again. Before I could get up, I was wearing a blue blanket. With about forty-five stone of coppers on my back, I was going nowhere. They quickly had the cuffs on and my crash helmet off. The copper who had stopped me with the car door was the same one I had called a wanker at the start of the chase. And he wasn't best pleased with me.

As they dragged me towards the car, they got a few sly digs in, and now the adrenaline rush was wearing off I began to feel the pain. By the time they got me into the car, three other coppers appeared, red in the face and out of breath.

'The driver got away,' I heard them say. I chuckled.

One of the coppers reached into the car and punched me in the face. 'Think it's fucking funny, do you?' he shouted at me.

I tasted blood in my mouth, so I spat it through the door at him. It splashed on his chest and he went fucking berserk. He came into the car like a torpedo, head-first, and began swinging wild punches at me and cursing. My hands were cuffed behind my back, but I dodged him as best I could, and due to the confined space and his rage, he never caught me with a clean blow. The other coppers dragged him out of the car and tried to calm him down.

I noticed that two old ladies had come out of the nearest house and were standing watching with shocked faces. I sprayed out a bit more blood and allowed it to trickle down my chin, then I looked at them with a frightened and plaintive face.

'Please help me,' I cried. 'The police are trying to kill me, and I haven't done anything! They say they're going to give me a terrible hiding at the police station. I'm scared.'

It did the trick. The two old dears went marching up to the group of coppers, who were still busy trying to calm their mate down, and began verbally laying into them. One of them hurried back into the house to get a pen and paper to take down their numbers. I was dying to laugh, but I had to keep a sad face. The coppers quickly dispersed, leaving the motorbike cop to wait for the van to pick up our wrecked Honda. Two of them jumped into the front of the car in which I was a prisoner and tried to drive off, but one of the ladies stood in front of the car until her mate was able to write down the registration number. The coppers were swearing under their breaths, but there was not a lot they could do. As we eventually pulled away, I turned a scared pathetic face towards the ladies, and I knew they would be on the phone to the police station right away.

By the time we got to Streatham police station I knew the cops were worried by what the old ladies might say. The driver turned to me when we pulled into the compound.

'You know I never laid a finger on you, mate? I'm just the driver.'

His mate was quick to jump in with his story. 'Yeah, that's right. It wasn't us. The blokes in the other car done all the damage. We pulled them off you, remember?'

I had to milk this situation for all it was worth, so I tried to look slightly confused. 'I can't really remember,' I said. 'All I remember is a lot of policemen beating me up. And my head hurts.'

The coppers got out of the car, but I could hear them talking.

'He's probably got concussion.'

'Yeah, but he'll have got that from coming off the bike, that's nothing to do with us.'

'I don't know, you hit him pretty hard with the car door . . .'

'Fuck off, mate! It was fucking Tony who steamed into him . . .'

I heard every word and I so wanted to laugh out loud. It was nice to see the Old Bill shitting themselves for a change.

When they got me out of the car I pretended to be weak and fell to my knees.

'Oh,' I moaned. 'The handcuffs are cutting into my wrists, please don't hurt me any more, mister.'

They looked at each other, and then one of them leant down and unlocked the cuffs. It was more than I'd hoped for. As they helped me to my feet I gave them a hard shove, which they were not expecting, and legged it through the open gates of the compound. I was so fast that they didn't even chase me. Within minutes I was hiding in a garden four streets away from the police station. And despite trying to keep quiet, I just couldn't stop laughing.

I stayed hidden until it got dark and then carefully made my way home. Micky had got clean away and was waiting for me round the estate. We compared wounds. Micky had badly grazed knees and hands from coming off the Honda and a couple of bruises around his ribs. He had rolled a few times and come up running the same as me, but the coppers who had chased him were on foot and out of condition. As well as a few bruises and a cut lip, I had a nasty graze on my right buttock from skidding on the ground. My jeans were ripped and there was quite a bit of blood. It would leave a nasty scar, which I still have, but I would live.

I felt great about having escaped right out of the lion's den, but I knew it wouldn't take the police long to put two and two together and come up with my name. I had left my fingerprints on the bike. But this just gave me the excuse I needed to go on the run again. That night I stayed at Micky's gaff and didn't go home. I had only been out of Send for two days. So much for the Short Sharp Shock.

I was back to living on the streets and thieving anything that wasn't nailed down, and some things that were. In the small hours of the morning I would carry out smash-and-grab raids, mainly on electrical-goods shops. My methods were very unsophisticated, just a case of finding a likely-looking target with big shiny things in the window and then smashing out the glass with a 2 lb ball-pein hammer and scooping up whatever was portable and saleable. By the time the police got around to investigating the alarm bells, I was long gone. Grundig tape-decks were a great seller, as were pocket calculators, all the rage at that time and very expensive to buy retail.

I had no trouble selling stolen goods, and what the local fences wouldn't buy, I could always sell in second-hand shops. The money wasn't great but I was getting the stuff for nothing so I didn't really give a shit. I knew the petty thieving was only temporary. I had ideas, and plans to go into the big time. All I needed was a couple of sensible partners with plenty of bottle to carry out my plans.

It was around this time that I met up with a kindred spirit, Peter Mayne, aka Pete the Nut, Potty Pete or Choo Choo. Pete was a couple of years older than me and as mad as a hatter, in a kill-'em-all-let-God-sort-'em-out kind of way. All the kids of our age were terrified of him because of his propensity for unprovoked violence. He would not hesitate to use a tool if there was one handy and he didn't like the cut of your jib. Pete was not the full shilling, and maybe not even sixpence, but he definitely had plenty of bottle. I always got on great with him, but I think that was because I didn't have any fear of him and I would tell him when he was out of order.

Pete's brother, Harry, was a good mate of mine, and a great thief. Harry also had plenty of bottle, and he was not as violent as his brother. It was Harry I was looking for when I ran into Pete. He told me that Harry was serving a borstal sentence for GBH on a copper and that he himself was on the run after jumping the fence at Stamford House remand home. He was living in a groundsman's shed on Tooting Bec Common.

I always believed that Pete was misunderstood. Yes, he was a violent lunatic with a hair-trigger and a deep-seated paranoia, but nobody bothered to look any further than that. He was absolutely fearless, loyal and generous, and had a bit of a sense of humour as well. He was never the brightest bulb in the display, and a lot of his violent behaviour was to cover up the fact that life had him confused. He got the nickname Choo Choo after trying to steal a Ford Corsair from a railway station car-park. The keys had been left in the ignition, so Pete jumped in, threw the car into gear and gave the accelerator some welly. Unfortunately, he had thrown the gearstick into reverse, so he crashed through a chain-link fence, down an eight-foot embankment and on to a railway line. He escaped with a broken toe, but caused the South-East rail network to be closed down for four hours while they tried to move the wreckage from the tracks. Knowing that Pete couldn't drive, I asked him what had possessed him to try and steal a car in the first place. He replied, 'Well, I thought that once I was in the driving seat, the old driving game might suddenly come to me.'

That's the kind of blind faith from which religions spring.

Pete and I soon became a win-double. If anything was worth thieving, then we were the boys for the job. Phone boxes and milk machines were always good for a few quid. In the 1970s, before twenty-four-hour supermarkets came along, there were machines on most highstreets that dispensed cartons of milk and orange juice, and an enterprising thief with a large screwdriver could relieve these machines of their cash. It was never a lot, just survival money when you were living on the streets.

We knew a fence who was into antiques in a big way and would pay good money for anything we could get our hands on. We didn't know a jardinière from a jar of peanut butter, but we were willing to learn. Top of the fence's wish-list were a Georgian silver tea-set and a grandfather clock, but this was not the sort of gear we could easily find on the streets of south London, so we had to go out to the sticks.

We would bunk on to the trains without a clue where we were going and just get off when it looked as though we were in the country. We realized that a sure-fire way of knowing if something was an antique was to nick it from an antique shop. Once we spotted a grandfather clock in a small shop in Caterham and decided to try our luck after the shop had closed for the evening. We managed to break in with no trouble, but the clock was too big and bulky for us. Neither of us could drive, and the plan to get the clock back to south London on the train was a bit unrealistic. We dumped the clock two streets away and went back for a couple of bags of reasonably sized objets d'art.

We soon found that the most profitable and portable antique items to steal were carriage clocks, silver items and netsukes (small ivory carvings from Japan). We invariably got ripped off by the fence because we had to take whatever he was willing to pay and there was nowhere to punt these sorts of specialist items about. Later, in the mid-1980s, when ivory dropped out of fashion and became a news issue due to the ban on elephant hunting, I thought again of all the ivory pieces I had stolen in my younger days. I must have nicked at least twenty elephants' worth.

Before long I got pissed off with being cheated by our fence and decided it was time to up our game and step up to the big time. I had the contacts who would get us started.

It was around this time, the long hot summer of 1976, that I became a teddy-boy. I had always been a big fan of the rock 'n' roll of the fifties, and I thought the young Elvis was the dog's bollocks. He had a mean and moody style that I tried to emulate, and I loved the clothes. Not the Vegas jumpsuits, I'm talking about the sharp sports jackets, pegged pants and white bucks of the early fifties, before the army took him. I got my hair cut in a quiff and DA (duck's arse), and started to frequent the Edwardian Club in Brixton, which was run by an original teddy-boy named Tommy Hogan. Pete followed suit.

I loved a lot of things about the ted lifestyle, not least the acceptance. Being a ted was like being in an elite brotherhood; wherever you went you were accepted. If you met another ted on the street, even if you had never seen him before, you would stop and talk. If you saw a ted in trouble, you would help out. In the clubs, nobody gave a fuck if you were under age, someone would buy you a pint, and if you could jive, pulling birds was as easy as asking for a dance. I got right into the teddy-boy thing, and even went as far as buying a cut-throat razor from a second-hand shop. The teds were a violent lot, and often there would be fights with other subcultures, like the skinheads or soul-boys. Punk rockers had not come on to the scene at this stage, but in 1977 they would become our main enemy.

I loved the excitement of a bit of violence and so did Pete, so we slotted right in as teds. Up until now I had been a bit reluctant to use weapons, with the exception of trying to brain the farmer screw with the shovel in DC, but that had been a spur-of-the-moment thing. My dad had instilled in me a belief that your head, hands and feet were the only weapons you needed in a fight, but some of the fights the teds got into involved weapons of every description. I chose the razor just because it was the weapon favoured by a lot of the old teds. It could be easily concealed and, unless you cut someone across the throat, it was unlikely to land you with a murder charge. The cut-throat razor is a slashing tool which causes a lot of pain and a lot of blood but leaves clean wounds that are very easily stitched up. A trick I learned from the old teds was to grind down the rounded end of the blade into a point – you can do this by rubbing it on a wall or lamppost – and then wrap a bit of masking tape around the blade about an inch from the end; this means that when you slash someone, the blade can't go in more than an inch and cause too much damage. We may have loved a bit of violence, but we weren't complete fucking nutters. We had no intention of killing anyone.

I practised religiously with my razor until I could whip it out and flick it open as quickly as any Western gunslinger. I thought I was Jack the Biscuit. And with all that practice, it was only a matter of time before I put it on someone. The first time was outside the Edwardian Club when a group of soul-boys steamed us one night. Most of the soul-boys were blade-merchants, and their favoured weapon was the sheath-knife. During the fight I was cornered by a soul-boy who didn't have a weapon but was getting the better of me with his fists, so I pulled out my razor and struck out blindly. I felt the blade bite into his flesh and stop at the bone, and I jerked my arm back, opening an eight-inch wound from his forehead to his chin. For a moment nothing happened and he carried on throwing punches at me, then his face just seemed to fall apart, and the blood was like a water-fall. He screamed and staggered away holding his face. I felt sick. I just stood there with my mouth open, not believing what I had done. I wanted to run after him and say I was sorry, but someone bounced a pool cue off the back of my head and I instinctively lashed out with the razor again, this time missing the target.

By now the soul-boys were getting the worst of the fight, so they legged it and left us to the post-battle euphoria. One of the older teds had witnessed my slashing of the enemy, and he put his arm around my shoulders and sang my praises to everyone. I wasn't feeling too great. The shame and sickness of slashing an unarmed opponent was coming over me, and I kept seeing the moment when the skin of his face came away, and the look of agony in his eyes. I felt there was no honour in what I had done.

'He didn't even have a tool,' I said quietly.

The ted who had been praising my actions lifted up his shirt and displayed a terrible-looking scar that dissected his stomach.

'That's what those cunts did to me last year. Stuck a fucking bayonet in me guts and left me for dead. I was with me bird and they were mob-handed. I'd be happy if you slashed every fucking one of them!'

I seized on this justification, and it helped to ease my conscience. He was right, it could just as easily have been me that was cut. I rationalized it for a while and by the end of the evening I was boasting about my first cutting.

After that first slashing the rest came easier, until putting the blade across an opponent's face became almost routine to me. I was getting a reputation as a 'tool-merchant', which was no bad thing when every second kid on the manor was secreting a blade somewhere on his person. I was still game for a 'straightener' if the occasion called for it, but most of the time there wasn't room for formal discussions before the ruck kicked off. I further enhanced my reputation when I stormed a skinhead club on Bedford Hill single-handed and slashed everyone in sight. It was in revenge for the skins almost killing a pal of mine. I was steaming drunk and the club was almost empty at the time, but I laid the stripes down on anything that moved. By the time the tale had done the rounds it was gospel that I had taken on fifty skins and turned their club into an abattoir. The truth was a lot less glamorous, but whenever anyone brought it up I would just give them a hard look and say nothing. That's how reputations are built. People started calling me 'Razor', and it stuck.

It was at this time that I decided to get in touch with my old DC pal from north London and find out what was on offer. I had lost his phone number but remembered that he lived on an estate in Highbury, not too far from the Arsenal football ground, so off I went with Pete, on a quest for the blagger's tools of the trade — guns.

I don't know what the statute of limitations is on supplying firearms, even crap ones, so I'll forgo the details of what happened next. Suffice to say we parted with forty crumpled green pound-notes and came back across the river with a holdall containing a sawn-off 16-gauge shotgun and a WWII German Luger. Both guns were in a decrepit state: the barrel of the Luger had a slight bend in it, and it was just as well I had no ammo or I might now be typing these words with my toes; and the shotgun was a Stevens, dating from 1916, and had more rust than the average Ford Cortina, but we had two bird-shot cartridges for the shotgun, so that made it 'real'. Now we had the guns and the attitude, but we were deficient to the tune of one getaway driver. We could hardly make our escape on the bus. Enter George.

George was part gipsy, part gorja and all car-thief. Cars were his main interest: if it had wheels and an engine, George could hot-wire it and drive it away quick as a wink. He loved driving and was fast gaining a reputation as a pukka wheel-man, or 'dragger'. He would steal a fast motor of the day, like a Cortina 2000E or a Rover 3.5 litre S and go looking for Old Bill motors to instigate a chase. Nine times out of ten George could leave the police standing with his extraordinary driving skills, but he also had certain manoeuvres which would guarantee his escape. His favourite trick for shaking off a persistent squad-car was known as 'the reverse ram'. He would bring his own vehicle almost to a stop and then throw the gears into reverse while jamming his foot on the accelerator; speeding backwards he would smash into the front of the police car causing crippling damage to the radiator and engine. The disabled police car would have to abandon the chase, but George's ride would suffer only rear-end damage and be able to escape.

I think the term 'joy-rider' was coined with people like George in mind. For him, being behind the wheel of a fast car was all the joy he needed in his life. He was another kid who had grown up close to poverty and had suffered discrimination, because his father was a gipsy. To a lot of people in this country the gipsies are as undesirable and unwelcome as the blacks and the Irish, so I had a great affinity with George, and when it came time to find a driver, he was the first one I thought of. The only trouble was that at that time George was on remand in Stamford House Remand Centre, for Taking and Driving Away, naturally.

Stamford House was, and maybe still is, a juvenile jail for boys between the ages of twelve and seventeen, run by the local authority rather than the prison system. It was a lot softer than the likes of Send or Latchmere House; there were no beatings or drill routines, but if you are holding someone behind locked gates against their will, then you are just running a prison by another name. Most of the boys at Stamford House were petty, non-violent offenders, but it also had a 'Closed Unit', which held a few hard cases.

Situated at the lower end of the Goldhawk Road in Shepherd's Bush, Stamford House had a bad reputation in the seventies, the hangover from a much-publicized paedophilia ring that was discovered there in the 1960s, so the prisoners were treated with kid gloves. I had been remanded to Stamford House several times before I was sent to DC, and on each occasion I had escaped and was back on the streets before the ink was dry on the warrant. Security outside the closed unit was minimal and consisted of a twelve-foot chain-link fence. One time, after my fourth escape, the staff confiscated my clothes and put me in a pair of striped pyjamas, hoping to deter me. It did no good. As soon as I got the chance I was up and over the fence and running down Goldhawk Road like a fugitive from a chain-gang.

I decided that me and Pete would break into Stamford House and get George out. George's brother was going to visit him, so we got him to pass the word that the cavalry was on its way, and when to expect us. Breaking in was even easier than breaking out. We scaled the fence with ease and dropped inside the darkened compound in the small hours of the morning. We knew that George was in Church House, which was situated opposite the gym. As we crept past the gym I spat. During one of my short stays I had laced on the sixteen-ounce gloves in that gym to settle an argument I had with a little black kid from east London. The gym staff were very big on letting kids settle their differences by duking it out in the ring, and as I had some boxing experience I was eager to throw plenty of leather at this other kid. I entered the ring supremely confident of victory and got the shit knocked out of me for three long rounds. He hit me with so many rights I was almost begging for a left. What made it even more embarrassing was that the kid had never boxed before. That was the last time I ever got in the ring. I'd like to say that the other kid went on to become lightweight champion of the world, but he didn't. He became a part-time pimp and full-time crackhead, and I heard he got stabbed to death with a six-inch nail in HMP Long Lartin twenty years after our fight. He coulda been a contender.

George was supposed to be waiting for us, but when we reached the appointed window he was nowhere to be seen. We tried a few whispered calls, but we couldn't get too loud as each houseblock had a night-patrol officer. Eventually I knocked on one of the windows to the dorms and got a kid out of bed.

'Which dorm is George in?' I whispered to the sleepy-eyed con.

'George the till-merchant, from Plaistow?' he yawned.

'No, George the car-thief, from Mitcham,' I replied.

'Oh, him. Yeah, he done a runner this afternoon when we were on the yard.'

We had come all the way over to Shepherd's Bush in the middle of the night to break him out of jail and the inconsiderate cunt had made his own way out. There's gratitude for you. We climbed back out of the jail and began the long trek back to south London.

The next day we found George pulling wheelspins in a stolen Mini Cooper on the New Park Road estate. We gave him a bit of grief about not being in when we called, but he just shrugged it off.

'Gotta take your chances where you find 'em,' was his reply. I liked his attitude.

We put the proposition of driving on a proper bit of work to him and he almost took my arm off.

'Cor! Not fucking many, mate! I'll have some of that! All day long, and twice on Sunday! When do we start?'

We now had the tools and the team; all we needed was a target.

Our first job was a small record shop in Streatham Hill. I had picked it because I had been in there on previous shoplifting forays and knew it was a one-man operation. I felt we had to start with something easy and work our way up. The record shop did pretty brisk business, so there was bound to be ready cash on the premises, and we knew the area like a dog knows its own shit. It would be sweet for a getaway. Another plus was the fact that the sound system in the shop was kept under the counter, which meant that the owner had to duck out of sight in order to change the records. This figured prominently in our plan.

George nicked us a lovely Ford Corsair 2000 for the job and swore he would get us away, even if he had to ram every police car in London. The biggest mistake we made was taking ourselves too seriously. We approached the job as though we were hitting the Bank of England. It was all 'synchronized watches' and 'alternative getaway routes', but I suppose it was a learning process and it would all stand me in good stead for the future.

Pete and I approached the shop like a pair of extras from a bad British gangster film, both wearing long overcoats we had got from an Oxfam shop and cheap plastic sunglasses. I had on a trilby that was about four sizes too big for me and Pete a flat cap, but neither of us looked half as suspicious as George, who was parked in the busy street with his collar turned up and a stocking-mask over his face, busily revving the engine of the car in an impatient and nervous manner. As we were in the midst of the hottest summer in living memory, you could say that we all looked very out of place in our heavy garments, sweat dripping out of us, but we had never heard of a blag being pulled off by a gang in shorts and T-shirts, so overcoats and hats were de rigueur as far as we knew. I had the Luger in my inside pocket, and Pete was carrying a plastic bag that contained a cosh, some lengths of twine to tie up the shop-keeper, a pair of pliers to cut the phone line and another rolled-up plastic bag to transport the money away. We had left nothing to chance.

Ignoring the curious stares from passers-by, we quickly walked into the shop. As we went in, the owner, who was behind the jump polishing LP covers with a J-cloth, gave us an amused look. I guess he saw his fair share of weirdos, even though the punk-rock movement was still some months away. The only other person in the shop was a hippy-looking geezer who was obviously a customer. He was at the back of the shop, riffling through the Wynder K. Frog LPs, and I saw him exchange an amused glance with the proprietor.

We shuffled over to the rack furthest away from the counter and pretended to be interested in the stack of records. I glanced at Pete. He looked as frightened and uncomfortable as I felt. 'Wait till the hippy fucks off,' I muttered through the side of my mouth. Pete nodded.

Now we were actually there, I didn't know if I'd be able to go through with it. My heart felt as though it was going to burst right out of my chest and slither out of the door. My mouth was so dry that every time I tried to swallow, my throat made a clicking sound.

The hippy finally picked a record he wanted and took it up to the counter. He said something to the owner and they both looked back at us and laughed. They knew! I was sure that the police would come bursting through the door at any moment and nick us. I was ready to leave. Then I thought about how word would get around that I had lost my bottle on the job. I would be a laughing stock on the manor. The reputation it had taken so long to build would be in tatters. I felt my cheeks go red at the thought. In the middle of this self-administered whipping I felt a dig in my side. It was Pete giving me the elbow. I looked up and noticed that the hippy had left, and the owner was on his own. I swallowed hard and forced my leaden limbs into life.

This was it. Win, lose or draw, I wouldn't be shot for not trying.

I plucked an LP from the rack and walked up to the counter on shaky legs. Pete followed. The owner was a tall man, maybe six foot two, but thin. He had medium-length hair and a bit of a wispy moustache; I noticed he had a large wart in the crease of his left nostril and I focused on that rather than look at the rest of his face. I truly believed that if I looked into his eyes he would be able to see my intentions writ large and would immediately press an alarm. I handed him the record.

'I . . . er . . . I want to hear this,' I croaked.

'Which track?' he asked.

Shit! I glanced at Pete, who shrugged and found something of profound interest to look at down on the floor.

'Er . . . track six?' I ventured.

The man nodded, then flipped the record expertly from its sleeve and ducked below the counter to put it on the deck. I reached into the inside pocket of my overcoat and gripped the butt of the Luger. The foresight snagged on the lining of the pocket and I was still struggling with it when the man popped up. The first crystal notes of Roy Orbison's 'Only the Lonely' filled the small shop. By sheer coincidence I had chosen a track that I knew well and had danced to with many a one-night-stand at the Edwardian Club. When I picked up the LP it had been at random. This was all getting a bit surreal. I was still struggling to get the gun out of my coat and the man was looking at me with a puzzled smile on his face. I was again on the verge of abandoning the whole thing, when the pistol came free with a loud ripping sound. I pointed it at the man's face.

'Stand and deliver!' I shouted triumphantly.

As soon as the words left my lips I wanted to cringe. What the hell had possessed me to use such a corny phrase? I can only assume it was the ghost of Dick Turpin.

The man looked at the gun, and then at me, his smile growing wider.

'Is this a joke?' he asked.

I looked down at the barrel of the gun and saw there was a swathe of red overcoat lining hanging from the foresight. This was going from bad to farce. I quickly snatched the material away and steadied the gun. I took a deep breath. And that was when it came over me – the 'buzz'.

Maybe it's something as simple as the adrenaline level reaching a certain point or the brain kicking in with a potent spurt of seratonin, I don't know what it is, but armed robbers call it the buzz. I felt deathly calm and full of confidence. Every nerve ending was alive and fizzing. I wanted to laugh out loud. I cocked the empty pistol.

'Get your fucking hands up, or I'll shoot you.'

I knew it was me speaking but I barely recognized my own voice.

The smile slid off his face like oil from a hot pan, and his hands shot into the air like someone had pulled a string.

I gave Pete a shove. 'Do your job. Guard the door.' He scuttled over to the door and turned the sign to 'Closed', just as we had planned.

'Now,' I said calmly, 'this is a robbery. All we want is the money. Hand it over and you won't get hurt. OK?'

He nodded like an epileptic at a Status Quo concert. I gestured with the pistol at the till. He put one hand down and pressed the key to open it.

'Take the money out and put it on the counter,' I said, 'but do it slowly.'

He reached into the till drawer and pulled out one £20 note and placed it squarely on the counter.

'Not one at a fucking time,' I said. 'We don't have all day.'

He swallowed, hard. 'That's the lot,' he said. 'The rest went to the bank at three o' clock.'

'Well, where's the safe?' I asked.

He shook his head. 'We don't have one. That's why I bank the takings every day.'

I knew he was telling the truth but I made a cursory search of the till and the space behind the jump. I was disappointed with the haul, but it was sugared by the buzz I was feeling.

Pete was nervously hopping from one foot to the other over by the door.

'Hurry up, for fuck's sake!' he almost shrieked.

I slipped the twenty into my pocket. So much for bringing a bag to cart away the cash. I gave the man my hard stare, the slow-burn that says 'I don't want to kill you but I will if I have to.' I've perfected it over the years but even back then it was pretty effective.

'If you leave here within the next ten minutes you will be shot,' I said. 'We have a man with a sniper's rifle on a rooftop across the street, and he'll be watching you.'

He nodded again, as though he actually believed every word of my fanciful claptrap. I gestured with the pistol. 'Now lie down on the floor.'

In a split second he was hugging the ground like it was a long-lost relative who owed him money. I nodded to Pete and he was out of the door.

As I reached the door myself I noticed that Roy Orbison was just reaching the final crescendo of 'Only the Lonely'. The song was no longer than three and a half minutes, but it felt like I had been in the shop for hours. This was my first experience of that criminal phenomenon known as 'buzz-time', a theory that Albert Einstein never got around to investigating. From the moment I pull a gun on a robbery, it seems as though time itself seems to stretch out, like warm toffee. I live a whole lifetime in minutes, aware of every breath that leaves my body and every beat of my heart. The world seems to suddenly pop into clear focus and my every sense is heightened. I don't want to seem as if I'm investing the experience with mystical qualities because, when you break it right down, it's just nicking a few quid at the point of a gun, but I would compare it to something like free-fall parachuting. You psyche yourself up to step out of a plane thousands of feet up in the air, knowing that there is a possibility that something could go wrong and you are jumping to your death. But you step out anyway, spitting in the face of death and knowing that once you leave the plane there is no changing your mind and turning back. And in the few minutes of free fall, you're aware of everything, but you cannot stop.

From the moment I put my hand on the gun I am in free-fall and everything must run its course. My liberty, and maybe even my life, is in the balance, and that's the rush I have always craved. Had I been born into more financially comfortable circumstances, I might have achieved my fix in more acceptable pursuits, such as skiing down mountain slopes, big-game hunting or free-fall parachuting, but on the streets and council estates of south London I took my fix wherever I could find it. It wasn't a game; the danger was real. If you choose armed robbery as a career, you had better be aware that there's a possibility that you'll end up face-down on a dirty pavement with your lifeblood running into a gutter. And many do.

As I stepped out on to the sun-baked street, I winced at the whining of the engine as George stomped on the accelerator pedal of the getaway motor. I was no sooner in the car than he took off like a rally driver, fishtailing across the road and barely missing a 137 bus. I settled back into the seat and let out a deep breath. Pete was laughing next to me and I felt a lot like laughing myself.

'What the fuck are you going to do with them?' he asked.

I looked down and for the first time I realized I was clutching a bundle of LPs in my hands. I vaguely remember grabbing them from a rack by the door. I examined them and found I had eight copies of the Bay City Rollers' *Greatest Hits*. Win some, lose some.

Like a mug-punter getting his first win on the horses, I couldn't wait to get at it again. Next time would be even better. It didn't matter that the prize wouldn't even cover our expenses, it was all about the experience itself. During the short drive to safety I began to plot our next robbery. I was well and truly hooked.

5. Summer of '76

As I've said before, I do like a good gun. I find them fascinating. There is something satisfying and strangely intoxicating about the way a good pistol fits into a human hand. I can appreciate the weight and power of a decent shooter in the same way that a craftsman gets a kick out of handling the tools of his trade. Don't get me wrong, I don't have the desire to wank over them, it's just that I find them aesthetically pleasing. I suppose there are no end of 'ologists who will frown at my penchant for firearms and swear that it makes me a mother-fixated, bed-wetting psycho with a small penis. Fuck 'em. If I was offered the choice between the complete leather-bound works of Freud and Jung and a nickel-plated Desert Eagle automatic, I know which one I'd find more useful. Does that make me a sexual deviant?

Back in '76, though, when I purchased my first firearms, I had a healthy fear of guns. It was the shotgun that frightened me the most, simply because we had ammunition for it, which made it a genuine killing machine. When it was loaded with one of those stubby red cartridges, it would be deadly. And though I may have been young and reckless, I had no desire to actually hurt anybody who hadn't hurt me. Guns didn't inflict a shallow cut that was easily stitched up; guns were final, and I was not prepared to go that far.

Violence was part of my life, but it was a hot-blooded, spur-of-the-moment type of violence. Throwing a few digs at someone who shaped up to me or swinging a cosh or a razor in a gang fight was acceptable, but cold-bloodedly setting out to deliberately do someone severe and maybe fatal damage just wasn't in me. The shotgun made me gun-shy, and that was a good thing, but I wasn't yet familiar with firearms, and mixing that with my cocky bravado was dangerous. I was an accident searching for somewhere to happen.

I had no intention of shooting anybody just to nick a few quid. Money wasn't that important to me. I had no rent or bills to pay and I could get drunk on the fumes from a barmaid's apron, so every night was a cheap night out for me. It was nice to have money, but I was more into the buzz of thieving. As I grew older, that would change and money did become important, but it was always secondary to the buzz. In '76 my only extravagance was clothes. Being a teddy-boy, I was into the whole sartorial elegance thing, but I could get a drape-suit hand-made for £60 and I could steal that much from one night of smash-and-grabs. So, though I took armed robbery fairly seriously, it was still a big adventure to me.

Obviously Pete and George were disappointed with our take from the record shop, and though they were euphoric at having got away with armed robbery, they didn't seem to have the same enthusiasm as me about it. I tried to explain to them how great it had felt, but all I got from them was funny looks, so I shut up about it. I scanned the local paper looking for any news of the robbery, getting George to read out any article that might be about it, but there was nothing. I was disappointed but that only made me more determined to make my next job a big one – and this time I would be carrying the sawn-off.

The rent office was a one-storey cinder-block building on an estate, just off Kings Avenue. Thursday was rent-day for the surrounding council tenants and most of them paid in hard cash. I guessed there would be a sizeable prize just waiting for a young team of daring blaggers and, as far as I was concerned, that prize was ours. The plan was simple: we would burst into the rent office just before closing time, and I would fire a blast from the shotgun into the ceiling, creating panic among the staff and showing them from the off that we meant business. Pete's job was to vault the counter and load the money. George would be outside in the getaway car. What could go wrong?

I gave the shotgun a good scrub-up to get the worst of the rust and grime off it, making sure I paid great attention to the cleanliness of the barrel. I didn't want it blowing up in my hand as soon as I pulled the trigger. Pete thought it would be a good idea to take the gun on to the common and test-fire it to make sure there was nothing wrong with it, but I shrugged off his fears, thinking he was losing his bottle and stalling for time. I was eager to go again.

At the appointed hour we were in position outside the rent office in a hot Austin 1300, supplied by George. I had persuaded him that it was a bit sussy for him to pull his stocking-mask down over his face before we had actually entered the building. He wasn't happy about it, but he kept his mask rolled up on his head. Pete and I wore the same outfits as before.

Though late in the day, the street around the rent office was fairly busy, so we sat in the car for a while. George couldn't sit still and kept fiddling with the rear-view mirror. Pete was chewing bubble-gum and kept blowing and bursting bubbles. They were both getting on my nerves, but it was only a bit of pre-job tension. I was shitting myself as much as the other two, but I was hoping that once we started moving, I would regain the feeling of excitement I got on the first job. Finally, the last two customers left the rent office. This was it. I pulled the sawn-off out of the bag at my feet and, somewhat gingerly, put it under my coat. It was now loaded, and I had an extra cartridge in my pocket for the reload.

I opened the car door and had one foot on the street when I heard a sharp intake of breath from George. I knew exactly what that sound meant even before he spoke.

'Old Bill!' he whispered.

I quickly pulled back into the car, my heart beating like a lambeg drum at an Orange march. My eyes scanned the surrounding area for signs of danger. 'Where?' I asked urgently, my limbs turning to lead.

George was staring into the rear-view mirror, his hand poised over the ignition key like a buzzard hovering over a carcass. He suddenly exhaled loudly and visibly relaxed.

'It's all right,' he said. 'It's only an ice-cream van!'

As if right on cue, we were treated to a blast of 'Popeye the

Sailor Man', as the van turned on to the estate. I looked at Pete and he looked like he was going to vomit. I felt the same.

'Anyone fancy a 99?' asked George.

I slapped him on the side of the head. 'You cunt,' I snarled. 'Don't fuck about.'

He rubbed his head and gave me an aggrieved look. 'I wasn't,' he said. 'I really thought it was a bill-wagon. It's white with an orange stripe down the side, and I only saw it in the mirror.'

I took a deep breath to calm myself a little. 'OK,' I said firmly. 'No stopping this time, let's go.' And I was out of the car before anyone could change their mind.

Pete and I went across the pavement like MPs chasing a free lunch. My senses were so in tune that I could actually feel the grain of the wood on the door as I pushed it open and the change from concrete paving to carpet as I took my first step inside. My blood was fizzing and my nerve ends were singing. The buzz was on me, strong. There were four staff on the other side of the counter as we burst in. One of them was on the phone and I clearly heard him say 'Wait a minute.' I fancied I could hear them all breathing, but maybe that was my imagination. Everyone froze for a moment and then, as though someone had shouted GO!, it all came to life. I pulled the shotgun from under my coat and pointed it at the ceiling.

'This is a raid!' I shouted at the top of my voice and braced myself for the explosion as I pulled hard on the trigger.

Nothing happened. I pulled again; still nothing. I silently cursed the descendants of all north London-dwelling gun-dealers. And one in particular.

Hoping that no one had noticed, I lowered the gun and pointed it at the staff instead. 'All of you,' I growled. 'Get over in that corner.' I gestured with the gun and they all rushed to comply.

The fella who was on the phone was still clutching the hand-piece as he ran and pulled the rest of the phone off the desk with a crash.

'Drop it,' I snarled. And the rest of the phone hit the deck.

I tapped Pete on the shoulder. 'Get to it,' I shouted. He jumped over the counter like he had been in training for the Olympics and began emptying the cash drawers into a plastic bag.

There was a medium-sized safe in the corner, but the door was shut.

'Who's got the safe keys?' I demanded. One of the men raised his hand.

I pointed the gun at him. 'Open it,' I said.

By now Pete had all the cash from the tills bagged up and he was waiting expectantly beside the safe. The key-man cleared his throat nervously.

'I can't,' he said. 'It's on a time-lock.'

All the other staff members nodded their heads in confirmation. I frowned menacingly. I had never heard of a time-lock.

'Oh yeah?' I said. 'Just fucking open it before I get the hump.'

The key-man swallowed loudly. 'I can't,' he said again. 'It will only open at certain times. There's nothing we can do. Honestly.'

The staff all nodded again, this time more vigorously.

I looked at Pete, who shrugged. He had obviously never heard of a time-lock either. 'So when does it open?' I asked.

The key-man glanced at the clock on the wall. 'In about forty minutes.'

Pete looked dubious. 'We can't hang around for that long,' he said, stating the bleeding obvious, as usual.

There was nothing more we could do. I ordered the staff to hug the carpet, and we lit out like a couple of two-bob bangers.

Our take was just under £400, which was a bit more respectable than the first job. Like British Rail, we were getting there. After we had dumped the hot Austin and carved up the proceeds, there were smiles all round. As a celebration we headed down to a chip shop in Bedford Hill where they served up the best spareribs in the whole of south London. George was driving a MkII Cortina he had bought from one of his many cousins. It was a straight motor, but as he was under age, had no licence or insurance and was already banned from driving for seven years, we might as well have been in a nicked car. We collected our portions of chips and ribs and sat in the parked car to eat. I still had the bag with the shotgun in it, and I was complaining loudly that we had been sold a dud. As I spoke, I reached into the bag and pulled the gun up on to my lap. I pointed it towards the roof of the car and told how I had pulled the trigger like a Christmas cracker but had been left wearing the paper-hat. George leant over the back of the driver's seat, mouth full of prime rib, and looked at the gun. 'Did you have the safety-catch off?' he asked.

I was puzzled. 'I dunno,' I said. 'Whereabouts is it?'

George flicked a small lever with his greasy fingers.

I then committed one of the most stupid acts of my life, and in a life as littered with acts of blatant stupidity as mine, that is some claim. I pulled on the trigger.

It was as though a bomb had detonated in the car. A bright orange flame shot six inches out of the end of the barrel and at the same time a loud booming sound seemed to physically knock me backwards. Daylight appeared through the roof of the car and bits of burning vinyl highlining began falling on to my legs.

It seemed as though the car was filled with gunsmoke, and I could taste it in my throat. I looked about me; there were chips and spare-ribs all over the place, and George was staring at me, open-mouthed and eyes as big as saucers. As I looked at him, a trickle of blood ran out of his nostril. Shit! I thought, I've fucking shot him! I looked at Pete. He was scrabbling at the door handle and mouthing something at me. That's when I realized I had gone deaf. I wondered if I was dead.

Then the door beside me was pulled open and a pair of strong hands dragged me out of the car and laid me on the road. I looked up and saw a small crowd standing around me, looking down, their mouths moving but no sound coming out. It was then that I realized my own nose was bleeding; I could feel the blood flowing down my throat. I rolled on my side to cough it up, and with the first cough I heard a distinct popping sound, and suddenly I could hear again.

'Just lie still,' someone was telling me. 'You may have internal injuries. Someone phone an ambulance . . .'

I struggled to my feet despite the protests from the crowd. My head was spinning and there was a ringing in my ears, but otherwise I felt OK.

Pete was nowhere in sight, but George was leaning on the bonnet of the car with a dazed look on his face and a small crowd around him.

'Police and ambulance are on their way,' someone in the crowd shouted.

'. . . car bomb, I think . . .' I heard someone say. A man still had hold of my arm and was telling me to sit down and take it easy.

I spat out a mouthful of blood. 'I'm all right,' I said. 'It was just a firework that went off in the car.'

A few people looked dubiously at the two-inch hole in the roof of the car and then looked at me. 'A Roman candle,' I said hopefully.

This was going from bad to worse. I knew we had to get away, and it had to be now. I shrugged off the helping hands and leant back into the car. I found the shotgun on the floor where it had fallen and got out again.

As I turned around with the vicious-looking sawn-off in my hands, the crowd were not shy about scattering off to places unknown. Within a couple of seconds the street was empty except for me and George. I could hear the sirens in the distance, so I grabbed George by the arm and dragged him away. It was lucky that we knew all the alleys and back doubles in the area and we soon put plenty of distance between us and Bedford Hill.

Pete was already back at the flop. He had been uninjured and followed his first instinct, which was to run. Neither George nor I was injured either, the nosebleeds and temporary deafness had been from the pressure of the explosion in such a confined space. George was pissed off about losing his car, as we could hardly go and claim it back. We had had a very lucky escape. But a few hours later, after the shock had worn off, we were laughing about the incident and cracking jokes about my stupidity.

But I learned more important lessons that day. I learned to become intimately familiar with any weapon before I had to use it. I learned that when carrying a gun, death and danger are just one small pull on the trigger away. I learned never to point a firearm at another human being unless I was confident in what I was doing. In short, I learned the greatest respect for loaded guns. In future I would always test-fire any gun I bought.

To this day I have never discharged a firearm during the commission of a robbery, my philosophy being that if you have to resort to the big bang, then you are not a very convincing robber and you should seek alternative employment. I have cleaned out every till in a bank with no more than a scowl and my fingers making the shape of a gun in a paper bag. Robbery is all about confidence and attitude, and if you don't have the bottle in the first place, then no amount of firepower will make you a good blagger. A frightened man with a gun is a danger to everyone. End of lesson.

Throughout the rest of that long hot summer of 1976, we struck all over south London. Nowhere was safe from us – shops, rent offices, betting shops, off-licences – anywhere there was ready cash and minimal security. We still weren't ready for banks, post offices or building societies, but it was only a psychological thing. The main money institutions were too big and intimidating for us. It was as though we had to serve out our apprenticeship first. Anyway, we were happy with the few quid we were making, and every day was a party day.

We were still into the teddy-boy thing, and we all had tailor-made drape-suits. Mine even had a custom pocket under the velvet lapel for my razor. As well as the Edwardian Club, we started to frequent other rock 'n' roll clubs, like Bobbysox in Wood Green, the Lyceum in the Strand and the George in Shepherd's Bush. The scene was really picking up and the clubs would be packed to the rafters every night of the week. This was when a lot of the ted gangs were making their names and the future hard men of the scene were coming up. West London had the best-organized and most violent gangs; the Bushwackers from Shepherd's Bush were led by two guys called Shades and Stud. Stud received a ten-year prison sentence in 1979 for stabbing a punk rocker through the neck with a sharpened screwdriver. Then you had the White City Wildcats, known for their prowess with bicycle-chains, and the Chiswick Chaps, who favoured the baseball bat. Every part of London had its gangs and, when not battling with other teen subcultures like the mods, skinheads and soul-boys, they would fight each other. In my part of south London we had a couple of fledgling gangs, the Streatham Teds and the Brixton Rebels, most of whom I had grown up with. So there was plenty of fighting going on after drink had been taken, and Pete, George and I were normally in the thick of it.

But all good summers must eventually come to an end, and that year the end came for us in September. George had used some of his ill-gotten to buy a MkII V6 Ford Zodiac. It was a lovely motor, two-tone dove-grey and scarlet paint-job, with tail-fins and white-wall tyres, and he had used it to drive down to visit some of his relatives on the Lonesome Depot gipsy site in Mitcham. Unfortunately, as he was pulling into the site, he was recognized by one of the coppers who regularly kept watch there for stolen vehicles. He knew that George was wanted on warrants for car theft and absconding from Stamford House. The police waited for George to drive off the site – they couldn't really miss his car – and got him boxed in before he could take off. He was nicked and remanded in custody, this time to Latchmere House in Surrey, an altogether harder gaff to break out of.

We found out later that the Old Bill never made George for any of the robberies. As the driver, his face had never been on offer, so they didn't have a clue that he was anything but a car thief. He was charged with eight counts of TDA and eventually ended up with three months' detention. But in the meantime, Pete and I were a robbery team without a getaway driver.

There was no one we trusted enough to bring on to the team at this late stage, so Pete and I decided to cut down on the robberies and only hit targets that we could get away from on foot. This meant mainly small shops. A week after George was captured we had our first failure.

Our target was a newsagents on Balham High Street, which was bound to have a bit of cash in the till as it was close to the railway station and caught the commuter traffic. We planned our getaway, making sure we knew all the side-streets to duck down, and then we struck.

We walked into the shop when it was empty of customers and took up our by now familiar positions, Pete by the door and me in front of the counter with the Luger in my fist. The owner of the shop, who sat, impassively, behind the jump, was an Asian man, complete with turban and pointy beard. I waved the gun under his nose and told him to empty the till.

'No,' he said, simply.

I could hardly believe it. This had never happened before. I decided he didn't understand what I was saying. So I said it again, louder.

He shook his head.

I looked at Pete, who shrugged, as usual.

'Look,' I said reasonably, 'this is a gun, and if you don't hand over the cash, I'll be forced to shoot you. Now, come on. We don't have all day.'

He shook his head again. 'If you want money,' he said, 'you should get a job.'

I pretended to cock the pistol, hoping to frighten him, and stepped closer to the counter. 'This is my fucking job,' I snarled. 'Now get the fucking money on the counter, or I'll blow that fucking turban right off your head!' By now I was shouting.

He crossed his arms and leant back in his chair.

'I don't think so,' he said. 'In Uganda I saw many guns, and I see that your gun is unloaded. You are minus the magazine. And you swear far too much for such a young man.'

He had me. What could I do? It was a ludicrous situation, and it was time to make a dignified exit. I tried to salvage some of my pride. I put the Luger into my pocket, and threw a ten-pence piece on to the counter. I picked a Mars Bar from the display and walked to the door.

'Keep the change,' I said, over my shoulder.

That's the way it goes sometimes. If someone calls your bluff, you have to shit or get off the pot. Over the years I have been refused sometimes; it happens to every robber sooner or later, and why start shooting up the gaff when you know that you can get the prize elsewhere? There are a million banks in the world, and as a career robber I later learned to identify the places that will hand over and those that won't. There are certain highstreet banks in this country that actually have a policy of not handing over cash to raiders; they find it more financially prudent to put their customers at risk than give up the fully insured money in their tills. These companies train their staff to drop down behind their bullet-proof screens as soon as they get a whiff of a raid. No such luxury for their customers, who are stuck out in the banking hall with a now-frustrated armed criminal. But it keeps their insurance premiums down and the shareholders happy. That's business for you.

I was now eager to up our game and start hitting the banks rather than keep going as small-timers. I needed the buzz, it was an addiction that would gnaw at me for the rest of my life. But without a driver we were fucked. While George was still in Latchmere, we were approached by a fence who had a bit of work for us. It was a motorbike showroom on Bedford Hill, and he was ready to pay cash-money for all the leather-wear and crash helmets. We went down and took a look at it, and it looked a stone-ginger, so that weekend we spent four hours sledgehammering our way through the rear wall of the premises. It backed on to a railway line, so we would wait for a train to rumble past to cover the noise. Finally we got through. The reason for breaking through the wall was because all the doors and windows were alarmed.

We got in late on the Saturday night and made eight trips back to the fence with the gear loaded up in an old baby pram. By the early hours of Sunday morning we had the whole gaff cleared of leather gear and crash hats and had earned ourselves a nice few quid. There were also some very nice bikes on display, but we had no market for them. The pride of place in the window went to a pair of gleaming Harley Davidson trial bikes. They were 250cc twins in gold and maroon livery.

Even though neither of us could drive a car, we had both nicked our fair share of motorbikes. I wonder now how we never thought of using bikes for a getaway on our robberies, but I can only put it down to the fact that we were novices and were following a set pattern in our blagging, a tried-and-tested method we had seen in films and on the telly. Robbers always wore long coats and made their getaway by car; those were the rules.

We found the keys to the Harleys in the office, but there was no way we could get them out through the same hole we came in through, so we decided on a kamikaze mission. We tossed a coin to see who would break the window. I lost. We had kept back boots, a leather riding-suit and a crash hat each from the loot, so we got suited up. Pete mounted his bike and got ready to roll. I got a brick from the wall we had broken and a large monkey-wrench from the shop's toolbox. It was getting light outside, but there was no traffic on the road and all was quiet. I waited for a second, listening to the silence, then I nodded at Pete, who keyed his bike and began to rev. I launched the brick, as hard as I could, through the plate-glass window.

The window exploded with a loud crack and I stepped forward and quickly bashed out the shards that were left hanging, clearing a path with the monkey wrench. As soon as the brick had breached the glass it set off the burglar alarm, and it was whooping like a police siren. The noise was a tremendous and sudden intrusion in the quiet of the morning. As soon as the way was clear, Pete threw his Harley into gear and wheelspan out of the showroom and off up Bedford Hill, leaving exhaust fumes and a wall of sound in his wake. I ran to the second Harley and jumped on. I keyed it up and threw it into gear, and shot across the showroom floor at full revs. Unfortunately, a piece of glass punctured the back tyre and as I came at high speed out on to the street, I lost control of the bike.

The Harley shimmied this way and that as I tried to hang on and regain control, but the front wheel hit the opposite kerb and I was launched over the handlebars with some force. I sailed through the air and straight through the plate-glass window of a dry-cleaners, head-first. Luckily I was wearing good-quality crash hat and leathers. I was uninjured but badly shaken up. I picked myself from the wreckage and stumbled out of the shop. Now the burglar alarm on the dry-cleaners was also wailing, and the pavement on both sides of the street was littered with broken glass. I was doing a pretty good job of attracting attention to myself. Windows were starting to open, and the hue and cry would soon be up. Right on cue, an old man poked his head out of the window of the flat above the dry-cleaners.

'The police are on their way, you fucking vandal! The police are coming!'

I acknowledged his shouts with a wave. I quickly righted my bike and tried a running bump-start, but I could see that it was a write-off. The front forks were buckled from hitting the kerb, and the back tyre was in shreds. I dropped it. Above the din from the burglar alarms I could hear a police siren. It was definitely time to facilitate my egress. I legged it.

As I ran I ripped off the crash hat and launched it into a garden. I was in serious shit; it wouldn't take too much detective work to make me for this job, as I was running through deserted streets in a set of bright-red motorbike leathers. I got a couple of streets away from the scene of the crime and decided I had better get out of sight. I dived into a front garden and burrowed my way into the middle of a thick hedge. And not a moment too soon. Through the leaves I saw a jam-sandwich cruise slowly and sneakily up the street with three big coppers on board keeping 'em peeled. I waited until they went past and then I struggled to get the incriminating leathers off. I was wearing a T-shirt and shorts underneath, which would not look out of place in the unseasonably warm late summer, but there was no way I could disguise the high-leg motorbike boots unless I wanted to go barefoot.

I stayed in that hedge for over two hours, making friends with half a million insects, until I was sure it would be safe to come out. Then I made my way back to the flop. The shorts and boots ensemble got a few funny looks, but I think I managed to carry it off with a bit of panache. Ten years later shorts and biker boots were all the rage on the gay scene (so I'm told), so in the fashion race I was way ahead of my time.

I should have seen the writing on the wall after the bike fiasco: motorbikes and reckless attitudes are a deadly combination – but I wasn't taking too much notice. Pete had got clean away on his Harley, and with me on the pillion we got into a couple of entertaining police chases in the next couple of weeks, before he sold the bike to a Road Rat. Pete really got the buzz for bikes the night he got the Harley from the showroom, and he wouldn't leave them alone after that. He got the same buzz from bikes that I got from blagging. I remember him once telling me that he never felt more alive than when he was on a straight stretch of road with the throttle flat out and the engine screaming. In 1986 Pete was riding his own Honda 250, when a Ford Granada jumped a red light and hit him side-on at 60 mph. He was killed instantly, and his younger brother, Robert, who had been riding pillion, was crippled for life. Sometimes your addictions will kill you.

By the start of 1977, I was a seasoned criminal. I had committed a variety of crimes, some of them very serious, and I knew that it was only a matter of time before I was nicked. I knew there was a warrant out on me for a GBH charge, as the police had been around questioning people about me. As far as I knew, Old Bill had yet to make me for any of the robberies, but that didn't mean I would be handing myself in for anything. Going into a police station voluntarily was anathema to me. I would run for as long as I could. I was having a great time.

But nothing lasts for ever, as the poet said, and my destiny was looming large. I was on a trip into trouble in a stolen car and I didn't have the sense or inclination to take my foot off the accelerator.

In February 1977 things finally came on top for me and Pete.

We were casing an electrical-goods shop in Streatham Hill with a mind to burgling it later that night, when we were spotted by a patrol car. The cops recognized us on sight and called for reinforcements. Before we knew what was happening we were cuffed and on our way to the police station. And this time there was no way they were going to let go of me until I was safely inside the cell.

Both Pete and I were on the wanted list: Pete for being on the run from Stamford House on a weapons charge, and me for the stolen-motorbike crash on the day after I got out of Send. I was also wanted for GBH on a skinhead during a gang-fight outside the bowling alley in Streatham. I had coshed him with a length of lead pipe, splitting his forehead open, and someone had put my name up for it. But the only thing I was worried about were the armed robberies we had carried out. The other charges were minor in comparison.

They put me and Pete in separate cells and left us there for a couple of hours to await questioning by the CID. On one occasion the hatch on the cell door opened and I recognized the copper who had taken my cuffs off on the day I escaped. He stared at me for a moment, then shook his head and slammed the hatch.

Eventually the CID men took me out for questioning. It was the usual routine, two of them, one standing behind my chair in a menacing fashion while the other one fired questions at me and banged his fist on the table a lot. I denied everything: I never even knew there was a bowling alley in Streatham, and I had never allowed myself to be carried on a stolen motorbike that crashed during a police chase. I never coshed anyone and I never escaped from anywhere, and on the days that such incidents occurred I was probably in church. It went on and on; they fired off questions and I fired lies straight back. They knew I was guilty, and the only thing that surprised me was that they never laid a finger on me.

In those days there was no videoing of suspects or taping of interviews, and the police could hold a suspect for seven days without access to a solicitor. In my experience, almost all confessions were gained by mental and physical torture. And why wouldn't they be, when the police had to answer to no one and the courts decreed that a police officer's word was sacrosanct? It doesn't surprise me in the slightest that most of the worst miscarriages of justice ever to come to light in this country date back to the 1970s. If you were at it in the seventies, you accepted beatings and torture from the police as an occupational hazard, particularly from the CID, and if they didn't beat you up and try to frame you, you'd think it was unusual.

My interview lasted about an hour, with not one mention of armed robbery, so I thought I was safe when they told me I was to be charged with GBH, TDA and escaping from police custody.

But then they dropped the first depth-charge into the murky waters of my mind.

'You've been out of DC a long time, and we know you haven't been living at home. So how have you been getting your money?'

I shrugged. 'Doing casual work,' I said. 'Building sites and that.'

They both laughed out loud. 'Yeah, all right,' said the interrogator.

There was an uncomfortable silence.

'What about a bit of bail on these charges?' I asked.

The interrogator shook his head slowly. 'I don't think so,' he said. 'The robbery squad want to question you about something.' He smiled, and the smile told me everything.

Back in the cell I surveyed my options. I would deny everything, that was a certainty. But if I was made for the robberies, then they would no doubt put me on an identity parade. I had worn a minimal disguise so I knew that the witnesses would have little trouble picking me out. In short, I was fucked. So I did what I often do when locked in a police cell: I went to sleep.

I was awakened by the cell door clanking open. There were two plainclothes men at the door. Big, craggy-looking faces and rumpled suits. The robbery squad. They took me to an interview room and, instead of a beating, the first thing they offered me was a cup of tea! The interrogation methods of the robbery squad were more subtle than what I had been used to from the police. There was no shouting or banging on furniture. They seemed laid back and very confident. They said their main concern was recovering the firearms used in robberies and finding out where they had come from originally. I wished them luck in this endeavour and denied all knowledge of anything connected to it. They told me that they had witnesses who would pick me out on an ID parade, and I said, 'Well, let's go then.'

The interrogation went on for about an hour before they announced that I was to be charged with armed robbery on the Streatham record shop and on the rent office and attempted robbery on the newsagents in Balham. Plus a charge of being in possession of a firearm with intent. I just shrugged. There was little else I could do. As they put me back in the cell I heard them instruct the jailer to get Pete out for interview. I knew he would also deny everything.

We were both picked out by every witness on the ID parade, and after three days in police custody we were charged with armed robbery and refused bail. I began to rationalize my situation. OK, so I was well and truly nicked, but they still had to prove the charges. I would be locked up on remand until the court case, but after my stint in Send, I had little fear of being locked up. I had heard that in juvenile remand the screws left you alone, there was none of that marching everywhere and getting the face punched off you every five minutes. I would survive. If the worst came to the worst I would end up with a borstal sentence and be out in nine months with good behaviour. How bad could it be?

Little did I know.

6. Rebel with a Cause

Our court appearance at Camberwell magistrates court was no more than a formality. The charges were read out, the police strenuously objected to bail, and we were remanded in custody for seven days by a mean-faced old magistrate. Pete was over seventeen, so he was sent to Ashford remand centre, in Middlesex, which took seventeen- to twenty-one-year-olds. I had just turned sixteen, so it was Latchmere House for me.

Latchmere was my first taste of real prison. Unlike at Send or Stamford House, the screws at Latchmere wore full uniform, including the slashed-peak cap. There were two wings at Latchmere. A-wing was for kids doing short YP (Young Prisoner) sentences, and as they were already convicted they did all the decent jobs, like working in the kitchen and dining-hall and cleaning the yards. B-wing was for kids on remand but not yet convicted. The bottom landing, known as B-One, was segregated from the top landing, B-Two, and housed what were known by the prison system as USLAs (Under School-Leaving Age). The residents of B-One were not allowed to smoke and had to attend classes every day. B-Two landing was for older kids, and they were allowed to earn canteen-money by working in the workshops whenever there was staff to man them, which wasn't often.

After going through the usual reception procedure of being stripped and examined, forced to bathe in two inches of tepid water and being issued with a second-hand prison uniform, I was allocated to a cell on B-One. Though I had left school, I was still officially under school-leaving age. I wanted to smoke and mix with serious criminals, not a bunch of school-kids. I pulled the landing officer and politely requested a transfer to B-Two, but the screw in charge of the landing laughed in my face.

I went into the cell, fuming and humiliated. I wasn't going to stand for it. If I was going to get what I wanted, then it was best I started by letting the screws know I wasn't going to take any shit. I didn't even bother to unpack my kit.

At every meal time the cell doors would be unlocked and all the kids had to stand to attention beside their door for a roll-check before being marched across the exercise yard to the dining-hall. I decided not to participate. When the door opened I just lay on my bed with my hands behind my head and waited. I could hear the count going on and the consternation as they came up one short. Eventually a screw poked his head into my cell, his face incredulous.

'Are you a fucking moron, boy?' he shouted. 'It's roll-call, you stand to attention by your door to be counted! Now, up, up, up!'

I yawned. 'I don't think so, mate. You've got me on the wrong landing.'

The screw almost hopped in rage, his fists clenched and his face went puce.

'Have you gone fucking mad? Did you call me "mate"? We'll fucking see about this.' And with that, he slammed the door.

I was shitting myself, but at the same time I was also looking forward to seeing how far I could push them. I knew I might have to take a beating, but I was determined not to back down. I felt really alive for the first time since I'd been nicked, thriving on the adrenaline.

After everyone had been marched off to the dining-hall, I heard several pairs of marching boots enter the wing and stop outside my door. It swung open and there was a dam of screws in the doorway, headed by a senior officer.

'OK,' he started, reasonably enough. 'What's the problem?'

I explained that I was on remand for some very serious charges and I would be fucked if I was going to attend classes and knock about with a load of gas-meter bandits. I wanted a move to B-Two.

The SO was very understanding. He told me, 'You don't dictate to us, you little prick. If you're not off that bed and standing to attention by the count of three, we'll make you wish you'd never been born.'

I had no choice now. I was off the bed when he got to two, I backed up to the wall and put my fists up and did my best to look as though I meant business. 'You ain't dealing with some cunt here,' I growled. 'I'll fucking fight you all, from here to the block if I have to.'

I was never going to win, but that wasn't the point. My situation didn't require victory, it only forbade surrender.

The screws wasted no time in rushing me, and they didn't fuck about. I managed to get a couple of digs in, but I was soon overwhelmed and caught in head- and wrist-locks. They dragged me out of the cell, down some steps, and across the exercise yard to the block in A-wing. All the way there, they were punching and kicking me, so it was a relief when they launched me head-first into a block cell. But I was off the floor and kicking the door as soon as it slammed.

'You fucking wankers, I'll fucking kill you all!' I shouted until my voice was hoarse, and kicked the metal door until my legs were too tired to carry on. Then I curled up in a corner of the bare cell and fell asleep.

The next morning I was in agony. My ribs were so badly bruised that it was painful just to breathe. I managed to get on my feet and walk up and down the cell a few times without collapsing. My face felt sore and swollen, but nothing was broken. I was determined not to let the screws see that they had hurt me. So when they opened the door to put in my breakfast, I was on the floor doing press-ups, even though it nearly killed me. With my plastic bowl of porridge was a nicking sheet, the official charge-sheet that tells you what prison rule you are accused of breaking. I was charged with refusing a direct order and threatening behaviour to a senior officer.

Later that morning I was taken in front of the governor for trial. Before I could appear in the governor's presence, the screws took my shoes and gave me a pair of size twelve slippers to wear. This is so you cannot attempt to attack the governor, the idea being that you can barely shuffle along, let alone leap over the desk and kick him in the head. I was glad of the slippers, as I used the shuffle to smother the fact that I was in pain and wouldn't be able to move fast anyway.

I was taken into the adjudication room by two screws and made to stand in front of a desk and give my name and number. There was a picture of the Queen up on the wall, and the governor sat behind another desk about ten feet away from the one where I was standing. The two screws who had marched me in stood slightly in front of me, one at each shoulder, facing me. If I made any sudden moves towards the governor, they would be ready to leap on me.

The governor was fat and bald but with a bristling RAF-type moustache. He didn't even bother looking at me, but spoke to the chief officer.

'Read the charges please, Chief.'

The chief, a big man running to fat with plenty of braid on his uniform, stood and cleared his throat, before reading from a piece of paper in a bored voice, 'Sir, on 23 February of this year, remand prisoner 160 Smith refused a direct order to vacate his bed for the roll-call on B-One landing. When ordered to present himself by Senior Officer Morgan, Smith put up his fists in a threatening manner and stated, "I will fucking kill every one of you". He was then removed to the punishment block.'

The chief sat down. All through his reading the governor had been writing it down, or maybe drawing little pictures of Spitfires, for all I knew. He put down his pen and smiled at the chief.

'Thank you, Chief,' he said, and finally looked in my direction.

'Are you guilty or not guilty?' he asked, and the tone of his voice and the look in his eyes told me that he didn't care what I said. This was routine for him; I would be pronounced guilty, as there was no way on this earth that he was going to take my word above that of his officers.

'Guilty,' I said.

He nodded slightly, as if to acknowledge that I had done the right thing. He marked my guilt on the official paperwork, and then considered my sentence for a few seconds.

'Seven days' solitary confinement, fourteen days' loss of canteen. Off you go.'

I was grabbed by the elbows and hustled back to my cell by the two block screws. And that is how justice is dispensed behind the walls of HMP every day of the year.

I was satisfied with the outcome. I had made my point and the screws had got the message. I was willing to risk physical punishment and official sanctions in order to get what I wanted. In the screws' eyes I was dangerous and therefore one to be avoided. Even though I had ended up hurt when the weight of numbers was in their favour, they had to take into consideration the fact that I would be willing to attack them in a one-to-one situation. In any prison there will always be windows of opportunity when a determined con can seriously hurt a screw, and the screws are well aware of that fact. My actions had planted the slightest kernel of fear in their minds, and now I just had to make sure it would grow.

To put it another way, there are plenty of growlers in prison, people who can put on a good show of verbal and body language but stop short of physical violence. The screws soon get to know who they are and learn to take their antics with a yawn. But there are also a minority of cons, myself included, who have previous for actually assaulting them. And with that minority they must take every threat seriously. If one of the growlers threatens to knock a screw out, they will normally leave him to calm down and take no further action. But if someone like me, with a track record for throwing digs, makes the same threat, they will start putting on the riot gear and preparing a cell in the punishment block. So any polite request that I make is given serious consideration and not just fobbed off like those from the majority of the prison population. The only way to earn a grudging respect from the uniformed arm of the prison system is to fight for it.

My seven days in the block passed quickly. I spent the time doing sit-ups and press-ups, working out the pain of my bruised body. And once again I began to build up my hate and harness it for daily use. On the eighth morning I was released from the block and marched back over to B-wing. This time I was allocated to a cell on B-Two. I had achieved my objective, but I'd had to wade through shit to get it.

They put me in a cell with a short kid with curly hair. I noticed he had proper tattoos on both arms, not the Indian ink prison variety but real coloured professional jobs. I was impressed. When the door was closed I put my kit on the empty bunk and turned to my new cell mate, and so began the age-old prison ritual of finding out who I was banged up with. Names, hometowns, crimes and what sentences we were expecting were exchanged over the next five minutes. I found out his name was Jerry Keeble, Jel to his mates, from Chelmsford in Essex, in for burglary, and expecting a borstal. He also hated the screws and was game for a tear-up. I had a feeling the screws were going to regret putting me and Jel in the same cell. And I wasn't wrong.

In order to beat the boredom of being banged up for most of the day and all of the night we hatched plots to escape. We had heard that very few kids ever escaped from Latchmere, but the fact that a few had made it out encouraged us in our plans. When we weren't plotting our bid for freedom, we tried to cause the screws as much trouble as possible.

Every morning the inmates were supposed to vacate their beds, fold all the bedding into squares, turn the mattress on its side and lay out all kit for inspection. The piss-pot had to be scrubbed clean and placed with the lid open on its side. Of course, me and Jel fucked up the inspection every day. Sometimes we would rig it so that as soon as the inspecting screw stepped into our cell he would trip a thread that pulled both kit and mattresses over in a heap, or we would sprinkle sugar all over the polished floor, so the screws, in their big shiny hob-nailed boots, would slip or at worst make a loud scrunching sound as they walked. If we were feeling particularly nasty, we'd leave a big steaming pony in the piss-pot.

At night the screws would regularly patrol the outside of the wings, and we would hurl terrible abuse at them. There was one horrible little screw, who everyone hated and who we called

Hitler, and he would wait until three in the morning and then walk around the wing banging his truncheon on a dustbin lid to wake us all up.

One night when he was on duty, both me and Jel had a pony in a paper bag and waited up all night for him to start his banging antics. Sure enough, in the small hours there he came, marching along with a big grin on his face. We waited until he was under our cell, then launched the shit-parcel down on top of him.

The bag burst open on his hat and showered him with shit. He stopped dead, shit running down his face and on to his uniform, his grin frozen but twitching. Then he let out a huge howl and scampered off. Me and Jel almost shit again from laughing. The word soon spread around the cells and kids were banging their cups on the window bars and cheering. 'Hitler's been bombed!' was the cry. The whole wing was awake, there were burning sheets and papers being thrown out of the windows, and the celebration went on for a good half-hour. Every time it died down someone would shout, 'Hitler's copped a parcel!', and it would start up again.

The only other time I saw and heard middle-of-the-night celebrations like this in a prison was nine years later at HMP Brixton, when it was reported on the radio news at 2 a.m. that a Brixton screw had been stabbed to death at a boxing match in Thornton Heath. That night the whole of Brixton erupted in cheers and jubilation and the cry was, 'One off, sir!', which was the phrase that screws used when they had carted a prisoner off to the block for a beating. Prison breeds a them-and-us mentality in people if it does nothing else.

The next morning, Hitler's bombing was the talk of the nick. The screws did not look happy as they lined us up for inspection. The PO took the opportunity to strut the landing and warn us that unless the culprit owned up, there would be dark days ahead for B-Two. Sure enough, after breakfast everyone was given a spin. The screws had a hard-on to find the phantom bomber and thought that by wrecking our cells they would get someone to give them the whisper. But the only people who knew who had done it were me and Jel, and we weren't talking. We all endured the search with prison-bred stoicism, and the further kit-inspection that followed ten minutes after the search.

After a couple of weeks the incident was almost forgotten. It had gone into Latchmere folklore, so it would never be forgotten by the cons, but the screws had eased up and it seemed as though it had passed them by. So Jel and I decided to try it again. We plotted up with our bag of shit and waited for the night patrol to pass, but this time they were on guard. We missed the target completely. Not only that, we were also spotted by the screws who, unbeknown to us, had secreted themselves to watch for just such an eventuality.

The cell door burst open and a gang of screws manhandled us to the block. We were too surprised to even put up a struggle. Caught, bang to rights. We were charged with assault and attempted assault.

The next morning we appeared before a grave-faced governor for trial. In the funereal atmosphere of the adjudication room, Officer Hitler read his evidence.

'Sir, on Wednesday 8 March 1977, I was on duty as night patrol. At approximately 3.06 a.m. I was heading in a westerly direction below B-Two landing when I became aware of an object landing on my hat. It was with some disgust that I discovered this to be a paper bag filled with excreta. At the time I was directly under the cell occupied by 160 Smith and 748 Keeble.'

He then held up a clear plastic bag, inside of which was a hat with a large stain on the crown.

Though I had been doing my best to avoid Jel's eye, the word 'excreta', which I had never heard before, in combination with the hat in the evidence bag, was the last straw. We looked at each other and burst out laughing.

The governor was incensed. 'SILENCE!' he shouted, banging his fist on the desk. 'This is a very serious matter.'

We managed to get ourselves under control, but it was an effort.

The governor took the bag from Officer Hitler and examined it for a moment with appropriate gravity. I so wanted to laugh that I nearly pissed myself. The governor put the hat bag on his desk and tutted.

'Have you any questions about the officer's evidence?' he asked.

I shook my head, afraid to speak lest I collapse with laughter. But Jel was made of sterner stuff.

'Yeah,' he said, seriously. 'I've got a question.'

The governor was wary. His eyes screwed up and he leant forward.

'Proceed,' he said.

Jel puffed his chest up and hooked his thumbs in his chest-pockets. 'This . . . "excreta", Officer. Tell me, was it still warm?'

That was it, the whole room erupted. The screws were growling, the governor was banging on his desk and shouting, Hitler was foaming at the mouth, and me and Jel were rolling around in hysterical laughter as the screws dragged us back to our cells.

Later that morning we were taken back in and pronounced guilty on both charges. We lost fourteen days' remission, fourteen days' canteen and were given seven days' solitary confinement each. But to this day I think it was well worth it. Nowadays I only have to hear someone mention the word 'excreta', and I have to stop myself from giggling.

I suppose there are some people who think that pelting another human being with shit is no subject for humour, and out there in the real world it is unacceptable. But tacky though the subject is, in prison, shit is still being used as a weapon. In the top-security dispersal prisons it is fairly common to 'shit up' screws, and governors if you can get them. It came into vogue as a type of assault after men on 'dirty protests' realized how disgusted and frightened screws were of getting shit on them. Covering yourself in your own shit was a good way of delaying or avoiding a beating. The next logical step was to actually throw it over them.

Prison is a hard, evil, dirty place, and don't let the tabloids tell you it isn't.

I have never been one to take incarceration lying down. I was always looking to escape, no matter what prison I was in. And

Latchmere House was no different. In May 1993 I appeared before Judge D. at Maidstone crown court on a number of charges, including escaping from prison custody. I attempted to use the Geneva Convention as part of my defence on this charge. I was defending myself and knew that the evidence on other charges was so overwhelming that I was going away for a long time anyway. It was the first time the Geneva defence had been used in a British court.

My argument was that the Geneva Convention made it the duty of every man to escape, therefore my escape from prison was legal and the charge should be dropped. The judge pointed out that the Geneva Convention was only relevant in times of war and referred to the duty of men serving in the armed forces who had been captured by the enemy.

I was ready for this. I had a stack of newspaper cuttings in which various politicians, including two home secretaries, police chiefs and newspaper reporters and editors, pointed out that they were 'waging a war on crime.' I then pointed out that if there was indeed a war on crime going on, then I was obviously a soldier in the criminal army, and I had been captured during the war and imprisoned. Therefore I *was* covered by the Geneva Convention.

The judge was intrigued and not a little amused by my argument. The prosecution was outraged.

'Your Honour, the defendant's argument is facetious. He faces criminal charges, and he brings these proceedings into disrepute by citing a ridiculous defence. This cannot go any further.' But Judge D. was enjoying himself.

'Let me remind you, Mr Brown, it is the prosecution's job to try to dismantle the defence's argument. Simply calling it facetious and ridiculous will not do.'

The prosecution couldn't believe it. And neither could I. After a whispered conference amongst the prosecution team they asked for an adjournment. I was over the moon at even getting this far.

The judge remanded the case over the weekend. I went back to prison with a spring in my step and a song in my heart at having got one over on the system.

On the Monday, the prosecution team all wore smug grins, and I guessed they had spent the weekend hitting the books. Court reconvened and, sure enough, they were ready for me.

'Your Honour, a study of the Geneva Convention has revealed a number of flaws in the defence's argument. It covers only opposing states who are signatories to the document and where formal declarations of war have been made. The prosecution cannot accept that the criminal underworld is an opposing state. At best it is a terrorist organization, and as such it is not entitled to the privileges afforded under the Convention. Also, it is not a signatory to the Convention, and there has been no formal declaration of war. We therefore move that the defence argument holds no water and it would be a gross distortion of justice to put this matter before a jury.'

The judge smiled, and I thought he was going to give it to me.

'Very well argued, Mr Brown.' He looked at me. 'Mr Smith, good try.'

And that was that. I had won a battle but lost the war, a war that the prosecution could prove did not exist. But for an all too fleeting moment I had tasted the heady nectar of victory over the system, and that was enough.

Back in Latchmere House in 1977 Jel and me were always plotting an escape; it kept us going through the long days and nights of boredom. One night I noticed that the brickwork in the corner of our cell was damp. When I dug into it with a biro, bits of the mortar started to crumble. We were very excited about this and set to work looking for a proper tool to dig out with. It was hard work finding a tool; in prison all cutlery is made of plastic. We eventually paid two ounces of tobacco for a four-inch nail that someone had nicked from the workshop. We had to pay such a high price because the fella who nicked it wanted it to stab somebody with, and he was loath to let it go. In the event, he ended up dropping a dumbbell on his victim's head while they were at the gym, so all's well that ends well.

Once we had the nail, we started digging in earnest. The brickwork was rotten and came out like a Tory minister caught wearing a dress. Soon we had removed three whole bricks and we could see the fence fifty feet away, beckoning us. In the daytime we moved a locker in front of our escape hatch, and at night we beavered away at our 'ole. Every now and again at Latchmere, as in every prison, there would be a lock-down, when all the cells were searched, but if our luck held out we would be gone before the next one. When the hole was big enough we set about making a rope to get us down to the ground, and a rope and hook for the fence. The ropes were no trouble as we could make them from plaited bedclothes, but the hook was another matter. But I had an idea.

Part of every prison cell's furniture, apart from an iron bed, a locker and a table, is a chair. These chairs are the type you get in schools, a hollow tubular frame with a wooden seat and back-rest riveted to the frame. I realized that if we were able to get hold of a hacksaw blade, we could saw diagonally across the legs of the chair and make a decent hook. The only trouble was that in Latchmere hacksaw blades were as rare as rocking-horse shit.

We finally found a bod who was willing to smuggle a hacksaw blade in from a visit, but he wanted £100 up front. That was a hell of a lot of money back in '77. It was while we were trying to beat him down to a more affordable tenner that the matter became academic. The lock-down search came.

It took the screws about three minutes to find our 'ole behind the locker. We were once again whisked off to the block. I denied all knowledge of the hole and said it must have been there when we moved into the cell. The governor wasn't having it at any price. We were kept in the block under investigation for a week, then they charged us both with damaging government property in order to escape. I still denied everything, but Jel stuck his hand up to it and said I knew nothing about it because he had made the hole when I was asleep. I didn't expect him to do it and I was surprised when the screws let me back on the wing and told me Jel had admitted it.

He was fined four weeks' wages and got seven days' solitary. When he came back on the wing they had us in separate cells on opposite sides of the landing. I asked Jel why he had stuck his hand up. He said, 'What was the point of both of us rotting in the block for months? At least this way one of us got a result, and that's what counts with these bastards; if you can't beat them you should at least get a result.'

Jel is still a good pal of mine to this day.

Even though they had split me and Jel up, we still caused mayhem whenever we could. One day they took about twenty of us from B-Two over to the workshop. Most of the time the workshops were closed due to lack of staff, and we were banged up in our cells for twenty-three hours a day, but every now and again there would be a burst of work and some of us would get to glue the bristles into yard-brushes for a couple of days. Another fella, who I also knew on the out, named Johnny Mac, was also on the work party with us. Johnny was good stuff. His dad was pals with my dad in the 1960s and 70s when drinking and fighting were their main occupations. Like most of us around the south London area, Johnny had been an amateur boxer, but unlike the majority of us, he had been good at it. The only trouble with Johnny was his hair-trigger temper. He would pick up the nearest weapon to hand when the red mist came over him, and he wouldn't be shy about using it.

In the summer of '76 I had been in the workshop at Stamford House with Johnny when he battered both the Bully brothers, leaving one blinded in one eye and the other one a nervous wreck. The Bully brothers had been picking on a few of the kids and getting away with it, but they came severely unstuck when they tried to bully Johnny Mac. He laid into the pair of them with the ball-pein hammer he had been using to make a copper ashtray. It took five screws to get the hammer out of his hand, and when the dust cleared the Bully brothers' reign of terror was over. For good.

Johnny was placed in the closed unit to await a police investigation, but just before he was charged with GBH with intent, he escaped with another well-known wild kid named Spanish Jimmy. They sat on the top of the fence, slagging the screws off for a good five minutes before dropping to freedom on the other side. But now Johnny was in Latchmere, awaiting trial for all the charges. The last time I heard anything about Spanish Jimmy was in 1992, when the newspapers reported he had been awarded compensation from the courts for being kept in a body-belt for three days at HMP Wandsworth.

That day, the first sign for the screws that the workshop party was going to be trouble was when they tried making us stand to attention and march to the shop. No way were we having it. We were all unconvicted prisoners, and we weren't taking any bollocks. The screws were shouting out the step as we strolled along with our hands in our pockets taking no notice whatsoever.

Once in the workshop we stood around and chatted amongst ourselves. The screw who was in charge told us to shut our mouths and get to work. Nobody moved, we just carried on ignoring him. With that, he made the mistake of grabbing Johnny by the arm. Johnny chinned him, and the fight was on. It was a spontaneous act, we hadn't said a word about steaming the screws, but as soon as Johnny landed the first punch it was as though a signal had been given.

One of the screws managed to press the riot bell, but before reinforcements could arrive the five workshop screws took a good beating.

At the sound of the bell, screws from all over the prison came running. They burst through the doors of the workshop to find their colleagues getting the worst of it, and immediately drew batons. The fight that ensued was like something from a western. Punches and kicks were flying everywhere with wild abandon. Jel grabbed a fire extinguisher and sprayed the screws with powder. It really was a grand mêlée.

Eventually, as always happens when you are outnumbered, the screws managed to drag us off to the block, still fighting. It took eight screws to get Johnny into the cell, he fought like a demon and spurred the rest of us to do the same. The screws were in bits, they had never faced a group of cons like us – and none of us was over the age of seventeen.

It took two days to parade us all in front of the governor for adjudication and we all received various punishments from loss of remission to solitary confinement. Five of us, who had been in trouble before, including me, Jel and Johnny, were kept in solitary for a month. At first the block screws tried to bully and intimidate us, but they soon realized it wasn't worth the candle. We didn't give a fuck and would throw punches at them as soon as they started their nonsense. We were all veterans of the DC system, and a beating from the screws didn't hold the same terrors for us as for normal cons.

When our solitary was finished we went back to B-Two to a hero's welcome. The workshop war was a talking point for months and even the YPs who served the grub in the dining-hall would give us extra helpings. I was fast becoming a 'face', and I loved every minute of it.

My time at Latchmere came to an end on 30 May 1977. In the early hours of the morning, four screws appeared at my door, put me in handcuffs and carted me on to a sweatbox. I was on my way to the Old Bailey to face charges of armed robbery.

And something told me I wouldn't be coming back.

7. Up the Bailey

The Old Bailey was a grim-looking gaff, and it didn't help that my first sight of it was through a sweatbox window in the rain.

The Bailey was legendary. It dealt with only the cream of the criminal world and all the high-profile cases, and here I was, still a teenager. Underneath the fear I had about what was going to happen to me here, there was also a strange sense of excitement and achievement. The majority of my contemporaries were being dealt with in juvenile court, but I had made it all the way to the top. It was a validation of my status.

The sweatbox turned off the street and down a long dark tunnel on to a huge steel turntable, and the engine was switched off. Then the turntable cranked into life and the whole van span slowly around. There's a shortage of turning space under the Bailey, and the turntable is needed to manoeuvre the prison transports. We parked; and then began the long wait.

The prison van has got to be the most uncomfortable vehicle ever built. It was obviously designed by sadists who probably have a wank every time they see one on the streets, trundling along with its cargo of human misery. The vans consist of fourteen cells, each one the size of a council-toilet cubicle but without so much leg room. The seat is moulded Perspex and about as comfortable as a ham sandwich at a Jewish wedding feast. The window is tinted so no one can see inside and anyone looking out thinks it's the middle of the night. They are freezing cold in winter, and chokingly hot in summer, hence the nickname. The suspension allows every bump and pothole on the road to jar the bones, and when the brakes are put on you bounce off the steel walls like a lottery ball. And every day there are hundreds of these vehicles on the roads all over this country full of men, women and children being moved somewhere by the prison system. Travelling in a sweatbox is bad, but the real nightmare begins when you reach your destination. The screws are in no hurry to unload the vans since they have more important things to do first, like sorting out the paperwork, chatting to their mates, having a cup of tea after the long drive, that sort of thing. On more than one occasion I have spent over three hours in a parked sweatbox, roasting and suffering from dehydration.

After twenty minutes' waiting I was ready to confess to the Great Train Robbery. I was unloaded by a surly-faced screw. He must have read my record, which travels with you from the prison, because he put the handcuffs on tighter than a Scotsman's sporran. I wouldn't have minded, but it was only a twenty-foot walk from the van to reception, and we were already thirty-foot underground behind two sets of locked gates. The screws in the Bailey were mainly veterans of nicks like Brixton and Wandsworth coming to the end of their careers. As such, they were a fairly easygoing bunch. I was told the score straight away:

'Keep yer fucking gob shut and don't cause us any trouble, and you can go in the same cell as your co-defendant and have as much snout brought down by your brief as you can smoke.'

That suited me just fine.

I almost didn't recognize Pete the Nut; he had certainly been in the wars. Because he was over seventeen, he had been remanded in Ashford YP Centre in Middlesex. A week before our court date, he had got into a fight with the screws and come off much the worse. Now he had a beaut of an eye that was every colour of the rainbow and a broken jaw. His jaw was wired up, so it was difficult for him to speak, but I managed to get the story out of him. It turns out that the screws at Ashford are mostly ex-DC stock, proper vicious bastards who aren't shy about swinging the batons. Pete had made the mistake of standing up to one of them when they tried to take liberties, so they had dragged him to the punishment block and set about him six-handed.

We were soon chatting about what our options would be in court, and things didn't look too good. The fact that at our ages we were at the Old Bailey could only mean that they meant to make an example of us.

Our barristers called us out. They had a deal to offer us. If we both pleaded guilty to burglary, one robbery, GBH and possession of a firearm, then the prosecution would ask for a borstal recall for Pete, and six months' DC for me. The alternative was a trial, at which the barristers assured us we would be found guilty, and a possible sentence of three to five years. We were strongly advised to plead guilty.

After we had spent some time together weighing up the pros and cons, we decided to accept the deal. I calculated that I would serve three months of my DC sentence, so I would be out for the end of the summer. It would be no picnic, but better take a sure three months than a possible three years if I went ahead with a trial and was found guilty. Three years seemed like an eternity to my young mind; I would never be able to do that long without going mad. We informed the briefs that we would take the deal and stick our hands up. There were smiles all round.

Court Two was a proper ancient-looking dump. It was almost as dirty as the cells we had come from. I had been expecting some sort of opulence from 'the greatest court in the land', but it was a kip. There seemed to be a layer of dust over everything, including the judge. He looked about 180, sitting up there with his manky old wig and a face so screwed up you'd think he'd spent the night sucking on fresh-cut lemons.

Me and Pete came up the steep stone stairs and found ourselves already in the dock. We were told to sit down, on a bench so uncomfortable it could almost have been ripped out of a sweatbox. There was a lot of mumbling going on and talking in stage whispers. Everyone seemed to be dressed in black cloaks and ratty-looking wigs. Finally they were ready to acknowledge our presence. We were ordered to stand, and the charges were read.

'Noel Stephen Smith, you are charged that on 10 July 1976 you did rob one Peter Deadman' (I almost giggled at this point) 'of £20 cash and a quantity of long-playing records. Contrary to Section One of the Theft Act, 1968. Do you say "guilty" or "not guilty"?'

'Guilty!' I shouted, a little too loudly. It made everyone look at me, and I was glad. If I was having my moment in court the least they could do was notice me.

They went through the other charges and I answered 'guilty' just as loudly. The judge was staring daggers at me for waking him up, but I didn't care, we had a deal, I already knew what sentence I was getting.

Next it was Pete's turn. They read out the first charge on the indictment and asked for his plea.

'Gngrhay,' he said, around a mouthful of steel wires.

There was a shuffle of paperwork and everyone looked puzzled. The clerk tried again. Again Pete managed something unintelligible.

Everyone looked at me. I whispered to Pete. 'Guilty or not, mate?'

'Guilty, of course,' he mangled.

I turned back to the court with my thumbs hooked in my armpits in my best barrister impression, and said, loudly, 'The defendant says, "Guilty", m'lud.'

The clerk told Pete to indicate by nodding if he was in agreement. This was a proper farce. On the last charge I listened carefully to Pete's 'guilty', then I turned to the court and shouted 'Not guilty.' Pete let out a wild howl; he was frustrated with trying to speak through his wired-up jaw and this was the last straw.

'Sorry, sorry,' I said. 'I meant "Guilty".' I was enjoying myself.

The judge asked for any mitigation to be put forward, and I was more than surprised when my mum was ushered into the witness box. I hadn't seen her, or any of my family, since the day I got out of DC. I wasn't one for having visits in jail, I never saw the point in it. Visits are nothing but grief, they remind you of what you have left behind and interrupt the flow of your sentence. Every time I had one I would feel as though I was starting the whole of my sentence again when the visit was finished. Also, I hated to think of my family coming into contact with screws and being ordered about and looked down on by them. I had done the crime so it was me alone who should do the time.

I smiled at my mum; she looked very upset and not a little overwhelmed by the surroundings. My heart almost broke seeing her standing in the box at the Old Bailey, telling the judge what a good boy I was if only I were given a chance. I didn't want her there, she was part of a different life, and I felt the two should never come together. As she stood there singing my praises and begging them to give me mercy, I had a crisis of faith. I wanted to go home with my mum and forget all this had ever happened. I would give it up and lead a normal life, I couldn't stand to see her like this. Things would change.

After my mum had begged for my life back, the judge thanked her for putting up with me. As she walked past the dock I managed a smile. Next up were the reports from Latchmere and Ashford. I was surprised to hear myself described as 'a border-line psychopath', and I wondered who had written the report. Probably one of the screws I had assaulted. The Latchmere probation officer recommended that I be sent to borstal. I smiled at this – unlucky mug, I'm going back to DC!

Pete's reports were not much better than mine, and they recommended an eighteen-month period of YP. Finally the case was over and it was time for us to collect our sentences. We waited expectantly.

The clerk ordered us to stand for sentencing. Even though I had already been told what it was going to be, I couldn't help but feel a touch of nerves. The judge dealt with Pete first.

'Peter Mayne, the only thing I can find to say to your credit is that you have pleaded guilty today. It is for that reason, and that reason only, that I propose to deal leniently with you. You will go to prison for three years.'

Pete was stunned, and I wasn't feeling too good myself. What had happened to our deal? As Pete was led from the dock the only comfort I could find was that I would have to get less than him. After all, I was still a juvenile. I prepared myself for nine months' borstal instead of six months' DC.

The judge turned to me.

'Noel Stephen Smith, I have read the reports compiled on you, and after viewing your conduct in this court this morning, I must say that I am in full agreement with the compilers of those reports. You are a career criminal in the making, and I feel it is time somebody stopped you in your tracks. That falls to me. Were it not for your young age, I would have no hesitation in sending you to prison for a great number of years. As it is, I propose to take a rare course and order you to be detained under the Children and Young Persons Act 1933 for a period not longer than three years.'

And that was that. We had been royally fucked over by the Crown. And the moral of the story is: British justice does not make deals.

I don't remember being taken down to the cells. At the age of sixteen, a sentence of three years seemed like a lifetime. It was 1977 and I would not get out until 1980! By then people would be flying around in jet-packs and taking holidays on the moon. It was a fifth of the life I had lived up until that day. I couldn't even remember three years into the past let alone look three years into the future. I would go mad. But the best part was yet to come.

Down in the cell we both put on a brave face.

'It's not that bad,' we said. 'At least we've already done five months' on remand, so that's got to come off. Plus remission of one third. That leaves nineteen months. Just a couple of borstal sentences back to back. No drama.'

Nineteen months was still a daunting prospect, but it cheered us up a bit. There was light at the end of the tunnel. Then my barrister came down and switched the light off.

It turned out that as I was sentenced under Section 53.2 of the CYP Act, I was not entitled to any of my remand time back. Not only that, but I was not entitled to any remission! I could only be released by order of the Secretary of State. I felt like I was stuck in a nightmare. My brief explained that Section 53.2 was a rare sentence and could only be given to '. . . a juvenile who is convicted of a crime that would warrant a sentence of fourteen years or more in an adult'.

I suppose I should have been chuffed. I had made it into the big time. But all I felt was numbness. Then anger.

'What about the deal you made with the prosecution?' I asked. 'I thought it was all sorted?'

The brief began to bluster, saying that we did the right thing by pleading guilty as it could have been worse.

'Worse?' I shouted. 'How the fuck could it have been worse? You fucking useless mong, get out before I knock you spark out.'

He scurried from the cell and I never saw him again.

After lunch the screws put me and Pete into the off-bail cell. It was a large room where all those who had been sentenced that day waited for the transport to take them to prison. In one corner was a table where five or six suited men played cards. They looked like right hard cases and seemed to know everybody in the room. I was the youngest one there, so I sat on the bench and kept my mouth shut, as did Pete. One of the card-players glanced in our direction and looked surprised.

'Bleedin' 'ell! You don't look old enough to shave yet. What you doin' 'ere?' he asked.

I shrugged. 'Just been sentenced,' I said.

The card-players were all looking at us now and I felt a bit self-conscious. The room went quiet.

'What did you get?' one of them asked.

I shrugged again. 'Three years' detention,' I said casually, knowing instinctively that to show any self-pity or regret would make me seem even more childish. 'Do it on me fuckin' 'ead.'

The card-players all laughed.

'That's the spirit, son. Fuck 'em if they can't take a joke.'

I felt proud that I had said the right thing.

'What was you up for?' asked one.

I straightened my shoulders and tried to look as hard and cool as they did. 'Armed robbery,' I said.

Again there was admiring laughter. 'Stone me, they're getting

into it young nowadays! Not even old enough to vote and he's
at the heavy! Makes me feel old. Here boy, how old are ya?'

'Sixteen,' I said.

'Well, keep yer chin up and don't let nobody take liberties
with ya, especially the screws. Here, for you and your pal.'

He threw me a pack of cigarettes and a box of matches. Then
they went back to their game, still chuckling.

I felt good.

During the afternoon I watched as the card-players went up
for sentencing one by one. As they came back into the cell each
one had something funny to say about his sentence.

'I got a twelve, boys. The beak must have had a good breakfast!'

'Fuckin' sixteen years, I'll be out in time for a holiday on
Mars.'

'I can't believe I only got an eight-stretch. The judge must
have mistook me for the grass!'

I studied the way they dressed – sharp suits, ties and highly
polished shoes – and the way they treated the screws, as though
they were merely errand-boys they were willing to tolerate. The
screws gave them whatever they asked for and treated them with
respect. This was what I wanted to be. Up until then I had
modelled myself on the American gangsters I'd seen in the Bogart
and Cagney films, but that afternoon at the Old Bailey I had
glimpsed the real thing: home-grown London blaggers in one of
their natural habitats. The Chaps, risking it all on a turn of the
cards, and then a smile and a wink when things went pear-shaped.
Taking it like a man. This was the life I craved.

Now I am older and wiser, and when I think about that day
I can't help but wonder how many of those men I looked up
to went back to their cells and shed a quiet tear that night. I'm
now able to understand the heartache and despair that must surely
lurk behind the façade of cocky bravado. I myself have laughed
in the face of public punishment and castigation only to weep
bitter tears in the privacy of my cell.

At around 5.30 that afternoon I was handcuffed and loaded
on to a prison transport. I heard them say that I was on my way

to a 'special unit' for Section 53s at Ashford remand centre. Pete was loaded on to a separate van, on his way to Aylesbury prison. Like me, incarceration would take a heavy toll on his mental health, but unlike me, he would serve only fifteen months of his sentence, being released on compassionate grounds when his parents died in quick succession, his mother of cancer, his father, a heart attack.

As the van passed through the sunny, crowded streets of London towards Middlesex, I wondered what was in store for me. I probably wouldn't see these streets again until I was nineteen years old. I thought about my family and silently wished them luck. Where I was going I would have no contact with the outside world. No use for love or any of the normal emotions that people take for granted. I didn't yet know it, but I was starting a journey that would take me into the very depths of hell. And, looking back now, the worst part was, I was actually looking forward to it.

Ashford remand centre is now a reception centre for asylum seekers. They did a lot of repairs, gave the gaff a new coat of paint and introduced a few facilities it did not have in my day, such as working toilets and a light switch on the inside of the cell. Back in 1977, Ashford was a disgraceful place, dirty, crumbling, and with an atmosphere of despair hanging over it like a cartoon stormcloud. The only other prisons I can think of that have the same ambience are the likes of Wandsworth, Dartmoor and Strangeways. Just looking at these prisons from the outside makes you want to cut your wrists, so imagine how much worse they are inside.

Section 53 was a very rare sentence, and I was only the third one to enter Ashford that year. Combined with my record from Latchmere, that meant I got special treatment in reception. All the incoming YPs were locked in a holding-room with a large window, and they watched, open-mouthed, as I was taken from the van, double-cuffed, and escorted into reception by six grim-faced screws. I couldn't resist playing to the gallery, sneering at the screws and giving everyone the old slow-burn.

The cuffs were removed after I was given the standard lecture by a fat PO about how violence against his staff would be met with worse violence and I couldn't beat the system. I did exactly what was expected of me, I yawned. The boys in the holding-room lapped it up. I was stripped, questioned, had my finger-prints and photo taken, then I was given a set of blues to wear. Prison blues consist of jeans, T-shirt and denim jacket, and are worn by all convicted prisoners. Unconvicted remand prisoners wear the same outfit, only in brown. When the routine was done the PO shouted, 'One for the Unit, sir,' and I was escorted by the six screws down various corridors and up endless flights of stairs.

The Unit was a small, enclosed landing consisting of eight cells, two small classrooms, a shower and a hot-plate area. The screws on the Unit were hand-picked for their ability to deal with violent juveniles. I was given the welcoming speech by the Unit SO: keep your gob shut, call officers 'sir', don't give us a hard time and we won't give you a hard time, etc. By now I had heard so many versions of this speech that it hardly registered any more.

I was allocated to a cell that was no different from any other cell I had been in before or since. There was an iron bed with a three-inch-thick foam mattress, a tubular chair, a plywood locker and table, and a plastic jug and piss-pot. The only good thing was that the piss-pot was brand-new. There was a small window high on the back wall, but all that could be seen from it was a strip of sky, as a large wooden board had been nailed to the outside to prevent us looking over the fence at the screws' houses. The door was closed behind me. I had survived day one of my sentence. Only another 1,095 to go. Jesus!

I was rudely awaken at seven the next morning by a screw banging on the door with a truncheon.

'Come on. Out of bed. Feet on the floor.'

I stuck my head out of the blankets and gave him a volley of abuse.

'You'll get yourself in trouble, lad, if you carry on like this,' he said, before moving on to the next cell.

'Yeah?' I shouted after him. 'What are you going to do then? Put me in fucking prison?'

Breakfast was at 8.15. It was the usual prison fare: grade three Canadian pig-meal posing as porridge, two slices of bread, a pat of marg and a cup of diesel. After this hearty repast it was time to slop-out. Slopping out was a terrible, degrading business that was still going on in British prisons up until the late 1990s. The last time I personally had to slop-out was at HMP Albany in 1997. Prisoners had to empty their piss-pots down a central sluice three times a day. On the Unit it wasn't so bad because it only held a maximum of 8 prisoners, but on a normal prison wing which housed up to 120 men it was fucking minging. Just imagine for a moment the smell of the contents of 120 chamberpots being emptied into one small sink just after breakfast. And of course the sluice itself is not designed to take such a large volume of waste three times a day, so inevitably it would overflow. Sometimes scores of men would have to wade ankle-deep through other men's piss in order to empty their own pot. Most times tempers would flare and you would end up with men rolling around in the mire trying to punch the faces off each other and splashing other men who would then join in the fight. How's that for a vision of hell?

The first of the other three detainees on Section 53 I met was a shy Irish sixteen-year-old who was doing four years for 'bomb-making'. He had been nicked, along with his entire family, in connection with the Guildford pub-bombing case, and the screws always gave him a hard time, referring to him as 'The Paddy Bomber'. In those days I didn't know whether he was guilty and I cared even less, but I liked him straight away because he was the first one in the Unit to offer me a roll-up.

The other two were proper off-key pieces of work. One was a fat, greasy-looking kid of fifteen who had been admitted the previous year and was serving eight years for aggravated burglary and raping an eighty-year-old woman. His nickname was the Turk, and he reminded me of a fatter, greasier version of the film actor Peter Lorre. He had a creepy way about him, and he was always licking his bright red rubbery lips. At the time, I didn't know he was in for rape, and if I had known, I would have had no hesitation in opening him up like a tin of beans. I classed all sex offenders as scum to be seriously injured whenever possible. My attitude was part natural revulsion and part learned from being in prison and seeing how it was.

The other detainee was a big public schoolboy of sixteen, named Charles. He was doing HMP, the juvenile version of life imprisonment, for strangling his best pal with his own schooltie. He tended to try to bully people who he thought might be weaker than himself and he was forever talking about his crime and how much he had enjoyed it.

It didn't take me long to establish my place in the pecking order on the Unit. Charles and the Turk were a pair of ice-creams and they soon melted into place when I growled at them a couple of times, so I was top rooster. The screws knew how things worked and as long as it didn't affect them, they sat back and let nature take its course. I was first for anything that was going: extras from the hot-plate, clean kit, showers and canteen. That's the way it works in every prison – survival of the meanest.

In a closed and essentially macho environment like prison you have to be prepared to fight for what you want. The only thing that will keep the rest of the animals at bay is the sure knowledge that they will get hurt if they try to take liberties with you. And every now and again this calls for practical demonstrations. Show one sign of weakness and they will rip you to pieces. Prison is great at stripping your humanity to the bone and sending you back to the Stone Age: if you want what I've got, you're going to have to club me into submission to take it, and then you'll have to watch your back, because I will make a come-back.

There are very few stand-up fights in prison. The Marquis of Queensberry would have a six-inch nail buried in his back before he could say 'Round one'. The reality of prison violence is that there is nowhere to run. If you come to blows with someone, there is no way to avoid seeing them every single day and the chances are, you will have to fight the same fight many times. So taking violence to extremes serves a dual purpose: it becomes a warning to others, and it also means you won't have to see your opponent again, as he will be shipped to another nick via the hospital. The creed of prison violence is get in first, get in fast and make sure you always put your opponent out of the game.

Prisoners can make a weapon out of almost anything, and they do. A razor-blade melted into the handle of a toothbrush, the Gillette bayonet, is a favourite. Any piece of metal can be sharpened up and used as a tool, and even a plastic toilet-brush becomes a formidable weapon if you shave the handle into a point. A tried and tested weapon, usually inflicted on sex offenders, is sugar and hot water. On every prison wing there is a communal hot-water urn that supplies boiling water to make tea. Put half a pound of sugar into a prison jug and top it up with boiling water from the urn, give it a mix, and you are ready to inflict horrific injuries. The sugar partly dissolves, so when the mixture is thrown in the victim's face it clings to the skin and burns all the more. This activity is known as 'jugging'. There is also 'jerking', which is a sharpened nail or half a scissors plunged into the lower body. And 'PP9-ing', which is a sock or pillow case filled with heavy PP9 batteries and smashed into the head or body. When it comes to inflicting violence on each other, prisoners are nothing if not resourceful.

Life in the Unit was routine and quickly became boring. After breakfast and slop-out we were taken to one of the classrooms, where we could paint watercolours or stuff soft-toys until lunch at 11.30. After lunch it was back to the classroom for more 'arts and crafts', until 3.30, tea-time, then at 4.00 it was bang-up for the night until the next morning. Day in, day out. After three days I was certain I would go mad long before I finished my sentence.

One evening after I had been in the Unit for about a month, I heard a loud commotion on the landing outside my cell. I stood at my cell door, looking through the crack to see what was going on. One of the voices sounded familiar, and suddenly I caught sight of a shock of curly hair and realized it was my old pal Jel Keeble.

'Jel! Jel!' I shouted. 'It's me, Razor! What's happening, mate?' Jel was locked into the cell next door to mine and in no time at all he was up at his window telling me what had happened.

He had appeared at Chelmsford crown court and pleaded guilty to burgling a café and stealing £100's worth of meat from the freezer. He had been expecting, at the very worst, to go to borstal, but after the judge read his report from Latchmere House, he was given three years' Section 53. And here he was.

It seemed very suspect that both me and Jerry had got exactly the same sentence within a month of each other, given that we both pleaded guilty to very different charges and that Section 53 was so rare. To this day I don't know if the authorities at Latchmere House had any say in our sentencing. If they did, then it is a sorry state of affairs that we weren't sentenced for the crimes we had committed but rather for our behaviour once banged up.

A week later the plot thickened when another ex-Latchmere House rebel turned up in the Unit. Tony was a lively fourteen-year-old from west London, who had a hundred previous convictions for theft, burglary and TDA. Despite his age, he had earned a reputation in Latchmere as one of the Chaps, and would take no shit from the screws. His case made the front page of the *Sun*, when he was sentenced to seven years' Section 53 for a £60 robbery. The rest of the bods involved in the shop robbery were all over seventeen and received six-month sentences, but the judge told Tony that his previous was too much and he deserved a wake-up call. His parting words were, 'You will be released when you are twenty-one. Perhaps by then you will have learned to be a man.'

With Jel and Tony on board we were a force to be reckoned with, and even the Irish boy started to come out of his shell and join in the slagging we gave to everyone – screws, tutors, and Charles and the Turk. One afternoon in the middle of the summer we demanded to be allowed off the Unit for a game of football in the exercise yard. This was unheard of, but we threatened to go on hunger strike if we weren't allowed out in the sun. The screws laughed it off, but after we had staunchly refused two meals, they called the chief. The chief was a big fat geezer with a purple nose who looked as though he wasn't interested in anything that he couldn't eat or drink. He listened to our demands and said he would see what he could do. The next morning at breakfast we were ready to refuse to eat again, when the SO announced that the governor had decided that we could have an hour on the exercise yard that afternoon. We were over the moon. It was a major victory. We had none of us been out in the fresh air since we came on to the Unit. It was like Christmas and all our birthdays had come at once.

That afternoon we were given an old leather football and marched down several flights of stairs by about fifteen screws. The moment I stepped out on to that yard and felt the sun on my face is one I'll never forget. The screws lined up around the yard and left us to it. We were dizzy with the excitement of it and had a great game of football. For an hour we were just kids again, enjoying our game and the weather. It was like being normal for a change.

But, like any concession granted by the system, there was a price to pay. The next morning there was the sound of movement on the landing before our doors were opened. When we came out for breakfast the Irish boy was gone. He had been shipped out. Maybe it was just his time to move on, or maybe someone had decided that we were getting a bit too vocal in our demands. Who knows? When I asked a screw why they had not told anyone that he was going, I was told, 'We couldn't tell anyone. Can't have the IRA trying to break him out, can we?' I never saw him again, but I was glad to read, many years later, that his family had been exonerated.

We never got out on the yard again. It was a one-off. August 1977 was a memorable month. The Queen's silver jubilee was all over the news, but it didn't affect me in the slightest. Elvis died, and that did affect me since I had always been a fan. Punk rock was also in the news, as was a case in west London, of three boys of sixteen convicted of raping a fourteen-year-old girl. We heard it on the radio and knew that they would be coming to the Unit if they got the sentences they deserved. We would be ready and waiting.

8. Gladiator School

The three boy-rapists got ten, eight and six years from the courts, but the stick they got from us when they reached the Unit was their real punishment. We attacked and abused them at every opportunity, until eventually there were two different factions on the Unit which could not be let out of their cells at the same time. Suddenly the screws had twice the work, as everything had to be done in shifts to avoid confrontation. It couldn't go on for long, and it didn't.

One morning in September the screws threw my door open at six o'clock, and I was on my way. They piled into my cell and watched as I packed my meagre belongings. As they put the handcuffs on, I asked where I was going. 'You'll find out when you get there,' was the reply. I was marched down to Reception and put into a holding cell. I had been in the cell about twenty minutes when the door opened and in walked Jel. They were getting rid of both of us on the same day.

We were more than happy to be moving on but hoped that Tony would be all right. He would now be on his own against the rapists, but he was a game kid and wouldn't allow anyone to take liberties. We discussed where we might be going.

'Could be anywhere, mate. I don't really mind as long as it's not Portland or Dover. I hear they're right bad.'

'Yeah, or Rochester, that's another kip. Maybe we're going on the borstal wing at Wormwood Scrubs! Fuck that.'

'Maybe they've had enough of us, and we're getting released?'

'Ha fuckin' ha. No, mate, they've got somewhere nasty lined up for us. No doubt about it. We'll be all right as long as we stick together.'

At 9 a.m. we were loaded into a green prison Transit van, with barred windows and six screws. The journey seemed to take for ever and there wasn't much to see out of the windows after the first ten minutes, just fields. Wherever they were taking us, it was definitely out in the sticks somewhere.

After what seemed like three hours, the van pulled up a long driveway and stopped outside two huge wooden gates. There was a sign to the left of the gates: HMBI Rochester. I looked at Jel, and he shrugged as if to say, 'It could have been worse.'

Rochester borstal was the first ever borstal built, in 1908, and was named after the nearby village of Borstal. It had a reputation as a hard place, where most of the trouble-makers in the south-east were sent. If you fucked up in another borstal you would end up in Rochester. Its equivalent in the south-west was Portland, which was rumoured to be much worse, so it was a result that we hadn't been sent there.

We were unloaded from the van and brought into the small reception area. And this was where I was given the bad news. They unlocked Jel's handcuffs, but when I held out mine for the same the screw shook his head.

'Keeble's the only one getting off here. You can stretch your legs for five minutes, and then back on the van. You're going somewhere else.'

I was gutted and I could tell Jel was too, but we put a brave face on it. We shook hands.

'Good luck, mate. Don't take any shit off these cunts.'

'See you again. Drop me a line.'

And that was it. I was loaded back into the van.

We had been travelling for about half an hour when I got the first idea where I was going. I saw a sign: DOVER 27 miles.

I tried to remember everything I had heard about Dover borstal. It was known as 'the riot borstal', because of the number of disturbances there. It was up on the top of a cliff overlooking the sea, and it was almost impossible to escape from because of a moat surrounding the grounds. Pete the Nut had done his first borstal sentence there and had told me plenty of stories about boys getting cut and bashed for the slightest offences. The only good point I could think of was that Pete's brother, Harry, was doing a borstal there. So at least there would be one familiar face, if nothing else.

Sure enough, as soon as I smelt the sea and saw the first seagull, the van started going uphill. We reached the top of the cliff known as Western Heights, and there it was. It looked more modern than Rochester but no less a place of incarceration with its high fences and huge gates.

I went through the usual reception routine, as well as the 'speech', this time from a skinny assistant governor with a facial twitch. Then I was marched to the induction house, which was called Romney. There were five houses at Dover, named after the Cinque Ports. All the houses except Deal had dormitory accommodation. The dormitories held either four or six 'trainees'. I was put into a dormitory with three hobbits, one of whom was suicidal. Suicide Sid had tried to kill himself on several occasions while on remand. His arms were a mass of scar tissue where he had cut himself so many times, and he had a permanent red ring around his neck from a hanging attempt that had gone wrong. He spoke constantly about how he missed his mum and his dad and his dog, and how he would not be able to survive his sentence. I felt some pity for him, but the constant whining got on my nerves.

The only thing on my mind at that time was escape, and I was willing to take any risk to get away. I questioned the other bods about the moat. I was told that it was thirty feet deep, with no water in it, and that the last boy who had tried to escape had ended up with two broken legs from falling into it. The news was not encouraging.

Every morning and afternoon a 'parade call' was held before inmates were allowed to go to work. Nobody in the induction house had a job yet, but we still had to go on parade. Borstal inmates were, on the whole, a mean and spiteful bunch who loved tradition, and the tradition in Dover was that all new boys in the induction house were to be hissed at and jeered at every opportunity. It was a form of intimidation and it was very effective. As the average borstal sentence was nine months, another tradition was that anyone who came in after the month of March would be greeted with the cry, 'Do your Christmas, mug!' Just a little reminder for kids who were probably already in bits over their sentence.

The first morning I went on parade call everyone began to hiss and jeer and tell me to do my Christmas, and I went into one. I rushed out of line and started swinging punches at whoever wasn't quick enough to get out of my way. This was unheard of, you were supposed to just take it and hope that it would pass, but I had three more Christmases to do and I wasn't taking any shit from anyone.

The screws pulled me off the parade square and back to the house. I was put into the dorm and left to cool off and I got another visit from the twitchy AG.

By the afternoon parade I had calmed down, and as the induction house marched up to the parade ground, there was silence. I got a few hard looks from the boys who considered themselves the Chaps, but nothing more. As we lined up to dress-off, the boy behind me tapped me on the shoulder and whispered, 'Over there.'

I looked in the direction he was indicating and was delighted to see Harry, Pete the Nut's brother, grinning at me. He gave me the thumbs-up and mouthed, 'See you this afternoon.'

I had grown up with Harry, sometimes known as 'Mad' Harry, or Harry the Hatchet. He was just as impulsive as his brother but nowhere near as thick. In fact, Harry had a genius for all things electrical or mechanical. He could hot-wire a car in seconds flat and disable a burglar alarm in the blink of an eye. The trouble with Harry was that he had a low boredom threshold; he would choose a topic and soak up every scrap of information about it very quickly, and then drop it and move on to something else. Had it not been for this flaw in his character, he could have made a good living at any profession he put his mind to.

Harry was doing his borstal for GBH and motorbike theft, and by the time I reached Dover he had already done fourteen months,

way above the average nine. He had been doing a plumbing course
and had almost completed it, when he got into a row with one
of the other boys on the course. He had taken an oxyacetylene
torch and heated up a pair of pliers until they were white-hot,
then picked them up with an asbestos glove and called the boy
he had argued with. When the boy turned around, Harry threw
him the pliers and said, 'Catch.' The boy followed his natural
instincts and caught the pliers. Harry lost three months for that.

The parade was a farce. It reminded me of one of those old
prisoner-of-war films. After the count and a lot of self-important
shouting by the screws – 'Deal house present and correct, sir' . . .
'Works party all correct, sir,' etc. – we were told to stand at ease
while the numbers were radioed to the control room. I had a
good look around at the other faces on the parade ground, and
there were a few that were familiar from both Send and Latchmere
House. I got a few grins and nods.

Once the count was checked again we were called to attention and marched away.

That afternoon Harry came over to the induction house to
see me. He was on the works party and worked with a civilian
plumber who had the run of the borstal. Harry got on well with
the civvy and could go anywhere he wanted. I was delighted to
see him, and we soon filled each other in on all the news. He
told me that there was one more Section 53 at Dover, a black
fella who was doing ten years for manslaughter, but he was a
proper hobbit and sucked up to the screws. He said everyone
was talking about me and my performance at the morning parade,
and the word was that I was in for some stick when I came off
induction and moved into one of the houses. He told me to try
and get into Deal house, where he was, and that it was the only
house that had single cells. I told him the names of a few of the
boys I knew who I had spotted on the parade ground.

'There's someone else who knows you here,' Harry told me.
'He's in the block at the moment for a tear-up, but he should
be out by Friday.'

'Who?' I asked, wondering if it was friend or foe.

Harry smiled. 'Johnny Mac,' he said.

I was relieved. Johnny was my old sparring partner from the workshop battle in Latchmere House. With both Harry and Johnny as allies I felt confident of making any move and getting back-up.

The borstal system worked on the carrot-and-stick principle. 'Trainees' were given a provisional release date of nine months, but if they toed the line and did a bit of sucking-up to the screws they could get their sentence cut to as little as six months. It also worked the other way, so if they kicked off and didn't conform, they could end up doing as long as two years. It was only a handful of very extreme hard-cases who ever did the full whack, and the average borstal boy did eight or nine months. But borstals like Dover, Rochester and Portland were specifically for the 'bad 'uns', boys who had already shown an inclination to 'buck the system', either through the type of crimes they had committed or by their behaviour in other juvenile institutions. Sticking all the worst cases behind the same walls led to massive problems for everybody.

Borstal was gladiator school for young criminals. Many of the major players on the heavy crime scene of the 1980s and beyond started their associations and reputations in Dover, Rochester and Portland. Borstal violence was vicious and frequent, and the bloodier the better. No one wanted to duke it out, and everyone was looking to 'stripe' the next man. Reputation was everything to us, gameness and bottle were revered, and backing down from anyone was considered cowardly, no matter what the reason. If there was one thing that was on a par with being a nonce or a grass to a borstal boy, it was being a 'sap', someone with no arse-hole. If you were not prepared to fight at the slightest insult, then you might as well just lie down and let everyone walk all over you; and they would. Show the slightest reluctance to put the blade about and within hours you would be stripped of all your personal possessions, be cleaning someone's cell for the rest of your time and handing over your canteen every week. It was as simple as that.

The screws didn't give a fuck if we carved each other into jigsaw puzzles; they had enough to do trying to dodge the flak themselves. They made a pretence of keeping order and discipline, and sometimes we went along with it, and sometimes we didn't. Of course, there was a percentage of trainees, even in the worst borstals, who just wanted to get on with their time and get out as soon as possible. So the screws mainly concentrated on them and tried to give the rest of us a wide berth.

I had only been in Dover a couple of days and I had already made plenty of enemies. I knew there were kids who would be out to test me, so I decided to get tooled up. Harry slipped me a razor-blade, which I snapped in half and made into a double-bladed Gillete bayonet. I was fully prepared to open the face of anyone who even looked at me funny.

Association time, when prisoners could mix with the rest of the cons on their own houseblock, was six till eight every evening. Some kids played pool on the battered half-size table, or table-tennis, or watched the black-and-white television that was located in a small room off the main hall. My jailhouse radar started tingling as soon as I walked into the association area. I spotted a couple of hard-faced individuals screwing me out over by the pool table. I had my tool handy, in the top pocket of my denim jacket, bristle-end up so it just looked like a toothbrush. By the way their eyes followed me across the hall, I knew they would be calling it on before the end of association, so I decided to get my retaliation in first. I walked straight over and fronted them.

'Do you know me?' I asked.

They both shook their heads, nonplussed at being confronted by their intended victim.

'Well, what the fuck are you looking at me for?'

I casually raised my hand and gripped the lapel of my jacket, my fingers a couple of inches from my top pocket. The shorter of my two would-be assassins swallowed hard, and his eyes roved everywhere except my face. The taller one tried a smile, but I could see bad intentions in his eyes.

'You're paranoid, mate,' he said.

I moved my hand over to my top pocket and they both flinched away as though I had splashed them with acid.

'Smith, 160,' the call came over the Tannoy system. 'Report to the wing office.' I stood for a moment, giving them the slow-burn.

'Mugs,' I said contemptuously, before turning my back and walking away.

An assistant governor was waiting for me in the wing office. 'Smith,' he began. 'You seem to have got off to a bad start.'

I stood in front of his desk and stared at the wall above his head. He paused as if expecting me to say something, but I kept my mouth shut. He shuffled a few papers on the desk, and waited.

'You're not the first hard-case I've had in front of me. Before I came here, I worked at Parkhurst, Chelmsford and Wormwood Scrubs. I've seen them all come and go. The Great Train Robbers, the Kray brothers, John McVicar . . .'

I made a great show of stifling a yawn.

'So if you think you can take on the system, I'm here to tell you that you'll come off a poor second.'

I began to whistle softly, under my breath but loud enough for him to hear and know that I wasn't interested in his speech. He shook his head in disgust.

'OK. Have it your way. But we'll be watching you. Dismissed.'

I strolled out of the office with my hands in my pockets.

The two hobbits I had fronted earlier were nowhere to be seen, so I nipped into the TV room to see what was on the box. The room was in semi-darkness and all the chairs were taken. It was *Top of the Pops* night. In those days *Top of the Pops* was almost a religious experience for borstal boys; not only did we get to see the latest hits performed by the artistes of the hour, but there was also Pan's People, a group of scantily clad dancers whose sexual gyrations could make any healthy trainee utter a cry of 'Oh, God!'

I stood with my back to the wall, just inside the door and watched the antics of Abba and the Boomtown Rats. I was still a teddy-boy and held in contempt any music that wasn't recorded between 1950 and 1960, but I was up for a bit of Pan's People. And I half-fancied the blonde bird in Abba.

The door of the telly room opened beside me and I just had time to glimpse the determined face of the hitman before sparks exploded in my head. I fell backwards, stunned and off balance but instinctively reaching for the tool in my top pocket. The hitman stepped further into the room and swung again. I caught the blow on my forearm and felt the vibrations right up to my shoulder as a sock full of pool balls bounced off the bone of my arm. I ducked the next swing and managed to get a good grip on my Gillette bayonet. I threw myself forward, using the wall as a launch-pad, and swung my tool at my attacker's face. It missed but whistled by his nose close enough to shit the life out of him, and he backed off. I wasn't feeling any pain, I never do in the heat of battle, but I knew he had caught me a good one on the side of my head, because my legs felt weak and uncoordinated, the sure sign of a near-knockout blow. As my attacker backed out into the light I saw that he was the taller of the two kids I had fronted earlier. He held the makeshift cosh ready for another swing, but there was panic on his face; he was losing heart because his first surprise attack had failed to put me on the deck. I gritted my teeth and lashed out again with the razor. He jumped back but tried a half-hearted swing with the cosh, and I managed to run the blades across his knuckles on his return swing. He screamed like a girl, and dropped the sockful of pool balls.

By now the gaff was in uproar. The boys in the telly room, hearing the commotion, had jumped up to get a better look, some of them standing on their chairs. The few boys who had been out in the association hall dropped what they were doing and rushed forward to get a ring-side view, and the noise had alerted the screws in the office, who had pressed the riot bell.

My attacker was now wounded and weaponless, leaking blood, and I was closing in for the kill. I feinted at his body, and when he dropped his hands to cover up, I whipped the blade upwards and across his face. His scream was gratifying. He bent at the waist, clutching his face and wailing. The mist was on me and I wasn't about to stop. I grabbed him by the hair and tried to lift his face so I could cut him again, and that's when two fifteen-stone screws crashed into me. I fell to the ground and lost my weapon in the process. All around me it was bedlam; my fellow borstal boys were cheering and whooping like a pack of jackals, buzzing on the violence and the smell of blood in the air. I tried to get up but caught a truncheon across the shoulders which knocked me back down. Then a couple of the fast-arriving re-inforcements fell on me, and all the fight left my body.

I was dragged to my feet, arms twisted up behind my back, and I could see a couple of screws administering first aid to the other fella; this consisted of pressing a prison towel to his wounds.

'You fucking mug!' I shouted at him. 'Next time I'll fucking kill you!'

The screws pulled me away, and I was taken on the long walk to the punishment block. As I left the houseblock I could hear the screws restoring order. 'It's all over. Come on, lads, disperse. *Top of the Pops* is still on.'

If it had been any other night except Thursday they might have had the makings of a mini-riot. The screws must have loved Jimmy Saville.

On the way to the block one of the escort screws asked me what it had all been about.

'I didn't like his haircut,' I said.

In any prison, the punishment block is where the screws get their own back on the prisoners. It doesn't matter who runs the main wings, it is the screws who run the punishment block. The punishment block at Dover was a particularly bad one. It was situated in the bottom of a dip in the ground, and you had to walk down a steep hill to get to it. It felt as though you were descending into an alien underworld. As I was frogmarched down the hill I heard the iron gate clang open; the block screws had been radioed to say I was coming.

'One on, sir,' shouted one of the escort screws.

On the whole, block screws are a strange and brutal breed. They choose to work in what is basically a prison within a prison, where the whole emphasis is on punishment. Not for them the bother of pretending to be interested in a prisoner's problems or trying to build a working relationship with their charges. They are the real 'screws' of the system, and they glory in it. Some of them are banished to work in the stygian gloom of the punishment block because their personalities are too abrasive for work with the main population: others, because they have been found out in their bullying and brutality and need to be hidden away; but still more choose to work in an environment where they have an opportunity to relieve the frustration of their sad, empty lives and impose their will on others. These are the same type of screws who, in the days when we still had capital punishment, were delighted to volunteer for the Death Watch – sitting in a cell for weeks, observing some poor bastard who was facing imminent death.

Dover punishment block was run by a crowd of the nastiest screws in the borstal system. Most of them were ex-military men, who loved a bit of discipline, as long as they were handing it out. From the minute I entered the block they tried to intimidate me, putting their faces right up close when they barked questions and trying to get me to double-time everywhere. They were wasting their time. I wasn't a borstal boy who could lose remission if I didn't knuckle under. I had already made up my mind that I would be doing things my own way in the borstal system; I had nothing to gain, or nothing to lose. As a Section 53, I couldn't get time off for good behaviour nor could I lose any for bad behaviour.

I strolled into a waiting cell and stripped at my own pace, ignoring the histrionics of the block screws. A strip search is standard procedure for entry into the block, and in some circumstances, like when you have assaulted a screw, this would be the moment when the screws would give you a beating, when you are naked and at your most vulnerable and psychologically disadvantaged. But I had only assaulted another con so, unless I got lippy, they had no reason to start any physical stuff. I was drained from the excitement of the fight and all I wanted was to get my head down. So I kept my mouth shut.

After the strip search I was locked into another cell with nothing but the clothes I was wearing and a plastic piss-pot. A mattress and blanket would be put in the cell at 9 p.m., and taken out again at 6 a.m. I sat on the stone-flagged floor with my back against a cold wall. I thought about the kid I had cut and felt no remorse whatsoever. Even had he not attacked me first, I would still have put the blade to him sooner or later. After my performance on the parade ground, I knew I would be a good scalp for anyone who wanted to enhance or build a reputation. And so, in order to survive, I had to prove I was more willing and vicious than anyone else. Talking a good fight is not enough, seeing is believing. I wondered how many more I would have to cut before everyone got the message. But the truth was, I didn't care. This was my world now.

When the mattress came in I got straight into bed. It had been a tiring day. I had sent my message out to the con population: drop me out or get hurt. And tomorrow I would begin getting my message across to the screws. If I had to serve every day of my sentence, I would do it on my own terms.

At 6 a.m. my cell door was thrown open and a bucket of cold water, a chunk of yellow carbolic soap, a rag and a scrubbing-brush were pushed inside. 'Get that bedding packed up, I'll be back for it in five minutes,' was the order. I got off my mattress and stretched. Despite the coldness of the cell, I had slept well. I packed up the blanket and mattress into the mattress cover and leant it by the door. I looked at the cleaning equipment, but made no move to touch it. There was no way I was going to scrub the floor.

The door opened again five minutes later and the screw pulled my bedding outside. He pointed to the bucket. 'Come on, chop chop. Get the floor scrubbed.'

I leant against the wall with my hands in my pockets. 'If you want it scrubbed,' I said, 'then you'll have to scrub it your fucking self.'

The screw stood in the doorway, hands on hips, and gave me a hard look. 'Listen, lad,' he said. 'There's two ways to do your time in this block, the easy way, and the hard way. And believe me, you will not like the hard way.'

I stared straight back at him. 'Bring it on,' I said, 'and then we'll see whether I like it or not.'

He shook his head. 'OK,' he said, and slammed the door behind him.

I heard them bringing the breakfast trolley around to the cell doors, but they went straight past mine. So, I thought, their first move was to try and starve me into compliance. I began to pace the cell to keep warm. As the block was underground there were no windows in the cells and it was cold all the time. Being a winter baby I didn't mind the cold too much, but moving about was better than standing still. I explored every inch of the cell and found nothing of any interest. It was four paces long and two wide, with a curved ceiling about eight foot up and a light covered by steel mesh in the centre of the ceiling. The walls were concrete, painted in a light blue and felt damp to the touch. The floor was stone flags.

After a couple of hours I felt very thirsty, so I dipped my hand in the cleaning bucket and tasted the water. It was icy cold and tasted of soap, but I managed to swallow some.

Around 10 a.m. the door was opened again, to reveal an old fella in a tweed jacket and crumpled trousers. He had a fag hanging from the corner of his mouth and a trail of ash down his front. There were two screws with him. He didn't come into the cell but stood at the doorway and squinted at me through a stream of smoke.

'Stand to attention for the doctor,' one of the screws barked.

I stayed leaning against the wall.

'Are you well?' the doctor enquired.

'Fuck off,' I replied. The door was slammed, and that was the extent of my medical examination.

By eleven, I had started to do a few press-ups, when the door opened again. This time there were six screws, and they looked as though they meant business. One of them stepped into the cell and cleared his throat. 'You are going to appear before the governor for adjudication. If you choose not to go, then we will take you forcibly. Do you understand?'

I nodded. I didn't mind appearing in front of the governor; it would break up my boredom. The screw who did the talking dropped a pair of oversized slippers on the floor and stepped back out of the cell. I changed into the slippers and the screws formed an escort to march me to the adjudication room. As I shuffled casually along, one of the screws barked out the marching order: 'Lef', ri', lef', ri', lef', ri', halt.' I ignored him and shuffled up to the desk.

'Name and number to the governor!' he almost screamed in his agitation.

I nodded to where the governor was sitting, ten feet away, with my file opened on the desk in front of him. 'He knows who I am,' I said.

The screws surrounded me, leaving a small gap between their shoulders so I could see the governor.

'Smith, 160,' the governor read. 'You were involved in an incident in Romney house where another trainee was seriously injured. This matter is in the hands of the police, and they will decide whether outside charges should be brought. While their investigation is going on you will be held in the block. Have you anything to say about this?'

I shook my head. He carried on.

'While you are in this establishment you will be expected to follow orders just like any other trainee, and that includes abiding by the block regime, for example, scrubbing your cell every morning. Is this clear?'

I took a deep breath. 'No, it's not,' I said. 'For a start, I am not a "trainee", I'm doing a detention sentence. So if you want me to follow orders like a squaddie then you better give me a fucking rifle and a weekend pass, 'cos I'm not playing your silly fucking games . . .'

The screws smothered me and started to drag me from the room. I lost a slipper and had begun to struggle when I felt a fist go into my back, and that made me struggle all the more. In the corridor outside my cell one of the screws slipped, which allowed me to free my right arm. I groped blindly and gripped on to the first bit of flesh I touched. One of the screws let out a yelp as I squeezed his nose as hard as I could. I got a good hold and jerked him sideways, and he lost his hold on me. I pulled my head back as far as I could and jerked it forward into the jaw of the screw in front. In seconds we were all rolling around the floor of the block. I managed to get a few digs into various uniformed body-parts before the screws once again got the upper hand.

This time I had gone too far. They dragged me into the cell and really set about me. They kicked and punched me from one end of the cell to the other, grunting and yelping with the exertion. There was nothing I could do except try to cover up as best I could. One of them kept stamping on my hands, and another had me by the hair with one hand while he punched my face with the other. In the mêlée the scrubbing bucket got kicked over and flooded the floor with cold water. The pain was so bad I was praying that one of them would knock me out. Eventually, after what seemed like two hours but could only have been five minutes, they grew too tired to hit me. With a final hard kick to the arse, they left the cell and slammed the door.

When they left I was in too much pain to get up. I lay on the floor in a pool of blood and cold water. I felt as though I had been beaten on every part of my body, and even the inside of my throat hurt from screaming. Anyone who says they don't scream when they are being beaten by six men is a fucking liar. I screamed like a little girl. As I lay sobbing in the cold, afraid to move in case I set off more explosions of pain in my body, and shitting myself in case they decided to come back for round two, I wondered if death might be better than this. Like Jesus Christ on the cross, I had my moment of doubt. I lay there and prayed for death. But it didn't come.

Later that evening my mattress and blanket were launched into the cell without a word. I managed to get on to all fours and mop up most of the water with the cleaning rag and squeeze it back into the bucket. I rolled on to the damp mattress, fully clothed, and wrapped myself in the blanket. It would be a long, cold, uncomfortable night. I thought a lot about my situation. OK, so I had taken a pretty serious beating, but it wasn't the first and I was damn sure it wouldn't be the last. I had declared war and lost the first battle, and now I had to decide if it was worth carrying on. The odds were heavily stacked against me, but I wondered how far the enemy would go if I continued. Would they dare to kill me? I didn't think so. Not on purpose anyway. I had probably already suffered their worst. I weighed up the pros and cons of giving up and conforming to the regime.

The way I saw it, if I was to knuckle under, they would probably leave me alone and I would have a fairly comfortable existence. There would be no more beatings, and I would be fed. I saw the reality of my situation very clearly. I was deep in the system; no one gave a shit about me. I received no letters and no visits, at my own request, and there were no outside bodies I knew about who might step in and save me. I should really just surrender and make it easy on myself. But there was a part of me that refused to surrender at any cost, a part that boiled and bubbled with hate and outrage. I had nothing, and still the system wanted more. Even if I became a model prisoner, a spineless, servile cur, I would still have to serve every day of my sentence. A sentence that, to me, seemed impossibly long. And though only hours before I had been wishing for death, I now wanted to live. And I wanted the system to know I was alive. I wouldn't give up. Hate would keep me going.

When the cell door opened the next morning the screws took out the mattress and replaced the cleaning equipment with fresh stuff. When the door closed again I took a long drink from the bucket. I was very hungry, but there was no way I was going to scrub the floor. I tried to do some press-ups, but I only managed two before the pain from my bruised body became too much.

I sat in a corner of the cell with my back against the wall and waited. I heard the breakfast trolley going around the cells, and my mouth watered at the thought of the food they were dishing out to other prisoners, no matter how unappetizing it might be in reality. Suddenly my door was opened and a plastic bowl and plate were pushed into the cell before the door slammed shut again. I couldn't believe it. I scurried over to the door and saw a half-filled bowl of porridge and three slices of bread with a pat of margarine. There was steam coming off the porridge. Like a starving animal, I grabbed the feast and dragged it back to the furthest corner of the cell. I ate quickly in case they came and tried to take it back. I only had a plastic spoon, and it was awkward trying to spread the marg on the bread, but it all went down with no trouble.

After I had eaten I felt much better. Life didn't look half so bad, and I even managed five more press-ups. The pain of the beating was receding to a dull throb. I had to keep moving around the cell so my body wouldn't stiffen up, so I walked up and down.

About an hour after breakfast the door was opened again and a couple of screws who I had never seen before took out the unused bucket and scrubber. They didn't say a word. I was elated. I had won a small victory, but a victory nonetheless. I was a Home Office cipher living in a hole in the ground, with the weight of a whole system bearing down on me, and still they couldn't beat me into submission! I felt like singing.

For the next two weeks the block screws left me alone. Every morning the bucket was pushed into my cell, and after breakfast it was taken out again, unused. I continued to receive my meals. I spent my time doing sit-ups, press-ups, running on the spot and shadow-boxing. After a few days my bruises faded and I felt as fit as ever. But in solitary confinement the days are long and boredom is the main enemy. I had seen a lot of films in my life, and I would spend many hours of the day acting them out in order to entertain myself. I would use all the different voices and characteristics of the people in them, and when I couldn't remember dialogue I would make it up. The screws must have thought I had really lost it, as they would peep through the spy-hole on the cell door five or six times a day and find me talking to myself and throwing shapes. I perfected my James Cagney and Humphrey Bogart voices and managed to stay just the right side of sane. Barely.

One morning the door opened and I was once again given the outsize slippers and shuffled off to the adjudication room. We went through the usual routine. The governor read from a piece of paper.

'Smith, 160. The police have now completed their investigation into an incident of grievous bodily harm in Romney House. The other trainee involved is refusing to press charges and claims he "cannot remember" what happened. Therefore the police have decided not to proceed with the matter, and have left it in my hands.'

I was delighted. It meant I could soon be out of the block and back in the general population. I suppressed a smile. I guessed that Harry or Johnny Mac had given the kid a warning. I knew that Johnny had got out of the block the day after I had arrived. I couldn't wait to get up on the houseblocks and see him again.

But the governor wasn't finished with me yet. 'Smith,' he began. 'You have only been at Dover for a short while, but already you have proved troublesome. I am of the opinion that you would benefit from psychiatric help, which you cannot receive in this establishment. I have already started proceedings to get you moved on. You will be held in the block pending transfer. That's all.'

Before I had a chance to take in what he had said, I was back in my cell. Psychiatric help? What the fuck was all that about? I wasn't a nutter! OK, so I had been a bit difficult, but psychiatric help? I paced up and down the cell wondering what it all meant. Surely they wouldn't send me to Broadmoor? I was too young, wasn't I?

The governor's words had me seriously worried. I had heard stories about Broadmoor. It was full of raving lunatics who would kill you as soon as look at you. This was frightening. Though I had kept my verbal contact with the block screws to a minimum, there was one old SO who always seemed friendly, so I decided to approach him the next time he was on duty to try and find out what was going to happen.

By luck, he was on that evening and put my bedding in the cell. I cleared my throat and engaged him in a pointless conversation about getting a clean blanket. He seemed happy to speak to me. After a while I got down to what was really bothering me. I told him what the governor had said and asked if he knew what would happen to me. He pushed the cell door lock down, a standard security move whenever screws enter a cell, so that a prisoner cannot pull the door closed and take them hostage. He pulled out a packet of Embassy No. 10 cigarettes. I remember them because they had a bright-red stripe on the packet, and it had been so long since I had seen a bright colour it really stood out in the gloom and drabness of the block. He looked out into the corridor to make sure none of the other screws was about, and then handed me one of the cigarettes. I could barely believe it, I knew he could get into serious trouble for giving anything to a block prisoner. I was so surprised by this little act of kindness that tears prickled in the back of my eyes.

The cigarette felt massive in my mouth after so long without smoking, and the first drag made me feel dizzy and light-headed. Up until that moment I had successfully managed to avoid investing the screws with any human dimension. To me they were just the front-line troops of 'the system', and all their faces blurred into one in my mind. I didn't want to know anything about them, except how I could hurt them. But now my defences were down and I was vulnerable for a short while.

The screw, Mr Black his name was, told me that as far as he knew, there were no plans to send me to Broadmoor. I was relieved at this. But he said I would be moving to a borstal or prison hospital for mental observation. He thought it might be Wormwood Scrubs, which apparently had the best hospital facilities in the prison system. He told me that I should just conform to the regime and make it easy on myself.

'Three years is not so long, Smithy,' he told me. 'I don't know why you insist on making it hard for yourself.'

I looked at the ground. I would never be able to explain myself to him, I was not that articulate and, besides, I had to remember that despite his kindness, he was still one of the enemy. When I finished my smoke, he took the butt and threw it out into the corridor. If it was found in my cell there would be questions asked.

'My advice to you is just get your nut down and do your bird. Keep your nose clean and stay out of trouble. OK?'

I nodded, but I had no intention of taking his advice. When he had gone, I vowed that if I had to cause any more trouble while I was here, it would be when Mr Black was off duty.

My smoke with Mr Black felt like that time the English and German troops came out of the trenches to play football on Christmas Day during the First World War, a temporary truce on the battlefield. On 10 November 1977, the screws came for me. I had been in Dover just over six weeks, five of which had been spent in solitary confinement. Breakfast came as usual, but as soon as I had eaten, my door was flung open to reveal the crumpled doctor, flanked by some of the biggest screws I had ever seen.

'Are you fit to travel?' the doctor asked from the doorway.

'It depends,' I said, 'on where you're taking me.'

One of the humungous screws shook his head. 'We don't have to tell you that,' he said.

This was it. In a way I was glad to be getting out of the block and out of Dover. But I was also scared of where they might be taking me. I went and put my back to the far wall of the cell and faced the knot of screws at the door. I didn't have to say a word, they were ready. One of the screws popped the lock, and they came into the cell and fanned out around me. I managed to get off one right-hander, but it must have been a good one because I heard a yelp of pain. I saw nothing though, because they fell on me and dragged me to the floor. I felt someone pull down my jeans and I panicked, but the more I struggled the tighter they held me. I felt something sharp going into my buttock, and cold began to creep up my body.

'There. All done.' It was the doctor's voice and it was the last thing I remember about Dover.

To this day I don't know what they injected me with, but it did the trick. I can't remember anything about being carried out of the block, or the van ride to Rochester borstal. My time at Dover had not been happy but, little did I know, there was even worse in store for me at Rochester.

9. Under the Liquid Cosh

My first conscious sighting of the hospital in Rochester borstal was a sea of nylon and rubber. I woke up on my back in a corner of a padded cell. The only sound was a slight buzzing coming from the mesh-encased strip-light in the centre of the ceiling. My mouth was dry and had a foul, faintly metallic taste, and when I swallowed I became aware of a dull pain in the back of my head. I didn't know where I was and the strangeness of the room threw me into a panic. I climbed unsteadily to my feet and ran my hands over the walls. The material felt slick to the touch, and cold. I could feel the slightly yielding padding-material behind the thick nylon covering. The floor was black rubber matting, and it felt gritty beneath my bare feet. I still had on my jeans and T-shirt, but my shoes and socks were missing.

There was a plastic, prison-issue piss-pot in one corner, and that helped to calm me down because it was so familiar – the only familiar thing in this alien landscape. My eyes sought out the faint lines in the padding that would tell me where the door was. After a long minute I managed to find the door and also a small bell-push, which I wasted no time in pressing. I heard no ring or buzzer, so I couldn't tell if the thing was even working. I pressed my finger on the button and kept it there, and after about five minutes I was rewarded with sounds: the door was being opened.

Three men stood in the open doorway, looking in at me like I was a particularly interesting specimen that might be slightly dangerous. The one in the middle was a small Asian with a bald head and round glasses. He was wearing a suit, shirt and tie, and shiny shoes, and he held a clipboard and a pen. The other two were both white men in long white coats.

'Ah, Smith,' said the Asian man, but he pronounced it 'Smit'. 'Up and about, I see. And no ill-effects from your little sleeping draught?' He sounded far too jolly, and I didn't trust him one bit.

'I've got a headache,' I said. 'And I need a drink of water.'

The Asian smiled.

'Naturally, naturally,' he said. 'Do you know why you are here?'

I shook my head. 'I don't even know where I am,' I said.

He marked something on his clipboard, smiling all the while. 'You are in the hospital block at Rochester. You are here for mental observation, as you have been showing signs of erratic and violent behaviour. We'll soon get to the bottom of your problems.'

He turned to one of the white-coats and whispered something that I didn't catch. The white-coat nodded and began to busy himself at a medical trolley that I had not noticed behind them.

'I am going to give you some medication now. It will help to calm you down. OK?' said the Asian.

I decided that this had gone far enough. I took a couple of steps back and shook my head. 'No,' I said. 'I don't want no fucking medication. There's nothing wrong with me.'

The Asian smiled even more widely and scribbled furiously on his clipboard. 'OK, Smit,' he said. 'We'll talk about the medication later. But in the meantime, take this for your headache, and some water for your thirst' (which he pronounced 'tirst').

He took a small plastic container from the white-coat at the trolley, half-full of a greenish liquid, and held it out to me. I was more than suspicious but my head was really pounding now and the pain was making me feel nauseous. The white-coat was now pouring a beaker of water from a jug, and my thirst kicked in when I saw it. I stepped forward again and reached for the medication. 'What is this?' I asked.

The Asian shrugged in a carefree manner. 'Just liquid paracetamol. Your headache will be gone in ten minutes. Drink. And then the water.'

I took a deep breath and then knocked it back. It was fucking vile and coated my throat all the way down like used motor-oil drained from a rusty sump. I almost gagged, but the beaker of water was thrust into my hand just in time and it flushed the medication down. I demanded, and got, two more beakers of water before I felt able to swallow my own saliva without vomiting. The Asian and his white-coated assistants all wore satisfied smiles.

'There now,' he said. 'We shall have you better in no time.'

The door was closed and I was left in the silence of the padded cell. I didn't know it at the time, but I had just had my first dose of Largactil, a heavy tranquillizer also known as Chlorpromazine. Within twenty-four hours I would be shuffling about like a zombie.

When I awoke the next morning there seemed to be a haze over everything. I had pissed myself in my sleep and my jeans were stuck to my legs, and because of the padding, the cell was waterproof, so the piss did not drain away, it just sat in the middle of the floor. I didn't really care, I just crawled out of the puddle of piss and sat looking at it. If I moved my head slightly, the puddle caught the reflection of the overhead light and made interesting shapes, and this kept me amused for ages. I couldn't seem to string my thoughts together in any logical way and even lifting my eyelids felt like hard work. I didn't hear the door open, but I became aware of voices and someone lifting me off the floor.

The next thing I can remember clearly is being in a different cell, wearing clean, dry, stripy pyjamas. I had never owned a pair of pyjamas in my life, and just the thought of wearing them had me chuckling for what seemed like hours. I was given food, but it was such an effort to eat it that I would doze off from the exertion half-way through the meal. I don't know what dosage of Largactil they had me on, or what other drugs they were mixing it with, but I lost a whole week, which to this day remains a white screen in my mind.

My next clear memory is of waking up on a cold December morning and looking out of the window in my cell at a bank of fog hanging in the air. The windows were wide open, although, as they consisted of plastic and metal strips about six inches wide, two of which were on hinges and opened outside, the term 'wide open' is a bit misleading, and the cell was freezing. I climbed out of bed and as the soles of my feet touched the bare floor I suddenly seemed to come back to life. I was aware of my surroundings. I knew that the medication was fucking me up and stealing my life, and with that awareness came a determination not to take it any more. But how could I stop? They had me where they wanted me, and there was nothing I could do about it. I was too weak and disoriented to fight back physically. The despair I felt at my situation in this moment of lucidity was like a crushing weight that left me breathless. I could feel the drug haze creeping back into my mind like a vampire-mist, filling every nook and cranny as it swept insidiously forward. And, in one last desperate move, I reached deep inside myself and grasped for something. And there it was, my old faithful companion – hate. I dredged it up from the depths and turned it loose.

I began to growl, deep-throated, wolf-like sounds that vibrated through my body and seemed to awaken my tired muscles. 'Fucking bastards!' I spat venomously into the cold, empty cell. 'Fucking bastards! Fucking no-good cunts! I'll kill the fucking lot of them! They can't have ME!' The words spewed out of me, growing harsher and louder and giving me strength. And pretty soon I was on my feet and marching around the cell, cursing the world and everyone in it. For the first time in days I felt truly alive. The drugs were still in my system, and when I switched off my hate and rage they would once more become dominant, but at least I could now think.

With breakfast came the medicine trolley. It was delivered by a white-coated medical SO named Wade. He was about thirty, with crafty eyes and a bushy moustache that I was sure was cover for a perpetual sneer. I would come to hate Wade, and the very thought of him would be enough to bring my powerful hate bubbling to the surface. He was a bully and a snide, and he missed no opportunity to assault or humiliate the patients under his control in the hospital.

He stood at the door of my cell and waggled the medication container at me. 'Come and get it,' he said, in a girlish sing-song voice that he must have thought was funny. I kept my eyes on the floor, shuffled over to the door very slowly and took the liquid from his hand. I turned to put it on the table, but Wade said, 'No, no. Straight down the hatch.'

I tipped the liquid into my mouth but didn't swallow it. The taste was terrible, but I shambled back to the bed and lay down with it still in my mouth. Wade chuckled and put the plastic bowl of porridge on the table before moving on. As soon as the door was closed I was off the bed and spitting the liquid into the piss-pot. I didn't know how long I would be able to keep it up before they became suspicious, but I was determined not to take the medicine.

At dinner-time Wade appeared again, this time with two yellow pills. The pills were easier to hide in my mouth and I dragged myself back to bed like a creature from the living dead, even though I was feeling a bit livelier. The pills went out of the window as soon as the door was locked. I had to get out of this hospital, or I would end up a drooling vegetable long after my sentence was over. I didn't like the feeling of not being in control, I felt helpless and physically weak from the effects of the medication. But for now I would have to act as though I was still taking it. Over the dinner-time lock-up period I heard screams coming from somewhere along the landing and I went over to the cell door and put my ear up against the gap. I could hear Wade's voice, and I heard someone laughing and a door closing, and then more screams. I guessed that they were probably taking the piss out of some poor unfortunate. The atmosphere in the hospital was even worse than the punishment blocks I had been in.

The hospital block at Rochester was a fairly modern building in 1977. Though there had been a prison on the site since 1874, it only began taking juveniles after the 1908 Prevention of Crime Act established the borstal system in England and Wales. Over the

years, buildings were added and demolished within the grounds
of Rochester. The oldest building still in use is the punishment
block, which dates from 1876, and the newest is the hospital block,
which was opened in 1971. The hospital is a square, two-storey
red-brick building, with cellular accommodation and a small ward
on the second storey. Out-patients were dealt with on the ground
floor. The hospital was also used by the female prisoners from
HMP Cookham Wood, which is situated right across the road
from Rochester. The most infamous prisoner in Cookham Wood
was Moors murderess Myra Hindley, and she was often to be seen
being escorted through the borstal when all the trainees were
banged up in their cells. She got plenty of verbal abuse from the
cells on E-wing, which was closest to the hospital.

The screws who worked in the hospital were called 'nurses',
but in reality they were nothing more than screws with a first-
aid certificate. They wore white coats over their uniforms, but
not one of them had what could be classed as a bedside manner.
Until the NHS started running prison hospitals in the late 1990s,
screws did most of the day-to-day work. I was once waiting to
see a doctor in the hospital at Wormwood Scrubs when one of
the prisoners had a fit and collapsed on to the floor, shaking and
frothing at the mouth. The white-coated screws just stood there
looking at him with puzzled faces, and it was other prisoners
who took over and made sure his head was supported and he
didn't bite his own tongue off. The cure-all in prison hospitals
is liquid paracetamol for physical ailments, and the liquid cosh
for anything psychological. God help anyone who really gets ill,
because the standard of care is atrocious.

After the dinner-hour lock-up, which is 11.30 to 12.30, allowing
the screws to go and have a few pints in their social club, which
is normally located just outside the walls of the establishment, I
was opened up for association. This was my chance to mix with
the other prisoners in the hospital and watch a bit of black-and-
white TV or play chess or table tennis. I had seen a film called
One Flew over the Cuckoo's Nest when I was outside. It starred
Jack Nicholson as a prisoner who was working his ticket in a

mental hospital, and when I saw the association area at Rochester hospital I immediately thought of that film. There was a rickety old ping-pong table with no net, a TV bolted on to a wall, a few vinyl chairs in various states of disrepair and a handful of raggedy zombies trudging around this palace of entertainment. I shuffled into the large room and the screw locked the door behind me. The screws were gathered in an office with a large wire-mesh window that looked out on to the association area, but they seemed more interested in telling each other jokes than in what might be happening to their charges.

I slouched around the room in my outsize slippers and took a closer look at my fellow patients. They all seemed to move in slow motion, as though they were in a Sam Peckinpah film instead of the real world. Three sorry-looking specimens were gathered in front of the fuzzy-pictured TV, staring at the almost indecipherable programme with their mouths hanging open. One of them reached up to scratch his nose and his hand seemed to take for ever to get there. The only sound was the voices coming from *General Hospital* – how apt – on the TV. Fuck this! I thought, this is a proper cabbage factory. I suddenly felt a tap on my shoulder. I remembered to turn slowly in case the screws were watching. I was faced with a black kid of about seventeen, but well-built, with powerful shoulders. His eyes were trying to focus on me, and the whites were an almost luminous yellow. His hair was piled up on his head in clumps and dusty lumps, with the odd dreadlock poking through here and there. His hand came up very slowly, and I noticed that he had a white table-tennis ball between his over-large fingers. 'Want a game?' he asked, slowly.

His name was Vince, and he was a rasta from Clapham, doing a borstal for GBH on the police and dipping (pickpocketing). He had ended up in the hospital on the 'slow-me-down juice', his words, when the screws had tried to cut his hair on reception. Up until very recently the prison service had refused to recognize Rastafarianism as a religion (they also refused to recognize vegan as a genuine diet) and would cut off the 'locks' of any rasta who entered the system. To the true rastafarian, dreadlocked hair and beard are sacred, so they would always put up a fight when 'babylon' (the screws) tried to shear them off. A lot of the really racist screws would volunteer for barber-duty whenever a rasta entered the prison. It gave them a real buzz to hold a man down, mob-handed, and violate his religion.

Over the next couple of days I got to know, and like, Vince. Though he was also drugged up and slower than a week in Wandsworth punishment block, he managed to retain his sense of humour. The first time I played table tennis with him he dropped the ball. It rolled about ten feet away from the table and it took him almost five minutes to reach it. And then another five minutes to get back to the table! We once sat down for a game of chess, and by the end of two hours' association he had still to make his second move. We seemed to be the only patients who were aware of what the drugs were doing to us, and though we could laugh about it, it wasn't really funny.

After I had managed to go for three days without taking my medication, Wade began to suspect. It happened that I had decided to write a letter to my family, telling them what was going on. I had no idea how I was going to get the letter out, as every piece of incoming and outgoing mail is read by the screws. I had hidden the letter under my mattress while I tried to figure it out, but when I was on association, the screws must have searched the cells and the letter was handed over to Wade. He came into the association room with a big grin on his face and my letter in his hand. I tried to pretend that I hadn't seen it before, but that only led to more enjoyment and laughter on the part of Wade and the two screws who were with him.

'So, you don't like it here, eh? Been writing to Mummy and Daddy and crying about the nasty staff?'

I kept my eyes on the vinyl-tiled floor, afraid that if I looked into his face he would see the hate and rage I was feeling. I began to shuffle slowly away, as though I was deep in a drug haze and didn't understand what was going on. But Wade wasn't having it; he followed me, waving the letter in my face.

'You fucking half-wit. A child of six could have written this better than you. You can't even spell! "Hospil"? What's a fucking "hospil"?'

The other two screws laughed aloud. Wade ripped the letter into pieces and threw it in my face.

I could feel my rage bubbling and boiling as it tried to force its way to the surface. I knew that if I let it loose now I would never get out of this hospital. I began to shake with the exertion of trying to hold it down. I so wanted to leap on Wade and rip his windpipe out, wiping the smug look off his moustachioed face. I kept my face averted and began to hum deep in my throat as a way of releasing some of my excess energy. Wade didn't have a clue. He poked me in the chest.

'You're a fucking imbecile, boy. What are you?'

I couldn't stand it any longer. I let out a roar that seemed to echo from every corner of the association room and startled everyone into motionlessness. Everybody froze. Even the cabbages around the television seemed to be affected; one stopped in mid-drool, leaving a string of saliva half-way to his chest. For me the roar was like venting an overheating steam engine. I looked into Wade's eyes for the first time. His mouth was open and he looked as startled as he should have been. He looked into my eyes, and he must have seen something of my rage there, a residue of absolute hatred, because he suddenly looked frightened and took a step backwards. I quickly looked at the floor again and began to shamble away towards the TV.

One of the screws by the door giggled. 'What was all that about?' he asked rhetorically. Wade marched out of the room followed by the other screws, but I noticed that every time I glanced over towards the office windows he was staring at me. I was glad that I hadn't attacked him physically, though it had been very close. Nothing more was said, and for the rest of the day everything followed its routine. But I knew there would be some sort of comeback.

The next morning, after breakfast, Wade kept a close eye on me, so I had to swallow my medication. I was taken to an office on the ground floor and told to wait outside. After what seemed like ages I was taken into the office by two screws. Behind a large desk sat a middle-aged man with thick white hair and a big nose. He was dressed in a grey three-piece suit, and I noticed that he had a gold chain looping from the pocket of his waistcoat. I was starting to feel the medication coming on and making me drowsy, so I sat down on the plastic-moulded chair in front of the desk without being told. The screws stayed in the office, but over by the door behind me.

There was a long silence as the suited man read through a file on the desk before him. I didn't have to be Sherlock Holmes to know it was my file. Finally he closed it and looked at me. He had a kindly face.

'So,' he began. 'You've had it pretty rough so far?'

I kept quiet, waiting to see which direction he was going to come from. I didn't trust anyone in authority, and that went double for anyone in this mad-house.

'It's understandable that you might feel hostile, but I'm here to help you.'

The medication was ushering banks of fog into my mind, so I began to grope for my rage to drive them away. I conjured up a picture of Wade's smug grin and immediately felt clear-headed.

'If you want to help me,' I said, 'get me off this medication and out of here.'

He looked closely at me. 'Do you think that's a good idea? You have shown yourself to be a very violent young man. Have you ever had thoughts of hurting yourself?'

The change of tack threw me for a minute. I shook my head. 'No,' I said.

He wrote something in my file. 'It's nothing to be ashamed of. I would understand it if you did have such thoughts. After all, you are serving a relatively long sentence. Three years can seem as long as life itself to a youth of your years.'

That struck a chord with me: 'as long as life itself', that's exactly how I felt about my sentence. I waited.

He nodded slightly and scribbled something else on my file.
'I am going to change your medication. We'll try something new.
You receive an injection once a month, and two pills every day.
The pills are merely to counter any side-effects from the injec-
tion, so you must take them. Understand? No more hiding the
meds, OK?'

I shook my head. 'What's in the injection?' I asked.

'That should be of no concern to you. As long as you take
the pills every day, I will let you out of the hospital, but I will
speak to you on a regular basis, and if you feel as though you
want to hurt yourself, or anyone else, you must tell me. OK?'

I nodded. The one thing I wanted was to get out of the
hospital, and if that meant submitting to medication, then so be
it.

To this day I don't know what medication they had me on.
The only one I'm certain of is Largactil, because the word stuck
in my mind and I later found out that lots of prisoners were
dosed with it. I once described the injection and pills to a fella
named Matty Wainwright, a Manchester lad who had done a
spell in Broadmoor for killing a fellow prisoner in Hull Special
Unit, and he said it sounded very much like the medication they
had given him for his schizophrenia. I cannot get access to my
medical files from Rochester, as the prison system claims that all
records are destroyed after a period of six years, but I bet they
would have made interesting reading.

The next day I was given my first injection. The new medication left me fairly lively and able to function properly, but I would
just suddenly come over tired and have to lie down and sleep at
odd times. It also made my throat very dry and I had to drink
plenty of water during the day, so I would be up pissing like a
horse throughout the night. But at least I could think again. My
main aim now was to get out of the hospital and on to one of
the wings, where escape was bound to be possible. From now
on, I was going to channel all my energy into getting away, any
way I could.

Three days after the injection and having taken my pills with no trouble, I had a visit in my cell from an assistant governor. He was very young, with a babyish face and shoulder-length hair, which was unusual for a screw. Most screws and governors were ex-services, favoured the short back and sides, and had a propensity for neatly trimmed facial hair. The AG entered my cell alone, which was also unusual, and sat on the end of my bed. He explained that he was in charge of C-wing, the newest of the wings and supposedly 'escape-proof', and that he was willing to take me on his wing as long as I promised to behave myself. To get out of that hospital I would have made a deal with the devil himself.

That afternoon, with my few pieces of kit packed into a pillow-case, I tasted fresh air for the first time in weeks as I was marched across the borstal grounds to C-wing. Outside the hospital, everything seemed bright and cool. Outside each wing were small grass verges that looked brilliantly green to my jaded eyes. I saw a group of trainees pulling a barrow full of kit, but I didn't recognize any of them. Their faces wore an expression of hostile indifference as they passed me. It was the usual mask of the borstal trainee. C-wing was as modern-looking as the hospital but without the aura of gloom hanging over it. The window bars and gates were disguised by a fancy grille-work pattern that gave the impression of being there for decorative purposes rather than security, but they would be hard to cut and even harder to break.

I was hoping that my old sparring partner Jel Keeble would be on C-wing. He was in the borstal somewhere, so I would get to see him sometime now that I was out of the hospital. I knew he'd be game for an escape, even if it was from the 'escape-proof' wing.

C-wing was a two-storey U-block, with cells on both storeys of the arms of the U-shape and offices and association areas joining the arms. The ground floor housed a large dining-hall and hot-plate area, with a television room and games room on the upper level.

The AG I had spoken to in the hospital was not on duty, so

I got a version of the keep-out-of-trouble-or-we'll-break-you speech from one of the senior wing-screws. I was shown up the wide staircase at the centre of the wing and into a cell half-way down one of the arms, known as spur-3.

After trying the mattress for lumps and checking that the piss-pot was clean, I began to look for a weapon. Getting tooled up in a strange environment was a matter of necessity for me. Who knew what I might be up against here? There could be kids from Dover or Latchmere who might have grudges to settle or scalps to take to enhance their own reps. Until I saw a friendly face, I would be on my own, and I had to be able to defend myself at all times. I checked through the kit I had brought from the hospital and found my pencil. It was perfect, sharpened to a nice point that would punch through flesh if I put enough effort into it, and well able to puncture an eyeball. I slipped it into the top pocket of my jean jacket and sat down to wait.

Entering a strange new prison wing can be a bowel-watering experience for even the most prison-hardened con. It's not half as bad for a first-timer who has never been inside before, because they will never have witnessed the stomach-churning violence that prisoners inflict on each other. Sure, they are bound to be apprehensive, but deep down they always believe that nothing nasty can happen to them, ignorance being the opium of bliss. But the seasoned con knows different. Very few men can blend into the background in prison without earning that right through drawing blood. There is always some predator looking for easy meat, or someone who bears a grudge by proxy for someone you have mixed it with in another jail. Before I can relax in prison I have to check out everyone on the wing, looking into each hooded eye for signs of recognition and intent. In prison, paranoia is king, and taking precautions becomes second nature. You must be aware of everything that is going on around you for every second of the day. The shower room is a favourite place for settling scores, the attack coming when you are naked and helpless and, as an added bonus, with soap in your eyes. I have witnessed, and participated in, many of these attacks over the years. One minute the victim is enjoying a shower, and the next there are two or three fully clothed men in there with him, all stabbing him with makeshift weapons, and it's impossible to defend yourself when all you have in your hands is your dick and a bar of Palmolive. It only takes a couple of minutes to leave a naked man with more perforations than the average tea-bag.

I entered the dining-hall at lunch-time, making sure to clock all the faces around me, my pencil lodged casually behind my ear within quick and easy reach. There were around sixty trainees on C-wing, and they were all gathered here. I recognized a few faces from other nicks, but they were neutrals, neither friends nor enemies. I quickly spotted who the Chaps were, the top-dogs of the wing. They have a look about them that is un-mistakable. If you can imagine a prison wing as a watering-hole on the dry plains of Africa and its denizens as the animals that gather there out of necessity, the Chaps would be the lions, haughty and dangerous-looking even when in languid repose, the other animals giving them a wide berth but always keeping an eye on them for any sudden movements.

I picked up my meal on a compartmentalized steel tray from the hot-plate. I was served by white-coated cons, with a couple of screws looking on. I would have to be very careful here, because I was an unknown quantity, and sooner or later they would have to test me. I didn't want to end up back in the hospital again, so boxing clever was the order of the day. I walked over to a table that had an empty seat at it and put my tray down. The three kids who were already at the table ignored me, so I sat down and began to eat. The dining-hall was noisy with voices and the clacking of plastic cutlery on steel trays, and I could feel eyes on me from all corners of the room.

At one of the tables to the side of me sat what was obviously a firm. The top-dog was a huge half-caste, who I later found out was a big man amongst the football hooligans and terrace fighters who followed Arsenal FC and was doing a borstal for slashing a couple of rival fans. I looked up and saw he was staring directly at me, and so were the rest of his firm. I gave him the dead-eyed stare that I normally reserved for screws. He nodded slightly, knowing that his unspoken challenge had been noted.

After dinner trainees were allowed free-association on the landings for fifteen minutes before the dinner-time bang-up. I went upstairs to my spur and stood outside my cell waiting. I wished I had a better tool than the pencil, in case it actually came to violence, but I decided the half-caste was going to lose an eye if it did.

I didn't have to wait long. The half-caste and one of his henchmen came strolling up my spur. They stopped in front of me.

'Where'd you come from, mate?' asked the half-caste.

I put my hand into my jacket pocket where I now had my trusty HB. 'South London,' I said.

'What you in for?' asked the henchman.

'Armed robbery and GBH,' I replied. 'I'm doing a three-detained.'

I could see they were impressed by this, though they disguised it well.

'Who do you know here? Who can vouch for you?' asked the half-caste.

If you are unknown in prison but you can get someone who is respected to vouch for you, that you are not a 'wrong 'un', a grass or sex offender, then you may be left alone. The only person I knew for sure was at Rochester was Jel Keeble. I told them.

'Keeble? Keeble . . .?' said the half-caste.

'I know him,' said the henchman. 'He's on A-wing. Game little fucker. You remember, he done that bully-cunt Jonesy with a ladle? Smashed him right in the mooey!'

The half-caste nodded. 'Oh yeah, curly-headed kid from Essex?'

'That's right,' said the henchman.

There was silence for a minute. Then the half-caste said, 'We'll see what Keeble says on parade this afternoon.'

And off they went. I let out a sigh of relief and unclenched my hand from the pencil. Once Jel had vouched for me I would be sweet.

When I entered the dining-hall at tea-time the atmosphere felt better. I collected my tray and was on my way to the table when the half-caste waved me over. 'I spoke to Keeble,' he said.

I nodded and said nothing.

He stuck his hand out. 'My name's Paul.'

I shook his hand and knew that it was being noted by every eye in the dining-hall.

'If you need anything, let me know. Keeble says you're to put your name down for RC church on Sunday, and he'll see you over there.'

'Cheers,' I said, and walked back to my table. I had been accepted, and though I would still be watched and judged on my behaviour in the next couple of weeks, it was a step in the right direction and I could relax slightly.

In the next couple of weeks I kept my eyes open and my mouth shut. I was looking for any weakness in the security of the wing that would allow me to reach the walls and the freedom beyond. I kept taking the medication and even got a job as a wing-cleaner, cleaning my own spur. It was great to see Jel again. He had been carving out a reputation for himself and was now regarded as one of the Chaps on A-wing. I told him about my desire to escape and he said he'd give me any help he could. As my plan was to escape from the wing, it would be impossible for Jel to escape with me, but I was delighted to learn that he had escape plans of his own.

On spur-3 there were sixteen single cells, but one of them, the one nearest to the entrance of the spur, was used as a 'hobbies' room. One of the screws was heavily into making pictures on boards using tacks and brightly coloured string, which he would then sell for charity. So a couple of the saps had volunteered to help out, in exchange for good reports and maybe a bit of time back on their next parole assessment. They worked in the converted cell, with access to tools such as a small hammer and a couple of screwdrivers. During my daily cleaning duties I noticed that they often wandered off and left the door to the hobbies room open. At the end of each spur there was also a small recess, or washroom, containing a couple of shower stalls, sinks and toilets, and this was also where the cleaning equipment was stored. Whilst cleaning out the recess I could keep an eye on the hobbies room and note the comings and goings.

The kid in the cell next door to me, a car-thief from Wimbledon named Robert, had worked in the hobbies room for a short while, so I questioned him on it, using the pretence that I might fancy doing a bit of picture-making myself.

'You don't want to work in there, mate,' he said. 'The bods who do it are grasses. They'll lolly you up as soon as look at you. I only went in there for a little while because I wanted to make one of them pictures for me bird. The fucking bastards lollied me up for nicking the materials. I lost three days.'

I asked him whether it was possible to get hold of the tools they were using. He looked worried.

'Listen, mate, if you want to do someone, you're better off making your own tool. The hammer in there ain't heavy enough to crack toffee, and the screwdrivers are blunt as fuck.'

I decided to throw a sprat. 'Anyone ever made it out of this wing?'

He looked around to make sure there was no one in earshot. 'I don't think so,' he said. 'It's escape-proof, ain't it? You thinking of trying?'

I knew I would need help to escape, and Jel had named Robert as one to be trusted, but I still had to proceed cautiously. I shrugged. 'Just talking, that's all,' I said.

He looked around again. 'Well, if you are thinking about it, you'll need a driver to get out of the sticks, and I can hot-wire anything.'

I nodded. 'All right,' I said, and left it there for then.

The cell doors on C-wing were different from the average cell door. Instead of the usual spy-hole in the centre of the door, so the screws could observe the prisoner when he was locked in, there was an eight-inch observation slit, length-ways and at head height. The slit was two inches wide and made of tough Perspex. But I noticed that the screws that held the Perspex in place were on the outside of the door, and could easily be exposed by levering up the plastic covering. The door was wooden, two inches thick, and apart from the observation slit, featured a heavy Chubb lock and an eight-inch bolt about six inches above the lock and two feet below the observation slit. This was all on the outside of the door, and once it was locked and I was inside, the door was smooth and featureless apart from the observation slit.

With one of the screwdrivers from the hobbies room I could lever the cover and unscrew the Perspex from the observation slit, but what then? I would still need to get through the lock and bolt. I checked out the lock when the door was open during the day, and I was pleasantly surprised to see that the metal cup which the bolt of the lock slotted into was set in wood! If I could hack out the inside of the wooden frame I would be able to remove the metal cup so that when the door was closed from the outside the screws would think it was locked, when in reality there would be nothing but the separate bolt holding it closed. And with the Perspex observation slit removed, I would be able to rig a bit of looped string to dangle out of the gap and hook the bolt and pull it open from inside the cell. The more I looked at the plan, the more I realized it could work.

I had another chat with Robert during association and laid out my plan for getting out of my cell at night. He was very enthusiastic and could find no flaws in the plan. We could do the work in the daytime, using the tools from the hobbies room. The screws rarely came upstairs during the day, except to lock us up over dinner- and tea-times, and as Robert was the television-room cleaner, he would be able to keep watch while I worked on the door. I would have to borrow the tools from the hobbies room, but as the mugs who worked in there spent a lot of the day either downstairs in the wing office sucking up to the screws or plotted up in their cells drinking tea and gossiping, I knew I would have no trouble. Robert thought we should bring someone else in to help out, and I agreed.

Swordy was a mixed-race kid, Malaysian father and Irish mother, who lived in the cell opposite me. He was doing his borstal for burglary, and had lost almost three months of it, mostly for back-chatting the screws, and a month for attempting to jump out of the dock and escape from the court building on the day he was sentenced. He was a good kid, though he didn't like violence, and neither did Robert. They did just enough to be left alone by the other trainees; nobody would take liberties with them because they had proved they would fight back, but they wouldn't go looking for trouble. Swordy was all for the escape, and I liked his sense of humour, so he was in.

The plan we worked out between us sounded like a goer. Once out of my cell, I was to creep down to the wing office and catch the night-watchman unawares. After nine o'clock at night, when all prisoners are locked in their cells, there is only a skeleton-staff manning the borstal. That was one night-watchman on every wing, and a two-man security patrol, a duty governor and a couple of staff in the gatehouse. I would tie the night-watchman up, and then come back up to the spur and break my confederates out of their cells, using one of the heavy floor-buffers to smash the doors in. Then we would use the night-watchman's keys to get out of the wing (he didn't have keys to the cells, only the wing gates) and make our way to the lowest part of the wall, between D- and E-wings, where the wall was about twelve feet high, liberating one of the kitchen barrows on the way. The kitchen barrows were wooden carts, about six feet long, used for ferrying the meals between the kitchen and the wings. We would then up-end the barrow against the wall and climb up and over. The barrows were always kept chained outside the kitchen, but if there was one kid in Rochester who couldn't break a padlock open with a length of iron bed-leg, then he didn't deserve to be in borstal. Once over the wall, we would nick a car and head back to London. With a bit of luck we would be home free before they knew we were gone.

I told Jel about my plan in the church at Sunday service. He said he had some goodies for me, as he had put off his own escape for a while, as his appeal against sentence was due to be heard early in the new year and he thought he had a good chance of getting his sentence cut.

Swordy was on the dustbin-party, the trainees detailed to collect the rubbish from all the wings and workshops, so he picked up a parcel from Jel on his next visit to A-wing. It was in the bin, wrapped in a grey prison sweatshirt, and he stuffed it underneath his donkey jacket and smuggled it back on to C-wing after work. When we opened the sweatshirt in my cell, we found two home-made chivs (knives) fashioned from six-inch lengths of pointed and sharpened aluminium with taped handles, three pound notes and, best of all, a genuine double-sided FS car-key. The double-sided FS key was a car thief's main tool back in the 1970s. It would open the doors and start the ignition of almost any standard saloon-car, and Fords in particular. To have one inside a top-security borstal was a major coup. I didn't know where Jel had acquired it, but it was an essential piece of kit for when we were over the wall. The cash would come in handy as well, but Robert and Swordy shied away from the chivs. It didn't matter, I would carry both of them. Just in case.

It was getting close to Christmas, and I decided we would make our break on Christmas Eve, when the screws least expected it. I also reasoned that I was bound to have a bit of luck on my birthday, of all days. On 23 December I nipped into the hobbies room while Robert kept watch and grabbed a screwdriver. In minutes I had the plastic strip levered off the observation slit on my door. I swiftly undid the eight screws and pocketed them. Then I fitted the strip back on and returned the screwdriver to the hobbies room. Now, though it looked no different, I would be able to knock the Perspex out of my observation slit with a hard push.

Stage one of the plan was complete, and I was now in free-fall.

On the twenty-fourth, I nicked the hammer and flat-head screwdriver and began work on my door-jamb. Once I'd cut out the first chunk of wood there was no stopping me. I smashed into the wood, levering out huge gouts of timber until I could get the screwdriver in behind the metal bolt-cup. But I was making too much noise, and one of the trainees who worked in the hobbies room came to investigate. Robert managed to stop him outside my door and, hearing the voices, I came out of my cell. The kid was big, but he had a frightened ferrety face.

'What's all the banging?' he was asking Robert.

I tapped him on the shoulder, and when he turned to face me I gave him the full-on hard-faced, mad-eyed look.

'What's your fucking problem, mug?' I asked, quietly but with menace.

He wanted to look anywhere but at my face so his eyes went down and he spotted the hammer and screwdriver in my hands. Outrage gave him back a bit of courage.

'You ain't supposed to have them tools, they're hobbies room only!'

I nodded. 'It ain't none of your fucking business, but I borrowed them to fix a new head on me broom. The screw in the office said it was all right. So, you got a fucking problem with that, have you, mug?'

He still couldn't look me in the face, but I could see by his body language he was willing to believe me. Anything I said, in fact. He swallowed and backed away. When he was half-way down the spur he said, 'You got to put them back as soon as you're done. We need them in about five minutes.'

'When I'm fucking ready,' I said.

When he was out of sight, Robert shook his head. 'I think he'll grass.'

'Go and keep watch,' I said. 'I'm almost finished.'

The hobbies kid either accepted my explanation or didn't fancy what might happen to him if he didn't, because no screws came to investigate. With a couple of minutes' hammering, I had the bolt-cup out of the wood. I slotted it back in temporarily and went and informed Robert that we would be spending Christmas in London!

Robert, Swordy and I spent the evening association period in a state of tense excitement. Instead of Santa coming down the chimney, we would be going over the wall for a present. At ten minutes to the eight o'clock bang-up time, I slipped down the spur and into my cell. I closed the door behind me and made sure the locking-bolt slipped into the metal cup. Then Swordy pushed the separate bolt home on the outside of the door. Now, as long as nobody shook it too hard, my door, to all appearances, was securely locked.

I heard everyone on the spur being locked up for the night. Then came my first test. The landing screw who was going off duty came around shaking the cell doors to make sure they were secure. I wedged my foot firmly against the bottom of the door, and when he shook it, it barely moved. Now I only had the night-watchman to come on duty and do his cursory test of the doors. The excitement was growing inside me. I was finally getting out of this place, and I felt like singing.

The night-watchman on duty that Christmas Eve was one of the better screws in the nick. He was always friendly towards the trainees and would slip a cigarette into the hands of any boy who had no snout. I'd had no dealings with him myself, but I had observed him in action. I felt a tinge of regret that he was on duty, but if it came to the choice between giving him a clump in order to get away or postponing the escape with the chance that the screws might notice my preparations on the door, it was no contest. I just hoped he wouldn't put up too much of a fight, or I might have to stab him. *C'est la guerre*, as French criminals are wont to say.

The night-watchman came around checking the doors and wishing everyone a merry Christmas, and I kept my foot firmly against my door when he shook it. Once he was done, he had no reason to come back up on the spur until 9 p.m., when he would do his rounds and turn his key in a contraption on the end of each spur to prove he wasn't sleeping on the job. He would have to turn the key at hourly intervals during the night, letting the control-room in the gatehouse know that everything was well. I planned to make the break after he had completed his 10 p.m. patrol. That would give me an hour to get out of the cell and creep up on him. And once he was tied up we would wait till 11 p.m. and turn his key ourselves, giving us a further hour to get off the wing, over the wall, and away.

I spent the next hour in a state of high excitement and tension. I gathered the escape kit, money and car-key in one pocket, knives down my waistband, and I put on an extra layer of clothes against the cold night air. I paced my small cell, thinking of all the things I was going to do when I got back to London. I had the shotgun and Luger from my previous jobs well hidden, and my first priority would be to get my hands on the shotgun. Next time, they wouldn't be taking me so easily. I planned to rob a couple of banks and then get out of the country, back to Ireland, where I had plenty of relatives who would hide me. I would live the life of Riley, slipping back into England a couple of times a year to carry out daring blags, and then back to Dublin to spend the loot.

As I paced the cell lost in my fantasy, I became hot, so I took off my donkey jacket and removed the home-made knives from my waistband and put them under the pillow on my bed. At five to ten I heard the night-watchman making his rounds. He walked past my cell and down to the end of the spur and turned his key. I heard him humming a tune as he walked back past my cell and on to the next spur. I said a small, desperate prayer that everything would go to plan. I got up to my door and looked through the observation slit. I could see Swordy's eyes staring through his own observation slit in the cell directly opposite mine. He would guide my looped piece of string to the bolt once the Perspex was out. He gave me a thumbs-up.

I spread my fingers on the surface of the observation slit and gave it a hard shove. It was as easy as popping a pea out of a pod. The plastic cover and the Perspex strip dropped to the floor outside my cell with a slight clatter. I put my ear up to the open gap and I could hear the sounds of the spur clearly: a radio in one of the cells was playing Boney M, and someone further down was having a coughing fit. I put my fingers through the gap and waggled them at Swordy. He was jumping up and down with excitement.

I had ripped a length of my bed-sheet and fashioned a noose that, when dangled out of the observation slit, would allow me to catch the bolt and pull it open. I got to work. Swordy used hand- and eye-gestures to let me know when I had reached the bolt. I managed to hook it on the fifth attempt, and by tugging sideways on the line I snicked it open. I stood still for a moment, listening. Then I gripped the door by the gap I had created earlier by the lock, and pulled. My cell door swept open with no noise at all. I took a step out on to the landing. It was my seventeenth birthday, and I was half-way to freedom.

I gave Swordy a grin, and then I stepped next door and looked directly into the excited eyes of Robert. I put my mouth up to the gap between his cell door and frame and whispered, 'Get ready, we're on our way!'

I slipped down to the end of the spur to see where the night-watchman was. I got down on my belly and crawled out on to the open landing at the top of the central staircase, and looked down. I had a clear view of the wing office and the night-watchman with his feet up on a desk and his eyes closed. He appeared to be singing along to a small radio that was on the desk. Satisfied, I slipped back on to the spur and undid the bolts on Swordy's and Robert's doors, in preparation for when I could break them out. It was strangely exhilarating to be loose on the landing after bang-up. I decided to go off the spur and into the television room opposite, so that I could get a view looking down on the office while I plotted my next move. If I came down the central staircase, the night-watchman would be able to see me and raise the alarm by pressing one of the panic buttons, which were situated on each landing and also in the wing office. I had to creep up on him somehow to catch him by surprise.

I was still trying to figure it out when the night-watchman came out of the office and headed up the stairs. There was no cover in the television room, and if I stayed there he would be bound to spot me, so I scurried along the landing and on to my spur. I ducked into the recess at the end of the spur. It was fairly dark in the recess, the only light coming from the spur, and I pressed myself against the back wall amongst the cleaning equipment. He came on to my spur. I saw his shadow pass the open door of the recess and heard his footsteps on the landing. It was way too early for him to turn his key, but one of the boys on the spur had a headache and had pressed his cell bell to ask for some paracetamol. The cell bell had activated a light on a board in the office, though at night it was silent.

I was starting to panic. I cursed the bastard with the headache and hoped it was a brain tumour. I could hear the night-watchman telling the headache-kid that he would have to go back down for the paracetamol and then slip a couple under the door. My heart was beating like a steel drum at the Notting Hill carnival. If he spotted my door open, the gig would be up. I reached down around my feet and the first solid thing I gripped was the handle of a steel mop-bucket. I cursed the fact that I had left the chivs under my pillow. I listened hard, waiting to hear the exclamation of surprise that would tell me he had spotted my door. But it never came. I heard him walking back down the spur. This could work out great. While he went back to the office I would be able to nip back to my cell and arm myself for his return. And then he walked into the recess.

The night-watchman had no idea that I was there. He just fancied a piss, and the recess had the closest urinal. He was whistling to himself as he unzipped. I pressed as far back into the shadows as I could and held my breath. He finished pissing and then, instead of just fucking off back downstairs, he moved to the sink to wash his hands. If that man had been any less hygienic, my life might have taken a different turn. The sink was exactly opposite the spot where I was standing, and there was a large mirror above it in which I could clearly see my own reflection.

I tried to slowly crouch out of sight as he bent over the sink scrubbing his hands and humming to himself. But, inevitably, he glanced at himself in the mirror. I froze, but he did an almost classic comedy double-take and spun around.

'What the . . .!' he managed to get out before I sprang into action.

I wrenched the mop-bucket up and outwards. It caught him on the shoulder and spun him out of the open door of the recess. I followed, the adrenaline flooding my body and lending me a fluid speed. Before he could regain his balance, I brought the bucket down on his head as hard as I could. In his shock and panic he turned to run, and went the wrong way. Instead of heading off the spur he ran deeper on to it. I had him, there was no escape except past me, and I wasn't going to let that happen. He was wearing a white uniform shirt, and as I chased him up the spur I saw it turn bright red with the blood that was flowing from his head. Half-way up the spur I brought the bucket down on his head again, and he collapsed like a dead weight. I stood over his unmoving body with the bucket raised, ready to still any movement he might make. But the only thing moving was the fast-flowing sea of blood that was spreading outwards from his head.

I stood there for a moment, breathing heavily and wondering what to do next, when I became aware of the noise all around me. All the occupants of the cells on the spur were up at their observation slits trying to see what was going on. They were all shouting and getting excited. By chance we had come to a stop right outside Robert's cell. I dropped the bucket and looked at his observation slit; there were large drops of blood splashed on it and the rest of the door. Robert's eyes were huge and frightened. I laughed nervously.

'Fucking caught me by surprise . . .' I said, in explanation for the carnage. Robert shook his head. 'Is he dead?' he asked.

I looked down at the night-watchman and noticed a deep gash on the back of his head, through which glinted the off-white of bone.

'I dunno,' I said. 'I think so.'

Robert started crying, big tears rolling down his face. 'Listen, mate,' he sputtered. 'Put my bolt back on, please. I don't want to be involved in this. Please?'

I felt drained, unable to think properly. I put Robert's bolt back into the socket, then looked at Swordy. He didn't want to go any further either, so I rebolted his door as well.

The adrenaline come-down was creeping through my mind and body, making me lethargic. I had to pull myself together. I took a deep breath and began to rationalize. OK, things had gone wrong and I was on my own, but the night-watchman was incapacitated (dead), and no alarm had yet been raised outside the wing. The escape was still on, though being unable to drive a car myself, it would be harder to get out of the area. There was no question I would carry on as planned. I nudged the prone body of the night-watchman with my toe. He didn't move, and the blood had formed an ocean on the floor, with his broken head as an island. This just made it all the more imperative that I escape. It would be HMP (Her Majesty's Pleasure, the life sentence given to any youth under the age of twenty-one who was convicted of murder) for sure.

I felt no pity for the night-watchman, only for myself. I would not have set out deliberately to kill him, and if things had gone according to plan I might have roughed him up a bit if he had resisted my attempt to tie him up, but nothing too serious. Before coming into the prison system I would have been sick and horrified at the thought that I might seriously injure someone, let alone kill them. But I was now hardened to almost any brutality. In just over two years I had changed from a normal human being into a desperate but uncaring animal who could dismiss the loss of a human life with a shrug. I genuinely thought he was dead.

I got my thoughts together and went into my cell to gather the rest of my escape equipment. I put on my donkey jacket and gathered the chivs from beneath my pillow. There was still a lot of shouting coming from the other cells on the spur. I took a look out of my cell window, but the rest of the borstal seemed to be quiet. I started to take one of the iron legs from my bed – I would need it to snap the padlock on the kitchen barrow – when a loud clanging noise echoed through the wing. I froze, unable at first to work out what it was, but then I realized it was the general-alarm bell. It would bring the night-patrol screws straight to C-wing as fast as they could run. My escape was over.

When I came out of my cell I saw that the body of the night-watchman was gone, but there was a trail of blood leading down the spur and around the corner to where one of the alarm buttons was located. I ran down the spur and around the corner. He was there, covered in blood and unsteady on his feet, but alive enough to keep his finger pressed firmly on the alarm. His eyes were bright in his blood-streaked face, and he slowly pointed a finger at me and mouthed, 'You bastard.'

My first feeling on seeing him was relief that I hadn't killed him after all; then I felt disappointment that my escape had failed, and then fascination at the amount of blood he had lost. I turned on my heel and ran back down the spur and into my cell. I could hear the sound of keys rattling in the downstairs gate as I put my arm as far out of the window as it would go and threw the escape kit, including the chivs, into the bushes below. It would not do me any favours to be caught with the stuff, and maybe someone else would find it and make use of it.

I closed the cell window, and all I could hear was a cacophony of sound: the general-alarm bell clanging, and trainees banging on their cell doors and shouting. I knew I would be in for a kicking from the screws, so I decided to get out on the landing to give myself space to fight back. But as I reached the door of my cell, so did the night patrol. They crashed through the door and knocked me flat on the floor. They had drawn batons and wasted no time in clubbing me into submission. I was dragged from the cell by my hair, and through pools of the night-watchman's blood, to the end of the spur. All the while I was being kicked and beaten with batons. As I was dragged out on to the landing at the top of the stairs the alarm bell was switched off. But from the noise, it seemed that the whole wing was awake and up banging on their doors. The two night-patrol screws stopped beating me for a minute and hoisted me to my feet. One of them had me by the collar of my donkey jacket and the other had my hands crossed behind my back, so I was defenceless. The night-watchman stood in front of me, a horrible vision in red-streaked white, and grimaced in pain and shock.

'Take a few shots,' said one of the screws that were holding me.

The night-watchman clenched his fists and launched a half-hearted flurry of punches at my stomach. He was weak from loss of blood and probably couldn't remember when he'd last thrown a punch. I barely felt his blows, but I made suitable noises of pain, which seemed to satisfy the screws. I had no desire to take any more punishment than I had to. I was in a very dangerous situation. These screws could quite literally kill me and justify doing so. I had attempted to murder one of their own during an escape attempt. Who would look twice if I happened to fall down the stairs and break my neck? At this juncture discretion was definitely the better part of valour, and for every blow I put up a dying scream, hoping they would think I'd had enough.

As it happened, I didn't fall down the stairs – maybe they never thought of it – and when I reached the ground floor alive but still getting a beating, I was almost looking forward to the block. I was frogmarched through the night, the riotous sounds of C-wing receding behind me. I could see the spotlit main wall with every step, and it seemed to mock me with its closeness. If I were walking twenty feet away on the other side of that wall my troubles would be over, I thought. I felt tears come to my eyes.

By the time I reached the punishment block, some of the night screws from the gatehouse and the block night-watchman were waiting for me. They wasted no time in steaming into me, but I was saved from serious injury by their berserker state. They were in such a hurry to give me a beating that they just got in each other's way, but I took a good few painful kicks and punches before they ripped my clothes off and launched me into the strong-box.

When the double doors of the strong-box were locked behind me, I was left in silence. I wrapped myself in the one blanket that was in there and lay down on the stone floor. I was in pain, but not much. I knew the real pain would kick in the next day when the natural anaesthetic of adrenaline was nothing but a memory. The worst pain was inside me. I had failed. And not only that, I would now have to face the consequences of my attempt. The only certainty in my life was that my days were about to get darker.

It was Christmas Day 1977, and I was seventeen years old.

10. Singing in the Strong-Box

The punishment block at Rochester is a long, gloomy, two-storey Victorian building, entered by going down several stone steps from ground level and through an iron-barred gate and solid oak door. The cells are on one side of the building, on both levels, and the entrance side is an almost blank stone-wall with two high, curved windows that let in little natural light. The first cell on the ground floor is the strong-box, a cell within a cell. To get into the strong-box you must unlock an iron gate, then a wooden door, then pass through a short vestibule and another wooden door. Inside the strong-box there is a raised concrete bed with no mattress and a dim light encased in wire mesh above the door. There is a plastic piss-pot and nothing else except a ragged and filthy prison blanket. The floor is stone flags and the cold, even at the height of summer, is bone-numbing. The normal attire worn in the strong-box is the 'zoot-suit', a slip-on top and shorts made from an unrippable nylon and vinyl mix and, if you're lucky, a pair of outsize slippers.

The strong-box is only supposed to be used for violent or suicidal prisoners, and not for longer than twenty-four hours without review by the governor, a doctor and the Board of Visitors, who are a supposedly independent body of local worthies who oversee the workings of a prison. I was in the strong-box for five days. On Christmas morning a group of screws came in and worked me over. They held me against a wall and took turns to punch me in the legs and body. Of course I screamed, but in the strong-box no one can hear you scream. I could do nothing but accept the beating, and even in the depths of my pain I understood that what they were doing was morally justifiable. In my world, or what had become my world, it was more than acceptable to get revenge on someone who had attacked one of your pals. In fact, it was essential. I would have done the same.

A couple of hours after the beating they threw in a zoot-suit and another blanket. I was fed at tea-time, a foul-looking stew that the block-screw took great pleasure in spitting in before he handed it over. I was given no cutlery, and I was starving, so I just ate the bits with no saliva visible, using my fingers to scoop up the gravy. I spent most of my time limping around the cell, talking to myself. The cold was almost unbearable, and the only way to generate heat was to keep moving. I ranted and raved at how my life had turned out. I knew I was in for a long stay in the block and it depressed me. I began to miss the relative comfort of C-wing and wished I had just got my head down and done my bird quietly. At other times I would spend hours cursing the borstal system, the courts, the police, probation officers, the screws and governors, and vowing to kill them all. I sincerely believe I was on the verge of total madness.

After three days in the strong-box without taking the daily pills that counteracted the effects of my medication, I began to feel strange. It is a feeling that is hard to describe: I desperately needed to see the colour red. My eyes flitted from wall to floor, from floor to ceiling, all the while searching for anything that might be coloured red. It was an obsession and I could not help myself. Then my head began tilting over to one side. I couldn't stop it, and I could hear the tendons in my neck creaking as I tried. Then my legs began to cramp and curl up under me. I lay on the floor and cried in pain as my head tried to turn in a complete circle. Next, my hands cramped and turned in on my wrists. I didn't know what was happening to me and I became more frightened than I had ever been. I lay on the cold floor, my body twisting itself into a cramped ball, and screamed for help. But no one came, until dinner-time.

When the screws opened the doors to put in my plastic dinner-plate, they thought my condition was highly amusing. One of them came into the strong-box and kicked me hard in the back. I couldn't move. After some minutes of discussion, they went to phone the hospital to find out if I was faking. About an hour later a doctor was ushered into the strong-box. With little fuss he stuck a needle in my arse and injected me with something.

'He'll come out of it in about twenty minutes,' he said, and then left me there.

Sure enough, after a while my limbs began to unknot and I could stand again. Within hours I was once again pacing the cell and cursing the world and everyone in it. And from then on I got my pills every morning with my porridge. I began to look forward to meal-times like they were parole hearings. My body became used to recognizing how close meal-times were, and I would increase my walking pace and begin to salivate about ten minutes before the doors opened. Once the meal was in and the doors shut again, I would attack the food like a wild animal, stuffing it in my mouth and barely chewing in my haste to get it down me. On the fifth day in the strong-box they gave me a plastic spoon, but I ignored it and kept using my fingers.

On the morning of the sixth day the screws gave me a pair of jeans and a T-shirt, and a pair of slippers. They brought me to the adjudication room and I went through the usual rigmarole of giving my name and number to the governor from ten feet away while being guarded by a bunch of screws. I was charged with 'causing gross personal violence' to a prison officer, attempted escape and damaging prison property. The governor explained that the charges were too serious for him to deal with, so I was remanded to the block to await trial in front of the Board of Visitors. The Board of Visitors included local magistrates, and though the governor of a prison could only take a maximum of twenty-eight days' loss of remission from a prisoner, the BoV could take unlimited remission for certain charges, one of which was causing gross personal violence to a prison officer. The BoV lost their disciplinary powers in 1991, as a result of the recommendations made by Lord Woolf in his report into the Strangeways riot.

I was marched out of the adjudication room and, instead of being put back into the strong-box, I was taken to a normal punishment cell. The punishment cells had two planks of wood screwed to the wall to act as a table-top and a seat, and a window high up on the back wall. The window was covered in scratched and filthy Perspex and could not be opened, but it had several small holes in it that allowed fresh air in, and it also let some natural light into the cell. Apart from the piss-pot, I was allowed to retain the jeans and T-shirt, and I would be allowed a mattress and bedclothes in the cell after eight o'clock at night. They were removed at 6.30 every morning.

In the punishment block the days were long and the nights even longer. They operated a rule of silence, and every hour was the same as the next. I got a shower once a week, on a Saturday afternoon, meals three times a day and a haircut once a month. I spoke to no one except the screws who brought my meals, and that was no more than grunted cursory routine questions. The governor came to my door every day, but it was never more than a fleeting visit. The door would spring open and the governor would be standing there with two block screws, one of whom would scream, 'Stand to attention, name and number to the governor!' I was supposed to stand to attention facing the door and present myself to the governor, who would then say, 'Good morning, Smith, any problems, no? Good', and then he would move on to the next cell. I refused to stand to attention and, after a while, I wouldn't even acknowledge his presence.

A doctor would also turn up at my door a couple of times a week and examine me from outside the cell with an 'Are you well?' Most times the door would close again before I could have answered, had I been inclined to do so. After a couple of weeks the pills stopped being delivered with my breakfast, but I had no ill-effects, so I assumed that the original injection had worn off and they were not giving me another one. I was glad of that.

I spent my days doing exercises such as shadow-boxing, running on the spot, and press-ups and sit-ups. I also spent hours playing football with my socks. I would take off my socks, roll them into a ball and then kick them around the cell; in my imagination I was on the green back home on my estate, surrounded by the kids I knew.

Singing was another way of passing the time. I would press

my face into the gap created by the corner of the back and side walls and sing all the songs I knew. Though we had little by way of luxuries when I was growing up, we always had a pile of records and a radiogram in the house. My mother loved country and western music, and my father was a big Sinatra fan, but we had plenty of 1950s rock 'n' roll and a few chart hits around as well. I grew up with music constantly in the background, and I knew the words to every song on the *Johnny Cash at Folsom Prison* LP, and I could sing the lyrics to the Frank Sinatra songbook, so I was never short of a song to sing in the block. Sometimes I would get a bit carried away and the screws would look through the spy-hole on the door and tell me to shut up.

One afternoon when, despite repeated warnings by the screws, I persisted in singing too loud, the screws burst in on me and gave me a few slaps. By now I was clear of my medication and almost healed from my last beating, so I put up a struggle. There were three screws, but I somehow managed to fight my way past them and out on to the landing of the block. There was nowhere to run as all doors were locked, except the screws' office at the end of the landing, so I headed for that. The office was about the size of two cells knocked together, and it was where the duty screws sat all day drinking tea and scratching their arses. I got into the office just ahead of the chasing screws and launched their table up in the air. Tea mugs and paperwork went everywhere as I bounced around the office like a mini-tornado, wrecking everything I could. The overturned table broke into pieces and I grabbed one of the table-legs and brandished it at the screws. It was a hefty piece of wood with two sharp nails sticking out of the broken end, which would no doubt do some naughty damage.

'Come on, you cunts!' I growled. 'I'll teach you to try and stop me singing.'

I was completely off my head and willing to kill someone if I had to. I just wanted to be left alone.

The screws backed off and one of them pressed the general-alarm button. At the sound of the alarm, screws came running from all over the borstal. They crashed through the door of the block and came to a halt in the corridor outside the office, milling about but not willing to risk a smack in the head from my makeshift club. By now my rage was starting to lose its impetus, and I realized that, once again, I was on a hiding-to-nothing. But I was trapped in a stand-off. I saw a couple of white-coated hospital screws at the back of the mob preparing an injection.

'Put down the weapon and come out of the office,' was the command.

'Fuck you!' was my reply.

They rushed me and dragged me, kicking and screaming, along the landing until they could get the needle in me. Just before the world turned black I distinctly heard a voice say, 'This is nothing but a fucking animal that needs putting down.' I had the urge to bite the speaker, but I was out before I could open my mouth.

Once again I woke up in the strong-box, only this time I couldn't move my arms or upper body. It took me some time to realize that I was locked into a canvas strait-jacket. My hands were encased in the thick, stiff material and crossed over my chest. I rolled over on to my front and banged my already sore face on the stone floor. I tried to figure out how I could get on to my feet without the use of my arms. I shuffled my way to the corner of the cell using my legs and shoulders to push along the floor. It took ages, and by the time I reached the corner I had to stop and rest for a while before levering myself up by using the walls to balance myself. When I was on my feet I took a couple of steps away from the corner and felt so dizzy I thought I was going to fall over. I panicked, knowing that if I fell I wouldn't be able to break my fall. I rested my back against the wall, and suddenly a terrible wave of claustrophobia washed over me. I began to struggle against the strait-jacket in my panic to be free of it, but that only seemed to make it tighter. After a few minutes of mindless struggling I was growing weak, so I began to shout as loud as I could for the screws to come and help me. But no one came; the strong-box was sound-proof.

Eventually I managed to calm myself down simply because I grew too tired to struggle. I slid down the wall so I was sitting in the corner of the cell facing the door. I took deep breaths and tried to relax. They would have to let me out of this sooner or later, and there was nothing I could do but wait. After a while I felt very calm and started humming a tune to myself. Then I realized that as the strong-box was sound-proof I would be able to sing as loud as I liked. So I did. And pretty soon I was no longer in the strong-box, trussed up like an oven-ready turkey, I was playing the Sands in Vegas, dressed in a crisp tux and cracking jokes with Dean Martin and Sammy Davis Jnr and singing to an appreciative audience.

Later that evening the screws entered the strong-box and took me out of the strait-jacket, and the next morning they put me back in a normal punishment cell. By then I had retreated so far inside my own head that I hardly noticed anything that was going on around me. I had learned the trick of shutting off the here and now. I had already blocked off all thoughts of the outside world, and now I was doing away with the inside world as well. I had created my own strong-box inside my head and I concealed myself in it, locking all doors and gates behind me. In my head I could do anything I wanted and talk to anyone I pleased. I would sit on the floor after breakfast and look at the blank cell-wall, and before I knew any time had passed the screws would be opening the door for dinner-time. I didn't know where the time went and I cared less.

At the start of February 1978 I was brought in front of the Board of Visitors for my trial. I was given a clean shirt and jeans before being marched into the adjudication room. It was almost the same set-up as trial before the governor, except there were three civilian members of the Board sitting behind the governor's desk. There were two middle-aged men in suits, who looked like a couple of bank managers, and a woman of about sixty who had hair like candy-floss. I didn't even have to hear their cut-glass accents to know they were local magistrates and that I had no chance of getting a result here. The governor sat off to the side of the Board, ready to offer help and advice, but not to me.

I was ordered to give my name and number to the Board, which I did, and then I was ordered to sit. Surrounded by screws who were really putting on a show of readiness for imminent danger from me, I must have been a pathetic sight. I weighed about nine stone in my clothes, my face showed signs of fading bruises, and I sat on a wooden chair in my clown-size slippers, hedged by the biggest, twitchiest screws in the nick. The civilians on the Board either looked at me like I was an exotic insect or, in the case of one of the men, didn't look at me at all. The woman sat in the middle of the trio, and she did the talking. The charges were read out by the governor, and after each one I was asked by the woman Board member how I pleaded. I mumbled 'Guilty' after each inquiry.

The Board were each given a copy of my prison record to read, and the room was silent as they absorbed the no-doubt damning document. There were a few ominous 'hmm's as they reached particularly troublesome passages of my life in incarceration thus far. I honestly didn't give a fuck what they were going to do to me, I was completely uninterested. I was thinking about dinner-time; it was fish cakes on Friday, my favourite. I stretched my legs out, and all the screws twitched and crouched in my direction as though I had pulled out a gun. It was quite gratifying to know that they took me seriously now. They could beat me until I screamed and crack jokes about it, but there wasn't one of them who would turn his back on me. I smiled.

'Do you find these proceedings amusing, Smith?' asked the woman.

I shrugged. She tutted and shook her head in annoyance.

'You do realize how serious this is, do you? You could have killed Officer Tuttle, and you might now be sitting in the Old Bailey, facing life imprisonment. What do you have to say about that?'

I just shrugged again. There was nothing I wanted to say.

After the Board had read my file there were a few minutes of whispered conversation between them. The governor leant in and joined the discussion a couple of times, and finally they all seemed satisfied.

'Stand up, Smith,' said the woman. 'This is a very serious case and, if you had been a borstal trainee, we would have had no compunction about taking away every last day of your remission. But it appears that you are a detainee under Section 53 and, in reality, you have no remission to lose. Perhaps it was this fact that encouraged you to embark on such a devious and savage act in the first place. You must be punished to the limit of our powers, so as to discourage you and like-minded others from such acts of indiscipline. You will forfeit all privileges for a period of six months, and you will remain in solitary confinement until such time as the governor deems you fit to be sent back to normal location. That is all.'

The escort screws marched me sharply out of the adjudication room and back to my cell.

The punishment meant little to me. I was now used to solitary confinement and, as far as I could see, I didn't have any privileges. I thought about what the woman had said. She actually thought that I did what I did because I knew I couldn't lose remission, like it was some sort of calculated-risk venture. She had no fucking idea! I wanted to be free, that was the long and short of it, the rest had just followed in the wake of that desire. Why was it so hard for them to understand that if you cage a human being, no matter what else you do, you can never snuff out his desire to escape? Imprisonment is unnatural and that's why it is used as a punishment; if we took to it as a duck to water it would have no impact. We adapt to prison, as we do to other harsh and unnatural conditions, but that doesn't mean we completely lose our natural instinct for freedom. We merely suppress it, and though I was slowly learning to suppress my own natural instincts, I was not yet fully mature.

Even in solitary, my desire for freedom was still strong. I felt it at odd moments, as you might feel a twinge of exquisite but fleeting pain from a bad tooth. I longed to be free. One night I was thinking about religion and how at odd times I had prayed to God with no result, and I suddenly had an idea. If God wouldn't deal with me, maybe the devil would. It was worth a try. I decided to try and call up the devil and offer him my soul in exchange for freedom. I was deadly serious about it; I figured that my soul was surplus to requirements anyway, and I was already in a hell of my own making, so why not cut a deal with the head honcho? I sat cross-legged on the floor and pleaded with Satan to appear and accept my offer, and I would not have been in the least surprised if he had manifested himself in that cold cell and sealed the deal with a spit and a handshake. Of course, he didn't appear. And I think it was at that moment that I decided there was no God and no devil. But that's how desperate for freedom I was. Desperate enough to trade my soul for it.

By March I had reached my lowest point. I was drifting in and out of madness, talking to myself constantly and spending my days crouched in the corner of the cell like an animal trying to hide. I stopped washing and brushing my teeth, and my thoughts were turning more and more to suicide. I had not tasted fresh air since the night I had been brought to the block, and my cell felt like a tomb in which I had been buried alive. The screws mostly ignored me, but one or two tried talking to me when they brought the food in. I wasn't having any of it. I knew they were plotting to kill me, I could see it on their faces. Sometimes I would listen for hours with my ear against the doorframe, trying to hear what they were talking about in the office at the end of the landing. I couldn't hear much, only a murmur, but I swear I heard them mention my name at least five times a day. I was certain that they were in that office, probably a gang of them, with my picture in front of them, planning the best way to murder me. Once when I had my ear to the door, I was certain that I heard my mother's voice. I knew that they had my mother in the office and they were going to kill her. I collapsed on the floor and cried for ages.

I decided to kill myself, and once that decision was made I felt a relief, like a heavy weight had been lifted off my shoulders.

The next morning I collected my bowl full of warm water after breakfast, and had a good wash and brushed my teeth for the first time in weeks. I even had a 'good morning' for the screws; there was nothing they could do to me now. I waited until I was locked up for the evening, knowing that the door would not be routinely opened for at least nine hours. I had broken the metal tab from the zipper on my jeans and sharpened it up by rubbing it on the stone floor. It wasn't perfect, but I knew it would do the job. I spent a while saying my goodbyes to my family, in my head, and then I started. My cell was never completely dark at night, there was a red light burning constantly, so that when the night-screw looked through he could see me. I got on to my mattress and pulled the blanket over me, then I put the sharpened edge of the metal against my wrist and slashed as hard as I could. There was a sharp pain, and then I felt a warm trickle of blood. I did it again, then twice more, and when I felt the blood flowing I closed my eyes and went to sleep.

The next thing I remember was the screw banging on the door the next morning, telling me to get up and get ready to put my bedding out. I couldn't believe I was still alive. The mattress and blanket were soaked in blood and I was sticky with it, but still breathing. I crawled out of bed and stood up. I felt slightly dizzy, but that was all. I looked at my left wrist and saw four deep cuts that were no longer bleeding. Then the pain hit me, a throbbing pain that was bad, but not life-threatening. I was gutted. 'Let me fucking die!' I shouted at the top of my voice.

The screws, alerted by my wail of despair, quickly worked out what was going on. They came into the cell, mob-handed, more interested in the whereabouts of the 'blade' I had used to try and kill myself than my distress. After a fingertip search of the floor they found the zipper-tab and bagged it. In the 1970s it was an offence against prison discipline to mutilate or self-harm, and a prisoner could lose up to fourteen days for it. I was locked back in the cell until a medic came down and cleaned up my arm and put a few stitches in the cuts. As he worked, a couple of screws stood around with smirks on their faces and contempt in their eyes. I had shown weakness and, to them, it proved they had broken me. My face burned with shame and humiliation and, close behind, came anger. These fucking bastards! They were loving it! As the last stitch went into my arm I resolved that I would never again allow myself to be beaten by these people. If they wanted me dead, they would have to do the job themselves. And once again, anger and rage helped to clear my head and give me direction. They had buried me in a concrete tomb, but I was alive, and I would keep on living just to spite them.

That afternoon I got a visit from the Catholic priest. He came to my cell on his own and spoke to me as though I was a normal human being. I told him I no longer believed in God and, though he tried to persuade me that He did exist, I was adamant. He asked me why I had cut myself, and I told him it was none of his business, which he accepted eventually. He asked what I did with my time and why I did not at least read. I explained that I wasn't a very good reader, but when he left he put a copy of the Bible on my plank-table. I remember thinking that it might make a good pillow when I lay on the floor during the day.

The next day he was back, and this time he had brought a couple of easy-reader books. They were Janet and Johns, which are used to teach young kids to read. He went through them with me, and though I struggled on some words I found the basics were coming back to me.

A couple of days later he turned up with a note-book and two black crayons. Now I occupied my time learning to read and write. Unlike my time at school, now I had few distractions and a definite hunger to learn. Reading and writing seemed to come easily and I couldn't get enough of it. It filled my days and nights, and soon it was all I thought about. With a word from the priest, I was allowed out of my cell once a week to pick a book from the block library. The block library is not as grand as it sounds – it was a filing cabinet in a disused cell on the second landing, and the thirty or so books were mainly ancient ex-navy stock with the names of the ships that had donated them stamped inside the covers. They were thrillers and westerns, all hardbacks with no dust-covers and smelling musty. But with my new-found ability to read, they looked great to me. The first book I read all the way through was Alistair MacLean's *Force Ten from Navarone*, and when I got to the last page I was so proud of myself.

Reading books was as good as watching films, and in the emptiness of that block cell I savoured every word. Each book was a new adventure that could take me outside the prison walls for as long as I was reading it. I became a voracious reader, and soon one visit to the book cabinet a week was not enough for me. It took me three weeks to read the Alistair MacLean book, but soon I was knocking them out in three days. Every time the screws opened my door I was asking to visit the library.

Once I had books, the time passed quickly for me. One day in late July, I had a visit from an assistant governor. He said they were thinking of letting me up on the wing if I promised to behave myself. By now solitary had become my life. I had adapted, and being able to read had made it easier, but I knew I had read almost all the small stock of books in the cabinet. And once they had been read, there would be nothing new. I kept quiet and nodded in all the right places as the AG spoke. And that was all they wanted – compliance.

The day after the visit from the AG, I was finally released from the block and took my first lungful of fresh air in over six months. The borstal hadn't changed much since I'd been buried. There were more flowers on the grass borders, the sun felt great on my face and I was glad to be alive. But as I was marched over to E-wing I couldn't help looking at the perimeter wall and feeling that same old longing for freedom.

My time in the block had left me slightly off-kilter. I suffered from severe paranoia, which came at irregular intervals, when I least expected it. And I found the noise and rush of the wing disturbing. But my reputation had gone before me, and there were people waiting to welcome me back. The story of my attempted escape and assault on the night-watchman had entered the annals of borstal legend. I heard that I had put up such a ferocious fight in the block that four screws had had to be hospitalized, and that I had spat in the face of the governor and attempted to attack the Board of Visitors. I did nothing to discourage these stories, because they meant that even the most dangerous of cons would think twice before challenging me.

E-wing was known as 'the end of the line', because almost every kid on there had been shipped out of either another wing or another borstal before ending up there. If you fucked up on E-wing you could only be sent to the borstal wing at Wormwood Scrubs, as no other borstal would take you. We were the dregs of the system: the mad, the bad and the downright dangerous, all cooped up together on one wing.

I am not proud to say that for a while on E-wing I became a bully. My reputation allowed me to take liberties, so I did. I singled out a couple of the weaker kids and demanded a percentage of their wages every week. I'm not going to try to justify my actions by telling you that 'taxing' was the norm, but it was. As I've said before, prison is no place for the weak.

Some kids became loan-sharks. The average borstal wage was 60p a week, and this would be paid in ten-pence pieces. For 60p you could buy half-an-ounce of Old Holborn tobacco, a packet of Rizlas and a box of matches from the canteen. And, if you made your smokes as thin as a match, and supplemented your

Rizlas with the thin pages of a King James Bible, and split your matches into four with a razor-blade, you might just reach pay-day without suffering too many nicotine withdrawals.

At least half the kids in Rochester were heavy smokers, so, on the day before pay-day, the sharks would offer single roll-ups for 10p a go. Included in the price was a split match. The trouble was, if you did succumb to temptation and purchased one of these roll-ups, it would leave you short on pay-day and unable to afford the complete smoker's package. That meant you would only be able to get a quarter-ounce of tobacco, and you would run out a couple of days earlier. You would then be tempted back to the loan-shark, who would give you his 'special offer', five stick-thin roll-ups for 30p. Once you accepted this, you were lost. The following week, you would owe two-thirds of your wages, and every week after that your entire wages would go to the shark, and in return you might get one roll-up a day – if you were lucky.

There were a lot of fights and violence over snout-debts. Every wing had at least one loan-shark, with a couple of GBH-merchants on his firm. Anyone who was late in paying would get a visit from the heavies, and a few digs as a reminder. Persistent offenders got coshed or, in extreme cases of piss-taking, they would be striped. A lot of kids took the easy way out and either went to the screws and asked for protection or, if they still had a bit of pride left, they would kick off outrageously, so the screws would have no choice but to nick them. Once on the block they would refuse to come back to the wing and usually got transferred to another nick. Those who did not pay their debts were known as 'knockers', or Tilbury dockers in rhyming slang. A reputation as a Tilbury would follow you everywhere and meant that you could never again get credit in jail.

I didn't bother selling snout. If the truth be told, the real Chaps looked down on the loan-sharks and classed them as mugs. Why bother going to all the trouble of hooking a fish by selling him snout when all it took was a few well-placed digs and a bit of growling? In my defence, I will only say that I never took all of my victims' wages, and they would always get a roll-up each on pay-day. Hard places make for hard times.

The kids in Rochester borstal in 1978 mainly belonged to the different teenage subcultures that were prevalent outside. A lot were skinheads, heavily into the National Front, but there were also punk-rockers, neo-mods, soul-boys, smoothies and teddy-boys. I still classed myself as a ted, and I would grease up my hair and wear the collar of my denim jacket turned up. If any of the other handful of teds on the wing had any bother, I would step in and help out, even if they were not classed as Chaps. I felt that being a ted, I owed them a certain amount of loyalty.

Racism was rife in borstal. Dover was the worst for it, and there had been a couple of race wars there that had developed into full-blown riots. Rochester was almost as bad. The black kids stuck together. Most of them were 'sticksmen', pick-pockets, which the white kids classed as no better than purse-snatchers. The black kids also had a very different attitude when it came to rapists. To them, rape was just another crime. White kids, myself included, saw rapists as the scum of the earth, and a lot of tension between the races came when the screws would let slip that there was a black rapist on the wing. For most of us, being a rapist was enough to warrant a striping, but a black rapist had all the NF boys intent on murder and mutilation. Most of the black kids would defend one of their number no matter what a scumbag sex-case he was. And then there would be trouble.

The crimes of rapists and sex offenders do not make sense to the ordinary criminal, so we call them nonsense-cases – nonces for short. Nonces raise the same level of disgust in criminals as they do in straight-goers. Natural revulsion. But a further reason nonces are not tolerated by ordinary prisoners is because they are grasses. Some refuse to go on to the special protection wings that the prison system has set up for them and request 'normal location'. Whether through arrogance, a refusal to admit their crimes or because they believe that what they have done is no worse than burgling someone's house or stealing their car, they refuse protection, as is their right. Some nonces even enjoy the dangerous game of living a secret life among packs of violent men who would cut their throats in a hot second. Like agents in a foreign country, they must watch everything they say and do in case they are found out and executed.

Once a nonce manages to slip on to a normal wing and is accepted as, if not one of the lads, certainly as part of the pond-life, the screws will make their move. Here's how it works. Johnny Nonce moves on to the wing, claiming to be in for 'GBH on the police' (the standard nonce cover-story, as it adds an air of danger and rebelliousness). Nobody knows anything about him, so he is left alone. Perhaps he will even produce a bit of paperwork, on request, to prove what he's in for – except the paperwork has been supplied to him by the prison system (standard procedure). So Johnny Nonce is free to mooch about and keep his ears open for who's doing what. The screws will have a word with Johnny Nonce and spell out that if he doesn't pass on any snippets of information he comes across, they might 'accidentally' let it slip that he is not all he seems to be. So now, not only is Johnny Nonce an undercover sex-case, but he's also a full-time grass.

Undercover nonces do a lot of damage with their informing. The screws find out who is doing the loan-sharking, the bullying and plotting escapes. Confusion is caused in the ranks of normal prisoners, as they try to find out who has been informing on their activities. Innocents end up accused and striped, and the screws sit back laughing at the trouble they and their tame nonce grass are causing. And that's another reason why nonces are not tolerated on normal location. If one is found out he will be severely dealt with.

I soon settled into the pace of life on E-wing, and before I knew it Christmas 1978 was upon me. I had served twenty-two months, including my time on remand, which was two-and-a-half borstal sentences, and I still had not managed to escape. I had been in a few fights, and I had done a few short stints in solitary. I still hated the block, but now that I could pass the time by reading it wasn't too bad.

One day a screw was trying to order me to march, and I told him to fuck off or he'd get a broken jaw. I ended up in the block again, five days' solitary. On the fourth day I was lying on the floor of my cell reading *Centennial* by James A. Michener, a thousand-page adventure that seemed tailor-made for solitary confinement, when a governor came into my cell. I had never seen him before; he was a big man with wide shoulders and a boxer's nose. He took off his coat and sat on the floor facing me. I was more than somewhat surprised by this, and when he began to speak, I listened.

This governor told me that he was new in the borstal, and he had taken a close look at my record and didn't like what he saw. Amen to that. He told me that if I made a deal with him to change my ways, he would recommend me for parole. But I had to conform to the regime, sign up for a vocational-training course and be free of adjudications for at least six months.

'And if I do all this, I'll get parole?' I asked.

He shook his head. 'Nothing is guaranteed,' he replied. 'But if you keep your part of the bargain, I will strongly recommend your release. You've caused a lot of problems for the system. You may not know it, but certain people in high places are very pissed off by your antics. If you can show a change of attitude, they might think that releasing you will be an end to the problem.'

I liked him. He spoke to me as though I was an adult. And when I thought about it later, I realized I was just about to turn eighteen. Maybe it was time for a change.

A week after I'd finished my solitary I was accepted on to the building-ops vocational-training course. My first choice was the draughtsman/technical-drawing course, but my maths weren't up to it. I made a mistake going for building-ops, and though I really did enjoy the work, I wasn't bright enough to see that I was training to be a builder's labourer. I learned the basics of brick-laying, concreting, scaffolding and woodwork, but not enough to become a tradesman in any of them. That's the trouble with all prison-based vocational training: they never teach you enough to be fully qualified at anything. Many ex-cons have been severely disappointed when they showed up for job interviews clutching their prison-gained certificates, only to find they're not worth a rub of soap.

Instead of the usual suspects, I began to knock about with the small group of teds and rockabillies on the wing. I played pool, discussed music, watched a bit of television and read a lot. I kept as low a profile as I could and avoided any wing politics or arguments. People left me alone because of my rep, and that meant I didn't have to make much of an effort to get whatever I wanted. I discovered the books of G. F. Newman, and they were a revelation. In the borstal system, and to this day in prison, there was a lot of censorship. For example, each wing at Rochester had a 'matron', some middle-aged biddy whose job it was to read all our incoming and outgoing mail and censor it. If there was any swearing or mention of sex or crime in our letters, it would be cut out, literally, with a pair of scissors. Some letters from girlfriends ended up as confetti by the time matron was finished with them. Ginger Reedman once got a letter from his girlfriend, and when he looked in the envelope there were two strips of writing paper, one said, 'Dear Ginge, hope you are well', and the other strip said, 'Love, Angela, XXX'. The matron had snipped out the rest of the letter because of its 'raunchy content'. The matron also had her say in what books, newspapers and magazines we were allowed to read. The *Sun* was permanently on her banned list.

The books that matron would allow in the wing-library were mainly westerns and *Boy's Own*-type adventures. But there were also some paperbacks that were known as 'floaters', which had made their way into the borstal through other routes, and they were the kind of books that would have matron foaming at the mouth and reaching for the petrol and matches. You could normally tell a floater by the fact that its front cover would be missing, usually to get rid of a lurid picture. And these books would be sold, bartered or hired out to the discerning reader who wanted a bit more than Miss Marple or the adventures of the Cisco Kid. By today's standards they were as tame as a toothless lion with a full belly, but to matron they were 'filth', which made them very attractive to us. *Lady Chatterley's Lover*, *Valley of the Dolls*, *The Lotus Eaters* and *Last Exit to Brooklyn* were all floaters, as was *A Profession of Violence*, the story of the Kray Twins. And top of the banned list were Harold Robbins and G. F. Newman.

When 1979 came around I was working hard on my latest escape plan, but this time I was hoping to escape through the front gate by earning parole. I still had a lot of hate and anger in me, but I was now a veteran at keeping it bottled up. One afternoon in April I was called out of work and taken over to the hospital. I asked the escort screw what it was all about, but he claimed he didn't know.

I was shown into an office and told to take a seat. Behind the desk sat an Asian man in a grey suit. I later found out he was a psychotherapist brought in especially to see me. No sooner was I in the chair than he started to verbally abuse me.

'You fucking little shit. Robbing people with a gun, assaulting fellow inmates and staff, what? You think you are a tough nut? You need a good thrashing! You bastard! Come on, let us see how tough you are. Do you want to hit me? Come on then, I dare you!'

I couldn't believe it. It was so unexpected, coming from this normal, respectable-looking man. I felt my rage rising inside me. I stood up, knocking the chair over, and clenched my fists. The doctor flinched but kept up his flow of abuse. I took a great gulp of air and tried to calm myself; at the same time I was automatically lining up the point on his jaw where my first punch was going to land. But something stopped me from launching my attack. I managed to get air back into my lungs. My whole body was shaking with suppressed rage, as I fought to keep it from erupting. I had to get out of this office or I would be right back where I started.

I turned my back on the doctor and, believe me, that took an almost Herculean effort, as every fibre in my body was screaming at me to attack, and I walked, stiff-legged, to the door. The door to the office was slightly ajar, which I hadn't noticed before, and when I stepped through it, I saw two screws waiting on either side of the doorway. They looked disappointed. I couldn't speak, and suddenly my legs felt like rubber and I had to sit down on a bench. Two of the screws went into the office without a word. The other two marched me back to work.

All afternoon I puzzled over it. It seemed surreal that I had been called to see a doctor who I had never seen before, just to be verbally abused. When I got back to the wing that evening I asked to see the AG. I explained what had happened and asked what it was all about.

'We're in the process of writing your parole reports, Smith,' he said. 'And you've had problems with anger control in the past. You've been very volatile and violent, and the parole board are going to want to know if you can face stressful situations without resorting to violence. Now we know, and the answer is "Yes, you can." You did well today. Keep it up.'

And that was it. I was dismissed. The system was playing a very dangerous game with me. I had been a split-second away from launching myself across the doctor's desk, and I know I would have done him some damage before the screws reached me. I was glad I held back. For all our sakes.

In the next few weeks I was wary of any more 'tests' the system might want to spring on me, but nothing else happened. I had started to correspond with my family, and one day I had a visit from my mum, my sister Samantha, my brother Mick and Mad Harry. It was great to see my family again, and I realized how much I had missed them. My mum was crying and saying how much I had grown. She made me promise that when I got out, I would never come back to prison again. But even as I made the promise, I knew I would be going back to crime. What else was there for me?

Mick and Harry were both dressed in teddy-boy finery, drape-suits, drainpipe trousers and waistcoats. Even Samantha was wearing a girl's drape-jacket. They filled me in on all the news. They had formed a gang and were at war with the local punk and skinhead gangs. There were clubs opening up all over London where you could hear fifties rock 'n' roll and rockabilly music, and the scene was really taking off. Listening to them I had a great longing to be out and part of it all. When the visit was over I went back to my cell. I felt depressed. The sun was shining and there was life on the other side of the wall, but I was still buried alive. It took me a couple of days to get over it.

On 10 June 1979, I was summoned to the AG's office. The AG read from a sheet of paper. 'Detainee D86160 N. Smith. The Secretary of State has decided to release you on licence, subject to conditions which will be explained to you. Provided circumstances do not change, you will be released on 2 July 1979 . . .'

I didn't hear the rest. I was going home. I felt faint. After all this time, I was finally getting out. I worked it out, I had just over three weeks left.

I didn't sleep that night, thinking about freedom, and I didn't think I'd be able to sleep for the next three weeks. But there was better to come. The next morning I was called back in front of the AG.

'Smith, it has been decided that, because of the amount of time you have been incarcerated, you should be granted seven days' home leave, in order to acclimatize yourself with the outside world before your release on parole. You will leave tomorrow. A travel warrant will be provided.'

And that was it. After twenty-eight months of hell on earth, I was walking out of the front gate. In all my time spent in solitary I had dreamed of this moment, and now that it was here, it was even sweeter than I'd dreamt it would be.

12. Rocking at the Chick-a-Boom

The summer of 1979 seems like another world now, long ago and far away. Margaret Thatcher had just won the General Election for the Conservative Party, and we were going through that short honeymoon period of new government, blissfully unaware of the horrors to come. The Yorkshire Ripper had claimed his tenth victim, and the police were still twenty months and three more victims away from catching him. Michael Jackson was still black and had all of his own body-parts. Punk rock had passed its peak, but was far from spitting its last. The Two-Tone revolution was underway, ushering in a new generation of ska-skins and neo-mods in tonic suits and porkpie hats. The biggest youth-film of the year was *Quadrophenia*, a story of rebellious youth set against the background of the 1960s battles between the mods and rockers.

The youth of the inner cities were restless. It would be two more years before the actual extent of their disaffection became apparent during the riots of 1981. But, in the meantime, they practised their violence on each other. Teenagers rushed to join gangs and form their own subcultures: teddy-boys, rockabillies, punks, skinheads, mods, soul-boys, rude-boys, smoothies, and casuals, hillbillies, psychobillies and disco-freaks all fought for the spotlight and their fifteen minutes of fame. Pubs, clubs and even the streets became their battlegrounds. If someone liked a different music or fashion from your own it was your duty to attack them on sight. Recruitment numbers were up for both the National Front and the Anti-Nazi League, and it was teenagers who were swelling their ranks. Football violence was on the wane, simply because there were better opportunities for a good punch-up joining a gang.

In my corner of south London, the ted and rockabilly gangs were outnumbered and in disarray. Ted-bashing had become a sport to the local skinhead gangs, and the latest refinement came when they started carrying scissors to cut off the quiff of any ted they came across. The teds and rockabillies had fought a much-publicized war with the punk-rockers in the Kings Road in the summer of '78, and now they were taking on all-comers, and losing.

When I stepped off the train at Streatham Hill station on 12 June 1979, I felt ready for anything. I had a lot of living to catch up on and a terrible hunger to make my mark. I still suffered from bouts of paranoia, and rage and bitterness bubbled just below the surface, ready to be unleashed at a moment's notice. I had changed. No longer the kid who had felt sick and sorry after his first slashing, no longer an advocate of fair play and decency when it came to my enemies, I was a bundle of spite and viciousness clothed in a teenage body, a war, looking for somewhere to declare itself. I wanted some sort of revenge for the months I had spent in solitary, for the beatings I had suffered at the hands of the prison system, and for the shit I had had to swallow in order to be released. Someone was going to suffer.

My family welcomed me back, as usual. But even they commented on how much I had changed. People kept asking me how it had been inside, but I couldn't even begin to tell them. I would just shrug, and say, 'It was all right.' I felt distanced from my family, as though I was not part of anything, just a shadow flitting through their lives. Mick was now a rockabilly and was in a gang called the Clapham Cougars, along with Pete the Nut, who had been released from Aylesbury YP centre in early 1978, when his parents died. Harry was also in the gang, as were several of the kids off the estate we had grown up with.

Pete hadn't changed much, neither had Harry, and it was great on my first night out to get pissed on Olde English cider and talk to people who had been inside and knew the score. Pete and Harry, along with their two sisters, had a council flat on Poynders Gardens Estate, near Clapham South. The party for my homecoming went on well into the early hours, and I met many friends who were now on the rockabilly scene, both new and old. There was drink, music, dancing and girls, and I ended up welcoming the dawn with a rockabilly girl named Elaine. It wasn't until much later that I found out she had been laid on, so to speak, by Mick, Harry and Pete, as my 'coming-out present'.

My seven-day home-leave seemed to go by in the blink of an eye. I got into one fight and ended up smashing a glass into a man's face. My level of violence was totally inappropriate for the outside but would have been yawned at in borstal. I noticed that people were a bit wary around me after that, but it was what I was used to. I knew that our little gang had the potential to be big on the gang scene; all they needed was the inspiration of a leader. And I had plans.

Going back to Rochester voluntarily was hard to do. The closer the train got to Medway, the gloomier my mood became. By the time I handed myself in at the gatehouse I was positively depressed. I had left the borstal seven days earlier dressed in my full teddy-boy outfit of grey drape-suit with black velvet collar and cuffs, but somewhere during the week I had evolved into a rockabilly and came back in black-leather gang-jacket, jeans and steel-toed boots. While changing back into my borstal uniform, I consoled myself with the thought that I only had two weeks left to do, and I had spent longer than that in the strong-box in the previous two years.

The next weeks seemed to last for ever. It was well-known that my release on parole was conditional on good behaviour, so my enemies came crawling out of the woodwork and seized their opportunity for a bit of kudos. Kids who only a month before would not have dared to look at me sideways suddenly found the bottle to try and front me. They knew that I couldn't risk losing my parole by putting the blade across their faces or even throwing a right-hander. I had to grit my teeth and swallow the insults, just as they had to in the past. A couple of times I was on the verge of kicking off, but I managed to stay my hand, though it nearly killed me to do so.

Finally, 2 July rolled around. At 8 a.m. I was marched from E-wing, past the hospital where I had spent such a terrible drug-fuelled nightmare in '77, and into the reception building. I changed into my own clothes, signed my parole licence, my firearms licence, which banned me from the possession of firearms or ammunition for the rest of my life on pain of imprisonment, and picked up my travel warrant and £12 discharge grant. As I walked through the gate I looked back at the perimeter wall, this time from the outside. It didn't look so big, and I wondered that it had ever managed to keep me in. I hoped never to see that wall again.

One month after my release from Rochester there was a warrant out for my arrest, for not reporting to my parole officer. I had reported for the first three weeks, but soon grew bored with sitting in a stuffy office for an afternoon a week, making small-talk about what I had been doing since my release. I had more exciting things to do, and there was no way I was going to tell my PO about them.

I had started to gather a gang of good fighters around me and organize raids on enemy gangs. Based in a squat, where I was now living, in Ferndale Road, Balham, we called ourselves the Balham Wildkatz. We were all tattooed with the gang name, and it was painted on the back panel of our leather jackets. We did a bit of burglary, the odd smash-and-grab raid and sold a lot of 'snide' to keep ourselves in beer, fags and clothes. There was me, my brother Mick, Mad Harry, Pete the Nut, my cousins, Ronnie and Eddie Regan, Popeye Willis, Joe Kennedy, Perry, Dennis and Alan Budd, Big Nose Eamon Armstrong, Gerry Suggers and Tall Paul, and maybe a dozen more rockabillies we could call on in a rumble. The Balham Wildkatz was a formidable gang.

It was Popeye Willis who introduced us to the snide-game, and he was mustard at it. Snide is the name for fake jewellery which was so good it could pass for the real thing – on a dark night, from half a mile away – sovereign rings, necklaces, gold ingots on chains, diamond rings, and every make of watch you could think of, in fake gold, platinum and silver. Where it came from originally, I never knew, but we got our snide from a fella named Belfast Joe who ran the protection in Balham market.

Belfast Joe was the big cheese in Balham in those days, and it was rumoured that he was an IRA man who had escaped from the Maze prison and was hiding out in south London. He was a short bull of a man with a face like a bulldog licking piss off a broken bottle, and he surrounded himself with a posse of henchmen, chief among them a scruffy, cockney motormouth named Johnny the Lip. I liked Johnny, he always had a joke or a funny story to tell and I never once saw him lose his temper, but it was strongly rumoured that he had once chopped a bloke's arm off with a garden scythe for insulting his brother.

Belfast Joe's normal hangout was the betting-shop on Bedford Hill, or Effy's Cafe about 200 yards away. He would sit there, like a fat spider in the middle of his web, and wait for the local tea-leaves to bring him stolen gear to buy. He would also buy information about likely targets for thievery and send his boys out on 'bits of work'. If you wanted anything, from a case of hooky vodka to a second-hand AK47, Belfast Joe was the man to see. He had a finger in everything, from illegal prize-fighting to taking protection money from stallholders. Popeye lived on the same street as Joe, just around the corner from Bedford Hill, and he became his gofer before getting into the rockabilly scene and joining the Wildkatz.

The snide-racket worked like this. Joe would sell us a mixed parcel of items on credit, and we would then punt them around for cash and pay him what he was owed. We made at least 100 per cent profit on every item. Popeye and I would work together as he had the spiel down to a fine art. We would walk into small shops and businesses – factories where plenty of women worked were best – and Popeye would spin a yarn about how we had just robbed a jewellers and needed to convert the loot into cash, sharpish. Not once, in all the time we were doing it, did anyone even threaten to call the police. Jewellery at cheap prices is hard to resist.

The fake sovereign rings cost about 50p to make; Joe bought them for £1 a piece and sold them to us for £4 a piece. We then knocked them out for £10–15 each as 'stolen property'. People just couldn't contain their greed; if you bought a real sovereign ring in those days it would cost you £35. Popeye's spiel never failed, and we could even afford to let some people haggle us down a couple of quid on every deal and still make a profit. We weren't earning fortunes, and punting the gear was very time-consuming, but we managed to hit a rock 'n' roll club every night of the week and end up pissed.

The trouble with Popeye was he could never resist selling the gear to anyone, no matter how close to home the buyer was, and at one time or another we had to dodge every shopkeeper on Bedford Hill because they were all looking for the impossible – their money back. Once the snide was sold, there was no legal comeback; you could hardly go to the police and tell them that the stolen jewellery you had bought from a couple of local tearaways had turned out to be fake. You had to either swallow your loss and chalk it up to experience, or try fronting us about it and end up bleeding. Most people swallowed, but a couple of leery shopkeepers ended up getting their faces stitched.

One regular punter for our snide was the Pieman, a bit of a dopey fella who delivered pies and pasties to the cafés and chip-shops around Balham. He had started off by buying a fake Rolex from us. These watches were real crap, they had Timex insides and their ticking was louder than a deathwatch beetle on a loud-hailer, but the gaudy, 'diamond'-encrusted cases made them glitter like a king's ransom. A week after he bought the 'Rolex', the Pieman sidled up to me and Popeye in Effy's Cafe. Here we go, I thought, thinks he can get his money back. But to our surprise, he wanted more. Over the months we must have sold him 20 lbs of snide jewellery, and he always came back for more. The Pieman was a mystery, but as long as he was keeping us in cash we didn't give a shit. I thought he must have been selling the gear on and earning a profit out of it. One day, after he had just given us £25 for a particularly gaudy bracelet, Popeye came straight out and asked him what he was doing with the gear he bought from us. He looked around to make sure no one was listening, and a crafty look came over his face.

'I've got it all stashed in a safety-deposit box,' he said. 'You don't think I want to be delivering pies for the rest of my life, do you?'

Me and Popeye were incredulous. I often wonder how the Pieman felt when he went to cash in his pension and found a bag of base-metal surrounded by flakes of gold- and silver- paint.

Another way we got our money was by robbing the queers on Tooting Bec Common. Bedford Hill itself was a red-light district, full of pimps, punters and prostitutes, who appeared after dark like a horde of ravenous vampires. But the top part of the Hill was flanked on either side by wooded areas of common and was a well-known homosexual pick-up point. We would secrete ourselves in the trees at the edge of the common, first sending Dennis Budd, the youngest and prettiest of the gang, to stand by the road as bait. As soon as a car stopped and its occupant began to chat Dennis up, we would swarm out of the woods and drag him from the car. The unfortunate victim would be given a beating, and we would drive away in his car, with his valuables. For me there was nothing personal in this, I wasn't a rabid 'queer-hater' like some of the gang professed to be, I just saw these men as a legitimate source of income.

Our days were spent hanging around the indoor market, where my brother Mick was the manager of a record shop called the Living End. We would drink cider from the bottle and chat up the numerous rockabilly girls who came to buy records or listen to the jukebox, or buy original 1950s clothing from a shop that was run by a teddy-boy called Moses. At night we would be out drinking, dancing and fighting at clubs such as the Chick-a-Boom in Carshalton, Bobbysox in Wood Green and the Greyhound in Croydon. We would travel all over London to the rockabilly clubs, usually by tube but sometimes in stolen cars. Wherever we went, we went as a gang, all flying colours (displaying our gang name on the backs of our jackets), so inevitably we got into plenty of fights with other gangs. By now we had teamed up with another gang of rockabillies from Battersea called the Battersea Rebels, and we were thirty-strong, with another twenty hangers-on who would turn up for fights to make up the numbers.

The Battersea Rebels started on the Patmore estate off the Wandsworth Road and, like us, they were originally a teddy-boy gang who evolved into rockabillies. The first leader of the gang was Tony 'Bopper' Hogan, whose dad was an original 1950s teddy-boy and a well-known disc jockey on the rock 'n' roll scene. He had run the Edwardian Club in Brixton, outside which I had carried out my first razor-slashing in 1976. Tony was a great dancer and a game fighter, and had been smashed in the head with a claw-hammer by a skinhead when he was thirteen. The attack with the hammer had fractured his skull, and he had to have extensive brain surgery. After that, Tony was 'off-key' and very unpredictable. He always carried a knife and had no hesitation about using it. Even seasoned gang-fighters were a little wary around Tony 'Bopper' Hogan.

I had first met Tony in the summer of 1975, on the yard at Stamford House Remand Centre. He was nicked with a couple of black kids for 'dipping' (picking pockets) in the West End. We got on well because we were both teds and had a lot in common. The next time I saw him was in Send DC, where he never stopped getting into fights. He was also in Rochester hospital for mental observation when I left the borstal on parole. Tony continued to be a very violent and volatile character, and in 1986 he stabbed his best friend to death and was sent to prison for life, with a recommendation that he serve a minimum of fifteen years.

In '79 the Battersea Rebels were being led by Tommy Hogan, Tony's younger brother, and they had some game fighters on their firm. It was the Battersea Rebels who introduced us to drugs. Up until then I had never smoked a joint or even known anyone who had. Being second-generation Irish, as most of our gang were, we came from mainly Catholic families, who were drink-oriented and classed anyone who smoked a joint a 'junkie'. To this day, my parents both think I am a junkie because I smoke the occasional joint.

The Battersea Rebels all smoked cannabis, and did a bit of speed, amphetamine sulphate, now and again. It was new to us, and personally I didn't get on with cannabis, as the only time I tried it was after a few pints, and it just made me feel sick. I didn't mind the speed though; it meant I could drink more and still be pretty lively when it came time to fight. Apart from hash and speed, we all loved to drink, and that was the full extent of our drug-taking.

Life was great for me during that summer, even though I was on the run again and living in a squat. I was rushing to catch up on all I had lost, and I found the time to fall in love with five or six different girls. In late summer me and a few of the gang gate-crashed a party in Sutton, and there I first laid eyes on a girl who was going to be a big part of my life for many years to come. Her name was Denise Anne Young.

The first time I saw Denise I could see she was pretty, but I didn't think she was anything special. I was more interested in her best mate, Melanie, because she looked like she was more likely to succumb to my animal charms and drop her drawers. To my mind, there were girls who would and girls who wouldn't, and Denise definitely had the look of a girl who wouldn't. I turned out to be wasting my time with Mel as well, so I did the next best thing and started a fight with a couple of rockers.

All too soon the summer was over, and so was my time at large. In November 1979 I was on my way to burgle a Burton's clothes shop in Tooting Broadway, at three o'clock in the morning. Belfast Joe was waiting for all the leather coats I could get, with cash in hand, but I was spotted looking suspicious by a patrol car. I gave a false name and details, but the coppers recognized me from my mugshot, which had been circulated to all London police stations along with a warrant for my arrest for violation of my parole conditions. I was taken to Amen Corner police station, and when I was searched they found a cut-throat razor in my jacket pocket. Luckily I had managed to dump my burglar's kit over a garden wall when I first saw them. I was charged with possession of an offensive weapon and breaching my parole licence. The next day I was taken to Lavender Hill magistrates court and remanded back into custody.

Latchmere House had not changed much, still the same dog-faced screws in slashed-peak caps and sad-faced young prisoners marking time on the bare, concrete yard. This time I was over eighteen, so I was located on A-wing with the YPs. I knew plenty of people there, from previous prisons, and within a couple of days I had everything I needed for a long stay. The offensive-weapon charge didn't really worry me, as they were usually dealt with by way of a £10 fine. But now I had broken my parole, I would have to serve every day of the remainder of my three-year sentence. My release date was 25 May 1980. But still I was in fairly good spirits.

Late in November I was taken for a court appearance on the offensive-weapon charge. When the magistrate heard I was already likely to be in custody for the next six months, he gave me a deferred sentence. So on 25 May 1980, the very day I was to be released, I would have to appear in court to be sentenced on this new charge. The magistrate made it quite clear that if I came back to court with a good-behaviour record from prison, I would not receive another custodial sentence.

At Latchmere I met up with my old mate Micky again, the kid who had been with me when I had my fingers broken by the burglary squad. He was now doing a nine-month YP sentence for stealing a motorbike and assaulting the police. It was good to see Micky again, but I had to wonder if either of us would have been meeting up in prison if it hadn't been for the beating we received from the police. I know it was an important factor in my own criminality. Micky was working on the hot-plate, serving up the meals, and he made sure I got the best of what was going. I'm glad to say that by 1983 Micky was going straight and had a good job as a mechanic and has not seen the inside of a prison since.

The day after I appeared in court and got my deferred sentence, I was handcuffed and loaded on to a van. They wouldn't tell me where I was going, but when I spotted the signs for Medway, I knew it was back to Rochester.

This time my stay on E-wing was pretty uneventful. Rochester was coming to the end of its time as a borstal institution. There was legislation going through Parliament that would do away with the borstal system and replace it with short detention sentences for young offenders. Rochester finally reverted back to a local prison, the original purpose for which it was built, in 1982. When I returned the atmosphere was no longer so tense. E-wing was now made up of mainly run-of-the-mill borstal boys with hardly any of the hard cases who had once stalked the landings. It was more laid back, but there was still the odd punch-up. I settled back in and began to wait for my release date.

Before I was nicked I had been going out with a girl named Alison, a gorgeous little bottle-blonde rockabilly chick who worked on the cosmetics counter at Woolworths in Tooting. We had sworn undying love to each other, and once inside I spent a lot of my time writing her letters. I also got back into reading, and read anything I could get my hands on. The days seemed to fly by.

In March 1980 Alison suddenly stopped writing and visiting. I applied to make an emergency phone-call to her, telling the AG that she was seven months pregnant. In those days you had to have a good reason in order to be able to use the phone. I was granted the phone call and when she picked up the phone I said, 'Guess who?'

She sounded surprised and delighted. 'Oh, is that you, Steve?'

I was devastated. I immediately let loose a torrent of abuse and demanded to know who Steve was. The screw who was in the office with me, supervising the phone call, leapt to his feet and tried to snatch the phone from my hand. I put my hand on his chest and shoved him back into his seat. I was part-way through telling Alison what I was going to do to her and Steve when I got out, when she hung up. The screw was pretty shaken up and told me that by rights he should nick me for assaulting him, never mind abusing the phone-call privilege to issue death threats.

After I had calmed down, the screw came to see me and told me he was not going to report the incident, but he was marking my file to indicate that I was never to be allowed another phone call. He was a fairly new screw and less militant than most of the dinosaurs working on E-wing. If I had been nicked for assaulting him, I would have ended up back in solitary, probably for the remainder of my sentence because of my previous record. I raged about Alison's betrayal for a couple of days and wrote her a few nasty letters which would never have made it past the scrutiny of matron if I had bothered to try and send them. But in the end I became pretty philosophical about it. There was nothing I could do from behind bars. But in my mind I promised Steve a good kicking when I got out.

Out of the blue I got a letter from Mel, asking for a VO so she and her mate could come and see me. I remembered her mate Denise, with the long chestnut hair and slightly husky voice. I sent the Visiting Order. At that time it was the vogue for rockabilly girls to wear donkey jackets, the most unflattering garment for a female since the sack-dress, but Denise looked great in hers. Mel did most of the talking and made it obvious that she fancied me, but I couldn't take my eyes off Denise. They told me that Alison was now going out with Turkey-Neck Steve, one of the Battersea Rebels, and that they had gone to a rock 'n' roll weekender at Caister together – so it must be true love. When it came time for the visit to end, Mel fell into my arms for a kiss, but it was Denise I really wanted.

I thought about Denise a lot in the next couple of months, but what really kept me going were my plans for revenge on Steve. Every night before I went to sleep I savoured the moment when I would confront him and give him the beating he deserved. Part of it was the fact that he must have known that Alison was my girl, and making a move on her was like calling me a mug. Everybody knew about it, and that galled me. Taking my girl was a direct challenge and if I let it pass, I would lose whatever respect I had from the gang. No, Steve was going to get it, and get it hard.

In the world of the Chaps, stealing another man's girl is a punishable offence and, at the very least, calls for a straightener. But to make a move on the girl of someone who is locked up and unable to defend his corner, well, that's a cardinal sin. I can honestly say that I have never made a move on a girl who was already in a relationship with someone else, and when any of my friends were in jail and I had cause to visit their wives or girl-friends I would always make sure I had someone with me. It's bad enough trying to keep a relationship going from behind bars, and the last thing you need is rumours that one of your pals has been seen sniffing around your wife.

I was once again released from Rochester borstal on the morning of 25 May 1980. My sentence was over, but it had been a long and eventful three years. I had turned nineteen, and I had nothing on my mind but getting back to the gang and living it up a little. But first I had to report to Lavender Hill magistrates court over my deferred sentence for the offensive weapon.

When I got to the court that afternoon, some of the gang were waiting. Mick, Harry, Pete, Joe Kennedy and Gordon were all there in their rockabilly summer mufti, gaudily coloured Hawaiian shirts, sunglasses, jeans and steel-toed boots. I got a great welcome and felt really good to be back. Also at the court waiting for me were Alison and her mate, Jeanette. To say I wasn't pleased to see her would be an understatement. She told me that her fling with Steve was over and all but begged me not to seek revenge. In my most charming manner I told her to go and fuck herself and to hire out a wheelchair for Steve while she was at it. She left in tears.

My court appearance was a formality. The judge read my reports and then gave me a conditional discharge, and I was free to go. For the first time since I had left Send DC, I was actually free. I had no outstanding court cases, no parole officer to report to and, as far as I knew, I wasn't wanted by the police for anything.

The gang told me that they had been having trouble with a skinhead gang called the Balham Bootboys. There was a turf war going on and things were starting to hot up. We went back to Poynders Gardens for a bit of a party, and I made plans to stoke the fire a bit more. If there was going to be a war, I would make sure that I was in the thick of it. After a quiet six months I was more than ready for a bit of excitement.

The Chick-a-Boom club, held every Wednesday and Saturday night at the St Helier Arms pub in Carshalton, Surrey, was the premier rockabilly gig. On a Saturday night there would be up to 500 rockabillies, teds and rockers packing the place out. Gangs from all over London and the south-east would fly their colours and show-out at the Chick-a-Boom, and there were many fights, usually in the large car park at the rear of the club. The front bar was used by the locals, the younger of them being casuals and football hooligans, and they resented the influx of what they called 'greasers' on to their patch. The atmosphere between the front- and back-bar occupants was always tense. But, to their frustration, the locals were heavily outnumbered, so they had to stand back and just watch as their unwelcome guests turned their turf into a carnival of drunken revelry and violence twice a week.

I loved the Chick-a-Boom, and I was involved in a lot of the incidents that led the *Daily Telegraph* to describe the St Helier Arms as 'the most violent pub in Britain'. There was always someone who wanted a fight, and I was always happy to oblige. Many times I ended up getting the shit kicked out of me, but it was all part of the game; no one can win every fight. There was no shame in being beaten in a straightener, and quite a few of the rockabilly crowd were amateur boxers at one time or another. One of my best pals at the time was Joe Kennedy. Joe had it all; he could box like Rocky Marciano and dance like Fred Astaire, though his enemies would have it the other way around. The girls loved Joe, and Joe loved the girls, sometimes two at a time. The only trouble with Joe was that he couldn't handle his drink; two pints of snakebite and he wanted to fight the world. When I had been on the run from my parole licence in '79, Joe and I had watched each other's backs in many a gang fight. I was as close to Joe as I was to my own brother.

Turkey-Neck Steve was lying low, having heard the skinny that I was out and looking to open him up. I knew where he lived, but the code was clear on such matters: you never take a fight to where a man lives. Family homes are sacred, and if you attack someone in their home, it all becomes way too personal and non-combatants can be injured. If you want someone bad enough you will always find them in some pub or club, or just walking to the shops. I don't ever involve anyone's family in my fights, and I expect the same respect. If someone attacks you in your home, then all bets are off and you'd be justified in seriously hurting them.

I saw Alison from time to time, in the clubs, but I ignored her. Then one Saturday night at the Chick-a-Boom I was accosted by a drunken girl who used to hang around with Alison but had fallen out with her. She was dying to dish the dirt and tell me all about her indiscretions while I was locked up. I was yawning and watching an argument that was developing between one of the Road Rats MC and one of the Deptford Alley Cats, contemplating following the crowd out into the car park to watch them duke it out, when she said, 'I don't suppose she told you that she got off with Joe Kennedy, as well?'

I couldn't believe it! My best pal and my bird! They had mugged me off and were probably having a good laugh about it. I wondered how many other people knew about it. I felt the old familiar rage rising.

Joe was on the dance floor with a couple of girls. As I watched him, my face burned with humiliation and rage. I was going to kill him. I walked out into the middle of the dancefloor, knocking a couple of jivers flying. I tapped Joe on the shoulder, and when he turned around I hit him full in the face with a right hook. He went down but was up very quickly and into a boxing stance. He looked bewildered but ready to rumble. Barney, the bouncer, and his team had spotted the trouble and they got between us. 'Come on, lads. You know the score, take it outside.'

I headed for the car park, followed by a crowd of sightseers and a confused but angry Joe Kennedy. Joe was a good boxer; he had boxed in the Junior ABA southern finals at the Café Royal, losing on points. As we stripped off our leather jackets I felt the old buzz coming on me. People were crowding around our space in the car park, jostling for a good view. Joe was bare-chested and flexing his not inconsiderable muscles for the girls who were watching. I left my white T-shirt on.

Joe gave me a searching look.

'What are we rucking for?' he asked.

'Alison,' I replied, and I saw a look of enlightenment flick across his face.

'Do you want to box, or fight?' he asked.

'Fight,' I replied.

He nodded.

There was no referee. We just steamed into each other, throwing punches, headbutts and kicks. The fight was brutal and bloody. I broke his nose with a headbutt, and the crowd grew excited when they saw the blood flow. A few times we both ended up wrestling on the ground, before breaking apart and getting to our feet for a restart. After a while I could hear nothing except my own grunts of exertion and the blood singing in my ears, but I felt every blow from Joe's sledgehammer fists. In fighting terms, sixty seconds is a long time, because when you are on adrenaline overload you use energy and resources very quickly. Three minutes of continuously throwing and dodging blows can leave the fittest athlete gasping for breath, which is why professional boxers have a break between three-minute rounds. But in a fight situation every second seems like an hour. Afterwards Mick told me that we had fought for a quarter of an hour, and believe me, that's some feat.

In the end, me and Joe fought ourselves to a standstill, both of us covered in blood, sweat and snot and barely able to lift our arms to throw another punch. Barney the bouncer jumped between us and declared the fight a draw. And now that my rage had been spent and my pride upheld, I shook hands with Joe, and we staggered back into the club to have a drink together. We were still pals, but it was never the same after that. Because of a silly little tart who couldn't keep her legs closed when I was away, I had fallen out with my best pal. I vowed that if I ever went back inside again, I would immediately sack any bird I was with. It wasn't worth the trouble.

The morning after my ruck with Joe Kennedy, I was awakened at seven by my mother. She had a worried look on her face and urged me to get up and dressed as quickly as I could, as my father wanted to speak to me. I had only got to bed at 3 a.m., and I was in bits from the fight and dying with a hangover. I struggled out of bed and shuffled into the front room where my grim-faced parents sat.

My dad indicated a small wad of banknotes on the coffee table. 'That's all we've got at the moment,' he said. 'I'll get on the phone to your uncle Michael, in Dublin, and he'll put you up for a while. Until the heat dies down.'

I was confused. 'What? Dublin? What heat?'

My mother pulled a plastic bag out from behind her chair and tipped the contents on to the carpet. It was the jeans, socks and T-shirt I had been wearing the night before, which I had dumped in the laundry basket in the bathroom before falling into bed. They were absolutely smothered in dried blood. The white T-shirt looked red with small white patches, and there were even spatters of blood on my white socks. I looked at the clothes, then at their serious faces, and I started to laugh despite the pain I was in.

My dad shook his head. 'It's not fucking funny. No one loses that amount of blood and lives. If you've killed someone, and anyone saw it, the police'll be looking for you.'

I explained that the blood had come from Joe Kennedy's broken nose, and that when I had left him at 2 a.m. he was singing 'Be-Bop-a-Lula' at the top of his voice in the back of a mini-cab. They were still sceptical, but relieved. My mother taped up the bag of clothes and threw them down the dust chute anyway, and the old man went off to work. I went back to bed. I was touched that their first thought had been to get me out of the country.

At this time, Popeye was running a breakers yard on a bit of land off Balham High Road. He had a caravan on the site, and the gang used to meet there to drink cider, shoot the shit and plan our moves on other gangs. We had had a bit of trouble at the Chick-a-Boom club with a gang called the Crawley Cats, who were led by two boxing brothers named Seamus and Lenny. Most of their gang were members of Alan Minter's old boxing club in

Crawley, and they were awesome fist-fighters. I had glassed one of their gang, known as 'Snake', in a scuffle inside the Chick-a-Boom a couple of months earlier, and since then they had picked off a couple of members of the Wildkatz and dished out beatings. The Crawley Cats were in need of a lesson. We put the word out that we were going to take the Crawley, and that any gang who had a grievance with them was welcome to join in. We never knew they had upset so many people.

The Chick-a-Boom was heaving that Saturday night, but somehow the Crawley Cats had got wind of their impending demise, and had decided to give the festivities a miss. By ten o' clock most of the gang were steaming drunk and geared up to visit violence and mayhem on somebody. It didn't seem right to go to all this trouble for nothing. Small skirmishes broke out among the firms who had been allies at the start of the evening. I nipped out into the car park to watch Joe 'Psycho' Healey, one of the Battersea firm, take on a big rocker named 'Blue' in a straightener over a spilled drink.

No sooner had Joe Healey's little turnout finished than word came to us that Joe Kennedy was taking on one of the Norwood gang in a fist fight. The Norwood gang was a small but vicious gang who had their base in Stassi's Cafe in Brixton market. They were led by five brothers from Norwood, and they were all tasty tool-merchants. I pushed my way through the crowd in the car park in time to see a once again shirtless Joe Kennedy administering a terrible beating to the face and body of Tony from the Norwood gang. The crowd was loving it, baying for blood like Roman citizens at a circus. I caught sight of Alan and a couple more of the Norwood gang watching the fight in disappointment. It was a public humiliation for them, and one that would not be allowed to continue if they had anything to do with it. I saw Alan smash the pint mug he was holding on the kerb, leaving a handle and jagged shards of glass clutched in his fist. One of his henchmen, named Douggie, pulled off his bike-chain belt and wrapped it around his fist. They were going to put Joe Kennedy out of the game.

As well as my razor, I was also carrying a sawn-off pickaxe handle down my trousers. When I saw Alan and Douggie make their move through the crowd, I pulled out the pick-handle and moved to intercept them. Joe was still throwing punches at the now-drooping Tony, unaware that Alan was about to attack him from behind with the broken pint mug. I stepped out of the crowd and swung my weapon. Alan caught the full force of the blow upside his head and hit the ground without a sound. I had knocked him spark-out. I turned on Douggie and the other members of their gang, and suddenly it was a free-for-all. Joe realized what was happening and joined me as we took on five members of the Norwood gang.

Someone smashed a bottle across my head and blood was flowing freely down my face. I swung my pick-handle and hit Douggie across the chest. He fell backwards over the bonnet of a pristine Rover 3.5S, and as I swung at him again he rolled away and I left a large dent in the aluminium bonnet. Then I was hit in the knee, probably by a lead pipe, and I went down. The kicks came in hard and fast, and I was on the verge of unconsciousness when there was suddenly a space around me. Mick, Harry, Tommy Hogan and Dave C. had come to my rescue. I managed to get to my feet, and saw that the fight had come to an end. Alan was getting to his feet as well. The two gangs, bloodied but unbowed, faced each other across a few feet of car park. When the weapons had come out the spectators had moved well back for fear of being injured. We were all breathing heavily from adrenaline and exertion. It was one of those strange moments that sometimes comes in gang fights, when the violence has stopped but the atmosphere tells you that it can start back up again if someone says the wrong thing or makes a sudden move.

'You're fucking out of order,' said Alan, pointing a finger at me. I couldn't believe the brass neck of the geezer.

'How the fuck do you work that out?' I growled back. 'Joe was having a straight-go with your brother, and you wanna glass him from behind?'

Alan clutched the back of his head and winced in pain. 'I'm

talking about the car, you cunt. The fucking car! Look at it.'

He pointed at the dented Rover. Then I realized it was his car. He wasn't moaning about being smashed in the head with a pick handle, but about the damage to his motor! I couldn't fucking believe it.

'You're fucking paying for that,' he said, in a shrill voice.

There were shouts of 'fuck you', and 'take it out of this', from my side. We had now been joined by Joe Healey's boys, Popeye and the Kennington mob. The Norwood gang realized that they were now heavily outnumbered, so they made a muttering retreat. They piled into their cars and headed, in convoy, out of the car park. Alan pulled up next to me in his battered pride and joy and rolled his window down.

'Next time I see you, you're fucking dead,' he said.

'Yeah, go on, fuck off out of it, you mug,' I replied.

Eight months later, this moment would be back to haunt me.

The Rover wheel-spinned away and we all went back into the club for a drink.

We never did catch up with the Crawley Cats, which was very lucky for them. And the rest of the night was a haze of drink.

I was still living at home in my parents' flat, but I was only ever there for a few hours' sleep at night. I would roll in, invariably drunk, at all hours of the morning. Then, after a kip and a wash and change of clothes, I would be back out again. I was still working the snides with Popeye and a friend of mine called 'the German' because of his blond hair and doing the odd bit of burglary at night. The latest coup was burgling petrol stations. In those days there were not many petrol stations that stayed open for twenty-four hours a day. A lot of them kept the takings in a floor safe, which could be levered out of the floor using a putlog scaffold-pole. The safe could then be carried away and opened at our leisure. There was never more than a couple of hundred quid in them, but that kept us in beer and fags.

I've never really had a lot of luck with safes. I once spent an entire bank-holiday weekend nicking and opening a huge safe from a metalworks factory. We had been told by someone who worked there that it never contained less than £10,000. It took six of us to get the safe down three flights of stairs, then we had to break out of the factory, as we had come through a skylight, and then the bastard was too awkward and heavy to get up on to the back of the Bedford flatbed we had nicked especially for the job. We dropped the safe in the middle of the road and it left a dent like a moon crater. Eventually one of the mob pulled his own Rover saloon up and we managed to tip the safe into his boot. The back of the car was almost dragging along the road with the weight, and it absolutely ruined the suspension. Of course, we couldn't close the boot lid, so we had to drive to the flop with the safe sitting there in plain view.

Luckily we never got a pull from any nosy coppers, but we got some funny looks from other road-users. We got the safe back to some underground garages in Battersea and started to break into it. Twelve hours later we were still at it. The best way to crack a safe is from the back and is known as 'peeling'. First you cut through the outer skin with an angle-grinder and peel it back. Then you'll find another metal plate that has to be cut through, then steel-reinforced concrete that has to be broken up and ripped out, then the final metal skin.

Believe me, it is hard fucking graft. We eventually got into our big safe and found bundles of paperwork and a petty-cash box containing £150. We had sweated and strained for nearly two days and ruined a perfectly good car, all for £25 each. We could have earned double that by working on a building site for a couple of days. That put me off safes for good.

One afternoon I was in the Bedford pub, on Bedford Hill, which had become our local, playing pool with Popeye and the German, when we heard the sound of many sirens close by. We looked out of the window and saw several police cars and an ambulance flash by. Then some kid who used to hang around the market came into the pub and told us that Belfast Joe had just been shot. We rushed up to where he lived and found the roads all cordoned off and plenty of flashing blue lights. According to a witness we spoke to, Belfast Joe had been walking from the betting shop to his home when a car containing three men pulled alongside him and started blasting. One bullet creased his head, but he managed to get inside his house and the car screeched away.

It was some weeks before we heard the full story. It appears that, far from being an IRA gunman on the run, Belfast Joe was in fact one of the Shankhill Butchers, a Protestant paramilitary gang who specialized in kidnapping random Catholics off the streets and torturing them to death. We heard that Belfast Joe was given eleven life sentences for his part in the murders. The rumour was that it was actually members of the INLA who had tracked him down and tried to shoot him. Their bungled hit led to his identity being exposed and him being sent back to Ireland and jailed. A lot of people were glad to see the back of him, particularly the people who had been paying him protection money. We just shrugged. It would mean an end to the snide-game.

It was around this time that I started going out with Denise. She was celebrating her eighteenth birthday at the Chick-a-Boom club when I asked her to dance. I walked her home that night and we ended up kissing. It was never going to be a match made in heaven. I was a violent young thug from a council estate and had spent my formative years in the punishment blocks of the borstal system. I was unwilling to give up my wild and un-disciplined lifestyle. I liked stealing and fighting. And Denise came from a middle-class background. Her parents owned their detached house in Surrey, her father worked for British Aerospace, and Denise was starting a career in accounting, working at the Prudential in Croydon. And to top it all, her family were rabid loyalists from Portadown, a Protestant stronghold in the north of Ireland, and mine were uninterested Republicans from Dublin, in the south. You couldn't get much more opposite than that.

I didn't get on with Denise's family from the start, but a lot of that was my fault. My surly temperament and jailhouse manners did not endear me to normal people. Whenever I saw her parents I did no more than grunt a grudging 'hello'. I was way out of my depth in social situations that did not involve downing six pints of cider and throwing a few right-handers. I also sensed a bit of hostility when they found out their little girl was knocking about with a 'taig' (a disparaging name for an Irish Catholic, used by Protestants). But Denise was different from the slappers I had known up until then. She wasn't impressed by my macho posturing and constant violence. With a lot of girls, all I had to do was ask them to dance and I would be guaranteed a ride. After all, I was young, fairly good-looking and the leader of a gang of violent lunatics: what girl could resist that? But Denise did. For a longer time than I care to remember.

I moved out of my parents' flat, mainly because they were driving me mad to get 'a proper job'. My auntie Marie, my dad's sister, had moved back to Dublin and left her five-bedroom council house in Balham empty. Twelve of her kids had gone with her, but one of the boys, Ronnie, had stayed in London. He was living with his girlfriend Gaynor, who was expecting their first child, and the German took over the house in Carmina Road. Every day we would set out to steal or con enough money to get us by. It was a constant struggle, but I loved the freedom of it. If things got too desperate we would go up to the pond on Clapham Common and kill a duck. They were easy to catch, easy to kill and tasted great when cooked over a wood fire in the back garden.

The German had a good line in patter, which he used to great effect in the pubs and illegal drinkers, and a broad Dublin accent. One of our favourite haunts was an illegal drinking club around the back of a row of shops on Bedford Hill called Dublin Jimmy's. The club was open whenever the pubs were shut, and to gain entry you had to walk along a rubbish-strewn alley, down a flight of concrete steps and give a signal-ring on a concealed doorbell. Inside, behind a reinforced-steel door, was a long, smoky, low-ceilinged hall with a makeshift bar, a tatty jukebox and a bunch of mismatched tables and chairs. Dublin Jimmy himself was a slim dandy of a man, always jovial, except when he was swinging the baseball bat, which he kept within easy reach, at trouble-makers. The clientele was made up of some of the most villainous characters you could ever hope to see outside of a police mug-shot book.

Dublin Jimmy's was a watering-hole for blaggers, hoisters, draggers, conmen and thieves. The beer was sold by the can at £1 a time, there being no till for legal reasons, and spirits were sold by the bottle. The women who went to Dublin Jimmy's were, not to put too fine a point on it, slappers and off-duty prostitutes. Every now and again a fight would break out, usually in the early hours of the morning, and Jimmy would be swinging his bat like Babe Ruth. The club was like an ante-chamber of alcoholics' hell, but we loved it.

Dublin Jimmy's also attracted straight-goers, usually sub-contractors from the building trade, who were, on the whole, country Irish who loved a drink any time they could get it. The German would get in amongst these men and dazzle their already drunken brains with his false promises of stolen goods at bargain prices. It was a joy to watch him at work, weaving his tales as though they were delicate threads of fine gold: a joke here, a serious look there, a ponderous scratch of the head, he layered the threads until they were thick enough to slip around the target's neck. And then he would reel him in.

The con-story normally involved a hijacked van loaded with top-of-the-range power-tools, and the German was the go-between who was looking for a buyer. Of course there were no power-tools, but the German painted such a vivid word-picture of them that even I, who was in on the con, could almost smell the fresh coating of oil that adorned their non-existent parts. Even if the buyer were cagey, we would still end up with free drinks all night while the deal was being discussed. And sometimes they would be stupid enough or drunk enough to part with a deposit. The German hadn't just kissed the Blarney Stone, he had swallowed it whole.

We still frequented the Bedford pub, hanging around in the back bar on most days and selling stolen goods to the girls and their pimps. We got to know most of the girls, and I often thought I wouldn't pay a tenner for the whole lot of them, let alone a

quick hand-job on the common. Maybe some of the prostitutes who work the hotel trade in Mayfair are clean and good-
looking, but the girls on Bedford Hill were, as a group, filthy
and ugly.

Fights were frequent in the Bedford, and once or twice firearms
were brandished. We had our spot by the fire-exit picked out so
we could make a quick getaway if things got too hot. One night
a couple of pimps had a disagreement over one of the girls, and
a sawn-off shotgun was fired into the ceiling. I was in the toilet
when I heard the bang, and by the time I'd cracked the door
open to get a peek at what was going on, the whole pub had
emptied. All that moved was a cloud of gunsmoke and plaster-
dust floating in the air.

The pimps who used the Bedford were almost caricatures.
Predominantly black, they dressed and spoke like Huggy Bear,
who was probably their idol. They hated us, not only because
we ripped the piss out of them at every opportunity but also
because our presence on Bedford Hill was bad for 'bidness'. A
lot of the girls' clientele were straight-goers from outside the area
and could easily be robbed and intimidated by us. One night my
then girlfriend came into the pub shaken and crying because she
had been followed by a kerb-crawler who had made lewd sugges-
tions to her. The trouble with hanging out in a red-light district
is that the punters seem to think every female on the street is
fair game. She gave us a description of his car, and me and a
couple of the boys went looking for him. He wasn't very hard
to find, still cruising the Hill trying to get his rocks off. I stepped
out into the road in front of him so he had to brake to avoid
running me down. He was dragged from his car, given a sound
kicking and robbed. I used to wear Commando boots with steel
toecaps, and I used them to kick out every light on his car and
leave some choice dents in the bodywork.

There was always some sort of excitement to be found on
Bedford Hill, twenty-four hours a day if we wanted it, some piece
of skulduggery to get up to in order to earn a pound-note, or
someone looking for a tear-up. The Balham Bootboys, a gang of

punks and skinheads led by a huge, nappy-wearing punk-rocker named Junior, lived on the council estate at the top of the hill, and if we got bored we would mount a raid on the estate or the games arcade out on Balham High Road which was the Bootboys HQ. The Bootboys were always game for a rumble, and it was they who started the vogue for carrying scissors in order to cut the quiff from any rockers they managed to corner. To lose your quiff was a major embarrassment, a bit like Chuck Connors having his cavalry sabre broken at the start of that old TV series *Branded*. To us our hair was our identity as much as our colours were, and losing it was like being emasculated. Needless to say, once the Bootboys started taking scalps, the gloves were off and we would beat them unmercifully whenever we caught them.

With gang violence escalating and me having to scrape a living from the streets by any means necessary, it wasn't long before I ended up back inside again. By now it was becoming an occupational hazard.

13. The Battle of Morden

Wormwood Scrubs was my first taste of adult prison. It wasn't that much different from juvenile jail, except more of the cons had facial hair. I was back inside on remand for a violent episode that involved a bit of gang-fighting, but the evidence against me was pretty weak and I was expecting to have the charges dropped at my next appearance at the magistrates court. In the meantime I made myself as comfortable as I could in the Scrubs and did my best to explore my surroundings at every opportunity.

I put my name down for church services on Sunday morning. It was a chance to get out of the cell, in which I spent twenty-three hours of every day, and see a few new faces. The church inside the Scrubs is a magnificent building. Designed by Edmund du Cane, and built between 1885 and 1889, the chapel of St Francis of Assisi is the largest chapel in any English prison, with a seven-bay aisled nave and some top-notch stained-glass windows. Of course, it's only for use by Church of England worshippers. The Catholic flock worship in a one-storey prefabricated hut next door to the library. I dread to think where they put the Jews and Muslims – probably in a broom-cupboard on D-wing.

One of the attractions of church services was getting to view the lifers. We were allowed no direct contact with them, and when we got to the church they were already there, in six or seven rows on the opposite side. Lifers were a fascinating group to us. We knew that, by definition, the majority of them were murderers, and we would try to spot any of the 'famous' ones who had been in the newspapers. At that time, Reggie Kray, Donald 'the Black Panther' Neilson (who was convicted of murdering heiress Leslie Whittle and a couple of sub-postmasters) and 'Mad' Frankie Fraser were all in the Scrubs, though of the three I only remember seeing Neilson.

The lifers looked tough and a bit scary. They mostly wore tailored blue-stripe prison shirts with grandad collars and long grey prison overcoats, and they studiously ignored the staring faces and open mouths on my side of the church. I shuddered to think that one day I might end up on the other side. It could easily happen. Seeing as how I was in God's house anyway, I said a little prayer that it wouldn't happen to me. The lifers scared me, and though I might act tough on the outside and pretend that if my time came to get the big L, I would shrug it off, privately, I was shit-scared of going to prison for life.

A life sentence means you are completely at the mercy of the prison system. Although it is the Home Secretary who makes the final decision on your release, on the recommendation of the parole board, everything depends on the reports that the screws write about you. I have met lifers who have had their release delayed by decades simply because they do not get on with the screws. It is the work of a moment to mark a lifer's file 'Anti-authority, still dangerous'. The parole board tends to set great store by what is written by prison officers who have direct contact with the prisoner.

Contrary to what you might see in films, prisoners in British prisons do not go in front of the parole board to plead their case in person. All decisions are made behind closed doors and are based on written reports. A life sentence for someone with a bad prison record or who refuses to cooperate with the system can mean decades behind bars. I have seen the evidence of this with my own eyes. In Albany prison I met a lifer who had spent twenty-seven years in the system despite the trial judge recommending a tariff of nine years, because he refused to converse with anybody in authority. If he required anything, he would simply jot it down and hand the note to a screw. The amount of time this man spent in jail is by no means unique. There are prisoners in our top-security prisons who last tasted freedom when Harold Wilson was Prime Minister. Yet there are still people who seek to perpetuate the myth that sentencing in this country is 'soft' and that our prisons operate a 'revolving-door' policy.

When the Great Train Robbers received their thirty-year

sentences in 1964, society seemed shocked at the barbarity of such punishment. Nowadays thirty-year sentences for robbers or drug barons are commonplace, and they are rarely even thought newsworthy. For robbing less than £2,000 from a building society, using a cucumber in a paper bag as a 'gun', you can reasonably expect to receive a sentence of ten years and upwards on a guilty plea. Far from being the lenient old duffers that you read about in the tabloid press, British judges of the twenty-first century are just as harsh and punishment-oriented as their eighteenth-century predecessors who sentenced children to be flogged for stealing a loaf of bread. I can only assume that someone must have a vested interest in convincing the public that criminals are getting off lightly. You would soon spot the lie if you were to walk around the landings of the average prison and tot up the number of years on every door-card.

But now back to my story. After a couple of weeks on remand in Wormwood Scrubs, I was informed that due to lack of evidence, the case against me was to be dropped. To say I was pleased would be an understatement. Seeing the lifers in the chapel had given me a there-but-for-the-grace-of-God feeling.

A couple of days after my release, I bought a diamond engagement ring that had come from a parcel stolen from a courier at Hatton Garden, and Denise and I got engaged. We had an engagement party in the house in Carmina Road, but none of Denise's family came. Chris H. contributed two sacks of fresh prawns from the fish stall where he worked, and Johnny Williams gave us twenty flagons of cider, which I assumed were stolen goods. We all got pissed and ate prawns, and it all ended up in a fight. But me and Denise were in love.

The gang was still going strong, despite a few losses in the ranks. Harry got sentenced to a fresh whack of borstal and ended up back in Dover. Pete got nicked in a stolen car with a ted named Johnny Virgo, and they stuck their hands up to various offences to lighten their sentences by showing co-operation. They were both given twenty-one months' YP. So much for pleading guilty. Also while I had been locked up, there had been a major affray involving rockabilly gangs from the Chick-a-Boom club and a mixed gang of skins and punks. The punk gang had lain in ambush at Morden tube station one Saturday night, and then attacked the club-goers as they got off the M1 bus on their way to catch the last tube back into London. Morden High Street became a war-zone, with various factions fighting hand-to-hand and with all description of weaponry. The M1 bus had several windows put through, shops were damaged and the ticket-collector's box inside the station was pushed down a flight of stairs, with the ticket-collector still in it. There were thirty-six arrests for various public-order offences and the carrying of offensive weapons. The local papers headlined it 'The Battle of Morden Station'. Most of the Balham Wildkatz were involved, and arrested.

I attended the court hearing, which had to be held at Wimbledon town hall because the magistrates court could not accommodate all the defendants, as a spectator, for a change. Of the thirty-six arrested, thirty-four of them were rockabillies who had been at the Chick-a-Boom, including three girls. Joe Kennedy was there, as was my brother, Mick, Gordon, Alan and Dennis Budd, Ahmet, Big Nose Eamon, Chinese Chris, Little Roy Clarke and some of the Battersea boys. The inside of the town hall was an amphitheatre, and the three magistrates sat on a raised stage in the middle, surrounded on three sides by the leather-jacketed defendants and their legal advisers. The smell of Brylcreem, Brut and chewing-gum was almost overpowering in the teak-panelled chamber.

Things got off to a bad start when Joe Kennedy realized that the microphones in front of each seat were on and working. He gave a short rendition of the Johnny Burnette classic 'Lonesome Train', before the clerk could reach him and unplug the mic. He got a round of applause from the fifty-or-so spectators who were attired in various garments of 1950s vintage. The stern-faced magistrate called for all the microphones to be turned off at the mains before he would proceed and told Joe that he was close to being jailed for contempt. There were several boos from the public gallery. Each defendant had to stand up, state his name and plead guilty or not guilty when the charge was read to him. This took most of the morning, and everyone pleaded guilty to the lesser charges of causing a public nuisance and obstruction. No one wanted to stick their hands up to affray or possession of offensive weapons, even though most of them had been caught bang to rights. Joe and Chinese Chris pleaded not guilty to heaving the ticket-collector's box down the station stairs.

After the pleading there was a break for lunch, which most of us spent drinking cider straight from the bottle and hassling the bewildered shoppers in Wimbledon town centre. With our greased hair, leather jackets, chains and steel-toed boots, we must have seemed like an invading army of barbarians to the sedate middle-class folk of Wimbledon. We went back to the town hall for the afternoon session in high spirits, and found that the forces of justice had worked out a deal in our absence. In an effort to get the case over as quickly as possible, the magistrates agreed to bind all the defendants over to keep the peace for twelve months. This was less a slap on the wrist, more a finger-wagging. All the defendants and their solicitors agreed, as long as the more serious charges were just 'left on file' and not proceeded with. That was how the Battle of Morden Station ended, in a whimper from the court. We now felt that we were immune from serious punishment. Our gang had walked on a whole range of public-order offences. It was as though we had a licence to do what we wanted.

At this stage of my life I was no longer involved in gun crime. I still thought about armed robbery and the buzz I had got from it, but life in the gang was feeding my adrenaline addiction quite nicely. There was always something happening, every day was a new adventure and I was earning enough money from petty crime to get by fairly comfortably.

With my propensity to be at the forefront of anything that was going on, it wasn't long before I found myself back in prison again. One Saturday night I was one of the last stragglers out of the Chick-a-Boom club, along with Gordon and one of the Mitcham Hepcats, named Roy Sears. Gordon and Roy were chatting up a couple of Dutch teddy-girls who were on holiday in England, and I was lamenting the fact that Denise had not been allowed out that night. She was still living in her parents' home, and under their rules. Since she had been engaged to me I had kept her out all night a couple of times, causing her to miss work the next day. Her parents naturally cited me as a bad influence and were doing their utmost to keep us apart.

I was just lighting a cigarette when I became aware of raised voices. I came around the corner from the car park and saw Gordon, Roy and the two Dutch girls surrounded by a mob of smoothies. I recognized some of them as the boot-boys from the front bar of the St Helier Arms.

'We run this fucking pub, right?' I heard one of them say. Gordon and Roy were backed up against the wall of the pub and outnumbered by three to one. I pulled out my razor and jumped in.

'You fucking want some, you mugs?' I growled. The boot-boys backed off a bit when they saw my blade glinting in the street light. They didn't seem so eager now there was a chance they might get cut. One of them, a big fella with mad, curly hair like Harpo Marx, seemed drunker and braver than the rest.

'I'll fucking have some, Ted, if you wanna put that razor down and fight like a man.' His mates egged him on.

There was no way I could ignore a challenge like that. I handed my razor to Roy. 'Keep it open,' I said. 'And if any of these other cunts try jumping in, cut 'em.'

Roy was more than happy to oblige.

Harpo was faster than I expected, and his first punch broke my nose. I could taste the hot blood in the back of my throat and the pain was excruciating. I desperately dodged his next couple of swings and managed to get him in a clinch and hang on. We struggled around in a strange dance for a minute before toppling over. I was on top of him when we hit the ground and the breath was knocked out of him. I managed to get up on his chest and started launching wild punches to his unprotected face. I was just getting into the swing of it when a boot came crashing into his temple and I was dragged aside. It took me a few moments to see what had happened. Five or six rockabillies had come out of the club and, seeing the fight in progress, had decided to steam in. They were all around Harpo, kicking the life out of him. I got to my feet, covered in my own blood, and tried to stop them. They thought they were helping me out. They didn't really know me to talk to, but they were rockabillies and so was I, and that was enough for them to get involved. It was an embarrassment for me; despite my broken nose, I had had the situation under control. A couple of them turned on Harpo's pals, and within seconds there was a gang fight going on.

Barney and his team of bouncers heard the commotion and came running from the club to break it up. As I was the only one not fighting, they ignored me and grabbed hold of those who were. Things calmed down a bit. Harpo looked in a bad way; he was covered in blood and seemed to be unconscious. Barney shouted into the pub for someone to phone an ambulance. I took my razor back off Roy, folded it and put it in my pocket. A few of the fighters slipped off into the night, not wanting to be further involved. I was just about to leave myself, when Harpo gave a loud groan and sat up. His face was a mess and his hair was matted with blood, but other than that he seemed pretty lively for a geezer who'd just taken a good kicking. He spotted me.

'You fucking wanker!' he said. 'Had to have your mates to back you up!'

I was incensed at this. I hadn't asked anyone to help me, I'd had my nose broken, and now here was this prick calling me a coward. I felt the rage come bursting up inside me. I took a couple of running steps and kicked him straight in the face with as much force as I could muster. I was wearing Commando boots with steel toecaps, and I felt the bones of his face cave in as my boot made contact. There was a meaty thwack and his head bounced off the road, but he was out before that and can't have felt it.

I stood looking down at his ruined face. 'Fuck you!' I screamed at him. But of course he couldn't hear me. There was shocked silence from everyone present. The Dutch girls cuddled each other in fear, and Gordon threw up over his own shoes. My rage died out as quickly as it flared, and I realized I was in trouble. 'See ya later,' I said to no one in particular, and jogged off down Middleton Road.

I heard the sirens as I cut across the green and headed for Green Wrythe Lane. I knew I had to get out of the area as fast as I could, but by this time of night all the buses and trains had stopped running, and I could hardly turn up at a cab office covered in blood without attracting attention. I decided to walk the six miles back to Balham. I had reached the borders of Mitcham and Morden before I was stopped by a patrol car. They searched me and found my razor. I was taken to Sutton police station to be questioned 'about a serious case of assault'.

It turned out that Harpo was a lot tougher than I gave him credit for. He had a broken nose, a broken cheek-bone and had lost two front teeth but refused to press charges and even told the police that he had 'fallen over while drunk'. I saw him outside the St Helier Arms about a year later; his face was a real mess even though it had healed. We never spoke, but nodded to each other with that strange respect that former combatants have for each other. But in the meantime I was once again remanded in custody for possession of an offensive weapon and suspicion of GBH. This time I was sent to HMP Lewes.

14. Payback

HMP Lewes, just outside Brighton, is one of the Victorian 'hanging jails', local prisons where executions were carried out when the death penalty was still in force. C-wing was the young prisoners' remand wing, and it was much the same as Wormwood Scrubs YP wing, in that there was an eclectic mix of prisoners, from car thieves to murderers. I was now a veteran of prison life, though I was still under the age of twenty-one, and I settled into the routine of C-wing with no trouble. By pure coincidence I ended up being banged up in the same cell as one of the chaps from Rochester borstal, Steve Rorison.

Steve, from Wandsworth, was on remand for GBH, and had already been in Lewes for four months when I got there. He quickly filled me in on the wing routine, which involved at least twenty-two hours of the day locked in our cell. We passed the time by playing cards and bullshitting about how well we had been doing outside before we had the misfortune to be nicked. Steve's girlfriend was pregnant and due to have the baby very soon, and he seemed pretty blasé about it. Steve was the kind of guy who didn't really get worked up about much; he seemed to take everything in his stride. Even when he was punching the jaw off someone he looked as though his heart wasn't really in it. One night we were fast asleep when a banging on the cell door woke us up. It was a night-patrol screw to tell Steve that his girlfriend had just had the baby, and it was a girl. At this joyous news Steve yawned, scratched his head and said, 'And you're waking me up in the middle of the night to tell me that? What are you, some kind of fucking town-crier?'

The screw walked away with the right hump, and Steve was snoring again in a couple of minutes.

Denise visited, and told me she was pregnant. She hadn't told her parents yet, and I knew that was going to be no party. But I made up my mind straight away to stick by her. There was never any question in my mind that we could be together and make it work. I loved Denise more than I had ever loved anyone.

The rest of my time in Lewes was spent in the block, so I had plenty of thinking time. I realized how lucky I was that I was neither dead nor serving life imprisonment with the sort of life I had been leading. I had nothing but the clothes I stood up in, a reputation as a 'bad bastard' and a few nasty scars. Maybe it was time for a change. After all, I was about to become a daddy; I had responsibilities now.

Just before Christmas 1980 I appeared at Wallington magistrates court and pleaded guilty to possessing an offensive weapon and being drunk and disorderly. I was fined £20 and put on probation for a year. Denise was waiting outside the court for me. She had told her parents about the baby, and they had reacted badly. They told her to get an abortion or leave their home. I couldn't believe that any parent would really throw their daughter out on the streets, but they were serious. They gave her a week to decide.

My parents offered to put us up in their flat, but there wasn't that much room to begin with, and we wanted a place of our own. I sought advice from my probation officer, and she gave us a couple of addresses to try. We turned up at Lambeth housing offices and declared ourselves homeless. With me fresh out of prison and Denise pregnant, they offered us a room in a halfway-house overlooking Clapham Common. We took it. The rent was £6 a week, which was about triple what the room was worth. It was so small I had to go outside to change my mind, but it had the basics, a double bed and a sink. We moved in.

Denise was still working, so I set about finding myself a job. I got a couple of days, cash in hand, on a building site, and bought an old black-and-white television, which I carried on my shoulder from Balham to Clapham Common Northside. I tried to settle into domestic life, but there was just something inside me that craved action and excitement, so I started hanging around Balham

while Denise was at work. I was picking up the odd few quid from illegal sources, cons and thefts and the occasional burglary. I joined some of the Battersea gang in their car-stripping ring, which was fairly hard work but regular money.

The Battersea boys, Tommy, Dave C. and George, had a buyer who would take almost anything but specialized in spare parts. He owned a breakers yard, so he would sell us a cheap runner with no MOT or tax, and we would drive around in it looking for things to nick and bring back to sell to him. It was almost like a regular job. We would meet at a café on the Wandsworth road every morning and plan which areas we were going to hit that day and what we were looking to nick. Both Tommy and Dave C. were brilliant car thieves, and it was a pleasure to watch them at work. If we were nicking car stereos, which the buyer would give us up to £25 a piece for, we would pull up in a place where there were plenty of likely-looking motors, like a station car park or even a quiet residential street. Me and George would leave Tommy and Dave C. in our motor while we took a casual walkaround, scoping the targets. We were looking for top-of-the-range systems, mainly Blaupunkts, which the makers assure the buyer cannot be removed without a set of special Blaupunkt keys. Tommy could knock up a set of Blaupunkt keys in three minutes, using wire-cutters and an ordinary metal coathanger. We would also check for alarm stickers and any other valuables lying inside the cars. After our recce, we would come back and sit in our car and pass the info to Tommy and Dave C. They would then get out and go to work.

Sometimes the boys would use 'twirls', a set of double-edged FS keys, to get into the cars, but Tommy could open almost any car with a medium-sized pair of household scissors. The trick was to make as little noise and mess as possible so we could do half a dozen cars on the same plot without attracting attention. Sometimes the boys would be defeated by the locks on certain top-of-the-range models, then they would resort to a counterpunch through a quarter-light window. Once inside the car, it would take them seconds to slot in the home-made key and

disconnect the stereo. They would walk back to our car and hand the stereo in to me and George, and we would bag it up while the boys moved on to the next target. They always left the alarmed cars till last.

An alarm is no deterrent to a serious thief, it's just a bit of a nuisance. Tommy and Dave C. would simply ignore the burst of alarm noise and quickly lock themselves into the car, shutting it off. Then they would get the stereo and let themselves out again, locking the car behind them and shutting the alarm off again.

Sometimes we would go 'lifting' for mag-wheels. This was a bit more dangerous and involved heavy manual labour. We would cruise around in our old banger until we spotted a car parked up with expensive wheels. This could be anywhere, even parked on a high street or outside someone's house. The secret was to move as swiftly as possible. We would approach the target car, four-handed and each with a wheel-brace, and in broad daylight we would undo the wheel-nuts as quickly as possible. Then three of us would bodily lift the car, while Tommy pulled the wheels off. The last wheel was always the hardest because we would have to lift almost the whole weight of the car. Then we would load the stolen wheels into our car and drive off leaving the target car sitting on its rims. To pull this off we had to be faster than a set of Formula One pit mechanics and, because of the effort and luck involved, we could only do it a maximum of twice a day. We usually got £150 for a good set of wheels, but we only went after wheels when we were ready to trade our own car in, as it would be too hot to use after a wheel job. Too many people would have taken our registration number.

After a wheel job our car would go on top of a pile in the buyer's breakers yard, and we would hit the streets in a new banger. Sometimes we would steal a whole car, and we had various underground garages on council estates where we could strip them in comfort. We would take the doors, boot, bonnet, wheels, battery, lights and interior. We could strip a top-of-the-range Ford Granada in less than an hour. A four-door would stand us a couple of hundred quid in spares. I soon learned to

drive, in other people's cars. Sometimes we would steal three or four cars from a car park and then drive them down the side road where the breakers yard was situated, straight past the buyer, who would note down which particular parts he wanted stripped from each car. One of us would then double back in our straight car to pick up the list. He, the buyer, was always after Rolls-Royce parts and had a standing offer of £4,000 if we could steal and strip a Roller for him. But they were hard to find, and even harder to nick.

One day we nicked a Porsche Carrera three-litre from some underground garages in the West End. Our buyer offered us £200 to strip it, but we thought we could get more. Plus, it was great for posing in. We took turns in driving it around the estate for a couple of days, impressing the birds and racing other stolen cars. Then we tucked it up in our lock-up in Battersea and set about trying to find a buyer. We finally got put in touch with a heavy firm from Kent who specialized in stolen performance cars. This firm were typical Bermondsey-gangsters-made-good-and-moved-to-the-sticks, all leather coats, gold ID bracelets and talking out of the side of their mouths. A couple of them came up to Battersea to look the Porsche over. They did a bit of humming and hawing but finally offered us £1,200 in cash, on the condition that we deliver it to a pub car park in Sidcup. We agreed. It was decided that me and Harry, fresh out of borstal and raring to go, would follow them down to Sidcup. Harry drove, and I sat in the passenger seat keeping an eye on the sky-blue Rolls-Royce the Kent firm had turned up in.

We took a big risk, two scruffy rockabillies driving a £30,000 Porsche through rush-hour traffic, but we reached our destination without incident. We parked the Porsche up and followed the buyers into the pub to collect our readies. The pub was packed and our buyers seemed to know everyone. Me and Harry looked very out of place in the midst of so many sheepskin coats and gold chains. We met up with the two main men at the bar and accepted a drink. After about five minutes of chit-chat, we finished our drinks and wanted to be heading back to Battersea, where Tommy and Dave C. were waiting for their share of the money. We were going to get a cab back. I politely requested our money, and suddenly the Kent firm started getting a bit lemon.

'Hold your horses, son,' said the leader. 'There's no rush. Have another drink.'

I didn't like being patronized by this flash monkey, just because he had a few pals around him. We had done our part of the bargain, now I just wanted the money and to get away from the bad atmosphere that was developing. 'No thanks,' I said, reasonably. 'Give us our dosh and we'll be off.'

The leader looked around at his mates, with a big grin on his face. 'Suppose I just tell you to fuck off, and save meself 1,200 sovs?'

I wasn't having this. I had been through too much in my life to allow myself to be mugged off by this prick. I pulled my hand out of my pocket and flicked open my razor in one swift, practised movement. I heard Harry's flick-knife click open beside me. 'In that case, you've got a fucking fight on your hands,' I said.

At the appearance of our blades, the crowd went quiet and moved back from the bar. We were heavily outnumbered, and if they pressed the issue we were sure to get a bad kicking, weapons or not, but I would make sure to leave my mark on a couple of them. I knew Harry was game and had my back. I never took my eyes off the leader. Fair play to him, he didn't look in the least ruffled. He smiled and spread his hands out in front of him in a placatory gesture.

'All right, son. I was only pulling your plonker. There's no need for all that. Here you are.' He reached into his breast pocket and pulled out a wad of notes. 'I've got your spondulicks. Twelve hundred, weren't it?'

I nodded, still with the razor in my hand. There was no way I was going to relax until I had the money in my pocket and I was on my way back to London. He counted the crisp new £50 notes out on to the bar. I took them and started to back to the door, preceded by Harry.

The buyer smiled even wider and nodded in my direction. 'If you get anything else, give me a bell,' he said, then turned back to the bar and ordered a brandy. Everyone else in his group turned away and ignored us. I was never so glad to get out of a boozer in my life.

Harry wanted to put the windows through on the Roller, but I stopped him. We were a long way from home, with no transport to hand. It jarred me that the Kent firm thought they could try to rip us off, but it happens a lot in the criminal world and we could hardly go and complain to the police. The Kray twins built their reputation on such rip-offs. They didn't have the bottle to shoplift a Mars Bar, but they weren't shy about bullying the people who did. One of the reasons why so many people involved in the drug trade carry shooters is because the rip-off rate is so high. If you operate outside the protection of the law, then you have to provide your own protection. Once more my thoughts turned towards investing in a gun of my own, just as a bit of insurance.

In the 1980s you could pick up a decent handgun and ammunition in London for as little as £100. Some were stolen on burglaries of houses or gun-shops, some were smuggled into the country among parcels of drugs or by squaddies coming back from the Falklands War who had lifted them from Argentinian soldiers as souvenirs. Shotguns were going for as little as £25 and the price of a junior-hacksaw. A pal of mine, who I'll call 'Jimmy', had access to a parcel of brand-new Smith & Wesson pump-action shotguns and hundreds of rounds of ammunition for them. The story was that the guns had originally been stolen from a police armoury in California and were on their way to Northern Ireland for 'the Boys' when someone intercepted them and brought them to London and Manchester for sale. I don't know how true that was, but most underworld rumours contain at least some element of truth.

So Jimmy had thirty pump-actions for sale at £200 a piece, and the word was soon out on the streets. Jimmy would be propping up the bar in a well-known 'villains' pub' every Friday morning waiting for business. If you wanted to make a purchase and you had the right credentials, such as a good reputation of criminal staunchness or an intro from someone of that pedigree, you could approach Jimmy and state your needs. Say you wanted two 'items' with fifty rounds of 'food' for each, you would leave the cash behind the cistern in the pub toilet and pick up the key to a lock-up which Jimmy would leave in an ashtray on the bar. Outside the pub, you'd be approached by one of Jimmy's runners, who would give you directions to the lock-up and then walk away. In the meantime Jimmy would have been on the blower to another of his runners, stating how many items and where. The buyer would get to the lock-up, usually a shed or garage on one of the estates, and find his parcel bagged and waiting. The key would be left in the now empty lock-up, and that was it, deal done.

It might all seem a bit cloak and dagger, but each move was designed to distance all the participants of this criminal ballet from the actual crime of selling illegal firearms. If undercover police tried a sting on the operation, they would have a hard job convincing a jury that anyone was guilty of anything. The only people who knew in advance which lock-up was to be used were Jimmy and his most-trusted runner, who delivered the directions to the buyer. Even the fella who delivered the guns to the lock-up didn't know where he was going until Jimmy phoned him. Anyway, there were never any comebacks on the deals and Jimmy sold out in three weeks. I half-fancied one of the new pump-actions, but they were too expensive and impractical unless you were using them to guard drug shipments or going on a robbery. I went for something smaller and cheaper.

I ended up paying £90 for a Smith & Wesson Model Ten revolver. It was a five-shot model and just the right weight and size to carry comfortably in my waistband. Once I had the gun in my hand, the old familiar buzz began eating at me. I had avoided going back to armed robbery because I knew that with my previous I would be looking at a serious lump of bird if I ever got convicted again. But having the gun fit snugly in my fist was like letting a recovered heroin addict play with a syringe full of prime skag. It was always there, in a corner of my mind, a little voice that whispered enticingly, 'Just one blag, you won't get caught for just one, and anyway, it's not as if you couldn't use the money, just have a look at a few banks, as a theoretical exercise, looking won't hurt, it's not against the law to just check out the security arrangements, is it?' It was like having a cartoon devil sitting on my shoulder.

I was still living with Denise, in our version of domestic bliss. It was the honeymoon period of our relationship, and with us it lasted longer than most couples we knew. Denise wanted to keep on working as long as her pregnancy would allow, so every morning she would go off to the office, leaving me to a day of ducking and diving. She thought I was doing casual labour while keeping my eye out for a permanent job. We had to keep living in the room at Clapham Common in order to be eligible for a council flat, but despite the cramped conditions we did all right.

With a baby on the way, I started to move away from gang activities. Petty gang-fights and drunken violence were no longer my top priority; I was more interested in earning a few quid. But I still dropped into the rockabilly clubs now and then. The scene was starting to die out; a lot of the clubs were closing down because of the violence and because people were too afraid to go for a night out. It was the likes of me and the Balham Wildkatz who had ruined everything. But there were still some hard-core gangs hanging on till the bitter end. The Chick-a-Boom was still going, and one Saturday night I got suited and booted and decided to drop in.

I wasn't flying gang-colours, and it was one of those rare occasions that I wasn't even carrying a weapon. I just wanted a night out with no trouble, but things were about to catch up with me. Barney, the bouncer, seemed surprised to see me, as I had not been there for a while. He warned me that the Norwood gang had been looking for me and they had made it clear that they weren't looking to ask me to dance. I shrugged it off and, to be honest, at this stage I was arrogant enough to believe in my own reputation. I was Razor Smith, veteran of countless gang-fights. Why should I worry about a bunch of mugs who had already been bested?

Inside the club I saw a few familiar faces, but not many of the Wildkatz. Everyone seemed to want to tell me how the Norwood gang were looking for me. It went in one ear and out the other. There was always someone 'looking' for someone else on the scene, and I wasn't fucking hiding. About 10.30 a buzz went around the club that the gang were here. Apparently they had drifted into the club one and two at a time and were now grouped, ten-handed, up at the bar. I went to get a drink and have a look for myself. Sure enough, there was Alan, surrounded by his brothers and the rest of his gang, including their latest recruit, a mixed-race bloke named Gary G. Gary G. was well known on the scene as a proper flash monkey; he once had loads of badges made up with his own face on them and handed them out to girls to wear. He was reputed to be some sort of karate expert, but though I had seen him fight a couple of straighteners, I never noticed any karate moves. He could have a decent punch-up though. But I wasn't really worried about Gary, because we had always been pretty friendly.

I got plenty of hard looks from the gang while I was ordering my drink, but no one said anything so I went back to my table by the dance floor, where I was sitting with Roy Sears, Mitch and Snapper of the Mitcham Rebels. Within minutes Gary G. was over at my table with a big smile on his face. We shook hands.

'So,' I said. 'You're with them now?'

Gary shrugged. 'They're all right,' he said. 'But they've got a bit of agg' with you, you know?'

I nodded. 'Yeah, I know. So what's the story?'

Gary looked shifty. 'I've asked them to leave it out for tonight.'

It was my turn to shrug. I had a reputation to uphold and I'd be fucked if I was going to ask for any favours from these mugs. 'If any one of them wants a fucking straightener, I'll be glad to step outside. Tell 'em that.'

I fancied my chances against any of them in a fair fight. And even if I got my head punched in, it was no drama, just as long as I was game. Gary went back to the bar to relay my message and I saw them in a huddle.

Mitch offered me his own cut-throat razor. 'Don't trust these cunts,' he warned. 'They're bound to be well tooled up.'

I refused his offer. I still didn't realize exactly how much trouble I was in. Gary never came back, so I assumed that they were leaving it for tonight. I carried on drinking. About eleven o'clock Barney came over and told me that Popeye was outside and wanted to talk to me. At that time Popeye was in the middle of a long-running feud with Joe Kennedy. He had taken pot-shots at Joe with a sawn-off shotgun when a silly argument had blown up out of all proportion. Joe had been in hiding for a while, but there was no doubt that he would make a comeback at some stage. Anyway, Popeye had a habit of turning up at pubs and clubs and calling people out to find out if Joe was inside. Once he had found out that Joe was in Charlie Chaplin's in Elephant and Castle, but by the time he had driven home and got his shotgun Joe was long gone.

I went outside to talk to Popeye and found him sitting in his car just inside the car park, with his lights off. I was leaning down at the passenger window to say hello when I heard the door of the club open behind me. I heard someone say, 'Hi, Razor,' so I turned around to be confronted by five of the Norwood gang, including Alan and Gary G. Before I could make a move, I was hit in the face with a cosh. I don't remember much about the beating, but it was definitely a good one. One of them had a camper's axe and he scalped me with it. I was down on the ground getting the shit beaten out of me. I think they wanted to kill me, as most of their blows were aimed at my head. I tried curling into a ball, but they just carried on beating and kicking me.

I lost consciousness and Popeye told me later that when they got too tired to beat me any more, two of them picked me up, opened the back door of Popeye's car and threw me in. 'Take him to the hospital or a morgue, whichever one he needs,' were Alan's parting words. While I was being beaten, one of the gang had been holding a dagger up to Popeye's throat, daring him to get out of the car. I didn't blame Popeye for staying put, but I couldn't help feeling a bit of disappointment at him. I'm sure if our roles were reversed I would have tried to help.

I came to in the back of Popeye's motor on the way to St Helier Hospital. I didn't really feel much pain, but the amount of blood on me was horrendous. I went to put my hand up to my face and that's when I realized my wrist was fractured; it was hanging at a funny angle. I told Popeye to take me home to Denise, and after some argument he agreed. I had had beatings before and the lack of pain I was feeling made me believe that this time was not much different. I was a bit worried about my wrist, but there was a chance it was just dislocated. Popeye helped me up the stairs, and when Denise opened the door and saw me, she almost fainted. I sat on the bed and leant back, my head resting on the wall.

Denise begged Popeye to go and phone an ambulance, but I wasn't having it. I told her I would be OK after a night's sleep. I went to stand up and there was a ripping sound as I lifted my head. Where I had rested my head against the wall, the blood had become sticky and congealed, and as I pulled away, I left a patch of my scalp, complete with hair, stuck to the wall. I remember staring at it and thinking, Shit! That's going to leave a bald patch! Denise got a bowl of hot water and some disinfectant and began to bathe my head. By the time she had got the worst of the blood off, she was in tears and kept saying, 'It's bad, it's really bad.'

Popeye wanted to go home and get his shotgun and drive back to the club and shoot everyone. I told him to leave it, I would see him tomorrow. He left. Denise finished cleaning me up and told me that I was definitely going to the hospital in the morning. Maybe it was the amount of alcohol I had drunk, but I wasn't feeling too bad. Within minutes of getting into bed I was asleep.

The next morning I woke up to a world of pain and found

my head stuck to the pillow with congealed blood. Denise had to pour two pots of water over me to remove the pillow without starting the bleeding up again. I went straight to St James's hospital and got treated almost right away. My wrist was broken but, surprisingly, my skull wasn't fractured. I had two cracked ribs and various cuts and bruises on my face and body. The axe-wounds on my head took over sixty stitches, and I had a cast on my wrist. I told them I had been jumped by unknown assailants outside a pub.

Though I didn't like to admit it, that beating took something out of me. My paranoia got worse and I started to have dreams about dying. I would no longer leave the house without being tooled up, usually with both a gun and a knife. I planned to go after the Norwood gang as soon as my injuries were healed. And I got visits from other members of the Wildkatz who wanted to be in on it. For the first time I began to wonder where it was all going to end. It seemed as though I had been swimming in a sea of blood and pain for most of my life. I beat and cut people, who then came back and beat and cut me, and on it went in a vicious spiral. I had to put a stop to this. I was going to be a father soon, and I wanted to be there for my child.

15. Massacre at the White Swan

On 30 July 1981 Denise was admitted to St Thomas's hospital with labour pains, and on 31 July we had a 10 lb 2 oz son. We named him Dean Edward Smith, after James Dean and my paternal grandfather Eddie Smith. He was a fine healthy baby, and as I held him in my arms, for the first time I felt at peace. This was my son, and everything was right with the world. I was more optimistic than I had been for many years. Denise handled the birth well, and we were more in love than ever.

The council offered us a couple of flats, but they were proper dumps, and Denise was adamant that she would not live on an estate, so we held out until we were offered a newly decorated maisonette on Bedford Road, in Clapham. The place was perfect, and we soon moved in and settled down. Two months after Dean was born, Denise was pregnant again.

I was still ducking and diving for a living. Along with Harry and Big Nose Eamon, I bought a set of record decks that had been stolen from a well-known nightclub. Harry built a decent amplifier from salvaged parts, and we knocked up a couple of six-foot speaker boxes and got a bit of work in the local pubs, playing mainly rock 'n' roll and rockabilly from our combined record collections. Things went pretty well, and we got offered a few private gigs, weddings and birthday parties. But the money wasn't that great, especially when it was split three ways, so I didn't give up my day jobs.

I still did the odd car-job with Tommy and Dave C., but I also started getting into a bit of fraud and deception. I knew a little Irish firm who had a brilliant forger, who I'll call 'PJ', working with them, and they specialized in Giros. In 1979 a team of burglars broke into the offices at Wandsworth town hall over a bank-holiday weekend and cut their way into the main safe.

They stole thousands of blank Giro cheques, and these were still being cashed well into the mid-1980s.

The blank Giros would have an amount of cash filled in by PJ, using Letraset transfers and a steady hand. Each Giro also has a number-code which identifies which post office the cheque can be cashed at, but as the thieves had also stolen the code-book, this was no problem. As he had made the cheques out for such large amounts of cash, usually in the region of £1,200, PJ would knock up a very kosher-looking letter of confirmation, with a phone number that any suspicious cashier could phone to speak to a supervisor at the DHSS. Of course, the 'supervisor' would be PJ himself, and the number would be a phone box where he was waiting.

The Giro firm were always looking for new faces to take the cheques into the post offices, and I did a bit of that for a while. I couldn't believe how lax the post-office staff were. Some of them wouldn't even bother looking at my face or the confirmation letter, they would just stamp the Giro and count out the readies. I got a third of the face-value, the driver who waited outside the post offices also got a third and PJ got a third. With a good driver we could hit six or seven post offices a day. Years later, when the Giro game was all but dead due to the post offices waking up to how much they were losing from bent cheques, I bumped into PJ again. By this time he was an alcoholic wreck, having spent his fortune on booze, birds and betting, but he was still at the game. The stolen Giros had long since run out and he was reduced to buying straight Giros from people for 10 per cent over face value and filling in larger amounts. But the post offices were now too hot and would seriously scrutinize any Giro over £100, so pickings were slim. PJ begged me to take a cheque into a sub post office in Fulham for him. He told me that the staff were 'sweet', and they had cashed plenty of hookey ones in the past, but he needed an unknown face or they might get suspicious. I felt a bit sorry for him, so I agreed as a one-off, for old times' sake.

The cheque was for £1,500, and it wasn't a patch on PJ's early work. I almost refused when I saw how badly it was worked. PJ waited outside in his car and I went in and joined a queue of OAPs waiting to cash their pensions. When I finally got to the counter I slipped the cheque under the screen and waited. The cashier, a fat Asian man, looked at the cheque, then looked at me, then looked at the cheque again. I put on my best confident face and waited. The cashier burst out laughing, then he waved another cashier over, said something to him in his own language and handed him the cheque. The second cashier also had a good laugh.

I knew I was on a loser but I tried to bluff it out. 'Is there something wrong?' I asked.

The first cashier put the cheque back on the counter and pushed it back under the screen towards me. 'Not today,' he said.

I reached into my inside pocket. 'I've got a letter of confirmation.'

The cashier shook his head; he still had a smile on his face. 'Keep it,' he said. 'I've already seen it twice this week.'

I snatched the cheque up and marched out of the post office with as much dignity as I could muster.

PJ was a typical example of a criminal who had milked a crime for all it was worth and didn't have the sense to move on to something else. I had always been flexible when it came to crime. If something wasn't working I would look around for the next earner. I believe that if you make the choice to be a criminal then you should be a criminal all the time and not try to be a part-timer. And that means you should not be afraid to try any decent crime that might earn a quid or two.

A good coup at the time was stealing bricks, in particular yellow Stocks. Second-hand yellow Stock bricks were much in demand in the early eighties because there were not many new houses being built and the building trade relied almost solely on renovation jobs. Yellow Stocks were the favourite, and that meant that their price went from 7p to 40p a brick, and suddenly they were worth stealing.

Bricks were delivered to jobs on wooden pallets of five hundred.

They would usually be placed in the garden of the house being renovated or out on the pavement. Our usual routine was to drive around in an old J4 van with a magnetic sign on the side that said 'Mulrooney Bricks Ltd' and a bogus phone-number. We would have a clipboard with a fake work-order, and hard-hats and donkey jackets. When we spotted any pallets of yellow Stocks, we would pull up and just start loading them into the van, as fast as we could, in broad daylight. If anyone came out of the job and questioned us, we would just spin them a yarn about how we had been ordered to pick up the bricks by our boss. Most of the time the governors would be nowhere near the actual work-site and our story would be accepted. If anyone was persistent in their objections to us taking the bricks we would say, 'OK, we'll go back to the yard and check that we've got the right site.' Then we would drive around until we spotted another likely target. We could clear three pallets of bricks from the road-side in under ten minutes, and any builder's yard would buy them from us, cash in hand, and no questions asked.

I once came unstuck nicking a parcel of bricks. I was with my friend the German and Dave Brennan's brother, John, in a pub called the Windsor, having an afternoon on the piss, when someone came in and told us he had just seen five pallets of yellow Stocks being put down on a road nearby. Even though we were all half-cut already, we couldn't resist. We quickly found the bricks and began loading them into our van, forming a three-man chain and throwing four bricks at a time along the chain, when a bloke came out of the house and demanded to know what we were doing. We gave him our spiel, but he wasn't wearing it. It turned out that he was the governor on this renovation and he had just been up to a builder's yard and paid for the bricks in person.

He told us the police were on the way, so we packed up our operation and scarpered a bit lively. But on our way back to the pub we suddenly had a police car on our tail. There was no way we could outrun them in our manky old van, so we pulled up. We still had about a hundred stolen bricks in the van, so we were nicked. The German and John gave false names, but one of the coppers knew me from a previous nicking. We were charged with theft and released on bail.

The case finally came up at Maidstone crown court a year later. The German and John got clean away on their false names, but I had to appear for trial. The prosecution stated that the theft of yellow Stock bricks in the south London area had 'reached epidemic proportions', and said that some brick-thieves had even gone so far as to demolish entire buildings in order to steal the bricks. I thought he was stronging it a bit, but I knew people who had taken down large walls for the bricks. The judge took one look at my previous and jailed me for fourteen days. As I had already nicked around £20,000's worth of yellow Stocks up until that time I had to shrug my shoulders and take my two weeks in Canterbury jail.

Scaffold clips were another good earner. At 60p a clip we would even take on the hard graft of dismantling a whole scaffold to get at them. One night the German and I broke into a scaffolder's yard and spent five hours loading sacks with clips and stacking them on the back of a lorry. At 5 a.m. we broke into the yard office and stole the lorry-keys. Then we revved up the huge flatbed and rammed the gates of the yard. We took both metal gates clean off their hinges and drove the lorry to a lock-up a few miles away, where we unloaded the sacks before dumping the lorry in a side-street. Every scaffolder marks his equipment with a dab of paint so he can identify it by the colour of the paint spot, but our buyer had a huge water-tank in his yard which contained no water but always had a fire burning in it. He would dump all stolen scaffold clips into the fire, where the paint would be burnt off. Then he could mark them with his own paint colour before selling them on. He even had the brass neck to call his company 'Everyone's Scaffolding Company'.

Being a criminal was a great life. I worked the hours I wanted and I never got bored with my job. Denise wasn't too happy about it, and I was hardly ever home. A lot of the deals for nicked gear were done in pubs and drinking dens, so whenever I did roll home I was invariably drunk. I could be an aggressive and nasty drunk, and I often started arguments with Denise for no reason. She had been very close to her family, and when they threw her out when she got pregnant with Dean, it really hurt her. Now she had a young baby, another one on the way, and me taking right liberties. I was so selfish and tied up in what I was doing I never once stopped to think how she might be feeling. In my criminal activities I could show a degree of sophistication, but when it came to my relationship with Denise I was as immature as ever.

I still hadn't forgotten the beating I got from the Norwood gang. There was a lot of talking and planning going on for a revenge raid on their HQ, which was a pub in Crystal Palace called the White Swan. If I'm to be completely honest now, I wanted the Norwood gang wiped out, and I mean dead, not only in revenge for the beating they had given me, but also because I wanted the war to end. Anything less than a very serious assault on them might mean they would make a comeback, and things might drag on for another year. I now had a family to think of, and that meant earning a few quid, not getting nicked for silly gang-fights.

The Norwood gang finally got theirs one Sunday night in 1982, almost two years to the day they had tried to kill me. They were inside the White Swan when a gang of up to twenty-five armed men came into the pub through both entrances. The fight inside the pub was like something out of a cowboy film. Tables, chairs, optics and windows were smashed. Somehow, in a desperation born of panic, Alan and his brother Tony managed to fight their way out of the pub. Alan got clean away, but Tony was cornered in a shop-doorway just along from the pub. There, a mob of gang members attacked him with a viciousness that would sicken an Old Bailey jury twelve months later.

Tony had three separate fractures in his skull, and he was partly scalped. He had nine stab wounds to his body, and his right arm was severed at the elbow. There was no doubt that he was left for dead. The *South London Press* reported in their front-page story that it took over nineteen hours of microsurgery to reattach his arm, and he would never have full use of it again. The morning after the attack somebody phoned Alan at home and told him that though he might have got away temporarily, he was going to get the same as his brother. The police were at his house listening to the phone call.

A couple of months after the attack, Joe Healey, Steve Healey and Popeye were arrested in dawn raids. They were charged with attempted murder, GBH, affray and possession of weapons, and all remanded in custody to Lewes prison. The boys had been identified by several witnesses, who had made statements. It was said that Joe Healey had wielded the three-foot Samurai sword that cut off Tony's arm. My name came up several times in the statements and at the subsequent trial, but I was never charged with any part of 'The White Swan Massacre', as the newspapers were now calling it.

Before the trial several of the key witnesses received death threats, and a couple had their windows put through in the middle of the night. As a result, certain statements were withdrawn or changed. The *South London Press* reported that on the opening day of the trial the prosecutor directed the jury to look at the accused in the dock, dressed in their gang-colours and with tattoos on display, and uttered, 'Would not any right-thinking member of the public feel a shudder of revulsion and fear even passing these men in the street?' – which I thought was a bit strong coming from a geezer wearing a wig and a cloak. But the jury were not to be swayed. They returned not-guilty verdicts on the attempted-murder charges, but found Joe guilty of GBH with intent. They found both Steve and Popeye guilty of assault (ABH) and affray. Joe was sent to prison for five years and nine months. Popeye and Steve got six months each. And that was the end of the war with the Norwood gang. The White Swan massacre put an end to the gang era for most of us. It wasn't fun any more.

I have nothing but respect for Joe, Steve and Popeye. They did their bird without a murmur and didn't make any statements against anyone else involved. In our world, they were staunch soldiers. And the passage of time has even allowed me to feel a

Who you looking at? Me aged nine months

Two cocky kids ready to take on anybody. Me and my brother, Mick, aged nine and seven

Mum and Dad

1971. Clockwise from back right: Me, Steve, Samantha, Alan, Dennis, Mick. Who'd believe that eight years on from this photo we'd form the nucleus of one of the most feared teenage gangs in south London?

Her Majesty's Detention Centre, Send, where the 'Short, Sharp Shock' was meted out with a size twelve boot

The interior of Court Two at the Old Bailey. In real life you can almost feel the misery and despair seeping out of the walls

Gladiator School. Rochester Borstal, where petty delinquents were forged into hardened criminals. I was there from November 1977 to May 1980

The gang's all here! From left to right: Popeye, Sharon, Mad Harry, me with my arms around Denise, Dad and Mick with our dog, Friday. Christmas 1980

Mad Harry and me, 1981, about to start work on our Ford Zodiac 'Battle Wagon'

1981: Rebel with a cause. Me in my first Vauxhall Victor, with sister, Samantha, on the bonnet

1981: Three generations of Smiths. From left to right: Me, my baby son Dean, Dad and brother, Mick

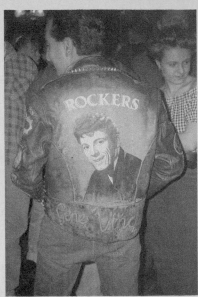

Rockin' at the Chick-a-Boom

'Big Beat' Kris (left) and pal. The Balham and Battersea Katz were the height of sartorial elegance

The Battersea Katz, boozing, doping and planning war

The proud father. Holding my firstborn,
Dean Edward Smith, 1981

My brief psychobilly phase. Joe's first
birthday

Two little boys: Joe and Dean in the
backyard at Bedford Road, 1984

Me and my boys on a rare holiday, to
Rhyl in 1985. I had to go back to London
half-way through the holiday to stand trial
for brick theft

Dean and Joe on the bonnet of my pink Rambler Classic, 1986

Lianne's second birthday. I met up with her and Denise in secret, as I was being hunted by the Flying Squad for armed robbery

'Members only, mate.' About to go and put myself on offer as a bouncer for £30 a session, 1988

HMP Albany on the Isle of Wight. It once had the dubious distinction of being the most violent dispersal prison in England. When I got there in 1990 there were an average of three stabbings a week

Me, Denise and the kids, HMP Albany
visiting room, 1990

HMP Wormword Scrubs

HMP Wandsworth, 'The Hate Factory':
a monument to prison brutality

The infamous centre at Wandsworth.
Charly Bronson was the only prisoner I
actually witnessed walking across it.
Prisoners had to walk clockwise around
the edge or brace themselves for a beating

Out on parole. Me and my dad, drunk as lords, August 1997

Dean, Joe and Lianne that same year

Out on parole again. With my daughter, Lianne, and my son Joe. Summer 1998

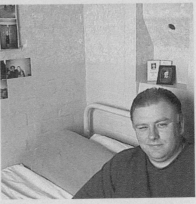

Me, in my luxurious cell at HMP Grendon, November 2003

grudging respect for our enemies. In the early 1990s I came across a centre-page spread about Alan in the *Sun*: his model girlfriend had chosen him over Sylvester Stallone, whom she was also dating. Just as well, I suppose, because I wouldn't have fancied Sly's chances if it had come to a tear-up.

The last time I saw Popeye was in 1998. He was handing out leaflets for a church meeting on Streatham High Road. He had changed a lot and was now some kind of born-again Christian preacher, though he still looked as though he might whip out a sawn-off and start blasting at any moment. I would hazard a guess that Popeye's God is the vengeful Old Testament variety. Joe and Steve still occasionally show up at what's left of the rockabilly scene, where they are afforded the respect they deserve.

As for Turkey Neck Steve, my desire for revenge wore off and we became friends. He's still a big hit with the ladies, and if I need any tips I know who to ask.

Joe Kennedy broke his neck in a diving accident in Spain in 1985 but recovered fully. He was last seen working as a ticket-collector for London Underground, which is somewhat ironic given his actions during the Battle of Morden Station.

Peter 'Pete the Nut' Mayne died in a road accident in 1986. His brother, Bert, was riding pillion and badly injured in the same accident. Three years later Harry Mayne was also in a motorbike accident that almost ended his life. It took him many years to recover and he will limp for the rest of his life. But the last time I saw him he was building a 750cc chopper in his back yard.

My brother Mick married and settled down. He has five kids and works for Lambeth Council. My sister Samantha married Tommy Hogan Jnr, and they have nine kids between them, including six from previous marriages. My cousin Ronnie also settled down and is now a successful businessman with his own painting and decorating firm.

Tony 'Bopper' Hogan is serving a life sentence for murder. He has been in prison since 1986. He escaped from the Court of Appeal in 1988 but was recaptured after two days.

As far as I know, the rest of the Balham Wildkatz, the Battersea

Rebels and the Norwood gang have all settled down to law-abiding lives. By 1983 the gangs had all but died out. And now that I had worked the craving for violence and revenge out of my system, it was time for me to go to work.

I was going back into armed robbery. And this time I was going to do it right.

16. The Little Firm

I made a lot of money from the various scams and cons I was involved in, but I spent it almost as fast as it was coming in. I had the typical criminal mentality about money, and that was the desire to spend it fast so that nobody can claim it back. If I had really worked for my money, like a straight-goer, then I would have been a lot more careful with it. Bent money just burned a hole in my pocket. I didn't live in the lap of luxury; we had a modest council house and took the occasional holiday in North Wales. I had a couple of decent suits and drove a succession of used cars, favouring the 1950s models such as Zephyrs and Zodiacs. Invariably I would start each day with the price of a cup of tea in my pocket, and end it with the same, having blown whatever loot I had managed to steal on drinking, gambling and living expenses. In short, I was surviving, but not really getting anywhere.

On 9 July 1982 my second son was born in St Thomas's hospital. We named him Joseph Stephen Smith, and he was just as beautiful as Dean. Denise was starting to patch things up with her family, but I would have little to do with them. I got on OK with her older sister, Margaret, and her two younger brothers, Christian and Raymond. Not that I saw much of them, as I was always out when they came to visit. But I didn't trust her parents. I had nothing in common with them, and to my dying day I will never understand the kind of parents who would turn their child out on to the streets for getting pregnant. My parents, in spite of what I had put them through with my wild ways, had never abandoned me. No matter what arguments or fights we had in the family, we all stuck together when it counted.

At this time, in south London there were quite a few robbery teams operating. One of them, known as 'The Little Firm' because most of its members were quite short in stature, were pals of mine. 'Scotch' Andy Philipson was a pint-sized Glasgow hard man who had moved to London in the early 1980s and was the leader of the Little Firm. He had already served a short sentence for robbery in Scotland, and he was almost a caricature of a Glasgow jock. He was game as a brace of pitbulls and would fight anybody at the drop of a hat, he loved a drink and a party, and was fiercely loyal to his friends.

I had worked a bit with Andy when he was into cheque-book and -card scams, and we had got on so well that he called on me whenever he got offered 'specialist' jobs. Once we picked up £500 a piece for bashing the granny out of a careless burglar who happened to burgle the home of a local villain. We got all his jewellery back and left the burglar with a broken jaw and three broken fingers.

Andy was very reliable and efficient when it came to giving out punishment beatings or putting the frighteners on other villains who had upset the applecart, and he usually took me along as back-up.

One time I went with him to an estate off Brixton Hill to give a 'message' to a firm who had hijacked a load of cigarettes that had already been stolen by a rival firm. The rip-off was seen as a 'dire liberty' by the first firm, but as they were working thieves and had no hard men on their books, they hired Andy to sort things out.

Andy phoned me up and asked me if I wanted to earn £250, and could I bring a gun? I didn't need asking twice. When I met him he was carrying a black holdall and dressed in his usual black crombie and black-leather gloves. I drove us up to the estate, and we went up to the first floor of a block and walked along the balcony. The estate was a rough place, full of burnt-out cars and boarded-up windows. The firm we were looking for had their flop there, where they kept stolen goods. Andy put the bag on the floor between his feet and knocked on the door. There was no answer. Then suddenly the brickwork next to his head exploded and there was the whine of a bullet ricocheting away. We ducked below the balcony wall in a hurry. Someone was shooting at us from the next block.

The firm we had come for had moved their operation into another squat in the block opposite and were on the look-out for any callers at their old flop. There was another boom and the sound of shotgun pellets peppering the wall above our heads. The first shot had been a pistol, now a shotgun; they must have been fully loaded over there. I got my revolver out and stayed crouched behind the wall. I only had five shots in the gun and no spare ammo. I didn't fancy my chances in a gunfight. I looked at Andy. He was smiling and unzipping his holdall. I was absolutely shitting myself, and amazed that he was so calm. He pulled a big black automatic pistol from the bag, cocked it and winked at me. Then he jumped up and fired off about fifteen shots in the direction of the other block. I put my hands up to my ears to block out the noise and squirmed about on the floor to dodge the hot cartridge-cases being ejected from his gun.

When his pistol was empty he ducked back down, popped out the magazine and began to reload. He was actually whistling a tune! Two shots came back from the other block, but once again they hit the brickwork above our heads. One of the most terrifying sounds in a gun battle is the whistling-whining sound that large-calibre bullets make when they ricochet off hard surfaces. They sound almost like a dying scream. I had plenty of bottle but getting my head shot off for £250 was not my idea of value for money. I hadn't fired a shot yet, I was too scared to put my head over the parapet.

'Come on, Andy,' I urged. 'Let's get the fuck out of here before Old Bill turn up.'

Andy nodded, slotted the now-loaded magazine into his pistol, and said, 'Give us a minute, just gotta teach these flash monkeys a lesson.'

He popped upright again and emptied his pistol into the other block. When he crouched back down he said to me, 'You're supposed to be doing this as well, you know!'

I couldn't believe it. 'Let's fucking go!' I shouted.

He put the pistol back into the bag. The other side was quiet now, having returned no fire after Andy's second burst. But instead of zipping up the bag and getting ready to move out, Andy pulled a sawn-off pump-action shotgun out of the bag. I was in a panic now. He racked the slide on the shotgun and pushed the bag over to me.

'Here,' he said. 'If you're no gonnie join the party, you can carry the fucking bag.'

I grabbed it and followed him down the balcony. He was firing and racking as we went.

We got back to the car and vacated the area without getting a pull. Andy laughed all the way home. 'That was fucking great, man. Just like a filum, so it was,' he said. I was just delighted to get away without being shot or nicked. Andy was as wild as they come, but there was no better man to have on your side in a bit of agg'. After that he used to call me 'the man with the virgin gun'.

The Little Firm was heavily into armed robbery, and besides the nucleus of the gang, which was Andy, Mark and Burt, they would also recruit other robbers for any big jobs. One such job was a Safeway supermarket near Streatham Common. One of their girlfriend's cousins had a job in Safeway stacking shelves, and he brought some very nice inside information about the security arrangements to the gang. He said the average weekend take was in the region of £80,000, and the money was taken to a strong-room upstairs from the shopping hall. He had once been sent up there to get a security guard to nick a shoplifter, and though the door to the strong-room was kept locked, there was a mirror above the door so that the guards and cashiers inside could identify who was at the door before opening it. Once they had seen his Safeway coat and official ID badge, they had opened the door with no problem. This info was well worth the five grand the kid was asking for it. So Andy began planning the job.

The inside-man was able to supply Safeway coats and official name-tags, stolen one at a time over a period of weeks. The Little Firm recruited a second getaway driver and another reliable heavy to carry one of the sawn-off shotguns they were taking on the job. A sawn-off shotgun is the perfect tool for armed robbery, because it is so frightening-looking, and putting the fear of God into those you are about to rob is essential. If you look half-hearted on a robbery it might encourage someone to 'have a go', and the last thing you want to do is make it harder for yourself by firing off shots and rolling around the floor with guards or members of the public. Plus, the more violence you use on a robbery, the more eager the police are to catch you, and the more inclined a jury becomes to see you locked up. The sawn-off shotgun is the best thing for dissuading people who might want to tackle you.

On the day of the robbery, the robbers donned their Safeway jackets and name-tags and slipped, one at a time, into the store. They spread out among the aisles and watched as the security guards took the last of the till-money upstairs. Andy was approached by a customer who, thinking he was a member of staff, questioned him as to where the 'dried onions' were kept. Andy tried to fob him off by pointing to the furthest aisle away from him, but the customer wasn't wearing it.

'I've already been over there,' he grumped. 'Can you show me?'

Andy was more interested in giving the rest of the team the signal to move upstairs, so without ceremony, he told the man to 'Fuck off!' The customer was incensed. He looked at Andy's name-tag, which identified him as Khan, and promised to report his rudeness to the management. Andy moved off and left the man fuming.

Up two flights of stairs, accessed from behind a rubber curtain at the back of the store, was the strong-room, and the takings. Burt stayed just inside the curtain, sawn-off at the ready, to guard the stairs in case anyone else tried to come up. Andy, Mark and the fourth gunman climbed the stairs. Andy marched up to the strong-room door on his own, while the other two got ready to rush the door from along the short corridor. Andy gave a loud knock and stood back so they could see him through the mirror from the inside. One of the security guards looked in the mirror and, seeing Andy's Safeway jacket, opened the door without a word. Andy reached under his jacket and produced his sawn-off and rested both barrels on the guard's chin. The others rushed up the corridor and burst into the strong-room. There were five people in there, two guards, and three cashiers who were counting and bagging up the money. The money was spread out all over a large table. Mark set about handcuffing the staff together while Andy and the other man scooped the cash into a large bin-liner. There were some Securicor packs already in the open safe, and these were soon bagged as well. They left the coins, which must have amounted to a good five grand, because they were too heavy. Four minutes after entering the strong-room, the team were on their way down the stairs with the cash.

Inside the curtain the team put their shotguns away. It was still a long walk to the front entrance of the supermarket, and they were hoping to walk out without attracting any attention. But as they came through the curtain and into the shop, the Tannoy system burst into life.

'All staff, be aware. We have a Code Red in progress!'

This was Safeway's security code for robbery. One of the staff in the strong-room must have been able to reach the Tannoy. The customers took no notice because they didn't have a clue what a Code Red was, but the staff were immediately on the alert.

The walk through the store now seemed even longer to the team, but they didn't panic, they just kept walking and tried to look as inconspicuous as possible. They were only about six feet from the doors when the two blokes from the fresh-fish counter, holding large filleting knives, decided to have a go. Andy was last in line when the robbery team sped into a run and burst out on to the pavement. The first getaway car was parked behind Streatham Common BR station, and to get to it the team had to cross the busy Streatham High Road, go down two flights of steps, run along an alley at the side of the station and out on to a back street.

When the job was being planned, the distance to the getaway

car was not an issue. Its location was perfect for a quiet getaway, it couldn't be seen by anybody in the shop or on the high road, and it wouldn't have to speed through heavy traffic to get away. The back street led directly to Streatham Common, where the changeover car was parked. But now it must have seemed like miles to the robbers as they fled with the loot, chased by two big have-a-gos armed with knives. Andy lost a shoe in the middle of the road and was cursing because they were £120 Bally loafers, but managed to dodge the heavy traffic and get down the steps and into the alley, the irate fishmongers close behind him. The front runners reached the getaway car and piled in. Looking back up the alley they saw the fishmongers close behind Andy, so they began to pile out of the car again, this time drawing their guns.

But Andy had had enough. He stopped dead and pulled his shotgun out. Pointing it right at the face of the first fishmonger, 'FUCK OFF!' he screamed. The fishmongers both dropped their knives and put their hands in the air. 'We thought you were one of our staff,' one of them said. Andy ordered them to the floor, then joined the rest of the team in the getaway motor.

The rest of the team had stripped off their Safeway jackets behind the curtain, but Andy had left his on. The fishmongers had figured that Andy was a member of staff bravely chasing the robbers and decided to help him out! They came a cat's whisker away from being shot.

The take from the Safeway robbery was disappointing. There was only £29,000 in cash. The Securicor packs taken from the safe contained over £40,000 in cheques, which the team burned. A lot of Safeway customers got their shopping for nothing that week.

There is nothing to be done when you get a disappointing take on a robbery, except pay off your expenses and adjust the cut accordingly. The inside-man who put the job up in the first place had to make do with £2,500 as his whack. He wasn't best pleased about that, as Safeway was saying that the robbers had netted over £70,000, but they were including the cheques, which were worthless, except to Safeway, obviously. The inside-man hooted a bit, and a couple of the robbery team, who didn't fancy spending the next decade in Parkhurst on the evidence of this disgruntled finger-merchant, talked up the idea of 'putting one in his nut' to make sure he kept his gob shut. But wiser heads prevailed, and Andy asked me to come with him when he put the frighteners on the man.

We caught him coming out of his local pub, a bit worse for drink. I held him in a bear-hug while Andy poured a bottle of ice-cold water over his head. Andy then struck a match and threw it at him. The match fizzled out as soon as it hit his sopping head.

'Keep your mouth shut,' Andy warned. 'Or the next time it might be petrol.'

And that was it. We strolled casually away, leaving a now very sober and soaking wet finger-man to contemplate the horrors that could quite easily befall him.

The Little Firm were prolific workers, sometimes doing three robberies a week. A couple of them had serious heroin habits which they had picked up on previous prison remands. I would say that 90 per cent of the heroin users that I know started taking the gear in jail. Time spent on remand in prison is the most boring, apart from time spent in punishment blocks, and a lot of prisoners turn to drugs to alleviate the boredom of twenty-three hours a day locked in a twelve-by-five-foot cell. Very few remand prisoners are given jobs inside a prison, so the days are spent lying in bed. Drugs are currency in this type of environment.

Andy had a serious coke habit and did a bit of acid now and again, but he loved a drink and was a real pub-man. All these vices took money, so the boys would be 'at it' almost on a daily basis. They robbed anywhere that held cash or valuables: banks, post offices, building societies, supermarkets, jewellers, bingo halls and cinemas. Andy even had his own personal favourite building society, which he would rob on his own if he needed a quick £500. He robbed the Gateway Building Society on Balham High Road at least six times, until it finally closed down.

The Little Firm were hotter than a £20 pistol; they were just too prolific to reign for long. And the purchase of a .22 rifle led to their downfall. It was known among the robbery fraternity that you could pierce the window of certain security vans by firing a long-case .22 rifle bullet at it. Once there was a hole in the glass you could widen it with a couple of blows from a pick-axe or a fireman's axe and put a sawn-off shotgun to the hole. The threat of red-hot twelve-gauge pellets flying around inside an armoured cab did a lot to persuade the security crew to open their doors and let the robbers in. So if you wanted to empty a few security or post-office vans, then a rifle was the thing for the job.

Stopping the vans to give you the time to do your work was as simple as blocking them off in a quiet street with a couple of stolen vehicles. With a well-practised team, the whole operation could take less than five minutes. Once inside the cab of the van, you could drive the whole lot away or enter the back where the money was kept and empty it on the spot.

The Little Firm put the word out that they were in the market for a rifle, which were not that common on the streets of south London. They soon got an approach and were offered a .22 sniper's rifle, complete with a snazzy aluminium briefcase and a sniper's scope. It was the kind of tool that a professional assassin might use, but the firm bought it anyway. Soon afterwards, the fella who sold it to them got nicked for something else and bought a bit of bail and a reduced sentence by rolling over on everyone he had ever had dealings with. Including the Little Firm.

The information that the police gained from the rifle dealer's treachery allowed them to identify the Little Firm as a team who were 'at it' in a big way. The purchase of the .22 also told them that the boys were looking to up their game, and go after security vans in the not too distant future. The Little Firm became a priority for the Flying Squad, and, based on this information, they mounted a surveillance operation on the boys that would lead to their arrest.

The Firm had decided to hit the National Westminster Bank

in Tulse Hill. On that job were Andy, Mark, Burt and a fourth robber. The driver was a nervous kid by the name of Chrissy. Chrissy had been bugging the boys to take him on a robbery for months, without success. He claimed to be an expert driver and wanted the money and glamour that he saw others getting. Eventually the boys found themselves short a driver on the bank job and Chrissy happened to be in the vicinity, so he was hired. Getaway drivers are always paid the same share as everyone else. Though they don't often carry firearms, they are still looking at a substantial sentence if they get caught. Chrissy was delighted to go on his first job, and he nicked a nice new four-door Vauxhall for it.

The bank robbery went according to plan. Four robbers entered the bank, three gunmen and a bag-man. They put everyone on the floor, scooped up the cash and prepared to leave. But on their way out, a man with a crash helmet in his hand blocked their exit. He was wearing a long waterproof jacket, and clearly visible underneath it was a police uniform. He was an off-duty copper who had come into the bank to do some business. The boys didn't panic; they held a shotgun to his head and ordered him to lie on the floor, then they left. Outside, one of the team noticed a moped and guessed it belonged to the copper inside, so he kicked it over. They piled into the getaway car and Chrissy pulled out into the busy traffic.

No sooner had the team left the bank than the off-duty copper was off the deck and out after them. He shouted to the bank staff to phone the police, as if they needed telling, and righted his moped before taking off through the traffic after the getaway car. In order to attract more attention, the copper was not wearing his crash helmet and was shouting at pedestrians to phone the police. The robbers, realizing their cover had been blown, opted for speed rather than trying to blend in. Chrissy was urged to put his foot down and lose the noisemaker on the moped. The getaway car was a top-of-the-range model and should have been able to outrun a moped very easily. But it wasn't happening.

Andy, perhaps suffering a paranoia hangover from his last coke binge, decided that Chrissy wasn't going for it and, worse, was deliberately trying to get them nicked. He put the barrels of his shotgun up to Chrissy's head, cocked the gun and told him in no uncertain terms what the result would be if they didn't shake off the moped. Chrissy was terrified, and rightly so, and began to sob loudly as he stamped on the accelerator pedal for all he was worth. But even on a clear, straight stretch of road he couldn't get the needle over 60 mph. Andy was on the verge of shooting him, when Mark came up with a better idea. He instructed Chrissy to take the next left-hand turn and stop the car.

When the copper on the moped followed them around the next corner he found the car stopped and three lunatic-faced gunmen running directly towards him, waving sawn-off shotguns like they meant business. He panicked, skidded his moped and fell off. One of the robbers stood over the downed moped and emptied both barrels of his shotgun into the engine. This effectively ended the chase and the robbers jumped back into their car and made off.

Chrissy's driving skills were vindicated after it was found that he had stolen a company car which had a regulator on the engine that would not allow it to go over 60 mph, so the rep who owned it couldn't thrash the bollocks out of it. Andy apologized for his threats, and Chrissy was accepted as part of the team. But his was to be a short career, because the Little Firm were to be nicked on their very next robbery. And Chrissy with them.

Andy phoned me at home and offered me a place on a bit of work they were doing, a supermarket in Surrey. Denise and I were going through a bit of a bad patch. She was pissed off about having to stay in all the time and look after the kids, while I was out living it up every night. She suspected, rightly, that I was seeing other women. In order to pour oil on troubled waters, I had agreed to look after Dean and Joe while she went and had her hair done for a rare night out – so I had to miss Andy's latest job. And that worked out very fortuitously indeed.

The supermarket job went without a hitch, and the team got all the way back to London before the Flying Squad sprung their operation. They ambushed the team's car at traffic lights in Tulse Hill, yards away from the last bank job, and bagged the lot without a shot being fired. They arrested Andy, Mark, Burt and Chrissy. They also reclaimed a carrier-bag containing £12,000 in cash from the supermarket robbery and two sawn-off shotguns. In the flop, which they raided at the same time, they found another shotgun, two revolvers, the sniper's rifle and a large amount of ammunition. The Little Firm were bang-in-it, as we say in south London.

Around this time I was also doing a bit of door-work in local pubs and illegal drinkers. Me doing door-work was a bit of a poacher-turned-gamekeeper deal. I could be a bit of a handful when I was drunk, just like my dad and my brother Mick, and all three of us were barred from many pubs in south London, mainly for fighting. One night I took on three Belfast men in the pool-bar of the Clockhouse pub on Clapham Park Road. I ended up getting a beating, but I managed to break one of the men's legs with a bar-stool and left a large gash in the forehead of another. My cousin, Ronnie, jumped into the fight and got hit on the head with a pool cue for his trouble. He also had a nasty gash, but we were both still standing when the dust had cleared. The governor of the pub decided enough was enough, he had already barred us a couple of times, but as the pub was only around the corner from my house in Bedford Road there was little he could do to stop me coming in other than physically remove me himself. Instead he offered me a job. He explained he would rather have me inside his tent pissing out than outside pissing in.

My work as a bouncer led to me being offered a couple of 'minding' jobs. Minding is just bodyguard work on the cheap for people who can't go to the police if someone rips them off. I did a bit of work for a notorious Brixton fence who specialized in stolen jewellery. All I had to do was stand around at meetings, looking tough and keeping my mouth shut. Sometimes I was told to make it obvious that I was carrying a gun, so as to make the sellers more inclined to accept whatever was offered for their loot. I also did some minding work for a great old thief called Jimmy the Hoister. Hoisting is shoplifting, and Jimmy was very good at it. He could have retired a very wealthy man if it wasn't for his penchant for booze, betting and gold-digging birds. Jimmy was poetry in motion when he was on the hoist, no fucking about at all, he would march into a large store and march straight out with a rack of cashmere coats or silk shirts. It was my job to make sure nobody tried to stop him. I would draw the heat of security guards and store detectives by going into the shop first and acting in a very suspicious manner. Jimmy couldn't fight his way out of a soap-bubble, so if he did get grabbed by anyone it was my job to get in there and make sure he got away.

I also did a bit of minding work for a team of female kite-merchants, girls who bought goods with stolen credit cards and chequebooks. They would normally pay me in goods purchased on the kite – suits, shirts and shoes.

One day we were in a shoe shop in Croydon, having loaded a van with goods purchased on the kite all that day, when a shop assistant became suspicious of the credit card. I used to go into the shops separately from the girls and just pretend to browse while keeping an eye on what was going on. Anyway, I noticed the shop assistant showing the card to the manager and then going over to lock the doors. They were obviously going to hold the girls in the shop while they phoned for the police. It was time for me to earn my fee. I followed the manager into his office, where he had just picked up the phone. I gave him my most intimidating smile and took the phone out of his hand.

'You're going to unlock your doors and let those girls out,' I told him, 'or I'm going to rip your head off and piss down your neck. Choice is yours.'

He just nodded, unlocked the doors and let us leave. That was the only time I had to do anything to earn my whack.

With my door-work, minding, the occasional disco gig and the odd bank robbery, I was doing pretty well financially. But there was trouble on the home front. I had had a brief affair with a bar-maid from Limerick named Miriam, and she had fallen pregnant. She went back to Ireland to have the baby, a girl she named Leah, and I haven't seen her since. But Denise found out about it and went fucking crazy. She cut up all my clothes and threw me out of the house. I still loved Denise, but I just couldn't resist other women, and most of my work brought me into contact with them.

I eventually made it up with Denise and moved back in with her and my two boys, but things were never the same. Then Denise fell pregnant with our third child, and I decided that it was finally time to get a straight job and stop fucking about.

But the best-laid plans . . .

17. Blood on Brixton Road

Throughout the early to mid 1980s I was in and out of prison for short periods, either on remand or sentenced. For example, I did two lots of twenty-eight days in Pentonville and Brixton for not having a television licence. I refused to buy a TV licence on principle. I had already paid for the set and didn't see why I should now pay to watch the fucking thing. I drove almost every day and I didn't have a driving licence either. Nor did I pay tax or have a passport or know my National Insurance number. I figured that the State knew quite enough about me from the Criminal Records Office without me volunteering any more information. The biggest single sentence I served during this time was two months in Pentonville for the theft of a set of Rolls-Royce hubcaps, valued at £800. We were getting £200 for every set we nicked. The set we were convicted for was taken from the Rolls-Royce of Adam Faith. He happened to be stuck in a traffic jam on Chelsea Bridge when we swiped them.

I was doing pretty well out of my semi-legitimate work, bouncing and deejaying. I was running music nights, playing everything from 1940s swing to contemporary reggae and soul at various pubs and clubs. I was also given the old Edwardian Club in Brixton, where I had hung out in the 1970s. Tommy Hogan Snr gave me the club as a gift after I did a few sets on one of his pirate-radio stations. The club had been losing business despite its late licence, mainly because the rock 'n' roll scene was going through its death throes at the time, and nobody really wanted to go for a night out in the heart of Brixton dressed up like a time-traveller from the 1950s. Since the riots of 1981, 'nice' people considered Brixton a no-go area at night. But I fixed up the club and started trying to attract some of the older and hardier rockers from my days on the scene.

Harry and Big Nose Eamon had long lost interest in the disco business, so I hired Tommy Hogan Jnr as a deejay for a lot of gigs. We were getting quite a bit of work at private parties, weddings and rugby-club bashes. I bought a big pink Yank motor, a 1962 Rambler Classic, and we used to transport the gear around in that. But by the time we had paid for petrol for the gas-guzzler, bought the latest twelve-inch releases and splashed out on drinks, the money wasn't that great. Sometimes I had to do a bank robbery just to subsidize expenses. The money was flying out of my hands at a rate of knots. This was when Denise was pregnant again and nagging me to give up all my criminal work and concentrate on legit stuff. I decided to give it a go.

My cousin Joe Regan was working as a hod-carrier and said he could get me a job on his site. The pay was pretty good, and it would leave my nights free for disco and bouncing work, so I took it. Denise was truly happy that I now had a 'normal' eight-to-five job. I started work on a site in Wandsworth, where they were building five hundred luxury apartments from scratch. Toting hods full of bricks and mortar all day is fucking hard work, but I soon got used to it and began to enjoy it. It was great working with Joe, who has a marvellous sense of humour, and the time just flew by. For the first time in my life things were really going well. Denise and my boys were happy, I wasn't doing anything they could send me to prison for, and we were financially sound. This lasted for five months.

One Friday night I finished a disco gig in a pub called the Acre Tavern at about 11.30 and, as a few of my friends there were going on for a drink in Brixton at an after-hours pub called the Loughborough Hotel, I decided to go with them. We piled into a couple of mini-cabs and off we went. There was me, my brother Mick, Dave C., Mark Murphy, my cousin Michael, a guy called Tony the Hippy and a couple of girls. The Loughborough was packed, as usual, with all sorts of people, young and old, black, white, Asian and a lot of Irish. There was a band playing on the stage, and crowds four-deep at the bar. We found a couple of tables in our usual corner and just generally had a good time, drinking and dancing.

At one stage during the night Mick went up to the bar to get a round in, and I saw him talking to a youngish bloke who I had never seen before. When he came back I asked him who he was, but Mick said he was just some mug trying to start a fight. Now Mick can have a terrible tear-up when he's in the mood, but he's normally quite a happy drunk who will laugh off most liberties. I'm the exact opposite, I get mean and nasty when I've had a few and I don't forgive anything. I looked over at the bar and noticed this geezer was with a crowd of five or six other blokes. I told Mick that I was going to pull the fella, but Mick made light of it and said it wasn't worth the agg'.

For the rest of the night I kept my eye on the group of blokes at the bar and soon sussed that they were out for a fight. They were 'screwing out' everybody and bumping people on purpose. I went up to the bar to get a round in and bumped into the main man on purpose myself.

'Why don't you look where you're fucking going?' he sneered at me.

I gave him my slow-burn look, all mad eyes and clenched jaw muscles. 'Why don't you try and fucking make me?' I replied.

His arsehole dropped right out. He turned away, mumbling something, and pushed through the crowd and back to his mates. I was satisfied that he was no more than a wanker who'd had too much to drink.

The Loughborough usually closed around 3 a.m., and by 2.45 most of my mob had pulled birds and drifted off. When I left the pub I was with only Dave C. and Tony the Hippy. We decided to walk down to Brixton High Street to get a kebab before getting a cab home. I was served first, and I was standing outside the kebab shop waiting for Dave and Tony when I heard a shout from the other side of the road. I looked around and saw the bloke I had fronted in the pub with four or five of his mates running across the road towards me. I dropped my kebab and hooked the first one in the side of the head. It was a lovely punch and he went down like a sack of spuds, so I moved on to the next one and stuck the nut on him. I was grappling with the second man when someone hit me from behind and I saw stars. When people say they 'saw stars' when hit with a headshot, they really mean it. It's like a sudden flash of bursting lights inside your head.

The other men piled into me and I was getting the worst of it. I went down on one knee and the boots came in hard and fast. I managed to cover my face with my hands, and I was struggling to stand when Dave C. saw what was happening and came flying out of the kebab shop and into the fray. Tony the Hippy was a confirmed non-violent pacifist and took no part in the fight, but Dave was a battler of old and would never see a friend without back-up in a tear-up, no matter what the odds. He jumped on the back of the biggest man and began to bite his ear. This gave me the space I needed to get back on my feet and, as I stood, I reached for the razor in my back pocket. I flicked it open and laid a stripe down the face of the man directly in front of me. He didn't feel it at first and kept throwing punches at me, so I slashed him again, across the forehead.

The cuts opened, and he staggered away screaming as he felt the warm freshets of blood flowing from his face. I was raging now and quickly moved on to my next target. I slashed another one across the cheek and he went down clutching his face. I saw the biggest of them still struggling with Dave on his back, so I ran over and tried to lay my razor across the bloke's face, but just as I slashed, Dave got his hand in the way and I ended up opening a wound across his knuckles. Dave felt the sting of the blade and pulled his hand away, but he still had his other hand around the man's neck. I slashed again, and this time I opened Dave's other arm from wrist to elbow, and the pain made Dave drop off him, leaving me an open target. I slashed again at the bloke's face, but he ducked and I cut him across the top of his head. He turned and tried to run but I was right behind him. I slashed his back and the blade cut through his shirt and into his flesh like it was melting butter. I felt the jar as the blade hit his spine, and heard a loud ping as the light blade snapped against the bone and fell to the ground.

The fight was over. One man was still knocked out in the middle of the road and three more were on the pavement nursing various cuts. I was breathing heavily, but my rage had left me. I picked up and folded my now-broken razor into my pocket. Dave was bleeding heavily from the wounds to his hand and arm. Now Tony leapt into action. He grabbed an apron from inside the kebab shop and began to bind Dave's wounds. The whole thing had taken only a couple of minutes, but it was definitely time to leave, as there were plenty of witnesses gathering. Me, Dave and Tony fucked off through Stockwell Park estate and thought no more about it.

This kind of fight wasn't unusual to us, in fact it was pretty routine. I had slashed plenty of people in the past, and I had had people attack me with all sorts of weapons. If you start a fight with a stranger and you get striped, you just chalk it up to experience, get your wounds stitched and are a bit more careful next time. No drama, as we say in south London. So I went home to bed, and Tony took Dave to a hospital to get his cuts stitched.

So that was Friday night. On Monday at 5 a.m. I was awakened by a loud banging on my door. I knew instinctively it was the police, even before I looked out and saw them all over the garden. I let them in before they started breaking the door down. There were twenty of them, both uniformed and CID. They crowded into the house, waking Denise and the kids up.

'Noel Stephen Smith, I have a warrant here for your arrest on a charge of serious assault that occurred on Friday last on Brixton High Street. I also have a warrant to search these premises,' said the man in charge.

I just shrugged. What else could I do?

While I was getting dressed, the police were searching every inch of the house. They found the jeans I had been wearing on Friday night, and the razor in a box on top of the medicine cabinet in the bathroom. They also had the bonus of finding a .22 Remington semi-automatic rifle by the side of a chair in the front room. The gun wasn't loaded, but the barrel had been sawn off. As I was leaving the house, in handcuffs and surrounded by coppers, I told Denise to phone my brief straight away. It looked like I was well in the shit.

I was taken to Brixton police station and locked in a cell for four hours before they were ready to question me. When I was finally taken out to be questioned I glanced up at the roll-board that tells you who's in the cells and saw an entry saying 'Attempted Murder, GBH with intent, Firearms with intent', and thought, Fuck me! He's in trouble. Then I noticed it was my name next to the charges.

The two CID men who questioned me seemed happy. One of them, a DC named Duncan Redpath, was rubbing his hands together in glee. 'You're bang to rights, Razor,' he said. 'We've got bundles of witnesses, we've got the weapon that was used, and to top it all off, you're white! Do you know how refreshing that is for Brixton police, going into court with a defendant who can't scream racial harassment for a change? Crying to the jury about how those nasty white policemen only picked on him because he's a poor black boy? This is a dream case.'

I looked at him. 'I ain't saying nothing until my brief gets here,' I said.

Redpath laughed out loud. 'Well, I hope he's a good one,' he said. 'Because you're in it up to your neck, my son.'

I was locked back in the cell to wait for my brief.

In the presence of my solicitor I made a 'no comment interview'. I was charged with GBH with intent Section 18 x2, GBH Section 20 x1, possession of a firearm with intent and being an 'unauthorized person', having served a sentence of three years or more and being banned from keeping firearms for life. The police informed my brief that they would 'strenuously' object to bail, in order to 'protect witnesses'. I was locked back into my cell to appear at Camberwell magistrates court the next morning.

Later that same evening I was interviewed by two Flying Squad officers from Tower Bridge office. They showed me a book of evidence photographs from various robberies, some of which I recognized and some of which I didn't. Almost all of the suspects were masked, and they tried to intimate that I appeared in several of the pictures. I recognized several members of the Little Firm and also a team of Dubliners that I knew were hitting a lot of Rolex jewellers in London, but I kept my mouth shut and acted bored, so they soon got tired and fucked off. Before they left they told me that they knew that I was 'at it', and that they would get me sooner or later. The next morning I was remanded in custody to Wormwood Scrubs.

The Scrubs hadn't changed much and I soon settled into the routine of C-wing. As I was unconvicted, I was allowed to wear my own clothes and have a visit every day. I could also have food and drink brought up, though the drink was limited to two cans of beer a day. My family kept me well supplied, and Denise came to visit at least twice a week. It was during this stay in the Scrubs that I started smoking dope. I bumped into a bloke named Terry, who was a couple of cells away from me, on remand for a diamond robbery in Hatton Garden. I knew his brother, Johnny, very well, and they were both well-known faces on the Patmore estate in Battersea. I had met Terry a couple of times in Harrington's pie and mash shop on Wandsworth Road and knew him to say hello to. When we met up in the Scrubs, Terry assumed that I was into a bit of puff, simply because most of the people he knew I ran with on the out were big puff-heads. Before I could put him right, he had bitten a chunk off his own parcel of hash and slipped it into my hand. It would have been churlish of me to try and hand it back, so I just said, 'Cheers'.

I wasn't really that interested in cannabis, because the only times I had ever tried it, I was always steaming drunk and it just made me feel sick, so I put the chunk of hash that Terry had given me into a matchbox and threw it in the drawer of my locker. The only trouble was that the next day, and every time I saw Terry, he gave me another piece, and by now I couldn't refuse without looking stupid. After a couple of weeks I had three matchboxes full of grass and hash.

One evening my cell door was opened and I was told that I was getting a cell mate. I wasn't too pleased about this, as I prefer my own company in jail, but there was fuck all I could do about it. I decided I would stand it for one night, but tomorrow I would kick off if they didn't move him.

My cell mate turned out to be a tall, stringy Asian fella named Bob. He was from north London and had been nicked for running a 'speed factory', manufacturing amphetamine sulphate. Within twenty minutes we were getting on like old pals. I just took to him straight away as soon as I found out he was into 1950s rhythm and blues music. We got talking about records and I found out he had a decent collection. He also had a good sense of humour. Later on in the evening he was saying how he could do with a joint, as he had just spent a traumatic three days in a police station. I went to my locker and pulled out one of my matchboxes full of grass and hash, and his face lit up. He made two huge joints and gave one to me. I didn't really want it, but I accepted just to be sociable.

It was the first time I had ever smoked dope without a skinful of beer first, and it was a revelation. All my worries and troubles seemed to drop away, and I laughed so much that my stomach hurt. Even better, when I woke up the next morning there was no hangover. From that night on I was a confirmed 'puff-head' whenever I was in prison. Cannabis mellowed me out and turned me into an easy-going sort of dude. If I had discovered it when I was fifteen, my story might have been very different.

I was celled up with Bob for the next five months, and we smoked a lot of dope and had some great laughs. Every time I appeared in court for a hearing I got my brief to apply for bail. The police objected every time, saying that if I were released, 'the streets of south London will be running with blood', as I was bound to seek to silence the people who were going witness against me. They pointed out that when they arrested me, three days after the cuttings, I had a semi-automatic firearm in my front room, and intimated that this was proof that I'd had plans to silence any witnesses. The police were so melodramatic about it all, it was almost amusing.

The fight on Brixton High Street had been nothing. I had done a lot worse and never been nicked for it, and I'd had worse done to me and never had a thought of getting the police involved. My dad had been glassed in the face three different times, and kicked from one end of London to the other, but he never, ever went to the police. It was unheard of. If you go mob-handed to an after-hours drinker and try your luck starting fights with strangers, how can you turn around and cry 'copper' when you come unstuck? There was no honour in what these men were doing. They were quite happy to steam into me when they thought I was unarmed and alone. But now they were whinging like teenagers and trying to get me put away for a long time.

GBH Section 18 carries a maximum sentence of life, Section 20 carries a maximum of five years, the gun could get me another five years, so it wasn't as though I was looking at a slap on the wrist if I got found guilty. After the committal to Inner London crown court, I was finally given copies of the evidence against me. There were full-colour photographs of the injuries suffered by the men, but the pictures were taken within hours of the cuts being stitched, so they looked more horrific. The statements were a load of old bollocks. Apparently I had attacked these five men for no reason, carved them into jigsaw puzzles and walked off.

I felt a lot more confident after I had read their statements, but I knew the one thing that would be hard to explain was the Remington in my front room. The good thing was that it was unloaded and they didn't find the ammo. As I explained earlier, rifles were in vogue as an aid to robbing security vans. If I was seriously going to shoot someone, I would use a pistol or a shotgun, not a fucking rifle. But I couldn't tell a jury that.

I was pleading not guilty to all charges, so I was committed to trial. My brief made an application to a judge-in-chambers for bail for me, but the police painted a picture of blood and bullets and all but went down on their knees and begged the judge not to grant it. So I remained in custody. Denise had given birth to our third child, a daughter who we named Lianne Margaret Smith, the day before I was released from Pentonville on the hubcap-stealing charge, and though I was now back inside, we were still getting on well. Denise knew the score on street- and pub-fights, having witnessed plenty of them at the Chick-a-Boom club and other rock 'n' roll venues and, like me, she felt it was a bit of a liberty me being locked up for what was basically defending myself. Although, to be truthful, I did a bit more than defend myself.

But then Denise got a phone call, from a woman I had been running around with for a while, detailing our 'affair'. The woman was Debbie Adams, who Popeye and Joe Kennedy had fallen out over all those years before. I had met her at a party and decided to renew our acquaintance. Debbie was a real femme fatale, with a big mouth. Fuck knows why she had phoned Denise and told her about us. Maybe she thought I might leave Denise for her. Well, that was never going to happen.

I was called for a visit in the Scrubs, and I was shocked to see both Denise and Debbie waiting for me at the table. Denise had Lianne in her arms and an evil look in her eyes. It was one of the worst prison visits I've ever had to sit through. Denise told me to choose between her and Debbie. I chose Denise, obviously, but I knew that wasn't going to be the end of it. After the visit I went up to the hatch, as Denise told me she had brought clean clothes up for me. The two screws behind the jump could barely conceal their glee as they placed two plastic bin-liners on the counter and asked me to sign the property book. They tipped the bags out, and there were most of my clothes, cut into shreds, once more. Suits, shirts, ties and even shoes had been hacked into confetti. Denise was never one for half-measures.

My trial was due to start on 22 December 1986, and after months on remand I was eager to get on with it. The brief thought I had a 70/30 chance of getting a not guilty – that was 70/30 in favour of the prosecution. The police had been overconfident and failed to put me on any ID parades, and for a case that would hinge on identification, that was a big mistake. Then a strange thing happened. On the opening day of the trial the prosecution asked for a further remand because one of their crucial witnesses was missing. I had a brilliant young barrister who was fast making a name for himself, Jim Sturman. He immediately objected to this and told the judge that I had already been on remand for months and been refused bail on numerous occasions due to police objections. Surely it would not be right to send me back to prison when the defence was ready and eager to prove my innocence? The judge agreed, and told the prosecutors to either start the trial or work out a deal with the defence for conditions of bail.

I was delighted. I knew they couldn't get their main witness to court or he would have been there already, so I was released on bail, two days before Christmas. The prosecution wanted me to put up two sureties of £50,000 each, a security of £30,000 to sign on at a police station twice a day, to live outside the London area and to have no contact with witnesses. Jim Sturman told the judge that their demands were unreasonable. The judge agreed. He released me on my own recognizance, but I had to stay out of SW9 and sign on at Clapham police station once a day. A new trial date was set for the middle of January. The police were as sick as dogs.

My brother Mick was waiting for me outside the court. I had let my hair grow while I was on remand and had also grown a huge moustache, just in case they put me on an ID parade. Mick drove me down to see my dad in his local pub on Stockwell Road, and he didn't recognize me at first. If my own father didn't recognize me, what chance would the witnesses have had?

It was great to be out, but I still had to face Denise. I turned up on the doorstep with a bunch of flowers and, after some persuasion, she let me in. I promised never to cheat on her again, and we made it up. But deep in my heart I knew that no matter how much I loved her and the kids I wouldn't keep my promise. I had a couple of chequebooks and a card that I had been saving for emergencies, and I went out and ironed out every cheque in both the books, buying presents. We had a good Christmas.

By the time my trial came up again, the prosecution was ready to proceed. But now they only had two witnesses. Patrick Hannon, on whom I was charged with committing the lesser GBH Section 20, had withdrawn his statement and said he could no longer remember anything about the fight. Two other men had disappeared back to Ireland, and a female witness said she was 'too scared' to give evidence. Before the trial, the prosecution offered a deal: if I would plead guilty to one Section 18 GBH, possession of a firearm with intent and Actual Bodily Harm, they would drop the other charges. I would get seven years' imprisonment or less. I told them to poke their deal, I was pleading not guilty to everything and I was ready for trial. I had learned my lesson about doing deals at the Old Bailey in 1977.

Before the jury was sworn in, there was a lot of legal argument. It turned out the prosecution was forced to alter the charges anyway, because they were now short of witnesses. My brief argued that possession of the rifle should not be on the same indictment, so I agreed to plead guilty before the trial began to possession of a firearm without a licence, without intent. This was a major result as I was bang to rights with the gun, and possession without intent carried a maximum of only three years. And even if the judge were to give me the maximum, I'd almost certainly win on appeal because I had pleaded guilty.

The jury was sworn in and the charges were put to me. As I had already pleaded to the gun charge, the jury did not know anything about it. The clerk read the charges.

'Noel Stephen Smith, you are charged on Count One on the indictment that on 5 March 1986, in the Greater London area, you did maliciously wound Michael Heaney, causing him grievous bodily harm, with the intent to do so. How do you plead?'

I stood up straight and looked at the jury. 'Not guilty,' I said, firmly and clearly. Next he read the same charge but with Joseph Heaney as the victim. 'Not guilty,' I replied again. Next he read a charge of Actual Bodily Harm on Patrick Hannon. Again I replied not guilty.

The trial was on.

The jury looked as good as gold. There were plenty of youngsters on it and they didn't bat an eyelid when the full-colour photographs of the injuries were handed around. One of them, a young bloke in a leather jacket, even shrugged as if to say, 'I've seen worse down the Old Kent Road every Saturday night.'

Michael Heaney told how he looked at his brother's face after the fight and was sick when he could see his teeth and jawbone through the flap of skin that had been carved out. He said he still had nightmares about that night and had been unable to work since. This evidence was somewhat negated when my brief questioned him as to what his job had been before the incident, and he had to answer, 'Unemployed, sir.'

It was even better when Joseph Heaney took the stand and the jury saw that far from being the bearer of a grotesquely face-altering scar, he had a very thin white line across his cheek which could barely be seen in certain light. He, too, apparently had nightmares about the incident. Under cross-examination it came out that both the Heaney brothers were amateur boxers and veterans of 'some' pub- and street-fights. They also admitted to liking a drink and had had 'a skinful' on the night of the fight. They both pointed me out as their assailant, but as I was the only one in the dock, their identification didn't carry much weight. It became pretty clear that they both had claims pending in the Criminal Injuries Board's calendar, and the police had given them the impression that if no one was convicted of the cuttings they wouldn't get any compensation.

It came out that the police had got my nickname, Razor, from one of the girls who had recognized me. They ran Razor through their computer and came up with me. I was the next one to go into the witness box, and my cross-examination went on for two days. I denied that my nickname was Razor. I denied that I had been carrying a razor on the night in question. I denied starting the fight but said I had been jumped by a gang I did not recognize and had thrown several punches in self-defence. I said that as far as I knew there were two different gangs fighting on the pavement outside the kebab shop, and I just happened to get caught in the crossfire. The kebab-shop owner had already testified that he saw several men fighting but couldn't recognize any of them. In my final plea I turned to the jury and said, 'I took a beating that night, and believe me, if I'd had a razor I would definitely have been tempted to use it. But I didn't. This whole case is a get-up by the Heaney brothers to nick a few quid in compo'. I hope you'll do the right thing. Thank you.'

The last witness was the surgeon from St Thomas's hospital who had stitched all the wounds. The prosecutor asked him if the wounds were consistent with the kind of wounds caused by a thin-bladed instrument such as a cut-throat razor? The surgeon replied 'Yes,' but qualified it with, 'or a Stanley knife.' The prosecution had already shown the jury the boxed razor that had been seized at my home. Forensics had found no trace of blood on it, nor on the clothing I had been wearing that night. But he said it would be an 'incredible coincidence' for an innocent man to be accused of an attack with a cut-throat razor, and then for the police to find just such a weapon in his home three days later.

Jim Sturman cross-examined the surgeon and delivered the *coup de grâce*. He took the razor from the evidence bag and handed it to the surgeon.

'I would like you to open that razor and look at the blade for me.'

The surgeon opened the blade, which was broken and jagged from hitting bone on the back of the last victim.

'Doctor,' said Jim, 'in your expert opinion, bearing in mind that you treated the wounds of the men involved in this unfortunate incident, is that the implement that caused those wounds?'

The surgeon gave a little smile and shook his head. 'No, Mr Sturman,' he said, 'it most certainly is not. This blade is jagged, it would make a ripping wound in flesh. The wounds I treated were perfectly even and clean.'

Jim looked at the jury. 'Thank you, Doctor. That will be all.'

The judge had little choice but to sum up in my favour. The jury went out to deliberate, and I was taken down to the cells to wait. Underneath Inner London crown court is a maze of corridors and passages, and because I had a quick word with Jim before leaving the courtroom, it took about ten minutes for me to get back to my cell. The jailer was just unlocking my cell door when the phone at the end of the corridor rang. He locked me in and went to answer it. Two minutes later he was unlocking my door again.

'Well,' he said, 'you've set a record. The jury is back with a verdict. I've been here twenty-three years and that's the quickest GBH verdict I've ever seen.'

I was nervous going back into court. No matter how much you think a case has gone in your favour, there's just no accounting for a jury. There are people serving decades in prison who bet their liberty on the whims of a jury. The great British public is more unpredictable than the National Lottery. So I couldn't help feeling a touch of trepidation as I watched the jury members file back in and take their seats. The young bloke in the leather jacket winked at me, but I didn't know if it was the kind of wink that said, You're OK, mate, or the kind that meant, We've seen right through you and you're going to jail.

I gripped the dock-rail and waited.

The clerk asked the foreman of the jury to stand. It was the kid in the leather jacket. The clerk went through the routine in a loud voice.

'On Count One, Grievous Bodily Harm with intent on Michael Heaney, do you find the defendant guilty or not guilty?'

There was a hush that seemed to stretch into infinity.

'Not guilty,' said the foreman. And I heard the police officers at the back of the court groaning.

They found me not guilty of all the charges and I couldn't keep the smile off my face. I bowed to the jury, like a dickhead, and said, 'Thank you very much. You've done the right thing.'

But it wasn't quite over yet. All through my time in the box, the prosecutor had tried to get me to admit that I had been convicted on offensive-weapons charges, including possession of a razor, before. He kept reminding me that I was on oath and trying to lead me into answers that would let the jury know that I was anything but a man of good character, but I had thwarted him. British law states that the prosecution cannot bring up anything about a defendant that might lead the jury to presuppose his guilt. For example, the jury couldn't hear that the police had got my nickname from police records because that would lead them to know that I had a police record, so they call it 'information received'.

But now the trial was over, and the prosecution couldn't wait to let the jury know that they had been too hasty in finding me innocent.

Before the judge could dismiss the jury, the prosecutor stood up and said, 'Your Honour, there is the matter of the second indictment, and I ask that the jury be allowed to remain and hear it. The defendant had already pleaded guilty to it before this trial started, so it won't take long.'

The judge shrugged and told the jury to remain seated. The clerk stood again and read the charge.

'Noel Stephen Smith, you are charged that on 8 March 1986, you had in your possession a .22 semi-automatic Remington rifle, without a licence for said firearm. And you have entered a plea of guilty, is this correct?'

In the euphoria of the not-guilty verdicts, I had forgotten about the gun charge. 'Yes,' I said, and I noticed some of the jury were now looking none too pleased.

The prosecutor picked up a sheaf of papers and spoke to the judge, but it was the jury he was looking at. 'Your Honour, I would like to draw your attention to the defendant's previous convictions before you pass sentence.'

The judge nodded and looked through his own sheaf of papers.

This was the prosecutor's big moment of revenge, and he was loving every minute of it. 'I would point out that he has several convictions for the possession of offensive weapons, including two for carrying cut-throat razors.' He looked at the jury one by one as he spoke as if to say, 'See what you've done? He was guilty all along.' I felt like a right prick. 'He also has convictions for armed robbery, possession of firearms and GBH.'

If he'd had a trumpet he would have blown it at this point. I could no longer look at the jury, but I could feel their eyes on me. The judge didn't seem too pleased either. My brief stood up and tried to minimize the damage with a bit of mitigation, but the judge wasn't wearing it. The maximum for possession without a licence was three years, and that's what he gave me.

Later that afternoon I was called back in front of the same

judge. He said that on advice from his clerk on the possibility of my appealing a maximum sentence, he was reducing my sentence to two years' imprisonment with one of those years suspended. This left me two months to serve in prison. All in all, I had had a good result all round.

This was when I got my first taste of HMP Wandsworth, one of the worst hellhole jails in the entire prison system.

18. Enter the Flying Squad

The nickname given to HMP Wandsworth by the many unfortunates who had passed through its gates was 'The Hate Factory', and it was well chosen. Many men had faced 'the long drop' at Wandsworth before capital punishment was abolished in 1966, and it is the only prison in England still to house a working gallows. They test it every six months, to make sure it will be ready in case they should ever need it again.

In Wandsworth, prisoners were treated little better than cattle, and anyone who complained or tried to fight back was quickly stamped on by the screws. The screws of this country mainly belong to a very powerful union called the Prison Officers' Association, or POA for short, and Wandsworth prison is classed as their 'flagship', as it has the most militant screws in the country. In Wandsworth the screws would openly flout racist tattoos and wear NF badges on their ties. They classed all prisoners as 'scum' and treated them as such. The punishment block was a dark, evil place where men were beaten until they cried out for mercy, and beyond. One infamous screw, who was still working in the jail in the 1990s, was reputed to have been investigated for beating prisoners to death on three separate occasions. It was certainly true that he was the only screw in the prison not allowed to carry a truncheon.

Many prison memoirs of the last twenty years have described the hell that was Wandsworth prison. Frankie Fraser, in his book *Mad Frank*, tells how he was almost murdered in the punishment block, and how the screws tried to break his legs by repeatedly slamming a cell door on them. And none of it is exaggerated. I endured, and witnessed, things in HMP Wandsworth that would have shamed the devil himself. But that was later, on my second visit there. For now I was only a short-termer, in for a 'shit and a shave', as we say in prison.

Funnily enough, when I got to Wandsworth, I was located on A-wing, three doors away from Frankie Fraser, who was doing three years for some gold coins and VAT scam. I never really spoke to him, but I was surprised to see how small he was. After all, this was a man whose violence was legendary amongst criminals and prisoners. This was before he began to rent himself out as a talking head on the celebrity gangster circuit.

Even though I was only in Wandsworth for two months, I saw enough to know that I didn't like it. The screws talked to people as though they were shit, and would press the alarm bell for the slightest thing. When it went off, the screws would come from everywhere, swinging batons and asking questions afterwards, if at all. The food was absolute shite, and kit change and showers were once every two weeks. You could end up in the block for not having your shirt tucked into your jeans or for having a button missing. Everywhere you looked there were dog-headed screws shouting and screeching. It was a fucking nightmare.

There was no in-cell sanitation, and the edge of the exercise yards under the cell windows was knee-deep in shit-parcels. When prisoners are locked in their cells for twenty-three hours a day, it is preferable to shit in a newspaper and throw it out of the window, rather than do it in the piss-pot and have it sit in the corner of the cell for hours. Most prisons had a party of prisoners, usually sex offenders, whose job it was to clean up these parcels. They were known as 'the Bomb Squad', but the screws in Wandsworth were, on the whole, too lazy to bother with organizing such things.

Wandsworth was also infested with mice and huge cockroaches. The mice weren't too bad, but after dark the cockroaches would come in under the cell doors, climb the walls and on to the ceiling. Then they would drop on to your face as you lay in bed in the dark. It was terrible. The light switch for every cell was outside, so the screws would come around at ten o'clock every night and switch off until six the next morning. And in the dark the roaches would come creeping. One night, after lights out, I heard a scurrying in the corner of my cell. Thinking it was a mouse, I felt around and found my matches and a bit of newspaper on the chair next to my bed. I stood on the end of the bed and rolled the paper into a torch and lit it. I held it up, expecting to see a mouse, and was horrified to see hundreds of cockroaches on the floor, like a black, shiny, moving carpet, all scuttling about to avoid the light.

One prisoner complained to a woman from the Board of Visitors about the mice and cockroaches, and she told him that he was 'fantasizing', and that there was 'no vermin problem in HMP Wandsworth'. He set about collecting evidence, and when she came back the next week, he emptied a pillow case full of dead mice and cockroaches on the floor in front of her. He was nicked for threatening behaviour to a member of the BoV.

The only good that came of my time at Wandsworth was that I got a chance to meet up with the members of the Little Firm again. They were on D-wing, having been weighed off at the Old Bailey to forty-three and a half years between the four of them. 'Scotch' Andy Philipson got thirteen years, Mark got thirteen years, Burt got ten years, and poor unlucky Chrissy got seven and a half. They had all pleaded guilty to various robberies and firearms offences.

Two months in Wandsworth jail is like a two-year sentence spent in any other, but at last my release date rolled around and I was back on the streets once again. I had no job, no money and no prospects. I tried claiming the dole, but they offered me £7, as I had not paid a stamp in my life. This was supposed to be an 'emergency payment', but I told them to poke it. I would do what I had always done, rob something.

I had decided to go back into armed robbery full time. In those days there was cash to be had, but first I would need a few quid to buy a gun and a decent getaway car. I had lost everything when I got nicked on the GBH charges. My trusty old Smith & Wesson revolver had been sold to cover expenses while I was on remand, so some sort of firearm was top priority.

I went back to live with Denise and the kids at Bedford Road,

but we were going through another one of our sticky patches
and Denise wanted me to move out. She was sick of having the
police kick our door in whenever I was wanted, and it was not
good for the kids. One thing I can honestly say about Denise
was that she always put the kids first. Our relationship was fiery,
but it was never boring.

I heard about the latest scam that all the lads were into to earn
a few quid and decided to try my hand at it. The interest-free-
credit game was easy and lucrative. A lot of shops offered interest-
free credit of up to £3,000, just on the showing of three bits of
ID and a bank-account number. You could walk in off the street,
flash your false paperwork, fill in a couple of forms, pay a deposit
and walk out with three grands' worth of goods, all brand-new
in the box and with a genuine receipt. It was a gift. All you
needed was a medical card, which could be cleaned by soaking
in brake-fluid, with a false name and address on it, a forged
driver's licence, which cost £50 in most south London boozers,
a gas or electric bill, which could be cleaned the same as the
medical card, and a building-society book with £1 deposited in
the account. The Woolwich Building Society was the only place
where you could open an account and they would print up the
book there and then and hand it to you over the counter. For
a £1 deposit you would have a genuine book with your false
name and address printed in it, and a genuine account number.

The shops who were giving you the credit were not allowed
to know how much money you had in your account, and if they
phoned the building society to confirm your account number
they were only allowed to know that you did have a genuine
account there. They would enter your details into their computer,
which would give you an instant credit-rating. Then you would
choose your goods – computers, television sets, video-recorders,
microwave ovens, whatever you knew would sell – pay a £30
deposit and the goods were yours. There were certain pubs in
south London that were like warehouses on some days, with boxed
electrical goods being sold to the highest bidder. Stolen goods
normally sell for one-third of the retail price, but with this stuff,

you were getting the box, the receipt, and no one was going to be looking for them, so we got as much as two-thirds of the retail price. Even if the police had checked them out, they would never come up as stolen. It was so easy that people were even using their own ID to get the stuff, knowing that the worst that could happen was that two years down the line they might get a County Court Judgement against their name and a poor credit rating. No one was ever going to prison for it, that was for sure.

I did a bit of interest-free and got a bit of money behind me, then rented a room from a pal of mine named Mark O'Brien. Mark had a three-bedroom flat in Tulse Hill, where he lived alone. He was a whizz-dealer (amphetamine sulphate). He was never any more than small-time, grams rather than kilos, but he had a steady client-base who would be visiting the flat at all hours of the night and day. We had some great parties in the flat, and they would sometimes go on for days. At the weekends we would do a few lines of whizz, get a carry-out of beer and go to the twenty-four-hour snooker hall in Gipsy Hill. We would be playing snooker and talking bollocks until dawn. There was a good crowd who used to come to the flat, like Dave C., Harry and Peter's younger brother, Robert, known as 'Bert', Tommy Hogan and Big Tony Rawle, known as 'Tank' because of his six-foot-four and eighteen-stone bulk. It was a good time, but I missed Denise and the kids a lot, and I would go and see them often.

I bought a .44 Navy Colt revolver from one of the burglars who used to buy his whizz from Mark. I paid £150 for it, and it was worth every penny; it was a beautiful gun that would have set me back at least £1,200 to buy legally. I also bought a little Webley revolver for £50 from the same burglar.

One night I discussed robbing a bank with Dave C. and Mark. We were all broke, as usual, and they both seemed up for it. Dave in particular wanted to have a go, and I trusted him like a brother. He was one of the gamest men I knew and would stand beside you against any odds. I had known him since the rockabilly gang-war days and had seen him in action many times. I wasn't too sure about Mark. He had some front but he was using a lot of his own whizz and that made him a bit unpredictable. But I decided I would ease them into it and show them the ropes first.

I picked a small branch of the Chelsea Building Society on Leigham Court Road in Streatham, opposite the *South London Press* building. We didn't even have a car between us at this time, so I said I would walk in and do the actual robbery, while Dave would wait at a bus stop outside with the Webley and tackle anyone who tried to stop my getaway. Mark would wait in an alley around the corner, where I would meet him and pass over my gun and disguise. He was to bin the disguise and take the gun back to the flat while I jumped on a bus with the money. We would all meet up back at the flat.

I was already a veteran of many robberies, but I still got a touch of stage fright before I actually pulled the gun; then the buzz would take over. I was wearing a big suede jacket with the collar turned up, a trilby hat pulled low over my forehead and a pair of dark glasses. The gun was in my waistband. I waited till the boys were in position, then I walked into the building society. There were no customers in there, so I went up to the jump and pulled my gun. 'Get the money on the counter,' I told the shocked cashier. She placed a bundle of banknotes on the counter, which I slipped into my pocket. 'Thank you,' I said, and walked out. It was all over in less than a minute, and the getaway went like clockwork.

An hour later I was back at the flat counting the money. The boys were very excited when they saw the cash. And that was that: they were hooked. We spent some of the money on a second-hand Ford Capri to use on the next job, and we were in business. I had a good team and the world was once again my oyster.

Throughout the summer of 1988, me and the boys went on a spree of armed robbery, on banks and building societies all over south London. Mark was our getaway driver, but the more money he earned, the more erratic he became. He started using cocaine as well as whizz, and drinking heavily. His driving skills were also a bit suspect. He would wheelspin away from jobs, attracting attention when there was no need for it, and once, when me and Dave came out of a job in Mitcham, he had moved the getaway car further down the road and we had to search for it. I had a chat with Dave, and we decided that Mark had to go; he was just too much of a liability. We sat him down and gave him the news. He was OK about it and admitted he was on the verge of asking to quit anyway. The work was too scary for him, and he couldn't sleep at night for worrying that he might get caught. Mark just wasn't cut out for this kind of life, and you can't make a silk purse out of a sow's ear.

We decided to set Mark up as an ounce-dealer and invest in a parcel of puff for him to deal out of the flat, so after our next bank job me and Dave put up a couple of grand a piece and set up the business. We each had a third share, but Mark would be in charge of running it. We agreed that if me and Dave ever got nicked, Mark would pay the profits from our shares to our families, and make sure we got plenty of puff delivered to us in prison. We shook on it.

One day me and Dave were plotted up on a bank in Mitcham. It wasn't too crowded and looked like a goer, so we made our entrance in the usual fashion and demanded the cash. Unfortunately for us, the manager was on the ball. He heard what was going on in the banking hall and walked out behind the screen and told the cashiers not to give us the money. No matter how much I threatened, he wouldn't budge. This kind of thing happens from time to time, and short of standing there arguing until the police turn up or shooting everyone in the gaff, there is little that can be done except make an exit.

But as we reached the getaway car the bank manager came out on to the street and started shouting for people to stop us. We took off towards Tooting, with me driving. And it wasn't long before I noticed a huge lorry speeding along right on our tail. I stamped on the accelerator and pulled ahead, but the lorry also put on a burst of speed and stayed right with us. We were on a long straight road with few turn-offs, and our change-over car was at the end of it. If I didn't lose the have-a-go in the lorry we wouldn't be able to dump the car and change into the next one. It was odds on that with all the commotion back at the bank our number-plate would have been noted. I told Dave to climb into the back seat with the shotgun, and when I slowed down, to fire a burst into the lorry's radiator grille. That would certainly disable them and force them to give up the chase.

Dave climbed into the back seat as I struggled to keep the car on the road at high speed. The lorry grille was looming huge in my rearview mirror, so I began to pump the brakes.

'OK,' I shouted. 'Let him have it.'

Suddenly there was what sounded like a sonic boom and I lost control of the steering wheel for a second. The car shimmied and drifted towards the kerb, but I managed to right it just in time. I looked in my rearview mirror and saw that Dave, the fucking lunatic, instead of leaning out of the side window and firing the gun at the lorry, as I had expected him to, had fired the shot through our back windscreen! The lorry dropped back and stopped altogether. Dave clambered back into the passenger seat and gave me a thumbs-up. There was nothing I could say. I just shook my head and carried on driving.

Another time we were plotting up on a bank in Streatham. We weren't actually going to rob it until the afternoon, so we split up and took a walk around to check out the area. The high street was crowded with shoppers and I lost sight of Dave. I was walking past the bank to have a look inside, when I just got the sudden urge to rob it right then. I didn't even have a gun on me, but by now I had robbed so many banks I could do them with my eyes closed. I pulled a paper bag from a bin on the pavement and marched straight in. I held my hand in the bag and put on my mean face. I pointed the bag at the two customers and shouted, 'This is a robbery! Go and stand by the back wall.'

The customers quickly moved to comply, and I turned my attention to the cashiers.

'Get the money up on the counter and nobody will get shot. Move!' I walked along the counter, filling my pockets with one hand while threatening them with the paper bag that was over my other hand. I took over £6,000, and then departed. I just thought it was a bit of a laugh.

I had gone down to see Denise and the kids, and I was talking to her in the kitchen when my two boys came running in, shouting, 'Dad, Dad, you're on the telly, come and have a look!' Chuckling indulgently, me and Denise followed them into the front room where they pointed excitedly at the TV screen. And sure enough, there I was, in living colour. I was bare-faced and pointing my Navy Colt at a bank cashier. I remembered the robbery, I had tried to flick my hood up as I entered the bank but I hadn't noticed, or cared, when it slipped back down again and just carried on. TV presenter Shaw Taylor was doing a voice-over on the security video.

'Do you recognize this man? He and an accomplice have robbed several banks in the London area in the past five months. Police say they are extremely dangerous and should not be approached. If you know who he is then ring this number . . .'

I felt my heart sink. There was no way anyone could fail to recognize me. And not only that, but Shaw Taylor finished by saying there was a 'substantial reward' for information leading to my capture. I was in deep shit. Again.

I kissed Denise and the kids goodbye and drove back to my flat. I was sure that everyone on the streets was looking at me. Knowing that the police have your picture and are actively seeking you for a serious crime is a terrible feeling. It notches any existing paranoia you may have up to a serious level. Knowing that thousands of people have seen your face on the television gives you the feeling that everyone you meet is going to recognize you and inform the police of your whereabouts. I felt hunted. I knew I had to get out of London straight away. I packed a bag with a few clothes, a couple of ounces of hash and some fake ID. I had just over three grand in cash from my last robbery, which I took with me, and I phoned Dave to let him know that I was off. His face hadn't been shown, but I advised him to lie low anyway.

I bought a ferry ticket to Ireland, knowing I could stay with my relatives in Dublin. Then I jumped on a train to Holyhead. Unfortunately, instead of getting on the express train, I got on one that stopped at about twenty stations on the way. Six hours later, I was still on the same train. I'd had a few drinks from the buffet car and rolled and smoked a couple of spliffs in the toilet, so I was half wrecked by the time the train pulled into Rhyl station in North Wales. I decided to get off and spend the night in a hotel and resume my journey the next day.

There was one taxi waiting in the station car park, so I asked the driver if he knew of any decent hotels. He told me his sister owned a good one on the sea front, so I told him to lead on.

The hotel had no single rooms available, so I took a double for the minimum three nights. The room was large and clean, with an en-suite shower and cable television. I ordered food and drink from room service, had a shower and rolled a couple of spliffs. Then I slept until midday the next day.

I ended up staying in Rhyl for a month. I phoned Denise regularly, but the police had been nowhere near the house. The only thing we could put it down to was the fact that at exactly the same time as *Police Five* was shown on ITV, BBCI was showing *Neighbours*, which at that time was a very popular show. I could only guess that anyone who might have recognized me was tuning in to the antics of our Australian cousins. God bless Australia, I say.

I decided to go back to London and move in with my cousins, Michael and Alan Regan, who had a flat on a Clapham estate. They were both hard-drinking, puff-smoking skirt-chasers, so life in their flat was never dull. Now I was certain that it was only a matter of time before the police came for me, so I decided to live it up while I still could. By day I robbed banks, and by night I partied. I spent money like it was going out of fashion, and I carried at least one gun everywhere I went. When I slept, I kept a revolver under my pillow and a shotgun by the side of the bed, fully loaded and cocked. I was determined not to be taken by surprise and to put up a fight when the police came for me. I knew I was looking at a very long stretch in prison.

Then, in October 1988, I got a phone call telling me to look on page two of that week's *South London Press*. Under the headline, 'Do You Know These Men?' were pictures of me and Dave C., taken from a bank's security video. I was wearing a hood, but was in the process of pulling it off, so my face was revealed, and Dave was wearing a flat cap and dark glasses, but the pictures were unmistakably of us. And the reward had gone up to £10,000 for anyone who knew of our whereabouts. I packed a bag once again, only this time I took my guns with me.

Within an hour of the newspaper hitting the streets I was ensconced in a bedsit, rented with false ID, and settled in for a long stay indoors. I only just made it as well. As I drove past Denise's house with my bag in the car, I had to pass through a police roadblock. They had Bedford Road sealed off, and there were armed police everywhere. They weren't expecting me to be driving past in a car, so I got through the roadblock with no trouble. I found out later that the police squad who raided Denise included ten armed officers. They took every bit of money she had in the house, saying that it was the proceeds of crime, and they generally wrecked the place. Then they got a radio message saying that I was at my cousins' flat. They surrounded the flat, then smashed the front door off its hinges. When they realized that I had only been gone for twenty minutes, they lost their collective rag. They separated my cousins in different rooms and set about them. They clubbed Alan to the ground with a pistol butt and pulled a big wardrobe down on top of him. They also slapped Michael around, calling him 'Irish scum'. They told the boys that if they didn't tell them where I was, they would both end up in Brixton prison by the end of the day. And when they found my shoulder-holster and a couple of rounds of ammunition I had left behind in my hasty flight, the police broke the place up.

The only people who knew where I was now living were Denise and Dave C. I phoned both of them the day after the raids to let them know where to get in touch with me. Dave was also in a hideout and had bought a motorbike so he could get about unrecognized in a crash helmet. He came down to my bedsit and we discussed our next move. We still had our armoury of weapons, and we were still one step ahead of the police. They had also raided Dave's family and a few of our mutual friends. We decided to go on an all-out spree, doing a couple of banks a day until we had enough money to get out of the country. But we would lie low for a week first to give the heat a chance to die down.

I couldn't leave the country without seeing Denise and the kids first, so I asked her to come to my hideout. It was a big mistake. She arrived on my doorstep with a frightened look on her face, and she was sure she had been followed. She thought she had lost her tail before turning into the street where I was staying, but her nerves were frayed and it was all getting too much for her. The police had set up an observation post across the road from her house and even followed her when she was taking the boys to school. Lianne was only eighteen months old at the time, and as I watched her and my boys playing on the floor of my scruffy bedsit I had my first regrets about the life I had chosen. The kids didn't know what was going on, but they knew their mum was upset, and that it was my fault. I had never given them a thought when I was out enjoying my gangster lifestyle, but now that it was too late I finally realized what I was about to lose. Ain't it always the way?

On 11 November 1988, I left my hideout for the first time. I was going down to Brixton to get a haircut, and I had already started growing a goatee beard in order to disguise myself.

As soon as I stepped out on to the street I got the feeling something was not quite right. A life of crime, violence and paranoia breeds a kind of sixth sense that kicks in when danger is near. It's hard to explain, it's just the creepy feeling that something isn't quite as kosher as it might appear. I looked up and down the quiet residential street, and at all the cars and vans parked there, but nothing out of the ordinary registered. I walked to my car, got in, and started the engine. Still nothing. I put the car in gear and pulled out into the road, and heard the sound of many engines starting up. I looked in my rearview mirror and saw several cars pulling out behind me, including a black London taxi and a Budget rent-a-van. These two vehicles were the give-away. It was well known in criminal circles that the Flying Squad had an account with Budget and hired their vans for surveillance jobs. It was also common knowledge that they had their own small fleet of black cabs, to blend into the London traffic.

It was on me, and I knew it. I don't know why they didn't take me when I was out in the open on the pavement, but they had now shown their hand, and there was no way I was going to give up without a chase. I was unarmed and driving a shitty little Austin Allegro with all the power of a cheap hairdryer, but I would give it my best shot. I put my foot down, indicated right and then turned left. My manoeuvre didn't fool anyone and they were right on my tail. I drove along Streatham Place at high speed, then spun around a corner on to Tierney Road without indicating. The Flying Squad were all around me. Tierney Road is a long straight stretch with a bend at the end, and I thought that if I could make it around the bend I could get on to the South Circular and stand a better chance, as I knew all the council estates around there and I might be able to dump the car and run.

As I bombed down Tierney Road at my top speed of 70 mph, I saw that they had everything covered. I saw a MkIV Cortina reverse around the bend at the end of the road and park side-ways blocking the bend. Two coppers jumped from the car and went behind it and took up positions with their guns pointing over the roof and directly at me. I had nowhere to go. I briefly thought about trying to ram the car on the bend but dismissed it. I began to pump my brakes. It was all over; I was well and truly nicked. I felt sick. I threw the gearstick into neutral and pumped the brakes until I was doing about 5 mph, then I turned the engine off and let the car coast up to the roadblock. When I came to a stop I put my hands on the ceiling of the car and waited. For a split second there was silence as the following vehicles came to a halt and turned their engines off. In my mind I could hear the booming echo of a cell door slamming.

For a minute nothing happened, then I heard the sound of car doors opening and many feet running along the road. The two coppers on the roadblock kept their guns pointed at me through the windscreen, grim-faced and never wavering.

'Show your fucking hands! Show your fucking hands!' came the shout from right beside my window. I looked out and saw two more armed coppers, one with a pump-action shotgun, the other with a revolver pointing at my head. I waved my hands in front of my face to show that I was unarmed. Suddenly the passenger door was wrenched open and a copper jumped into the car and grabbed my wrist. I was showered in glass as someone smashed the window of the driver's door in with a baton. I was grabbed and dragged bodily through the broken window, but the copper who had come in through the passenger side refused to let go of my wrist, so there was a moment of confusion and struggle. Finally I was dragged out and laid down roughly on the pavement. One copper put his boot across my throat and pointed his revolver at my face.

'If you fucking move . . .' he growled.

He didn't have to finish his sentence, I got the picture.

I was quickly and expertly searched and then rolled on my front before my hands were plasti-cuffed behind my back. Then I was hauled to my feet and a police photographer set up his camera on a tripod in front of me. It is standard practice for the Flying Squad to photograph their suspects when arrested, for many reasons. If a suspect were to try and change his appearance in the months before getting to trial or to claim injuries inflicted at his arrest, then the photographs can be shown to a jury. They also like a souvenir for their rogues' gallery.

'Noel Stephen Smith, I am arresting you for a series of armed robberies that have taken place in the Greater London area in the last eight months. You do not have to say anything, but anything you do say will be taken down and may be used in evidence against you.'

'I ain't got a clue what you're talking about,' I said. 'And I ain't saying nothing till I've seen my brief.'

They searched my bedsit and recovered the guns. I was taken to Brixton police station. They kept asking me where Dave was hiding out, and it buoyed my spirits to know that they hadn't caught him yet. I refused to say anything without my solicitor being present, so I was locked in a cell. When my brief arrived I gave a no-comment interview. Later that evening I was charged with nine counts of armed robbery and possession of firearms. It was back to C-wing at Wormwood Scrubs for me.

19. The Hate Factory

The Flying Squad nicked Dave three months after I was arrested. They raided Mark O'Brien's flat and found him in bed with his girlfriend, Mary. He was charged and put on remand at Wormwood Scrubs. The case against us was very solid: they had the guns and the security photographs, and we were both picked out by several witnesses on an ID parade. But old habits die hard, and the Flying Squad couldn't help sweetening the evidence pot with fabricated verbals. 'Verbals' are words or statements contributed by the police but said to come from the mouth of the suspect so as to make them look guilty. Verballing is nothing new, and the police have probably been using this tactic since they nicked their first suspect. At one time, anything a policeman told the court on oath was considered sacrosanct, and judges, magistrates and juries absolutely refused to believe that the police were capable of lying. But in recent years, due to a surfeit of miscarriage of justice cases where it has been proven that the police had no compunction about torturing, beating and falsifying evidence against suspects, verbals are less likely to be believed.

When I got the bundle of statements after the committal to Crown Court, I wasn't surprised to see that I had been verballed. They claimed that after I had been cautioned I stated, 'I knew it had to come sooner or later. I'm just glad I've been stopped before I killed somebody.' It wasn't on a par with, 'It's a fair cop, guv,' but it was fucking close.

We were committed to trial at the Old Bailey, but there were so many robbery cases pending in the courts that we ended up in Knightsbridge Crown, which was the 'overflow' court for the Old Bailey. Dave had decided to plead guilty, and eventually I reluctantly agreed to do the same. But whereas Dave was sticking his hands up to ten armed robberies and related firearms charges,

I refused to plead unless it was to two armed robberies, one attempted robbery and possession of firearms with intent. The prosecution agreed. So on 25 July 1989 we appeared before Judge Steven Mitchell in court number one at Knightsbridge, for sentence.

Dave had very few previous convictions and none for robbery, so his brief told him to expect between five and eight years. Personally, I thought he was being wildly optimistic, and I told him so. But Dave set his mind on eight years maximum. I expected between twelve and fifteen, because of my previous record. Dave was the first up to be sentenced, and from Count One his illusions were cruelly shattered. He got nine years for Counts One, Two and Three, ten years for Counts Four and Five, eleven years for Count Six, twelve years for Counts Seven, Eight and Nine, and thirteen years for Count Ten. Making a total of thirteen, with the rest to run concurrently. So much for his brief's estimate.

I was next, and though I faced only four counts, Judge Mitchell took longer to sentence me because he couldn't resist slagging me off first. I was a 'vicious criminal', a 'danger to the public', a 'violent recidivist', and several more of those stock phrases beloved by Crown Court judges. Finally he gave me twelve years each on Counts One and Two, thirteen on Count Three, and two and a half consecutive on Count Four. Making a total of fifteen years and six months. And that was that. The very next case in front of Judge Mitchell for sentencing was a police officer who pleaded guilty to raping a sixteen-year-old girl in his patrol car. He was given seven years.

Both Dave and I were now long-term Category A prisoners and were taken to Brixton prison under police escort. I was pretty philosophical about my sentence. I had been expecting something in double figures, and though I wasn't exactly happy about it, I had at least been prepared for it. Dave was gutted. He hadn't done a lot of bird, and while on remand he had found out that Mary was pregnant with their first child. I tried to cheer him up, but he was devastated.

After a night in Brixton we were transferred to Wandsworth

prison. At that time Wandsworth was the main allocation centre for long-term prisoners from London and the south-east. I would be on D-wing. D-wing held 120 Category A and E men and long-termers. A long-termer is usually anyone who is serving over seven years' imprisonment. The official description of Category A prisoners is 'Any prisoner whose escape would make them a danger to the police, the public, or the government.' E-men are prisoners who have escaped, attempted to escape or have a history of either. Category A prisoners are given a high degree of security, including armed police escorts and security vetting of all mail and visits. The only good thing about being Category A is that you are entitled to a single cell, as you are considered 'too dangerous' to be put in with anyone else. Each Category A prisoner has a small book containing their photo and details, which is held by the screws and used to record their every move outside the cell. Prisoners call it being 'on the book'. E-men also have a book, and they in addition have to wear a high-visibility uniform which consists of normal prison blues but with a wide yellow stripe on every item of clothing. E-men also have all of their clothing and kit taken from their cell every night. And both A- and E-men are subject to sudden transfers to prisons all over the country. This is known as 'ghosting', as you can disappear at any time.

I was dreading my time in Wandsworth. There is a bad atmosphere inside the prison, and it settled on me as soon as I got off the van. Everything is old and cold, with hardly a hint of colour anywhere. The floors are grey, the walls are grey and the sad, beaten faces of the prisoners are grey.

There were a lot of infamous criminals on D-wing, like Freddie Foreman, who did a ten with the Krays for disposing of Jack 'The Hat' McVitie's body. He was now doing nine years for handling some of the £7 million loot from the Securicor depot robbery in Curtain Road, East London. Dogan Arif, the eldest of the notorious south London Arif clan, was also there doing nine years for a drug-smuggling offence. In the cell directly above mine was Great Train Robber Tommy Wisbey, back doing a ten for coke. Tom was fifty nine at the time but still fit as a fiddle. I saw him have a punch up with a fella named Paul Whitehead who was half his age, and he beat the shit out of him. One of my more surreal experiences was sitting next to Tom in the gym for our bi-weekly movie show when they showed *Buster*, the story of his fellow train robber Buster Edwards. Tom never stopped moaning all through the film, saying things like, 'That never happened!', and 'Who the fuck is that supposed to be?'

Denise had been visiting me regularly throughout my remand time, but I decided that there was no way I could ask her to wait for me. I was doing a long time, and she was a relatively young woman, and good looking with it. I got her up on a visit and spelled everything out to her, but she wouldn't wear it. She told me that she loved me, and she would visit and bring the kids no matter where I was sent. I was touched that after all I had put her through, she was still willing to stand by me.

I was eager to escape, as always, and so was Dave, so we spent all of our exercise plotting ways to get out of Wandsworth. We were slightly demoralized by the fact that the last escape from Wandsworth prison had been in 1966, when Great Train Robber Ronnie Biggs had gone over the wall with a lot of help from outside sources. Wandsworth was now considered to be escape-proof, but that didn't stop us from thinking up a lot of hare-brained schemes that might get us out. One of Dave's ideas was to climb on to the roof of D-wing, negotiating the anti-climb barriers and rolls of razor-wire with a prison mattress. Then he wanted to tie the mattress around his body with strips of sheet and take a running jump from the sixty-foot roof, across a gap of twenty feet, and land on the top of the perimeter wall, hoping the mattress would cushion his landing. I managed to talk him out of that one.

I was like a lion in a cage at Wandsworth, forever on the prowl and looking for any opportunity to escape or turn on my keepers. I detested the screws, and stoking up plenty of hate and rage against them helped to keep my mind off the amount of time I had left to serve. The food was atrocious. They served up something they had the brass neck to call 'savoury rice', which was normal rice with a carrot diced into it. Curried beans was another staple: baked beans with curry powder added, and plenty of corn-flour to thicken the juice and disguise the fact that there weren't many actual beans in it. The cornflour would be just thrown in and created a glutinous paste. Corned beef was another favourite of the 'cooks'; straight from the catering-size tin, with thick white fat and jelly all around the edges, and served up with powdered potato and stewed cabbage. Most of the trouble happened at meal times when they were serving this shit up. The screws thought the food was hilarious, and they always wore big grins while dishing it out. But the final insult was when one of them decided to take the menu from their own canteen and stick it up over the hotplate. It had things like steak and chips, pork chops and chocolate gâteau on it, and that was one piss-take too many.

My first attempt at inciting a concerted act of indiscipline was a bit touch and go. I was walking around the exercise yard with Dave, a robber out of Camberwell named Jimmy Wynter, and his co-defendant from east London, who we called 'Dex'. It was mid June with the temperature in the eighties. On exercise we were not allowed to stop or sit down on the yard, we had to keep walking in a clockwise circle, and we were not allowed to take our shirts off, no matter how hot it was. There were around two hundred prisoners on the yard and, as usual, a lot of the talk was about the liberties the screws were taking. The Strangeways riot was just over, and a lot of other jails had kicked off in the wake of it, including Dartmoor, Bristol, Pucklechurch and Risley. During the Strangeways siege the screws on duty at Wandsworth were doubled, but when it ended they had reverted to their old arro-gance and only had six screws on the yard. The screws were posi-tioned strategically in twos, next to the three alarm buttons. It was an irritating source of shame to me and many other prisoners that we had not seized our chance when Strangeways had kicked off and taken our revenge on Wandsworth. But the brutal atmosphere at Wandsworth had a debilitating effect on most prisoners.

Dave was moaning about the food and saying we should do

something about it before the moment was gone. We were all hot and sweating in our thick shirts and tired of walking in circles, so I decided I was going to sit down. Just like that, I had the idea and put it into action.

'I'm sitting down,' I said. 'If you boys want to join me, feel free.'

I walked off the paved circle and sat down in the shade. The lads just stood there looking at me.

'You'll get nicked, you fucking nutter!' said Dave.

I shrugged. I'd had enough of talking, it was time for action. I knew if I was the only one to sit down I would end up being hammered by the screws in the block, but I didn't give a shit. My pride wouldn't allow me to stand back up again, so I was fucked. Dave, Jimmy and Dex carried on walking for a few steps, then they turned back and sat beside me. The adrenaline was kicking in now, and the blood was singing through my veins. I was actually doing something, I was in control of my own destiny at last, and I would face whatever consequences there were. No one could say that Razor Smith knuckled under at Wandsworth.

At first, the circle of other prisoners just stared at us, open-mouthed, and carried on walking. Dave gave me a worried look and nodded his head in the direction of the nearest pair of screws. They had been busy talking and didn't see us sit down, but as the buzz spread through the crowd of prisoners the screws sensed the change in atmosphere and looked about for the source of it. I saw one of the screws adjust his sunglasses and look in our direction. The yard was big, so he couldn't identify us from where he was, but he knew he didn't like what he was seeing. I saw him put his radio up to his mouth and begin the long walk to where we were. Suddenly a group of about ten prisoners, led by a west London robber and prison escapee named Greg Crabtree, came out of line and flopped down on to the ground right next to us. Then, as if a signal had been given, at least a hundred prisoners broke ranks and came and sat down. Dave breathed a heartfelt sigh of relief and grinned at me.

'Simple as that, Dave,' I said.

But I was also relieved. There was safety in numbers, they couldn't beat and block all of us. Within minutes there were only about twenty prisoners still walking the circle. The screw who had started to walk over soon backtracked, talking urgently into his radio. Wandsworth was now seeing its first act of concerted indiscipline, and I had started it.

The sit-down had been on the spur of the moment, so we had no strategy worked out for what would come next. The screws were looking nervous, and that was gratifying enough on its own. To see the arrogance slowly seeping from their faces when they realized they had almost two hundred prisoners on a sit-down is a sight that I'll take to my grave. Five minutes after we had sat down, the heavy mob arrived. The yard was flooded with dog-handlers with big, snarling Alsatians on short leads. Every other wing in the jail was locked down and the screws deployed to D-wing yard. The screws didn't approach us, they just lined up on the opposite side of the yard in a show of strength. We just laid back and enjoyed the sunshine for a change, people stripped their shirts off and used them as pillows, casually ignoring the screws.

Half an hour into the sit-down a governor came out on to the yard flanked by six screws in riot gear and carrying shields. The screws lined up as a barrier in front of him, and the governor spoke to us from behind it.

'Who is the ringleader here?' was his first question.

Nobody answered.

'Well, what is it you want then?' was his next.

We were all too prison-wise to put ourselves on offer. Anyone who spoke would be singled out as the instigator and be punished.

'You can't stay out here all day?' he said, but it was more of a question than a statement. He shook his head, and I was close enough to see the sweat on his top lip. I was delighted. It was probably the first time this besuited prick had ever spoken to prisoners, and he was cacking himself. Greg Crabtree put his hand up. The governor looked relieved.

'Yes, you there, what have you to say?'

Greg smiled. 'I was just wondering, governor. Did you buy that whistle at Oxfam?'

It got a massive laugh from every prisoner on the yard, but I could tell by the looks on the screws' faces that Greg was going to pay for it later. But it broke the ice, and several prisoners began to talk. I kept quiet as a list of grievances came out about the food, the amount of time banged up and the attitude of the screws. There was no way I was going to offer myself up as a sacrifice, not twice in one day.

After a bit of conversation, the governor, looking much more confident now, said that if we returned to our cells quietly, there would be no reprisals and he would look into our complaints. There was a short discussion amongst the prisoners, which I was careful to take no part in, and we decided to go in. We had already been out an hour over our exercise time and got a bit of a suntan, so we classed it as a result. If we started fighting with the screws, plenty of us would be hurt and end up with extra charges. We had made our point, so better to go in quietly and live to fight another day. I felt I could now hold my head up, Wandsworth hadn't beaten me. And I was secure in the knowledge that if conditions didn't improve I could always kick it off again.

When we were all safely locked in our cells, the reprisals began. And sure enough, Greg Crabtree was the first to go. He was marched to the punishment block on GOAD (Good Order And Discipline), which is official prison-speak for being put in solitary confinement for no specific charge. The next morning he was shipped to Albany prison on the Isle of Wight, along with six other prisoners picked at random. I escaped the mini-purge.

The removal of Greg Crabtree and others after the governor had promised no reprisals did little to foster any good will between prisoners and staff – not that there was that much in the first place, but things grew more tense in the following weeks. And when the next major incident occurred, I made sure I was in the thick of it.

I heard a rumour that a firm of prisoners was planning a spectacular break-out. But prison etiquette does not allow just anyone to invite themselves on to someone else's coup, or even enquire too closely about it, so I wasn't involved in the planning.

Since the spring of 1990 work had been going on to lay a new path in the sterile area at Wandsworth. The sterile area of a prison is the piece of ground between the perimeter wall and the inner fence, where no prisoner should ever step foot. Only dog patrols are allowed into the sterile area, but at Wandsworth, when the work was going on, there were civilian workmen and a lot of equipment in there. Including a JCB. Every time we came out on the yard for exercise we could see them working away.

I found out later that the plan was to do the screws guarding the gate to the sterile area from the exercise yard, then hijack the JCB and use it to crash through the wall. The plan needed plenty of bottle and a bit of luck for it to succeed. The thing that made it feasible was that while we were on exercise, the dustbin party would normally come through the yard gate and bring their trolley across the yard to collect the bins from the mailbag shop at the end of D-wing. The ideal time to strike would be when the gate was opened by the yard screws to let the dustbin party through. The only problem was that the alarm was sure to be raised very quickly, so the boys had to get to the JCB before the screws could reach them.

Exercise occurred as normal on the morning of 29 June, and only the participants knew that the day was going to be any different. I was walking around and noticed the change in atmosphere. My prison radar told me that something was about to happen. I saw the screws opening the gate to let the trolley through, and then I saw the group of prisoners in front of me pull on masks made from the sleeves of prison-issue sweatshirts. They burst from the crowd of circling prisoners and attacked the three screws on the gate. The screws went down like ninepins, and the five masked men were through the gate and running down the short alley to the sterile area. A cheer went up from the massed ranks of prisoners, and I cheered right along with them. We all rushed over to the fence and watched as the escape team came out in the sterile area. The screws who were guarding the civilian workers, faced with five masked and screaming prisoners running towards them, legged it. The civilians, a bit slower on the uptake, just stood there, frozen. Two of the escape team picked up abandoned shovels and made threatening moves towards the civilians who, seeing which way the wind was now blowing, ran for their lives. The only one left was a big, fat bloke in the driver's seat of the JCB. Two of the escape team leaped up on to the vehicle and bodily dragged the driver out, and he waddled off after his mates.

By this time the noise on the yard was phenomenal. Alarm bells were clanging, and all the prisoners from the yard were packed against the fence screaming encouragement. The screws had quickly got the gate locked and were looking stunned. Screws from all over the prison burst out on to the yard, only to be confronted by a hundred and fifty prisoners in a state of uproar. They didn't know what to do. Nothing like this had ever happened at Wandsworth, at least not since the Ronnie Biggs escape in 1966. I was pressed against the fence, screaming the boys on.

The escape team were all on the JCB, an Irish robber called Tony the Rat in the driver's seat, but the screws had got out on to the sterile area, and twenty or so of them, with batons drawn, were heading for the JCB. The escape team were all armed with shovels now, and they swung them at the first wave of screws who tried to clamber aboard the JCB and repelled them. The JCB was up on its hydraulic legs and these had to be disengaged before it could move forward. But Tony the Rat had been lying when he said he knew how to drive the JCB. He didn't have a clue. He tried to go forward and stalled the engine. Screws were now flooding the sterile area. Tony started the engine again and this time disengaged the legs. He threw it in gear and went forward a couple of feet before stalling again. In the meantime, one enterprising screw had jumped on to an abandoned dump-truck and started it up. Tony got the JCB engine started again and rolled forward, but the screw in the dump-truck pulled in front of him and blocked his path to the wall. The JCB stalled again, and this time, when Tony the Rat tried to start it, the engine flooded.

Behind the fence we could see every moment of this heart-stopping drama, and contributed like kids at a pantomime with shouts of 'Behind you!' when the screws tried rushing the JCB from different angles. Collective cheers and groans went up when the JCB started and stalled. I looked around and saw that there were about thirty screws on the yard with us, but they were milling around not knowing what to do. It made my heart sing to see the confusion and demoralized and frightened looks on their previously smug faces.

The JCB now flooded and stalled, the escape team looked like the survivors of a shipwreck clinging to a lifeboat, the screws like a tide of blue serge ebbing and flowing as they darted back and forth trying to pull the boys from the digger. It was a stand-off. The screws couldn't get near the JCB, and the escape team couldn't go anywhere. Then one of the screws reached down to the piles of rubble from the work on the path, and picked up a fist-sized piece of concrete. I saw him do it, and I knew what his next move would be before he made it. He hefted the concrete in his hand and then launched it, over arm, at the JCB. It smashed straight through the side window of the cab and hit Tony the Rat in the head. He slumped forward on to the steering wheel, unconscious. And the rest of the screws started picking up rubble and throwing it at the escape team. In a second, the air around the JCB was black with flying rubble. There was an almost continuous clanging as the missiles bounced from the metal body of the vehicle, and every window was turned to glass confetti. The escape team took many hits. With prisoners being stoned to death under the hot sun, we could just as easily have been in some prison yard in Damascus in 200 BC as in Wandsworth in 1990.

The prisoners on my side of the fence grew silent. There were a few groans as the screws really got into the swing of it, but short of tearing down the fence with our bare hands, there was nothing we could do to help. I felt sick at what was happening to the lads, but I also felt my terrible anger and rage rushing to the surface.

When all the escape team were down on the ground, at least three of them unconscious, the screws rushed in with batons drawn. They were like animals. Knots of screws crowded around each prisoner, kicking and hitting him with batons. It was as though they didn't care who saw them. The screws had been seconds away from losing these five men, and it was as if they now had to be punished in front of the rest of us in order to send us a message about not taking them on. For me it had the exact opposite effect. The bloodied and beaten escape team were dragged away to the block. As the last man was dragged over the rubble, leaving bright-red blood glinting on the concrete, I turned to the screws waiting on my side of the fence. If I'd had a gun, I would have executed every one of them without blinking an eye. My head was completely gone.

The crowd was silent as it turned away from the fence. There were now around forty screws facing us. I could see by their faces that they were nervous. A fat PO stepped to the fore and put out his hands placatingly.

'Come on now, lads,' he said. 'It was a good try, but it's all over now. Let's have you all back to your cells.'

Nobody moved. A spark was needed to light the dynamite. I stepped out of the crowd and faced the PO.

'Anywhere you want me, you're going to have to fucking well put me,' I said, and was grateful that there was no quaver in my voice. The fat PO swallowed, hard, and looked back at the screws behind him. He then looked over my shoulder at the crowd of silent prisoners.

'There's no need for any more trouble. Just go back to your cells before things get out of hand. You've all got remission to lose. Think about it.'

There was a murmuring from the crowd, and I got the feeling that the moment was passing all too quickly. I decided the time for talking was over. I took a fast step forward and threw a right hook at the PO's jaw. I caught him right on target, and he went down. Without stopping, I stepped over his body and threw more punches into a crowd of screws.

I was well up for it, throwing lefts and rights like a pro and dodging truncheon blows. But I couldn't understand why there were so many screws surrounding just me, until I took a blow to the head and went down. I was put in painful wrist-locks and hoisted on to my feet. And that's when I saw that only one other prisoner had followed me on the attack, the rest were being held at bay by screws with raised truncheons. I couldn't believe it. All these so-called hard men and tough guys, classed as some of the most dangerous criminals in the prison system, and they had lost their bottle when it actually came down to it. How many times had I walked around the yard and listened to these same men mouthing off about how it would be if they ever got the chance for a bit of payback? Now they had watched five of their own being beaten half to death by screws they professed to despise, and they had done nothing. At that moment I lost faith in prisoner solidarity. It wasn't the first time I had been left out on a limb by big-talking wankers, but I made up my mind it would be the last.

Whenever I hear prisoners talking about 'solidarity' and 'staunchness', I just walk away. If every prisoner in the country woke up tomorrow morning and decided to walk out of prison, there is nothing the authorities could do to stop us. We have such a draconian prison system in this country simply because the prisoners allow it, and instead of doing something about it they just sit back and fucking moan. I learned all of this on the yard at Wandsworth on 29 June 1990. I proved I was willing to make sacrifices, and I can hold my head up high in any company and, to me, that is what being 'staunch' and 'game' is all about.

'That's it now. Back to your cells!'

The fat PO was off the ground and fully in control now. The prisoners began to slink quietly back on to the wing. I was being held in wrist-locks and surrounded by a group of panting screws. I watched the last of the prisoners go on to D-wing and I felt like crying with the frustration of what had happened. The fat PO stood in front of me, rubbing his jaw where I had hit him.

'Think you're a real fucking hard man, don't you?' he said.

I spat at him. And he hit me with a hard punch in the stomach that knocked all the wind out of me.

'Get him in his cell,' he ordered the screws. 'I'll phone the block and check if they're ready for him.'

I was dragged away. When we got on the wing one of the screws who didn't know me asked me what my name was so as to check what number cell I was in. 'Spartacus,' I replied. But he didn't see the humour in it.

I was locked into my cell while the screws went to check that their pals in the block had finished locking up the escape team. In the cell next door to me was a West End face named 'Gentleman' Johnny Rosen, and he banged on the wall. I climbed up on to my table to talk to him through the window. He swung me a line with a little bit of cannabis and some tobacco on it, for my stay in the block. I quickly wrapped the puff, tobacco and some Rizlas and match heads in a bit of plastic bag and bottled the parcel. 'Bottling' is the universal way that prisoners hide items from searching by the screws. It involves inserting the parcel or 'joey' into the anus. Short of sticking their fingers up your arse, which some do, it is impossible for the screws to find the parcel. It wasn't long before I heard the sound of many boots marching along the landing towards my cell. I got down from the window and stood at the back of the cell with my back to the wall and waited. The door opened and a different PO stood there with a six-screw escort, all grim faces and big boots.

'These officers are going to escort you to the block,' said the PO. 'You can either walk or be carried. It's up to you.' For the word 'carried' he meant dragged and kicked.

I knew I was odds on for a kicking no matter what way I went, but I decided to play along. 'I'll walk,' I said.

As I came out of my cell the prison was unnaturally quiet. I noticed the twenty-stone gym-screw waiting for me; at one time he had won the World's Strongest Man competition on the telly. He didn't say a word, he just stood looking at me. The unspoken message was clear: if I had put up a fight in the cell it would have been him who came in first. As it happened, he didn't lay a finger on me, and I was glad of that, because a punch from him would have been like being hit with a sledgehammer.

Wandsworth prison is built to the 'opticon' design, meaning that all of the wings radiate out from the centre, like spokes radiating from the hub of a wheel. The centre at Wandsworth was infamous among prisoners all over the system. The centre consists of a central tiled mosaic surrounded by metal grating and a tiled pathway. Prisoners were not allowed to walk 'across' the centre, but only on the tiled path around the edge, and only in a clockwise direction; and they had to observe a strict rule of silence on the centre. Any prisoner who disobeyed these rules would suffer a punch in the mouth at the very least. The screws had a saying about the centre: God may walk on the centre, but he only does it when the staff are not watching. To the screws at Wandsworth, the centre was sacred.

I reached the end of D-wing, followed by my posse of screws, and looked down at the centre. What I saw made me feel weak in the knees. Almost every screw in the prison was waiting there. They looked up at me in silence, but with hatred coming off them in hot putrid waves. It was at this moment that I realized I could quite easily die here today. These people were not playing. I was poked in the back.

'Walk down the stairs and clockwise around the centre. Move!'

I managed to find the strength in my legs to follow the PO's orders. I walked through the iron gates and out on to the pathway around the centre. The block was in the basement of E-wing, which was right next to D-wing, but to reach it I had to traverse the whole centre.

'Draw batons!'

I don't know who shouted the order, but my mouth went dry and it was a physical effort to keep on walking that seemingly endless distance around.

The screws on the centre drew their truncheons, crouched down and began to beat them against the iron grating on the floor. The noise was bowel-wateringly frightening. I kept walking, and they all kept watching me. I have never been so thoroughly intimidated in my life. I was actually glad to reach E-wing and the stairs that led down into the block without being attacked. But my relief was momentary. I stopped at the top of the stairs and looked down. The batter squad were waiting for me, big screws with their shirtsleeves rolled up and blood on their boots and knuckles. I was prodded in the back once again, and I descended into hell.

There were already puddles and smears of blood on the block floors and walls from the members of the escape team. My escort waited at the top of the stairs and as soon as my foot touched the bottom step, I was grabbed by the batter squad. They half-marched-half-dragged me into the block. A governor stood in his shirtsleeves behind the block daïs. He had a smear of blood on his shirt. Earlier I had witnessed him putting the boot into one of the escape team in the sterile area. He stared at me.

'Take him in that cell and wipe the fucking smirk off his face,' he ordered.

I wondered how he could mistake a look of pure terror for a smirk. But worse, he had just given the screws carte blanche to do what they wanted to me. Uniformed screws are basically drones who look to the governor grades for guidance, and if a governor grade gives them an order, no matter how indirect, to beat me, then, by God, they would beat me until their arms grew tired. Though there was no way my pride would let me show it, I was petrified. If they were to go over the top and kill me, I wouldn't be the first suspicious death to come out of Wandsworth block. Far from it. And as far as I knew, no screws had ever been prosecuted.

They started by running me, head first, into the back wall of an open cell. Then the real beating started. I was held against the wall while three screws punched me in the ribs and kidneys. They kept kicking my feet away so I fell to the floor and then they would pull me up by my hair and continue their beating. All through this phase, there was a block SO standing by the door, casually marking my details on the punishment block roll-board and shouting questions at me. Then they ordered me to strip for the search. As I took off my shoes one of the screws stamped on my foot. It was very painful and I'd had enough. I had a sudden burst of rage and grabbed the screw in a headlock and pumped a couple of punches into his face. They hadn't been expecting it, and neither had I, to tell the truth, but they soon had me on the floor again, and this time they gave me a proper stomping. I was hoping that they would knock me unconscious, but it never happened and I had to endure the pain.

When the screws left the cell I was in a bad way. When I lifted my head from the floor I found two of my own teeth lying there. I had some serious pain, but at least I was still alive, and that was something to be thankful for. I knew from experience that the pain would recede and I would heal. I'd had many beatings in my life, but never had I been subjected to such a well-thought-out process of intimidation first. When it came to instilling fear and dishing out brutality, the screws at Wandsworth were experts. Later in the evening of that day, my door swung open again, to reveal three of the screws who had administered my beating. I sat in the corner, unable to stand because they had stamped on my ankles. The screws popped the lock and came into the cell. They told me, in no uncertain terms, that if I caused any more trouble at Wandsworth I would end up hanging from the bars. And to back up their threat they dangled a crude noose made from prison bed-sheets in front of my face. I had no doubt that they were capable of it, so I kept my mouth shut.

I was charged with assaulting a prison officer by punching him in the head, and attempting to incite other inmates to riot. I appeared in front of the governor and pleaded guilty to assault but not guilty to inciting a riot. I lost another twenty-eight days' remission for assault, and I was remanded in the block for trial in front of the Board of Visitors. Prison Rule 47, para 22, inciting to riot, was one of two charges on the rulebook that carried the maximum penalty of unlimited loss of remission (the other charge is gross personal violence to a prison officer, which I was done for in Rochester for hitting the night-watchman). If found guilty of incitement I could well be forced to do every day of my fifteen-and-a-half-year sentence, probably in solitary confine-ment, so I petitioned the Home Office to be allowed legal repre-sentation at my 'trial'. My petition was granted, and to illustrate how serious my situation was felt to be, I can tell you that less than one per cent of prisoners charged with a disciplinary offence has ever been granted legal representation in the history of the prison system.

The escape team were all charged with various assaults on screws and civilian workers and attempted prison escape. Their charges were serious enough to allow the governor to call in the police and the Crown Prosecution Service to deal with them, which would be a long, slow process, allowing them plenty of time to recover from their own injuries. We were all held incom-municado, with no access to anyone outside the prison. The prison doctor who examined us in the block was only interested in checking our hands and knuckles to see if he could find evidence of us assaulting anyone and was not receptive to any of our injuries. He dismissed them as 'self-inflicted during the escape attempt'. I found out later that the attempted escape had been big news all over the world. Some of my relatives saw it on the evening news in Dublin, and Sky News even interviewed Ronnie Biggs in Rio about it. Biggsy said that if we had waited a few days, until the twenty-fourth anniversary of his own escape, we might have had a little bit of luck on our side.

Within two weeks, most of the escape team had been ghosted to other prisons all over the country. The screws were back to their previous arrogant selves. Our moment of rebellion had fright-ened the lives out of them, but they soon forgot it. I was a one-in-five unlock, which means that before they would even consider opening my cell door for any reason they had to have at least one SO and five screws present. I had a boot imprint across my face for a couple of weeks where one of the screws had stamped on it while I was on the floor. As well as losing the two teeth, I had lumps and bruises all over my head and body. But I was recovering. The screws in the block were typical of their breed, all slashed-peak hats, chewing gum and black-leather gloves, and

I detested them. Where some people fall asleep at night counting sheep, I would get to sleep by shooting screws in my head. I had almost a decade left to serve, and I'd been bitter and twisted against the system even before I came in. I knew that if I didn't get out of Wandsworth soon, I might end up killing one of the screws for real.

After five weeks in the block, I finally got to see my solicitor. Peter Cadman, of Russell-Cooke in Putney, had never handled a Board of Visitors trial before, but then again there were very few solicitors who had. He was soon on to the governor, asking why I was being held in solitary where I couldn't arrange to speak to any potential witnesses who might be able to help my case. The day after his phone call I was released back on to D-wing. It was like getting parole. I knew it was almost impossible to win a case in front of the Board of Visitors, but with Peter Cadman representing me, I thought I might have a chance. I also knew that if I lost the case they would lock me so deep in prison that they'd have to pump air to me. There would be a lot riding on this trial.

20. On the Island

It was while I was at Wandsworth prison that I first came across Charly Bronson, 'Britain's Most Dangerous Prisoner'. Charly is a legend among prisoners and is even now known by the general public through his various books and documentaries on his life. He has been committed to Broadmoor twice, and both times he managed to get on the roof and rip it to shreds. That would be some achievement on its own, but when you add to it his other antics over the years, such as hostage-taking and being the most transferred prisoner in the British prison system, you begin to see that Charly really is an extraordinary character. I could fill a book with the stories I have heard about Charly over the years, but I'd never be able to say which were true and which were just part of the legend. But I will say this, I've rarely met a prisoner who didn't have a good word to say about Charly.

After I got back to D-wing from the block, things had quietened down a lot. Prisoners who had been waiting, sometimes for years, for transfers to other prisons suddenly found the process speeded up after the JCB incident. There were also firm plans to empty D-wing and begin modernizing it, putting toilets and showers in the cells. The system had been shaken up by what had happened on 29 June, and I was proud to have been part of it. I still had the trial to face, but I was more optimistic now that I was legally represented and out of the block.

The inquiry into Strangeways and other related riots was started by Lord Woolf, and for the first time in many years it seemed as though the powers that be were going to take a critical look at the state of our prison system. And not before time. Also, the European Commission on Torture in Prisons and Special Hospitals was touring the country and taking depositions from the people at the sharp end, and Wandsworth prison was near the top of their list.

One day I was sweeping the landing outside my cell when Dave called me over.

'You've got to get a look at this geezer!' he said, and pointed out of the recess window. Below the recess were the punishment-block exercise yards and a series of fenced and gated alleys that led on to the wing. I looked down and saw a big-shouldered prisoner with a bristling moustache, wearing a long prison-issue canvas raincoat, marching along. There were three screws with him, but they were struggling to match his pace. One of the screws was running ahead and unlocking the gates before the prisoner reached them, and the other two were locking the gates as he passed through without stopping, and then rushing to catch up at the next gate. The prisoner did not acknowledge the screws at all, and just kept marching forward at the same fast pace. It was like watching a loping lion with insects buzzing around it. I chuckled at this sight.

'Who the fuck is that?' I asked.

Gentleman Johnny Rosen had joined us at the window.

'That's Charly Bronson,' he said. 'He's done bundles of screws over the years, and they're shit-scared of him.'

I watched him march through a gate and on to the wing.

'Come on,' said Johnny. 'Have a look at this, you'll love it.'

We hurried out of the recess and down to the end of the landing above the gate Charly had entered through. And there he was. The front screw opened the gate that led to the centre and Charly marched straight through, and across it! There were plenty of screws about, but they all deigned not to notice this prisoner marching bare-faced across their holy of holies. Gentleman Johnny shouted out, 'Hello, Chaz!', and Charly looked up and waved, but kept his pace across the middle of the centre.

'Shut your fucking mouth, Rosen!' screamed a PO from the centre.

Charly came to a sudden halt and turned his head slowly to look at the PO. The three escort screws were panting with exertion and glad of the rest. Charly stared at the PO for about ten seconds. The PO swallowed.

'Morning, Bronson,' he muttered, and then turned around and walked away.

Charly looked up at us, gave us a nod, and then carried on his march to wherever he was going.

We were delighted. It was a lift to see that there were prisoners in the system who could silence a Wandsworth PO with no more than a look. And I was glad he was on our side. I would get to know Charly a bit better later on in my sentence, but for now just his presence in the prison was enough to make a lot of prisoners feel that the system wasn't having it all its own way.

One day an SO came to see me in my cell. The man had always been a 'dog' in any dealings I'd had with him in the past. A 'dog' is how prisoners describe any screw who will go out of his or her way to start trouble where none exists. So I was suspicious when he started coming over with a Mr Nice Guy routine, asking me how I was and which prison I was hoping to be allocated to. Finally, when he saw I was not playing his game, he got to the point.

'There are some people here who want to interview you,' he said. 'You don't have to speak to them if you don't want to. You're entirely within your rights to refuse.'

I was intrigued. 'Who are they?' I asked.

He shrugged. 'Just some busybodies from Europe, going around sticking their noses into things that shouldn't concern them.'

Then I twigged. 'The European Commission on Torture?' I asked.

The SO nodded. 'But if you do decide to talk to these people, you should be aware that it will be noted on your record.'

The unspoken threat was clear. I smiled.

'What can you do?' I said. 'Put me in prison and kick my teeth out?'

The SO slammed the door behind him.

Ten minutes later the door was opened again and I met two smart-suited men from the Commission. One was German and the other French, but they both spoke perfectly good English.

There was a security PO with them. After the introductions, they asked me if I was willing to talk to them. I said, 'Yes, but not in front of him,' and pointed at the PO. He went red in the face and began to bluster, but the men politely insisted that he leave. His parting shot was, 'I hope you know that this man is highly dangerous. He's attacked several prison staff, you know.'

The men told me that my name had been given to them by several prisoners who said I had been a victim of torture while in the punishment block. They also told me that since being in England they had taken depositions from several dozen prisoners and patients of special hospitals alleging the most 'horrific tortures'. They both stated that they had already investigated some South American prisons but found little as bad as what they were finding in the British prison system.

My deposition took over an hour. I told them everything about 29 June, and when I reached the part about the screws banging their batons on the centre as I walked around it, they told me that it was not the first time they had heard of this. Apparently it is a technique of intimidation taught in British Army riot control. The Commissioners told me that their report would take about a year to compile and be released, but that they already had enough to know it was not going to be very complimentary to the prison system. I looked forward to reading it.

Lord Woolf also sent a circular to prisoners asking for any information on the prison system that might be helpful to him in his inquiry. The screws were not happy with this, because any letter to Woolf was allowed to be sent out already sealed by the prisoner. Most of the screws got their jollies by reading our daily incoming and outgoing mail, and if we were allowed to send out a sealed letter, then who knows what we might reveal about them? But there was nothing they could do about it; the orders had come direct from the Home Office. But still most of us took precautions by wrapping most of the envelopes in Sellotape.

Finally, the day of my trial came around. I was marched down to the education block, where it was to take place, by eight screws. The screws were in a good mood, telling me how I had no chance of winning, but I just kept quiet. I had a good brief in Peter Cadman, and I knew he had put in a lot of work studying prison rules and procedures. I also had several prisoners to witness for me, even though the prison had done its best to ship out anyone who might have seen anything relevant.

It was a 'full board' sitting, which meant five members of the BoV, at least one of whom was a local magistrate. And because I was legally represented, the Home Office had sent in a Treasury Prosecutor to oppose us. There were fourteen screws who were going to give evidence that I had attempted to incite other prisoners to riot and attack prison officers. But right from the start it was obvious that things were not going to go to plan for the system. Screws are used to governor's adjudications, those mini kangaroo-courts that occur on a daily basis in every prison up and down this country. At these they just read out the evidence to the governor and the prisoner is found guilty and punished. Being cross-examined by an experienced legal advocate was a new and uncomfortable experience for them. Peter Cadman exposed their falsehoods with a couple of well-aimed questions. A typical exchange went something like this:

PETER: Officer, you say that my client was inciting other prisoners to riot? In what way exactly?

PRISON OFFICER: Well, he was waving his fist in the air and shouting 'Let's do it for Strangeways, lads.' And stuff like that.

PETER: And how many prisoners were on the yard at the time?

PRISON OFFICER: One hundred and fifty-four, sir.

PETER: And what were these other prisoners doing when the attempted escape was going on?

PRISON OFFICER: Er, they were cheering, sir.

PETER: And doing a fair bit of arm-waving themselves, I should think?

PRISON OFFICER: Yes, sir.

PETER: So, Officer, how did you manage to single my client out from one hundred and fifty-four shouting, arm-waving prisoners?

PRISON OFFICER: Erm, I knew him, sir. He's a bad 'un. He's assaulted prison officers before. He's no good. And if he gets away with this, he'll be seen as some sort of 'hero' by the rest of the scum we have to contend with, day in, day out. No, take it from me, sir, he's guilty all right.

PETER: Thank you, Officer. That will be all.

The first four screws gave the exact same evidence as each other, word for word. Peter asked the fifth screw, 'Have you got together with your colleagues before today and worked out exactly what you were going to say?'

And like the fucking dimwit he was, the screw answered, 'Yes, sir.'

The governor, who had been sitting off to the side of the room observing, put his head in his hands and sighed. The screws were not supposed to talk to each other about their evidence before the case. Peter moved that the rest of the prosecution witnesses not appear, and the Chairman of the BoV had to accede.

My first witness was an unsavoury-looking junkie called Taibe. He was serving six years for possession of heroin. I had wavered about calling Taibe, as he had a shifty look about him, like a cornered rat, and I was sure he wouldn't make a very good witness. How wrong I was. He was brilliant.

He told how he had been standing next to me throughout the incident and that I had done nothing out of the ordinary. As I had already pleaded guilty to assault in front of the governor, it was not allowed to be mentioned in the BoV case. The Treasury Prosecutor got up to cross-examine Taibe.

'Now, Taibe,' he began.

Taibe put up his hand to stop him.

'I really do think that I should be accorded the same courtesy that you have given the previous witnesses in this case, sir,' he said. 'I would be obliged if you would address me as "Mr Taibe", and not just "Taibe", as though I were some sort of lesser being.'

The room went quiet. I looked down at my paperwork to suppress a grin.

'Bravo!' said Peter Cadman.

The Treasury man coughed to hide his embarrassment, then

nodded. 'Very well, "Mr" Taibe. Why should we believe a word you have said in evidence? After all, you are a convicted heroin-dealer, are you not?'

Taibe smiled. 'I am, sir. I am also a convicted burglar, robber and thief. But I think you will find, if you check my record of thirty-four previous convictions, that not once have I been accused of perjury. Does that answer your question?'

I saw one member of the BoV hide a smile, and another nodding as if in agreement. The Treasury man had had quite enough of Taibe, the articulate junkie.

'No further questions,' he said, and sat back down.

As Taibe was being escorted from the room he gave me a wink. Taibe was shipped out of the prison the day after the trial, and I haven't seen him since. Good luck to him wherever he is.

I was taken out into the hall while the BoV made their deci-sion. The screws were not so happy now as they had been on their way down. After no more than five minutes I was called back in to stand in front of the BoV.

'Prisoner PJ2679 Smith,' the Chairman began. 'After careful deliberation of the evidence before us, we find you exonerated of the charge of incitement.' He then turned to the governor. 'Governor, I sincerely hope you will now speak to your officers and make sure they are cognizant with the rules of evidence in the future. Their performance here today was a shambles.'

The governor nodded, but I could tell he was less than pleased at being lectured in my presence.

I thanked Peter Cadman and was marched back to D-wing. I made sure to say nothing and keep my face neutral. The atmos-phere from the screws was terrible. They were looking for any excuse to jump me, I could feel it. Once I was back in my cell and they had gone, I allowed myself a cheer to celebrate. I had taken on the might of the system, and won. And the fact that it had happened in the POA stronghold of Wandsworth prison was the icing on the bun.

The next morning I was woken by a truncheon banging on my cell door at six o'clock.

'Pack your kit,' the screw informed me. 'You're being transferred.'

I had been in Wandsworth for over a year, and I can't say I
was sorry to be leaving – especially after my result had turned
me into a moving target for every screw in the nick. I packed
my gear as quickly as I could and sat on my bed waiting for the
escort. I wondered where I was going. Anywhere that wasn't
Wandsworth would be just fine with me.

Dave C., and a lot of my pals, like the Little Firm, had all been
shipped to Parkhurst, so I naturally assumed that I would be
going there as well, but the authorities had other plans for me.
There were only a handful of prisons equipped to take Category
A prisoners in those days, known as 'dispersal' prisons. The dispersal
system came out of the 1966 report on prison security by Lord
Mountbatten, in which he recommended that the most 'dangerous
and troublesome prisoners' in the system should be 'dispersed'
among a small group of prisons specifically designed to contain
them. By the 1990s there were seven dispersal prisons in this
country: Wormwood Scrubs, Parkhurst, Wakefield, Gartree, Long
Lartin, Frankland and Albany. HMP Wakefield, known as 'Monster
Mansion' to prisoners, held mainly sex offenders. The Scrubs held
mainly lifers. And Albany, next door to Parkhurst on the Isle of
Wight, held the most violent and troublesome prisoners of the
lot. You win no prizes for guessing that I was on my way to
Albany.

There had been many major 'disturbances' over the years at
Albany, and in 1990 the prison was still on a partial lock-down
that arose out of a riot in 1983. This meant that at any given
time at least one third of the prisoners were locked in their cells
and unable to associate. They worked it on a rota, so that every
prisoner got his share of solitary. Albany was not a popular destination for prisoners. It had a reputation for violence that was
unparalleled, even in the dispersal system.

But first I had to get there. I was loaded on to a van with
Dex O'Shaughnessy and an ex-probation officer turned security-
van robber named Ice. Security was tight, and we were chained

to the floor of the van. Only a month before, Greg Crabtree and several others had overpowered the screws on the van to Parkhurst and escaped into the wilds of Hampshire, so the escort screws were taking no chances. We were left chained to the floor during the forty-minute ferry-crossing from Portsmouth to the Isle of Wight, in very rough seas. If the ferry had sunk, we would have had no chance.

HMP Albany is fairly modern for a prison, having been completed in 1964. Unlike in the Victorian prisons, all five wings are on one long spoke and there is no centre. A, B and C wings were for 'normal' prisoners, but D and E wings were fenced off from the rest and housed some very bad sex-offenders. Everywhere I looked there were cameras, electronic gates and dog patrols. Albany was one of the very few prisons in the system that had never had an escape. There was a large contingent of IRA prisoners there, and its alumni read like a veritable 'Who's Who' of twentieth-century villainy: the Krays, the Great Train Robbers, Kenny Noye, the Richardsons, Freddie Foreman, Frankie Fraser – they had all passed through those electronic gates at some stage in their prison lives.

In reception I was told that the regime on the wings was a lot more relaxed than Wandsworth. But that wouldn't have been hard: the regime on the average Texas chain-gang would have been a lot more relaxed than Wandsworth. I was allowed to wear some of my own clothes, including my trainers. In fact, I was to find out that when it came to clothing at Albany, it was a case of 'anything goes'. Some of the Africans would walk around wearing dyed bed-sheets as robes, and there was a very good black market in 're-designed' prison clothing. Some of the lads who worked in the tailor's shop could make almost anything out of the basic prison uniform. My first purchase was a striped prison shirt which had been turned into a short-sleeve with two breast-pockets, a grandad collar and a pleat up the back à la Ben Sherman. It cost me an ounce of tobacco.

I met up with plenty of old prison friends at Albany, and made many more. My first evening on association I met up with my old mate from Wandsworth, Steve Daddow. Steve was a great brewer, and we shared a gallon of five-day-old hooch. After over two years without a drink, I was lagging drunk by the time I got back to my cell for bang-up. Like in most dispersal prisons, the prisoners at Albany were allowed to cook their own food, and there was a small kitchen on each wing. The prison still supplied meals at the hotplate, but we could use our wages to buy food from the canteen and cook it ourselves. There were also plenty of hooch-brewers at Albany who made some very interesting drink, some of which could bring on temporary blindness, but all of which could get you as drunk as a skunk.

The screws turned a blind eye to hooch and drugs, as they did to most things, but in the week before Christmas they would go through the motions of having a 'crackdown'. A couple of screws would come around the cells collecting illicit brew, but they would bargain with you. Their brief was to clear the prison of hooch, so if they brought plenty of it back to the security governor, they would have done a good job. They would come to your door, and if you had three gallons, you would give them one, and they would move on, satisfied.

The only time they would have a real crackdown on hooch was when one of their officers was attacked or injured due to drunkenness. Otherwise, they didn't really give a shit. It was the same with drugs. Though the main drug of choice was cannabis, there were also a handful of hard-core heroin-users, known as 'skagheads' to the prisoners, but they normally didn't last for long on the wings. With the price of heroin, it was very easy to get into debt and then have to go on protection when they couldn't pay.

I soon settled into the routine at Albany. I got a job in the woodwork shop, making prison lockers for £8 a week, and subsidized it by doing a bit of puff-dealing. Smuggling cannabis into a top-security prison was hard, but not impossible. There were screws who were willing and able to bring in the odd parcel, as long as it wasn't Class A, but they charged too much for the service. It was cheaper for me to bring it in myself, secreted up my arse on a visit from a couple of pals. Once it was in the 'bank', no amount of rub-downs or strip-searching would find it. At that time you could get an ounce of cannabis on the street for £70, but once that ounce came into prison it was worth almost triple the price. Some prisoners made more money selling drugs in jail than they ever made from their crimes, but I was not interested in great profits, I just wanted enough to make life in prison bearable. I would smoke a third of my parcel, give a third out to my friends as 'returns', which meant that if they got a parcel they would come and sort me out, and the last third I would cut into half-ounce deals. A half-ounce deal is enough puff for two joints, and will cost the buyer a half-ounce of tobacco or the equivalent in canteen goods, but what passes for two joints in prison would be what most smokers outside spill while building a joint.

By the early 1990s, cannabis had replaced tobacco as the preferred currency of prison. Most goods and services supplied by prisoners to other prisoners were paid for in cannabis. If you wanted a shirt altered, for example, you would pay cannabis equivalent to an ounce of tobacco. There were many cottage industries in prison, such as making jewellery boxes, doll's houses or rocking horses, which prisoners would buy to send out to their children. If you were a good cook, you could earn a weekly wage, usually an eighth of puff, by cooking for people. If you were a tailor, you could earn by altering and pressing clothes for people. A good artist could earn by doing portraits. There are plenty of very skilled people in our prisons, and they turn out top-quality work at cheap prices.

I got friendly with a Grenadian drug-smuggler called Les Victory, who worked in the furniture shop with me. Les was doing fifteen years for a couple of kilos of coke, and he had a good eye for business. Les had more money-making schemes than Del Boy Trotter. He was pals with an east London gunman named Matt Stanley, who was a good artist, and decided to set up a custom-made greetings card business on the wing. He would pay one of the boys on education to steal sheets of different coloured card from the art class, then Les would cut the cards and fold them into shape, and Matt would put some artwork on them.

Les knew that at this time I was writing a bit of poetry in order to try and win the £25 first prize in the annual Christmas poetry competition held by the Education Department, so he asked me if I fancied knocking out a few lines of verse for his cards. I wasn't really interested, until he said he would put me on a weekly retainer of a gallon of hooch. Les Victory made some of the best hooch in Albany, so I agreed to do a bit of poetry for him.

Our first customer for a customized card was a fella named Pat Tate. Pat came to the attention of the public a couple of years later when he was one of three men found shot to death in a Range Rover in a field in Essex. I read a lot about this case, and everyone said that Pat was a violent bully. I don't know about that. In every dealing I had with him he always behaved like a gentleman. I never once saw him raise his voice or his hands to anyone on A-wing. Pat was huge, and looked fairly intimidating, but when you spoke to him he was a nice fella. He ordered ten customized cards from us, and paid an eighth of puff with no trouble. And soon our cards were selling like hot soup on a cold day.

I developed certain stock rhymes that I would use in the cards that blokes wanted for their wives and girlfriends, one of which was, 'Throughout the realms of reason/ Across the spans of time/ My love for you, dear (insert name)/ Shall live and never die,' but some men wanted cards that expressed hatred rather than love. We did several for blokes to send to the person who had grassed them up and put them in jail in the first place, and even did one nasty one that the buyer sent to the judge who had sentenced him. The typical 'grass card' would have a noose and gallows on the front, and inside would be a suitably nasty piece of verse written by me, for example, 'Greetings, (insert name)/ How's the crack?/ Don't forget to watch your back/ My time is long/ But it will pass/ Then you'll get yours, you fucking grass' – not very subtle, I know, but it was the sort of stuff that people wanted. The card business was a very good earner and kept us in puff and hooch for a long time.

Many people I knew from other prisons turned up at Albany, including Kevin, the leader of the JCB escape team from

Wandsworth. It was here I also met Micky Harrold for the first time. When I was in Wandsworth there was a much publicized case in the newspapers about a lone security-van robber who had been tackled by some dossers who saw him robbing a Securicor van in the car park underneath the South Bank. The robber had been cornered by the vagrants and shot one of them in the head with his shotgun. There was uproar in the media about it. The robber escaped, but the newspapers decided that the victim, who had survived but was in a coma, should be lionized as a hero of the utmost bravery. They even attributed the words 'Let's do it for England!' to him, as he inspired the rest of the down-and-outs to chase the robber and make a citizen's arrest. This was how the newspapers told it, but the truth was very different. Micky Harrold, for he was the robber in question, wrote a very articulate letter to *The Times*, which they published, explaining how the shooting had actually come about. Micky was arrested a few months after the shooting and sentenced to twenty-four years in prison.

Micky was the most unlikely-looking armed robber I have ever met, a short, homosexual Scotsman with coke-bottle glasses and the features of a stranded fish, but very intelligent with it. Despite his odd looks, I liked Micky. What had really happened on the day of the shooting was that he had pulled his usual robbery routine. He couldn't drive and always worked alone, so he went to and from robberies on a mountain bike with a ruck-sack to hold his gun and cart the money away in. He would reach his target early, having already watched the guards' routine for weeks, and find a place to lock up his bike. He didn't want anyone stealing it. When the van turned up, he threatened the guard and took a bag containing £25,000, and made his way back to his bike. The dossers witnessed the robbery from their cardboard-box homes and decided to try and cash in. They followed Micky back to his bike, begging for some of the money, and when he refused, they tried to rob him. One of them threw a bottle at him and the rest picked up pieces of wood. Micky pulled out his gun and warned them twice, but when he bent down to unlock his bike another bottle hit him in the head and the dossers charged. Micky fired one shot that ricocheted off one of the pillars and hit the dosser in the head. And far from uttering the battle cry of 'Let's do it for England!', the dosser was Scottish. But the newspapers don't like the truth getting in the way of a good story.

At Albany I also met and became pals with Dave Croke, known in the press as 'the Armaguard Robber', because he had pulled off a spectacular robbery on the Armaguard security depot. Dave's MO was to strap a fake bomb on to the manager of the depot and get him and his staff to open the vaults. He loved the planning and preparation more than the actual robbery. He is a very good chess-player and highly intelligent, and it showed in his jobs.

There were a lot of IRA men in Albany, too, including the Balcombe Street men, who had admitted to carrying out the Guildford and Woolwich pub bombings, for which four innocent people spent many years in jail until they won their appeals. The IRA prisoners kept mostly to themselves. They were not unfriendly to other prisoners, but tended not to get involved in day-to-day wing-politics. They all seemed to be intelligent men.

Some of the violence in Albany was truly horrific. Stabbings and coshings, mainly over petty differences or debts, were everyday occurrences. There were also a lot of 'burn-outs' at Albany. It was fairly easy to get a coffee-jar full of petrol from the guys who worked on the gardens party. They would siphon it from the lawnmowers and bring it back to the wing for anyone who could pay the price. Burn-outs were mainly for suspected nonces or grasses and would normally be perpetrated in conjunction with a beating. It involved going into the victim's cell and splashing petrol over his property before setting it ablaze. Baby oil, available from the canteen, could also be used as an accelerant. Setting light to someone's property was a good way of making sure they would not come back to the wing. I was known for burn-outs at one stage, and was responsible for the Fire Brigade being called into the prison on numerous occasions. One case involved a Welsh lifer who was in for killing a little girl. He refused to go on 'the numbers' (Rule 43 protection), and despite several bad beatings, he wouldn't take the hint, so I decided to burn him out.

I waited until the Welshman was in the showers, then I went into his cell and splashed the four-star about. I had to be quick, so I lit a match and threw it into a pool of petrol on his bed and went to make my exit. It was then that I noticed that he had a pet budgie in a cage at the back of his cell, but it was too late for me to do anything about it. I left the cell and closed the door behind me. Within seconds the cell was an inferno. When the Welshman came back to find his cell on fire he tried to brave the flames to rescue his budgie, but it was too late. The screws dragged him out of the burning cell and called the Fire Brigade. The Welshman was inconsolable about the loss of his feathered friend and was led from the wing in floods of tears. I felt bad about the budgie, but at least we had rid the wing of a nonce.

About two weeks after the Welshman's budgie was roasted, I was in the visiting hall for a visit from a couple of pals. I noticed the Welshman sitting over in the nonces' section across the hall; he was also having a visit. I was telling my pals about how I had roasted his pet, when I saw a screw bring a bird-carrying box to the Welshman's table. It seemed he was getting a replacement budgie brought up by his visitors. In order to get it back to the wing, he would first have to transfer it from the carrying box into the cage. As I watched, he reached into the box and the bird jumped over his hand and flew up to the ceiling of the visiting hall. I couldn't resist this chance, I stood up and whipped off my jumper and waited. As the Welshman and the screw tried to coax the budgie from the rafters, it flew in my direction. I twisted my jumper and flicked the budgie out of the air with the sleeve. I picked the stunned bird from the floor and smiled at the Welshman. 'Two nil,' I said, and squeezed the life out of the budgie. I threw it in his direction and wiped the blood and feathers from my hand.

The Welshman went absolutely nuts. He roared, and began to charge across the hall towards me.

'Yeah,' I shouted. 'Come on, you fucking child-killer! I'll do you the way I done your birds!'

The alarm bell went off and the screws jumped him before he could reach me.

I'm not proud of what I did to those two birds; in fact, I felt terrible about it. I had two budgies of my own and always treated them well. But I was willing to stop at nothing in order to cause a bit of pain to this arrogant bastard who had murdered a young girl and thought he had the right to inhabit the same space as me. Sex offenders cannot be 'cured' or rehabilitated like ordinary criminals. Criminals can give up crime, because no matter how entrenched in it we may be, it is not really a set part of our nature. But sexual instincts are different. For instance, if you lock up a normal heterosexual man for a decade alone, then release him, he will seek out the company of females; and it is the same with your average kiddy-fiddler: they go looking for children because that is their sexual preference, and no amount of jail time can change that. There are certain treatments and courses they can do in prison that may reduce the risk of them reoffending, but you can't change their nature.

Sex offenders in prison get an easy ride from the system. They are bunched together on wings to protect them from the rest of the prison population, and generally treated more as patients than prisoners. As a result, we now have the largest population of paedophiles in Europe. It has been proved that even those sex offenders who volunteer for chemical castration still go on to reoffend. The urge cannot be erased.

While I'm on the subject of sexuality, although the public seems to think that homosexuality is widespread in prisons, contrary to popular belief, the prisoners in British jails do not spend their time buggering each other in the showers. There are a few openly gay men in prison, but being openly gay is not normally cause for concern. Nobody would consider a man a nonce just for being gay. Gay men are usually the butt of plenty of jokes and sexual banter among prisoners but, rarely, in the adult system, have I seen a man physically attacked for being gay.

And if there are heterosexual prisoners who turn 'prison-bent' and seek out the company of homosexuals, then it is done in secrecy and never spoken about. I have never heard of it happening, or witnessed any such thing, but I would guess that it does happen.

Of course, there are plenty of homosexual screws, very few of whom are openly gay. It is obvious why they are attracted to the job, and a lot of them seem to gravitate towards Reception or the Dedicated Search Team (DST), because these jobs involve the daily strip-searching of hundreds of men. In my experience, a good proportion of DST officers are closet homosexuals, who delight in wearing their 'special' uniform of black paramilitary-style clothing, trousers tucked into boots, and utility belts. They get to strip-search any prisoner who takes their fancy, and even have the power to order prisoners to perform erotic gymnastics such as squatting naked, pulling the cheeks of their arse apart, and even rolling back their foreskin on command.

I have been strip-searched by the DST on many occasions; in fact, they have probably seen me naked more times than all the women in my life put together. It's a very uncomfortable situation to be in a cell with two fully uniformed men less than two feet away from you eyeing every inch of your body. You can tell me that closet homosexuals are not attracted to this job, but you'll be wasting your breath.

One thing I can say about my time at Albany was that it was never boring. There were plenty of memorable characters, like Gary 'the Growler' Andrews, who was a leading light in the Portsmouth FC football thug following, known as the 6.57 Crew, and Andy, a south London robber who would start a fight in an empty house and never back down from anyone. There were also plenty of memorable incidents, like the time the IRA planted a fire-bomb in the A-wing TV room. The bomb was on a timer and due to go off at evening bang-up time so as to throw the prison into confusion and delay the lock-up, but they miscalculated. It went off after we had already been locked up for half an hour. We were stuck in our cells as the wing turned into an inferno. It was only because the day-shift screws had been delayed by a search at the gatehouse that they were able to get back into the prison and get us out of the cells before we suffocated from the smoke or burned to death in our cells. If the bomb had gone off ten minutes later I might not be here now, along with 120 other men. The screws saved our lives that night, and put their own safety at risk to do it.

Albany was an education. It taught me just how many complete lunatics there are in the adult prison system. And it taught me that not all screws are dogs who wanted to see me dead. My next move was to Maidstone prison, but going via Wandsworth was a very bad omen.

21. Madness at Maidstone

People with no experience of prison may think that once you are sentenced to a term of imprisonment and enter a prison, that is where you will stay, but the system is a lot more complicated than that, and the average long-termer may be moved to as many as twenty different prisons before his sentence is over. While on remand awaiting trial you will be held in a 'local' prison, close to whichever court you have to appear in. Once you are sentenced you will be taken to an 'allocation' jail, where you will be classified and allocated to a 'dispersal' prison, if you are a dangerous Category A prisoner, or a 'training' prison, if you are an average Category B, or a 'semi-open' prison if you are Category C, or an 'open' prison if you are a Category D prisoner. Once a prisoner is placed in the dispersal system, he must then work his way down the system by a combination of good behaviour and time served. Very few dispersal prisoners ever make it as far as Category D. In all of my years in prison I have never been a Category D, but I was once a Category C for a short period.

My move to HMP Maidstone was seen as a 'progressive' move to Category B conditions, because I was approaching the one-third stage of my sentence, when I would be able to apply for parole. In theory, a long-termer can be granted parole after serving this proportion of his overall sentence, but in practice the only people who get their first parole are sex offenders and police informers. Most long-termers do not even bother applying. The only drawback in my move to Maidstone was that I had to go back to Wandsworth, as that was the pick-up point for Kent prisons.

I knew I was going to have trouble at Wandsworth as soon as the van pulled up to reception.

'Unload,' said a reception screw, 'but leave Smith till last.'

The other eight prisoners were unloaded and rushed through their reception procedure. Finally I stepped off the van and on to Wandsworth soil. I was wearing a tailored grey prison over-coat, a tailored short-sleeve shirt, bleached prison jeans and a pair of black, lace-up officer's shoes. By the time I left reception I was in the mankiest kit they could find for me. I bore the ill treatment and insults by telling myself that I was only here for one night, and tomorrow I would be off to Maidstone. They wanted me to bite so they could give me the beating they thought I richly deserved for making them look like mugs at my BoV trial, but I kept my rage bottled up.

The next morning I was waiting by my cell door as soon as it got light. I wanted out of here as quickly as possible. By ten o' clock I was still on the wing. I pulled a PO and asked what time the van for Maidstone was leaving. He gave me a smirk. 'Maidstone, you say? That van left at eight this morning. You appear to have missed it. Never mind, there's another one leaving in two weeks.'

I was gutted. I was stuck in Wandsworth for a fortnight, and I would be a target for any screw who fancied his chances. I was living a nightmare.

How I endured that fortnight without exploding into violence, I'll never know. But it did little for my feelings of paranoia, that's for sure. The screws dug me out at every conceivable opportu-nity. I had strip searches and cell searches daily, and sometimes twice a day. They shaped up to me, got in my face as much as they could and made snide comments, but I refused to kick off. And I got through it.

I made it on to the next transfer, but I didn't relax until the van pulled through the gates of the prison. The escort screws were all Wandsworth dogs, so I ignored them and thought about Maidstone. It was rumoured to be lax in the security depart-ment, and the perimeter wall was climbable. I wanted to escape, and Maidstone would be the ideal place to do it from.

While I was at Albany, there had been a successful escape from Wandsworth, and it was by none other than my old borstal pal

Steve Hostetler. Steve was back doing eight years for a security-van robbery when he spotted a weakness in Wandsworth security that had evaded everyone over the years. He wangled a job in the laundry, from where he was able to force a shutter door and scale the lowest part of the perimeter wall with a makeshift rope and grapple. He and another bloke got clean away before anyone could raise the alarm. The news delighted me. Unfortunately, Steve was only out for a few months before he was nicked for several more robberies and given a further twelve years on top of the eight he was already serving. But Steve went down in prison history as the first man to escape from Wandsworth since Ronnie Biggs.

Greg Crabtree had also been busy on the escape front. After being recaptured from his escape off the van to Parkhurst, he was sent to Swaleside, a top-security prison on the Isle of Sheppey. Despite being classed as a high escape-risk, Greg managed to walk out of the visiting hall in broad daylight. Using the flimsy subterfuge that he was a visitor rather than a prisoner, he passed through several electronic metal-detectors and gates and found himself outside the prison. Greg was fast gaining a reputation as the Houdini of the prison system.

As a result of these high-profile escapes, including the helicopter escape from the exercise field at Gartree prison in which Johnny Kendall and Sid Draper were lifted to freedom in a hijacked chopper commanded by Andy Russell, the system attempted to tighten up security. But with so many determined men in prison it was never going to be easy for them. Things were going to get a lot worse for the system before they got better.

Also while I had been at Albany, the European Commission on Torture had published its report on British prisons and special hospitals. I read in the newspapers that it was 'a damning indictment of the state of our prisons', but I never actually got to see the report myself. Very few people in this country did. It was deemed 'not suitable' for publication here, which makes you wonder what exactly the government was hiding. I knew. I was living in it.

When I reached Maidstone and got off the van I was told that my personal property had 'gone missing'. The Wandsworth escort screws had big grins on their faces when they told me that they must have 'accidentally' forgotten to load it at Wandsworth. This was the final insult, and I cracked. I gave the Wandsworth screws a mouthful of abuse. As soon as I opened my mouth I was nicked. I spent my first and only night in Maidstone in the punishment block. I was charged with 'threatening and abusive behaviour to an officer', and the governor of Maidstone told me that he didn't want prisoners like me in his prison. The next afternoon I was loaded on to the first van and ended up back at Albany. So much for my progressive move. I was back where I had started.

After I had been back at Albany for a couple of weeks, they found a place for me in a unit for lifers and long-termers at Bristol prison. At least I wouldn't have to go near Wandsworth to get there.

B-wing, the unit at Bristol, was a strange place. There were sixty prisoners on the wing, most of them lifers who had already served a couple of decades in prison, and a lot of them were on some serious medication. It was like a cross between a mental ward and an old lags' home. But the atmosphere was fairly relaxed and the screws seemed to leave us alone. After a week I fired off a letter to my pal Andy in Albany and told him to get himself down here. As an added incentive I told him, wrongly, that all the cells were equipped with televisions. Andy stood it, and drove the AG at Albany mad for a move to Bristol. When he turned up and saw the gaff, I thought he was going to fight me on the spot. But he took it in good heart and we set about carving out a niche for ourselves.

At first, me and Andy were the only Londoners in Bristol nick, but we were soon joined by an East End conman and fraudster named Stevie Horne. Stevie's claim to fame was that he was the man who had managed to get the exclusive photographs of jockey Lester Piggott while he was serving his sentence for tax evasion at HMP Highpoint. Stevie told us that he himself had been doing two years for deception when Piggott came to the jail and, never one to miss a money-making opportunity, he immediately instructed his brother to get in touch with the press to arrange a deal and smuggle a small, disposable camera in to him. One of the tabloids agreed to pay £20,000 for the photos, so Stevie got to work. First, he cut a hole in a cardboard box and hid the camera inside, then he casually plonked himself down where Piggott was eating his breakfast and surreptitiously snapped off a few frames. He handed the camera back to his brother on the next visit, but when the film was developed he had nothing but some pictures of the inside of a cardboard box.

Stevie wasn't one to be put off by failure, so he tried again. But every time he got Piggott in his sights something seemed to go wrong. Eventually, after days of Stevie shadowing the Queen's former jockey around the prison, Piggott himself took the initiative. He confronted Stevie and asked him if he was trying to take his photo. Stevie nodded, and Piggott said, 'Well, why didn't you just ask?', and proceeded to pose for several shots. The pictures duly appeared in a Sunday paper.

The screws at Bristol seemed to have a lot of trouble understanding our cockney accents. Every morning and afternoon on our way to work in the tailor's shop, we had to pass a screw who would mark off our names on a clipboard. Stevie would give his name and number, 'Horne, 326,' and the screw would invariably answer, 'What?', to which Stevie's standard reply was, 'Horne, you know, that thing you have in the mornings.' One day, a female screw was checking the board, and sure enough when she got to Stevie she asked, 'What?' when he gave his name. And when Stevie gave his standard reply, she thought for a moment, then gave him a quizzical look.

'Breakfast?' she said in a deep West Country accent. 'There's no name like that on here.'

We were also joined by a young south Londoner doing eighteen months for possession of ecstasy. His name was Warren Foy, and he was distantly related to the infamous Foy brothers, Micky and Danny, from Bermondsey. The Foys were the top blaggers of their day but fell victim to heroin addiction later in life. Warren was a good kid, so we took him under our wing. The 'carrot-crunchers', which is what we called the locals, were a bit in awe of our 'sophisticated' London firm and so gave us a wide berth. We spent our time in the workshop playing kaluki, a card game similar to rummy and the national pastime for prisoners, and smoking dope. The instructor was a Welshman who was forever trying to get us to sew our quota of mailbags, but he might as well have been talking Martian for all the notice we took of him.

Soon another Londoner joined our firm, and he was the unluck-iest bloke I've ever met. 'Lucky' Paul met a Bristol girl at a rave, fell in love and moved down to Bristol to marry her. His new wife got a job as a barmaid in a local pub and everything went great for a while. Then Paul started hearing rumours that his wife was having an affair with the governor of the pub. Paul was only a little fella, though game as a hungry lion, and knew he wouldn't have much chance against his rival, who he had heard was an ex-boxer and built like a shit brickhouse. So Paul got in touch with a local firm of villains and asked to hire a gun for a one-off job. The firm hired him a 5-shot pump-action shotgun but told him that if he did not have the gun back by a certain date he would have to pay for the gun and take a serious beating. Paul took the gun, got masked up and burst into the pub where his wife was working. He saw a huge pug-ugly behind the bar and, assuming this was the governor, he fired. His first shot missed, but he never got a chance to fire the second. The locals jumped him, took the gun off him and beat him half to death with bottles, glasses and pub furniture. The police arrived in the nick of time to save his life. He was charged with attempted murder and possession of a firearm. And to cap it off, he had fired at the wrong man. The governor had been upstairs with Paul's wife.

As if all that wasn't bad enough, while he was on remand on C-wing of Bristol prison, someone pointed out a bloke who was rumoured to be a nonce. Thinking he could make a few friends and warn off anyone who might try to take liberties with him at the same time, Paul decided to do the sex offender. He filled a jug with boiling water from the urn, added half a bag of sugar and threw it in the man's face – but once again he had got the wrong man. Worse, the bloke he had jugged was a big-time drug-dealer with plenty of mates in the prison, and he immediately put a contract on Paul's head. The contract was an ounce of heroin and, in a prison system where the price of murder can be as low as a £10 bag of skag, Paul was definitely in trouble. The screws moved him over to the unit for his own protection. When we heard his story we accepted him as a fellow Londoner and put the word out among the carrot-crunchers that if anyone tried to collect the contract they would be the next to go. Paul went up to court and pleaded guilty to the gun and shooting charges, and got seven years. The London firm had a sit-down on the yard with the B-wing representatives of the C-wing drug-dealer and explained that Paul had made a bad mistake, and that there was no need for a stabbing war that only the screws could win. The baron's court case was just about to be dropped through lack of evidence, so he was happy enough to call off the hit before he left the prison. He was still badly scarred from the jugging, but I think it had made him lose his bottle.

Then Paul got a letter from his wife, who he hadn't seen since the shooting. She wanted to come and visit him and try again with their relationship. I was tempted to tell him to tell her to fuck off, but I kept my nose out of it. On her first visit she brought a message from the gang that Paul had hired the gun from, and they said they would be waiting for him when he got out of prison. But other than that, Paul and his wife seemed to be getting on OK. Then, after about five visits, she told him that she wanted a divorce, as she had met someone else. I had seen it coming, but what I didn't see coming was that she had met her new love whilst visiting the prison. And it was a screw! Not only a screw, but a PO. She had met him while he was organizing prisoners' visits, and he had asked her out, knowing she was at the prison to visit her husband. It was a dire liberty. But again, worse was to come. Paul put in a complaint about the PO stealing his wife and found himself on the next van to Dartmoor, the arsehole of the prison system. As far as I know, the PO got nothing but a mild reprimand for his conduct. Paul's story inspired me to write a poem called 'Lucky Bastard', which was one of the first things I ever had published.

Both me and Andy had managed to keep out of trouble at Bristol. We were old hands at concealing our actions from the screws. We smoked plenty of dope, drank gallons of hooch and had a gamble on everything from the horses to wing pool-competitions. Andy was a top pool-player and he took every game very seriously, so a lot of his fights were over pool. But the fights always happened away from the screws' sight, with me as the referee to make sure he didn't go too far and kill somebody. We took part in all the offending-behaviour courses that were available, with the aim of getting downgraded to Category C so we would have a better chance to escape. We even agreed to appear on a BBC television programme called *Crime Ltd* about imprisoned armed robbers. The BBC sent a crew to Bristol prison and we were filmed talking to the victims of armed robbery. When this documentary was aired, we got an enquiry from *Guardian* journalist Duncan Campbell about being interviewed for his crime show on BBC Radio 5. The episode was about bank security, and both Andy and I agreed to speak on it. Of course it helped that the people they sent to interview us were two gorgeous assistant producers. The girls were a breath of fresh air in the stagnant atmosphere of prison, and I think we would have agreed to anything they asked.

With all the publicity we were getting, it was odds-on that we would get our Category C status, and we did. We were told that we were to be shipped to HMP The Verne, a closed Category C prison on Portland Bill in Dorset. The Verne is located at the top of the Portland cliff next door to Portland borstal. It is surrounded by a fifteen-foot wall, and the cliff itself can only be reached by a causeway that connects it to the mainland. But it was a Category C nick, and that meant it was possible to escape. My sentence had been cut to eleven and a half years at my appeal, Dave C. had his cut to ten, but I had no illusions about being granted parole with my previous record. By the time I reached the Verne I had served four years in prison and had a minimum of three years and ten months left to serve. I was determined to escape.

Since my early days in Stamford House I'd not been too successful in my efforts to escape from custody. You might think I'd have given it up, but the desire for freedom was always strong in me. And there is no freedom more heady than that which you have stolen. It seemed as though everyone I knew in prison was making their escape. Andy Philipson and Mark of the Little Firm had got home-leave from Parkhurst and were both on the run. Greg 'Houdini' Crabtree had been recaptured after his escape from Swaleside and sent to Maidstone, where he had promptly scaled the wall, and was on the run again. Another of my pals, Gary Staggs, had hijacked a coach carrying him and five other prisoners from HMP Blundestone to HMP Wandsworth. The prisoners beat the screws in the escort unmercifully, and abandoned the coach in Archway, north London. The *News of the World* ran a double-page feature on the escape. Johnny Kendall, who had been recaptured after his helicopter spectacular from the field at Gartree, along with Kevin, the leader of the Wandsworth JCB attempt, had had a good go at breaking out of an armoured Category A van on the motorway between Long Lartin and Winchester. They didn't succeed, but a prison dog was killed, a screw had his wrist broken, and the van was wrecked in the attempt. It seemed as though everyone was having a go.

Andy was serving ten years for armed robbery, and he wanted to escape as much as I did, so it was good that we were both shipped to the Verne on the same day. As soon as we got there we began looking for weaknesses in the security. The Verne is one of the prisons originally built during the Napoleonic Wars and is made up of five houseblocks and five dormitory accommodations. The houseblocks have single cells for prisoners serving over four years, and the dormitories are for those serving under four years. The regime is very relaxed compared to the prisons I was used to. There are no bang-ups and, in fact, the cells are called 'rooms' and prisoners have their own key to their room.

You can wander almost anywhere within the perimeter wall. There are a minimum of five roll-calls per day, when a horn goes off and every prisoner has to get back to their room and stand by the door to be checked. It was all very civilized, but it was still prison, and we were being held there against our will.

The only time to make a successful escape from the Verne was at night, after the last roll-call at nine o'clock. Any other time would mean we would be quickly missed, and the causeway would be blocked. At the bottom of Portland Bill, below the prison, was a Royal Naval base for submarines, and it housed armed naval police who would help in the event of any escape from the Verne.

Our first attempt at scaling the wall was a disaster. We crept out of our houseblock at night and broke into the woodwork shop. We got a fifteen-foot piece of timber and hammered six-inch nails into it to use as handholds. We managed to get our makeshift ladder out of the window, but on our way to the perimeter wall, we were spotted by a night-patrol. We had to abandon our ladder and get back on to the houseblock before the alarm was raised and they called for a roll-call.

For our next attempt we made a rope from prison bedsheets and a grapple from a sawn-up tubular chair. We climbed out of the window of Andy's cell and crept under cover of darkness towards the wall. It was a stormy night and the rain was lashing down, so we were soaked, and so was our home-made rope. There were screws in sentry boxes at regular intervals around the wall, so we had to crawl through the gardens to avoid them. But there was no way to avoid them when we were right at the wall; we would just have to trust to luck. The perimeter wall was well lit with spotlights, and there was no cover within ten feet. We were completely exposed as we stood under the wall and threw up our grapple. If either of the screws in the sentry boxes that were closest to us had been doing his job, instead of sleeping, we would have been captured straight away. It was very windy, so my first throw of the grapple was blown off course and fell back at my feet. My second throw was perfect, and hooked the top of the wall. Andy was a lot lighter than me, and he went up the rope like a ferret up a trouser-leg. He straddled the top of the wall and beckoned me up. At that time I weighed a muscular fifteen stone, my ideal fighting weight, and I was fitter than I had been since I was a teenager, but as I got half-way up the rope it snapped. We hadn't bothered to braid the sheets, and with the soaking they had suffered from our crawl through the rain, they wouldn't hold my weight. I was stuck on the ground with no way of reaching the tiny piece of rope left hanging near the top of the wall.

Andy held his hand out and whispered for me to throw him the rest of the rope. He caught it, but just did not have the strength to pull me up. I had already been standing out in the open for far too long. It only needed one of the screws in the sentry boxes to wake up, and the alarm would go off. I made a decision.

'Go,' I said to Andy. 'You get away, and I'll make it back to my cell.'

Andy shook his head. 'Not a chance, bruv,' he said. 'If you don't go, then I don't go.'

Before I could stop him, he unhooked the grapple and dropped it at my feet. Then he swung off the wall and dropped back into the prison. We grabbed our escape kit and scampered back into cover. It was starting to get light, so we made our way back to our cells and decided to try again when we had made a better rope. Once more I had been unlucky in an escape. It was like I was cursed never to make a successful break.

As for Andy, he was and remains a true friend, and the kind of bloke for whom loyalty to one's friends is everything. To this day I would trust him with my life. And I did, but that was later.

I had fallen out with Denise over a silly argument on a visit at Albany, and we had not been in touch with each other for over a year. I still loved her, and I knew that she loved me. She had been through hell with me, bringing three young children up on her own and having to work at two jobs just to keep them in food and clothes. I had never been one for saving the money I stole; I pissed most of it up against the wall, never worrying about the future. Denise had brought the kids all the way to the Isle of Wight to visit me every two weeks without fail, having to leave the house at 9 a.m. and get a series of buses, trains, taxis and a ferry, in all kinds of weather, just so I could see them for an hour. Sometimes they didn't get home until after eight o'clock at night. I now realize that being in prison was the easy option. It is the prisoners' families who really suffer, having to endure being treated as criminals themselves by the prison system in order to get in to see their loved ones. My Denise had committed no crime other than to love a prick like me, but she still had to submit to searching and being ordered about by the uniformed arm of the Home Office, and so did my innocent children. It was all my fault, but I didn't even give it a thought at the time. I was too interested in making sure that I was comfortable in jail and had everything I needed.

Both me and Denise were too stubborn to break the dead-lock and get in touch first. I was still getting visits from the rest of my family, and my dad and Mick came everywhere to see me. Mad Harry was now going legit: he had settled down with Sharon and his two kids, bought a house in Northampton and was working as a plumber. Harry would often come to see me with my dad and brother. On one visit he told me how his sister, Jenny, had been attacked by an ex-boyfriend. Harry and his younger brothers, Robert and Tim, had got hold of the attacker and tried to kill him. They beat him with baseball bats and then ran over him in a car. He survived and got them nicked for GBH. They were on bail, but it looked as though Harry might get a bit of time for it because of his previous. I was choked for him, and told him to pass on my best to Jenny.

A week after Harry's visit I got a letter from Jenny thanking me for my concern. I had known Jenny since we were kids on the Sinclair estate together, and I had always had a soft spot for her. She had grown into a beautiful woman, and we were soon writing each other a couple of letters a week. Our postal rela-tionship blossomed and I began to look forward to her letters. I knew that word would eventually get back to Denise, and deep inside I hoped it would force her to get in touch with me. But Denise was far too stubborn.

While I was plotting my escape from the Verne, my mother was going through a bad patch with her health. She was suffering bronchial trouble and had to be admitted to hospital on a couple of occasions. The prison probation officer came to see me to tell me she had been taken into hospital again. I was very worried and, out of the blue, he told me that I might be eligible for a one-day parole in order to go and see her. I got on the phone straight away and spoke to my family. My mum was ill, but it wasn't a life-threatening illness. I asked them to exaggerate her illness to the probation officer so that I could get a day out to visit them, and they agreed.

I have always tried to keep a sense of honour in my life, and believe me when I say that despite my craving for freedom, I would have honoured any one-day parole that was granted to me. I would have gone home and seen my family and then come back to the prison voluntarily, and on time. If trust is put in me, then I have to honour that trust; it's just part of my make-up. But the system was not prepared to grant me any trust, so as far as I was concerned the gloves were off. The security department at the Verne, on advice from Prison Service Headquarters, was not prepared to let me visit my mother unless I was handcuffed and escorted by two prison officers. This decision told me that even though I was in a Category C prison, where prisoners walked out of the gate unescorted every day, I was still *persona non grata* with the system, due to my past.

On the morning of 5 November 1992, I was handcuffed to two of the biggest screws in the prison and taken to a taxi waiting at the gatehouse. Three security screws, including the head of security, were waiting for me. As they double-checked my handcuffs, the head spoke to me.

'If we had our way, you wouldn't be going anywhere, but the governor made the final decision. But know this, if you try anything, my officers will come down heavy on you.'

I kept silent.

His last words to the two screws were, 'Do not, under any circumstances, let him off those cuffs.'

The drive from Dorset to south London was long and uncomfortable. The screws ignored me and I ignored them. The driver of the taxi, a civilian, engaged me in conversation.

'This estate we're heading for,' he said, 'is it a rough place?'

I smiled. My parents had moved on to Stockwell Park Estate in Brixton, which at that time was the murder- and crack-cocaine-capital of London.

'Well,' I replied. 'The locals will probably take a couple of pot-shots at you, and maybe try to nick your wheels and sell you a bit of crack, but it's not too bad.'

The driver was terrified, and even the screws, who had probably never been outside Dorset in their lives, began to look a bit uncomfortable.

Stockwell Park Estate looked as rough as a docker's armpit as the taxi pulled on to it. Near the entrance was a burning car with no wheels and the Fire Brigade hosing it down. I was delighted when I saw the two screws look at each other with worried eyes. We went deeper into the estate, past graffiti-spattered walls and undernourished dogs slinking around rubbish-bags. I told the driver where to pull up. My parents lived in a flat off one of the first-floor walkways. It was awkward getting out of the car handcuffed together, but as soon as we were out, the driver said he was going to find somewhere to get a cup of tea. He said he would be back in two hours. He pulled a wheelspin in his hurry to get away. As the taxi reached the end of the block there was a loud bang, and half a brick bounced off the roof of the car. The driver didn't stop.

So there I was, in the middle of this urban wasteland, handcuffed to two big and frightened screws who were already way out of their depth. I directed them to the staircase that would bring us up on to the next level. The stairs were narrow and dark and stank of piss. As we reached the top, with me in the middle handcuffed by both hands, there was the sound of loud rap-music. On the concourse outside the staircase were five or six of the local youths, all baggy trousers, baseball caps and bad attitude. Their huge stereo, known locally as a 'Brixton briefcase', was on the ground at their feet, pumping out Niggaz With Attitude. The youths noticed us and their eyes immediately went down to the handcuffs. They blocked our path to the next balcony.

'Hey, Babylon bwoy,' said one. 'Feel say you're bad?'

The screws didn't have a fucking clue what he was saying, but I got on it straight away. They thought the screws were CID from Brixton police station.

'I beg your pardon?' said the lead screw. 'Can we get past, please?'

The youths burst into laughter. 'Ear de country bwoy now, im beg us pardon!'

I helped out. 'They ain't Old Bill,' I said. 'They're screws taking me for a visit.'

One of the youths nodded. 'Yeah,' he said. 'You is Mr Smith's bwoy, innit?'

I nodded. He said something to the rest of them and they cleared a path for us. I heard the screw behind me breathe a sigh of relief.

My family had been living on the Stockwell Park estate since 1982 and were well known to most of the locals. In fact, my dad and my brother were the only white people who were accepted in the local black pub, Leroy's, and could be found there every Saturday afternoon playing pool. My dad was known as 'Irish' among the blacks.

When we reached my parents' front door my dad answered the ring. He looked at the handcuffs.

'What's that all about?' he asked the screws. One of them explained that he had orders not to let me off the cuffs.

'Well, this is my house,' said my dad, 'and if you don't take those cuffs off, you can turn around and go straight back to the prison.'

He winked at me. The screws knew they had no choice. The taxi wouldn't be back for two hours and they wanted to get under cover before anyone took it into their heads to attack them. They took off the cuffs. Once inside the flat, my dad directed the screws to the kitchen, where he had provided the day's newspapers, and my sister made them a cup of tea. I stayed in the front room talking to my mum and the rest of the family. Mick had come around, with his wife Julie, and we all had an enjoyable visit. I told the family that I wasn't going back to the prison that day. My dad was against me doing a runner, but I talked him around, telling him I wanted at least one Christmas out and then I would give myself up. My brother Mick was all for it and showed me a way down off the balcony that would leave me on the ground floor. Mick gave me £20 and everyone wished me luck. I followed Mick as he climbed down from the flat to the road below. I asked him what he was going to do and he told me he would just go back upstairs and back through the front door again as though nothing had happened. We said our goodbyes and off I went.

I had no plan, but I was free at last, free at last – thank God Almighty, I was free at last! I ran across Stockwell Road and up a sidestreet to a pub I knew called the Marquis of Lorne. I knew it wouldn't be long before the alarm was raised, and I wanted to get out of the area as quickly as possible. It also crossed my mind that I might be quickly recaptured, so I at least wanted to have a pint. Brixton police had been notified that I was coming for the home visit and, although they weren't supervising it, they did have a contingency plan in case I escaped. I wasn't just some burglar or car thief coming on to their patch, I was a long-term prisoner with a proven propensity for loaded firearms. I strolled into the pub and ordered a light and bitter. While the barman was pulling my drink, I asked him if he had the number of a local cab-firm who would pick me up. He gave me my drink and a number. I downed half my drink in one gulp and got on the payphone to the cab-firm. They said they would have a car with me in ten minutes. I looked out of the pub window and saw two uniformed coppers on horses on the road outside. As I watched, a police car with lights flashing but no siren pulled up next to the mounties and the driver of the car leant out and said something, gesturing at the next turning. My heart sank. It was the curse again.

I instinctively knew that this police activity was connected to me. It would be just my luck to be recaptured less than ten minutes after I had escaped. I drained my drink in one mouthful and ordered a double gin. At least I wouldn't be going back to prison sober. I picked up my gin and told the barman that if my cab came I would be in the toilet and could he call me. He gave me a funny look but agreed. There was no window in the toilets, so I had no escape if the police came in. I drained my gin and, out of habit, I wrapped my change from the £20 note up in toilet paper and inserted it between the cheeks of my arse. I opened the door to the toilets a crack and looked out. A black guy in a leather cap walked into the empty bar.

'Someone order a mini-cab?' he asked.

I came out of the toilets. 'Yeah, mate,' I said. 'It was me.'

I looked out of the window and saw a police Sherpa van cruise slowly by. The bastards were all over the place. I smiled at the cab driver. 'Where're you parked, mate?' I asked.

'Just outside the door,' he replied.

'OK,' I said. 'If you go and open your back door, I'll be right out.'

He gave me a quizzical look, but then shrugged and walked out.

I gave him a minute, then checked out of the window to make sure the road was clear. I came out of the pub like a rocket and flew into the back seat of the cab, slamming the door behind me. I crouched down out of sight.

'Take me to Battersea, please,' I told the bemused cabbie. It was the first place I thought of.

The cabbie shrugged again and pulled off. 'You in some sort of trouble?' he asked.

'What makes you think that?' I said, from the floor behind him.

'Well,' he replied casually. 'Everywhere I look I'm seeing police cars. And I get the feeling you don't want them to see you.'

I decided to take a chance. 'Yeah, they're looking for me,' I said. 'I've just escaped from prison.'

He whistled. 'What, Brixton?' I didn't want to go into details so I just said 'Yeah.'

'My brother's in Brixton,' he said. 'C-wing, his name's Colin. Did you know him?' I crossed my fingers. 'Er . . . Colin? In for dealing, yeah?' I asked.

He laughed. 'Yeah, that's him. What a small world! There's a police van at the next traffic lights, so keep well down.'

My gamble had paid off. He threw a few back-doubles and when we came out on Clapham High Street he told me I could sit up, as we had left the police activity behind us.

I got him to drop me on York Road in Battersea, close to Tommy Hogan's flat.

'How much do I owe you?' I asked when I got out of the car.

He shook his head. 'Nothing, man. It's a pleasure to help out. You take care.' And then he drove off. It was lucky he hadn't charged me. It would have been slightly embarrassing having to pull the money from my arse cheeks.

I looked around. I was free! Without a plan or any idea how I was going to stay that way. But the air I was breathing was the sweetest I had ever tasted in my life.

22. Running Wild

There is something enormously exhilarating about being 'on the run', the feeling that you can do anything you like and it won't count because you shouldn't be here in the first place. If I was arrested, having done nothing, I would still be going straight back to prison and I couldn't change that. So the aim became to stay out as long as I could and have a great time. And if that meant I had to rob every bank in London, then I was well up for it. I looked on my time unlawfully at large as an unexpected bonus ball in the lottery of life, and I was ready to collect my prize.

When Tommy Hogan opened his front door and saw me standing there, he didn't bat an eyelid. As laid-back as he ever was, he just said, 'So, you've escaped then? I guess you could use a spliff around this time?'

He brought me in and opened cans of lager and got busy putting a couple of spliffs together. It was great shooting the shit with Tommy again. We discussed Dave C., Tommy's old Battersea Rebels gang-mate and my co-defendant on the sentence I was serving. Dave did not take naturally to incarceration and had had a bit of a mental breakdown in Parkhurst. It happens to a lot more long-term prisoners than you would ever hear about. Dave had been sectioned under the Mental Health Act and was in a psychiatric ward. We toasted him with our lager, and also other 'absent friends'. Tommy let me use his phone to get in touch with my old friend the German. If anyone was going to be able to supply what I would need, it would be him.

The German was the best conman and fixer I ever met. He could charm the knickers off a beautiful woman as easily as he could charm a fiver out of the hand of the tightest bastard in existence. A dapper little fella, he had it all: the gift of the gab, good looks, a boyish smile and a left hook like Mike Tyson. I've

seen him earn and spend thousands of pounds in a single day,
and, if times were hard, he wasn't shy about putting in a day's
straight graft on a building site to earn a few quid. When I went
on the run, the German was doing particularly well. He had a
luxury flat in Croydon, a Porsche 911 and a gorgeous girlfriend.
If he had one weakness, it was women. He couldn't resist them.
Back in the 1980s he had started an unwise liaison with the wife
of Dublin Jimmy, the owner of the illegal drinker on Bedford Hill
we used to frequent. Dublin Jimmy was not the sort of man you
would want to cross, and when he found out about the German
and his beloved he came looking for him with a sawn-off shotgun.

I was with Andy Philipson and the German one night in an
Indian restaurant at Clapham North when Dublin Jimmy and two
of his henchmen suddenly sat down at our table. Jimmy never said
a word, he just stared at the German, then took out his shotgun
and laid it on the table, pointing towards him, with his finger
caressing the trigger. The German leapt from his chair, took three
running steps and launched himself straight through the plate-glass
window of the restaurant. He crashed to the pavement in a shower
of glass and was up and running before the noise of his break-out
had died away. I just looked at Dublin Jimmy and shrugged.

'There goes the German,' I said.

I finally got through to the German, who was at a party in
the Acre Tavern, my local pub when I lived on Bedford Road.
A lot of my mates were at the party and he told me to jump in
a cab and get down there. By now it was dark and I guessed that
the police search would have died down when they hadn't found
me within the first hour. The Acre Tavern was on the outskirts
of Brixton and the last place they would expect to find me, so
I decided to risk it. I phoned a cab.

When I walked into the Acre Tavern I really knew I was home.
It was crowded with my pals, and a huge cheer went up as I
came through the door. Bottles of champagne were popped and
I got a good old-fashioned south London welcome. This is what
I had dreamed about for all those years in prison, and I couldn't
keep the smile off my face. We had a toast for all the lads left in

prison, and then it was down to business. The German said I could stay at his flat in Croydon until I got something sorted out. A street-trader named Jimmy called me into the toilets and slipped me a .32 Star automatic pistol, fully loaded. 'It's brand-spanking-new,' he said. 'Never been fired. It's a coming-out present, son. Use it in good health.' I thanked him and went back to the party. People kept coming up and patting me on the back and slipping me a few quid, which is the traditional welcome-home from prison in what passes for the 'underworld'. I felt on top of the world.

Used to prison-brewed hooch rather than real alcohol, I was soon lagging drunk. The German pulled me to one side and told me that his girlfriend, Sue, was waiting outside in a cab with the keys to his flat. He told me to go with her to get myself offside just in case Old Bill were still mooching about. He was going to finish a bit of business and then bring a select few back to his gaff so we could carry on the party. I was only around the corner from where Denise and my kids lived and I had to see them. I knew it would be risky, as the police were bound to put her under surveillance, but I hoped they hadn't got around to it yet. I had a word with my cousin Ronnie, who lived nearby, and he said he would get his wife, Gaynor, to phone Denise and ask her to bring the kids over to her place.

We met in Ron and Gaynor's front room. We hadn't seen each other for nearly two years and our meeting was not under the best of circumstances. The kids looked great, they had really grown and I was amazed at how much love I felt the moment I set eyes on them. I hadn't realized how much I was missing them. Conversation between me and Denise was stilted. Neither of us wanted to admit that we had been wrong in the first argument. The cab was waiting, and after a few minutes I said my goodbyes to the kids and promised I would see them again now that I was out. I hugged Denise and I thought she was going to respond, but then she felt the unmistakable shape of the gun in my inside pocket and she pulled back. I loved her so much, but I had no idea what to say for the best. I left her there with a tear in her eye.

The German's place was the business. It was a two-bedroomed

flat on the third floor of a luxury block, with all the latest gear. I knew he was doing well, and he had come a long way since we lived in a squat in Bedford Hill and mooched drinks at Dublin Jimmy's. Sue made it plain from the start that she wasn't happy about having an escaped convict moving in, but I made an effort to be nice to her. About an hour after we arrived, the German and the rest of the gang turned up in a convoy of mini-cabs, and the party was on. It turned out that Sue was related to my old borstal pal Barry Rogers. The German phoned Barry and told him I was there, and Barry jumped in his motor and came to join the party. He brought a carrier bag half-full of speed with him, and we reminisced and got out of our heads on primo whizz, cocaine, champagne and hash.

The party was still going on the next day. The German had phoned his favourite Indian restaurant some time the night before and had them deliver thirty full meals and four crates of lager. I had fallen into bed around 4 a.m., not used to the excitement and late hours. The routine of imprisonment conditions people to sleep early and rise early, because there is little to do once you have been locked into a cell for the night at 8 p.m. When I woke up there was a woman draped across me in the bed, and for a moment I didn't know where I was. Then I noticed the lampshade on the light hanging from the ceiling and I remembered. I felt great again, just like that. The feeling of being free, with time stretched out in front of me to use as I pleased, hit me in a wave of euphoria.

By the afternoon most of the party guests had left. I had a long bath. Another thing you rarely get in prison is a bath. Most jails have only communal shower rooms which allow no privacy and are not the sort of places you would want to linger for too long in, so a bath was a luxury. The German was in his silk dressing-gown, sitting in his throne-like armchair making the day's deals over the phone. It was a pleasure to watch him in action. While Sue fussed around cleaning the gaff up and bringing us endless cups of tea, I sat back and watched the German at work.

He had two phones right next to his chair and he was constantly on one or the other. The first phone rang as I sat down, and the German snatched it up. He listened for a while, taking sips from his tea-cup, then snapped off a couple of questions.

'How many pairs? Two hundred, eh? OK, what sizes have you got them in? Six? What the fuck do you expect me to do with 200 pairs of size-six Doctor Martens? You think I might know a gang of feminine-footed football thugs who are in the market for new boots? You're off your fucking head.' He winked at me and listened some more. 'OK,' he said into the phone. 'I'll tell you what I'll do, I'll take them off you for a grand.' He sipped some more of his tea, the gold rings on his fingers sparkling as he adjusted his dressing-gown. 'Yes, I know that's only five quid a pair, but you got them for nothing. Look, I ain't got time for this bollocks, I don't even want the fucking things, I'm just trying to do you a favour. They'll only take up space in my lock-up for months and then I'll end up giving them away.' He listened some more, then gave me the thumbs-up. 'OK, then,' he said. 'I'll send someone over straight away.'

After putting the phone down he thought for a moment, sipping his tea. Then he picked up the phone again and punched in a number.

'Hello, Tony? Yeah, mate, not bad, how's yerself? Listen, I've got 200 pairs of Doc Marten boots, all boxed, in various adult sizes. The boys have just lifted them off a van in Essex, and I knew you'd want first shout. Yeah, they only want fifteen quid a pair. You'll have the lot? Nice one, mate. One of the boys will be over to you in a couple of hours. Good luck.'

He put the phone down and rubbed his hands together. 'There you go, mate. Two grand earned and I'm not even dressed yet. This is a grand country.'

'What about when he finds out they're all size six?' I asked.

The German smiled. 'He's buying nicked gear, he's got no comeback. 'Sides, by this time tomorrow he'll have knocked them out to someone else at a profit.'

The German did the majority of his business from his armchair in the afternoons, and the night was for partying. Though he bought and sold a lot of nicked gear, he also did a roaring trade in snide goods and 'ringers'. The snide gear all came from a sweat-shop in Blackpool, where whole families were working shifts to produce some of the best fakes in the country: Hugo Boss, Nike, Adidas, Air Jordan, Coco Chanel – all the best names in fashion and leisure-wear were being reproduced and sold at rock-bottom prices. Perfumes, aftershaves, Gucci watches – anything that could be copied and sold to a gullible punter was being turned out at a rate of knots. The German would buy vanloads of this gear, and he had a network of single mothers who would sell the stuff in markets, from home and even in pubs and clubs for him. It was a very lucrative business for everyone involved. The factory would sell the German Hugo Boss sweatshirts, for example, at £2 each. The German would then pass them on to the girls and ask for a return of £5 each. The gear was in what looked like the genuine packaging, so the girls could pretend they were part of a stolen load and ask a third of the genuine retail price, £10. The girls earned the biggest profit because they did the long job of selling the gear. The German just sat on his arse in the middle while collecting a pure profit of £3 on every sweatshirt sold, and he also got to look like a benevolent uncle to the girls for letting them earn such good money. It was perfect. He told me that as soon as I got hold of a couple of grand in cash, he would arrange a load for me to invest in.

The German's other scam was the ringers. He had two very good car thieves on a retainer. I've met many car thieves in my life, but these boys were the dog's bollocks. You only had to give them a make, year and colour of car and they would be back with it in hours. The German paid them £200 in cash for every car they brought him. For their 200 sovs they would not only steal the car and park it up in a designated car-park, but they would also 'plate' it as well. 'Plating' is changing the number-plates of a stolen car to the plates of a legit car of the same make, model and colour. Once the cars were stolen, plated and parked, the German would get one of his girls to type the new details into one of his forged log-books, using a Golfball typewriter the same as the DVLA's, and then use the log-book to buy a year's road-tax from the post office, using a stolen cheque.

So now he had a brand-new car, complete with straight number-plates, log-book and tax-disc. He would also pay to have a set of keys made for the car, using the serial number found on the car's ignition-barrel. *Voilà*, one car ready for sale. Most of the cars he dealt in were Volkswagen Golf GTis, Range Rover Vogues or Porsches. The people buying the cars, on the whole, knew they were getting a ringer.

The German's ringers were going all over the country, from Blackpool to Leicester to Birmingham and Manchester; some even went to buyers in Glasgow and Belfast. The German also swapped the ringers for parcels of snide goods with the Blackpool firm. The money was rolling in from all angles. The German offered me a partnership, but I didn't really have the right head at that time for anything long term. I wanted to make my own money and then do a bit of investing as a silent partner. I did, however, take him up on his offer of supplying me with the wherewithal to get back into the robbery game: guns, cars and getaway drivers. But first he said he was visiting his contacts in Blackpool and I should come with him. The German said it was to be a friendly meeting, and it would get me out of London for the weekend and away from any raids the police might be planning in their search for me.

First we drove into Croydon town centre in the German's Porsche 911, and he got me kitted out with a suit and a few bits and pieces for our trip. We were going by train and taking one of the German's drivers with us to pick up a car at the other end and drive it back to London. The driver was a half-caste guy named John, and he seemed OK. Dressed in my new suit, I was ready for anything. Just before we left, the German told me I had better take my gun with me, 'just in case'. This made me a bit suspicious, but he assured me that it was just a precautionary measure. I slipped the .32 into my pocket.

We had a few drinks in a pub near the station while waiting for the train, and the German pulled out a bag of coke and we had a few lines. I was feeling pretty good until we were on the train and well on our way; then the German told me the real reason behind our jaunt to Blackpool. It turned out that he and 'Steve', the head of the Blackpool firm, were having 'business difficulties', and there had been a few threats flying back and forth on the phone-lines. So they were having a meet to try and sort things out. My role would be as the German's minder.

'This is a fucking heavy little firm,' the German told me. 'If things start going pear-shaped, you'll have to start shooting.'

I was slightly less than pleased by his revelations. I had been expecting a relaxing weekend in Blackpool, but instead it appeared I was on my way to the gunfight at the OK Corral. The coke I had consumed did little to cure my paranoia.

I knew things were serious when the German made us get off the train at Preston and take a taxi the rest of the way. 'Just in case they meet us at the station. First rule of business, be unpredictable,' was his explanation. When we got into Blackpool, he handed John a wad of notes and told him to go and enjoy himself and meet us later at the hotel. Steve, among other things, owned several guest-houses, so we turned up on the doorstep of one of them for the meet. Steve was of average height and build and was wearing about half his weight in gold. The bracelets and watches he wore on each wrist would have turned Jimmy Saville green with envy, and I didn't fancy his chances if he fell into the sea. He seemed genuinely pleased to see us and gave the German a big hug that set all his gold clanking and shimmering. The German introduced me as his 'minder', so I played the part: respectful but alert. Steve invited us in and offered us a drink.

Negotiations went smoothly and I began to relax. It seemed that it wasn't Steve who had the problem with the German, but his younger brother, who he referred to as 'our kid'. The trouble stemmed from a Range Rover Vogue that the German had sent up. Apparently, it had a biscuit-coloured interior, and 'our kid' had expressly asked for a black interior, or some such bollocks. Anyway, 'our kid' was fresh off remand that very day, having had a case of manslaughter dropped against him through lack of evidence. He was celebrating round at his club and looking forward to seeing the German to apologize for all the bother. I relaxed even further when I heard this.

The club was within walking distance, so we set off on foot, but Steve had to drop in to his local pub to see someone, so we had a drink there. I was starting to enjoy myself. Steve was a nice bloke, and he seemed to be known and respected by everyone. In the pub people were queueing up to buy him drinks and shake his hand. He was like a northern Al Capone figure. But one thing bothered me. A few of the people who approached our table mentioned 'our kid' being 'out of his head' round at the club. And they all seemed to look frightened when they mentioned him. Steve chuckled indulgently at these comments.

'He's a fucking nutter, is our kid. But you can't blame him for enjoying himself, he were three month on remand in Preston prison for this manslaughter charge.'

I thought of something. 'What was it?' I asked, casually. 'A stabbing, or something?'

Steve shook his head. 'Nah,' he said. 'He were accused of beating a fella to death with his fists. He's into all that kung-fu shite, and bare-knuckle boxing, is our kid.'

I didn't want to hear that. I slipped my hand into my pocket to make sure my gun was still there.

The club was a large single-storey building the size and shape of an aircraft hangar, reached across a vast tarmac car park. You could hear the music from 200 feet away, and six of the biggest bouncers I have ever seen were guarding the main doors. The bouncers all wore tuxedos and head mikes and had the bovine features of habitual steroid-abusers. They greeted Steve like a long-lost brother and warned him that 'our kid' was making a bit of a nuisance of himself inside.

Steve laughed at this. 'What, you're telling me that you lot are afraid to go in there and sort him out? You fucking big nancy boys.'

It was said in good humour, but I noticed the undercurrent of fear in the bouncers and wondered exactly what I was letting myself in for here. We went inside.

The inside of the club was done up like the set of the Grand Ole Opry, all wagon-wheels and Western signs. The bar was made of huge raw planks resting on massive steel-banded barrels. The place was heaving with bodies, and the smell of chips and cheap perfume was almost overpowering. On one side of the large dancefloor was a hatch serving scampi and chicken in a basket. The dee-jay was positioned on a high platform overlooking the floor, and as we walked in he put on the big hit of the time, 'Achy, Breaky Heart' by Billy Ray Cyrus, and the floor was instantly filled with dancing women. The main bar was way down at the end of the room, and there seemed to be some commotion there. We made our way through and into sight of the bar. A group of men were gathered around one end and they parted when they saw Steve. In the centre of the crowd was a bloke with no shirt on. He was built like a body-builder, with thick slabs of muscle on his chest and arms and a light sheen of sweat all over him. He had long black hair pulled back into a pony-tail, a broken nose and deep-set dark eyes under thick ridges of scar tissue. He looked as though he could quite easily go ten rounds with any man in the room and hold his own, and he was launching two-handed punches into one of the huge wooden barrels that were supporting the bar, his features set in concentration as he smashed his rock-hard fists into the splintering wood.

Steve nudged me. 'This is our kid,' he said.

I had thought it might be.

'Our kid' stopped punching the barrel when he spotted Steve, and grabbed him in a bear-hug.

'I've just bet the lads a fiver that I could punch a hole int' this barrel,' he said, and it was obvious he had been drinking. Then he caught sight of the German. 'You fucking little bastard!' he roared. 'How are you, lad?' He lifted the German off his feet and swung him around, and I was glad to see he was friendly, at least. After his excitement at seeing the German had died down, he looked at me. 'And who's this then?' he asked.

Steve grinned. 'It's the German's minder,' he said, and I thought I detected an undercurrent of malice in his voice that hadn't been there before. 'Our kid' walked up to me until his nose was almost touching mine.

'Is that right?' he asked in an aggressive voice. 'You a fucking "minder", are ya?'

I slipped my hand into my pocket and flicked the safety-catch off my pistol. I knew that if I showed any sign of fear here things could turn very nasty.

'I'm a mate,' I said, evenly, keeping my eyes on his.

He turned away. 'He's only a fucking cockney as well!' he said to the crowd. 'A fucking cockney in my fucking club!' He threw a hard right into the barrel and splintered the wood some more. If he made one move towards me I was going to shoot him and take my chances. Steve grabbed him around the neck and whispered something in his ear. 'Our kid' turned to me and gave me a long appraising look. 'All right, Cockney,' he said. 'If you want to drink in my club, you have to arm-wrestle me.'

I knew that the northerners wanted to try and humiliate me. It was all part of the macho dance that I was well used to. 'Our kid' was second in line to Steve, who I recognized as the alpha male of this pack, and that's probably why he felt the need to go over the top all the time. I'd read enough cod psychology in prison to be able to see how things were. I looked at the rippling slabs of muscle in his arms and shoulders and knew I could never beat him in an arm-wrestle. I was in good shape from all the training I had put in to keep fit for an escape over the wall, but 'our kid' was in a different class. Ten years before I would have just shot him and put an end to it, but I thought, fuck it, let him have his moment of glory. I took off my jacket and rolled up my sleeves. The crowd around the bar cheered and 'our kid' grinned happily. It was over in seconds, he beat me in both arms and seemed to lose his aggression towards me.

'Unlucky, Cockney,' he said. 'Come on, let's have a drink.'

Once his dominance had been asserted, 'our kid' became very friendly towards me and we ended up having a good night, but I could never completely drop my guard in his presence.

The German got all his business sorted out, and on Monday afternoon we were heading back to London with a vanload of snide goods. I had been out of prison for five days and it was time for me to go to work and start earning my keep.

When we got back to the flat in Croydon, I had a nice surprise: Jenny was waiting there. Jenny was one of the girls who sold the snides. It was great to see her again after so many years, and she looked as gorgeous as ever. Jenny is the sort of female who just exudes sexuality but is completely unaware of the effect she is having on men. They just seem to light up when she looks their way, and when she smiles, you cannot help but smile right back at her. Within minutes of our meeting we were getting along famously. I felt completely easy in her company and we shared a slightly off-key sense of humour. It had been a long time since I had been in the company of a woman who I didn't have a tense history with, or merely wanted to have sex with, and I fell in love straight away. I arranged to go to her flat the next evening for a bit of a get-together.

After Jenny left I got down to business. A phone call was made, and twenty minutes later a briefcase was delivered to the flat. Inside the briefcase was a sawn-off, double-barrel, 12-gauge shotgun and six rounds of ammunition. The gun was in perfect condition and had obviously been cut down by someone who had taken a bit of time on the job, as the butt had been re-varnished after the sawing and the cut ends of the barrels had been completely smoothed. I slotted the gun together and found it was fifteen inches long and had a lovely heft. The metal made a satisfying *click* when I flicked the barrels closed.

John, who'd driven the German and me from Blackpool, agreed to drive for me, and we took a Volkswagen Jetta that was plated, taxed and ready for sale. I decided to do the job suited and booted. I knew of a National Westminster bank on Balham High Road that I had been about to rob before I went to prison, so

I directed John down there. We parked in the car park of a busy supermarket and I left John in the car while I went to take a look. The bank was still there, and doing brisk business. I went back to the car and told John to pull up outside the bank and wait for me. John had never been on a bank job before and I could tell he was shitting himself. Before I got out of the car I warned him that he was not to drive off without me under any circumstances.

At the last minute I decided to dispense with the mask I had brought along. It was a moment of madness, and I don't know what possessed me. Perhaps it was the fact that if I was caught I would be going back to prison anyway. My provisional plan was to get enough money together to get out of the country, so it was an all-or-nothing deal. This time out would surely be my last roll of the dice, and at that moment I felt as though I would never be caught.

Instead of a mask, I slipped on a pair of Ray-Ban sunglasses I had found in the car. I checked out my reflection in the bank window and straightened my tie. I looked pretty smooth. I pushed the door open and stepped into the banking hall. There were about twenty customers going quietly about their business. I stepped over to a table and set my briefcase down on top of it. Without any hesitation I calmly popped the locks on the case. The shotgun was inside, already pieced together but with the barrels open. I took it out and flicked it shut. The click of metal meeting metal was loud in the hushed banking hall. A couple of customers looked my way and then away as though they didn't believe what they were seeing. I took a deep breath and stepped further into the bank.

'Right!' I shouted, to get everyone's attention. 'This is a raid! I want all you customers to step to the back wall of the bank. Come on now, let's go.'

Some of the customers, mainly the men, complied straight away, but some just looked around in confusion. I walked forward purposefully with the gun levelled at chest height so everyone could see it.

'Come on now, move back. If anyone tries to pass me I will shoot you. I am not joking. Step to the back wall and keep your heads down. It will all be over in a minute.'

In seconds, I had over twenty customers standing at the back wall. I turned to the cashiers and found that they had all dropped down out of sight behind the bullet-proof screen. I tapped on the glass screen with the butt of the gun.

'If one of you does not get up here and start handing over the money right now, I will execute your customers one by one.'

There were audible gasps from the customers. I smiled at them and shook my head, as if to reassure them that I was just bullshitting. One of the cashiers popped up like toast from a toaster.

'Don't shoot, don't shoot!' he said, his hands held high.

I passed him a plastic bag. 'Fill it,' I said. 'And don't forget the fifties.'

As the cashier went about the business of emptying the cash drawers I stepped back from the jump and kept an eye on the customers. I was buzzing. I felt great. Completely in control of the situation. I noticed one of the customers had a nice watch on. I pointed the gun at him.

'Is that a Rolex?' I asked.

He nodded nervously.

'What, a real one?'

He nodded again. He must have thought that I was going to nick it, but I would no more steal from a customer than I would from a charity-box. I was just making conversation to keep everyone calm.

'You should be careful wearing that in this area, mate. Plenty of muggers about, know what I mean?' He swallowed hard and nodded again. I looked at the cashier. 'You on a fucking go-slow, or what?'

The cashier pushed the bag back through the drawer. I picked it up and put it inside the briefcase, then locked it. 'Thank you very much for your co-operation,' I said. I backed up to the door, then slipped the gun under my jacket before stepping out on to the street.

The first thing I noticed was a police car sitting in traffic across the road. It was a normal patrol car, waiting for the traffic lights to change. I didn't panic, though my first instinct was to run. I got into the passenger seat of the getaway car. John was in bits, sweat dripping off his face as though he'd just run a marathon.

'Old Bill!' was the first thing he said to me.

I looked hard at him. 'Just pull off as though you're a normal bod,' I ordered. 'Don't attract attention.'

I was hoping no one would come running from the bank and bring it on top for us. John put the car in gear and indicated to pull out. The traffic lights changed and the patrol car shot off in the opposite direction. We had made it. I knew that any minute now the patrol car was going to get the call over the radio to go to the bank, but once we had turned on to a side road and were headed for Streatham, we were well away. There were too many possible getaways for the police to check them all.

Once we were fully safe and on our way back to Croydon, I began to feel the comedown. I had a headache and my hands wouldn't stop shaking. It was the reaction to the adrenaline that had flooded my body during the robbery. I took a couple of aspirin and tried to relax. I had now crossed the Rubicon; in a couple of days the bank security-film would be handed over to the Flying Squad and the hunt for me would be stepped up a couple of notches. I was now not only a prison escapee, but they knew I was armed and at it. There would be no turning back now.

In the next seventy-three days I robbed fourteen more banks, including three in one day in early January. I was a one-man crime-wave. I was also involved in one stabbing and two shooting incidents, one of which involved a man getting twenty shotgun pellets in the face. I was running wild and loving every minute of it. I ended up moving into Jenny's flat, while still trying to maintain some sort of relationship with Denise. I was all over the place; sometimes London, other times Liverpool or Northampton. I was living out all the dreams I'd had while locked up in jail. I drove a Porsche, dressed in the finest of clothes, ate at the best restaurants, and got drunk and stoned every single night.

One night, after I had been out for over a week, I phoned Jenny and she told me that she and her mates were going out that night to a pub in Battersea called the Galleon, where Tommy Hogan Snr was the deejay. I decided to go with them. I hired a stretch limo, got suited and booted and picked up the girls from Jenny's flat. There were six girls including Jenny, all dressed in little black dresses and looking the business. I was in a black silk suit and had my .32 in a shoulder holster. When we pulled up outside the pub I arranged the girls around me like a cordon of bodyguards. We made quite an entrance. I felt like James Bond. Tommy grabbed the microphone up on the stage.

'Here he is, back from a sell-out tour round HMP! The One That Got Away!'

The place was packed with people I knew and I got a round of applause. I bought drinks for everyone. Things like that were a great buzz and would get me smiling at the memory of them, even in the darkness of a filthy strip-cell.

The more I got away with, the more over the top I went. One shooting incident started when I was having a drink with the German in a pub in Croydon. Barry Rogers came into the pub to meet us, looking the worse for wear. His nose was broken and he had two black eyes and severe lacerations on both wrists. He told us that the injuries had been inflicted by the police. He and his girl rented a room in a house in Brixton from a bloke who was half a gangster, called 'Peter'. Peter had owned the breakers yard in Balham where Popeye had once worked and where the old Balham Wildkatz had gathered. He had pulled a gun on Popeye when they had fallen out, and he was not averse to a bit of skulduggery. Anyway, Barry had been having a loud verbal argument with his girl when Peter had come to tell them to keep the noise down. Peter soon made himself busy and got involved in the argument, so Barry punched him in the mouth as an encouragement to mind his own business.

Two things you definitely don't want to do if you value your safety: one is to get involved in any fight between a man and a woman in a relationship; and the other is to then phone the police when you get a smack in the mouth. These rules are clearly understood by the likes of Peter, and why he broke them I don't know. But he did. The police arrived at the house in the shape of a male and female uniformed team. Peter told them that he wanted Barry removed from his premises, so the constables went upstairs to talk to Barry. Being an ex-borstal boy and lifelong criminal, Barry's agitation only increased when he was confronted by the constabulary in his own bedroom. There was a heated exchange, and when the police tried to put the handcuffs on him Barry went berserk. He punched the male officer down a flight of stairs and nutted the female officer in the face. Reinforcements were called and soon there was a full-scale battle going on inside the house. At that time the police were trying out a new weapon to be used on violent prisoners, called a Taser. The Taser dispensed a severe electric shock that was supposed to subdue and make pliable any raging felon. But the Taser just made Barry all the more annoyed. He was Tasered six times but still kept on struggling. In the end, it was sheer weight of numbers that bore him down, and the cuffs were put on as tight as they could go. He was dragged to the van by the chain between the handcuffs, which accounted for the lacerations on his wrists as the metal cut into his flesh. He told us that he was laid face down in the van and beaten by two police officers all the way to the station. Once there, and still roaring abuse at the police, he was thrown into a cell and Tasered three more times whilst helpless. The next morning, when the day-shift opened the cell and saw the horrific state he was in, they got him cleaned up and gave him bail.

When Barry walked into the pub he looked terrible, but he had already been to the hospital, so we could only imagine how bad it must have been before he was cleaned up. Both me and the German were outraged — certainly at the police for the beating they gave him, but we expected that from the police — but more at Peter for getting them involved in the first place. As we knocked back our third pints of the morning we agreed that something should be done about Peter.

We started off planning to go down to Brixton and give Peter a good beating. But the more the day wore on and the drunker we got, the more our thoughts and talk turned to giving him a 'real lesson'. I don't remember who first suggested shooting him, but it was generally agreed that a leg full of buckshot would be the best message to send. We started on the vodka and decided to move down to a pub in Clapham. Once ensconced in Clapham, just a short drive away from Peter's gaff, I made a phone call to a fella called 'Colin', who had driven for me on a couple of robberies. I ordered him to drive to Jenny's flat and pick up the shoebox containing the shotgun and my .32 and bring them to us at the pub.

By the time the guns arrived, me, Barry and the German were steaming drunk and as mean as a sett of half-gassed badgers. Colin was stone-cold sober and looking worried. He wanted to leave us the guns and go home, but I told him he was going to drive us on a bit of work later on. I gave him £500 in cash as an inducement to stay. He wasn't happy but he reluctantly agreed.

By now we were drinking with a crowd of people that we knew, and my cousin Ronnie came into the pub as well. Always the joker, he told me he had something to liven me up and gave me a pill. Thinking it was speed, I swallowed it down. I found out afterwards that it was Tuinol, a powerful barbiturate that shouldn't be mixed with alcohol. After that I was in a world of my own.

At around 9 p.m. I went into the pub toilets with the shoebox. I put the .32 in my waistband and snapped the shotgun together and loaded it. I always attached a lanyard to my shotguns, a trainer-lace that was tied to the butt and barrel that I could hook around my neck. It made the gun easier to carry as it could hang down to waist-level under an overcoat, and it ensured that the gun could never be taken off me in a struggle. I loaded both guns. I went outside the pub for some fresh air. Julie came outside to talk to me and beg me not to go. I don't remember it, but she told me afterwards that two blokes who were walking past on the other side of the road laughed out loud at something and, in my drunken stupor, I thought they were laughing at me. I pulled the pistol from my waistband and fired four shots across the road in their direction. I didn't hit anyone, but the blokes ran in two different directions. At the sound of the gunshots, a crowd came out of the pub, and it was agreed that it was time we were off.

Barry had taken three of the Tuinol and was spark out under a table inside the pub, so he wouldn't be coming with us, which was just as well, as he would be a prime suspect when Peter got shot. Colin didn't want to use his car on the job, so we pulled my Porsche out of the car park next to the pub. It was a ringer anyway and only stood me in £500 as a friendly deal from the German. The German took the shotgun from me, afraid that I might accidentally fire it in the car because I was so far gone. There then ensued an argument between me and the German about who was sitting in the front. The Porsche was a two-door, and any criminal worth his salt knows better than to sit in the back of a two-door motor on a bit of work. It's hard to bail out and you can get trapped if the car crashes during a police chase. In the end I won the argument and ended up in the front with Colin.

What we didn't know was that one of Peter's mates had been in the pub and overheard us plotting to do him. He phoned Peter, who, thinking we were just coming to give him a beating, gathered a few hard cases around to his house and lay in wait for us. They were armed with an assortment of weapons and intended to turn the tables on us and give us a good thrashing.

We pulled up on the darkened street and fell out of the car, making more noise than was prudent. Me and the German straightened ourselves up and checked our guns before heading towards the dark house. I was first. I pushed on the front door and was surprised to find that it swung open easily. With my pistol held out at arm's length, I entered the black hallway. If we had been sober we might have stopped to wonder why the door was unlocked, but in the state we were in, we just accepted it as a bit of luck. I reached for a light switch, but nothing happened when I clicked it down. The bulb in the hall had been removed.

I took two steps further into the darkness and suddenly I was hit in the arm with what I later remembered was a crowbar. The pistol went flying from my hand and I heard it clatter to the floor further up the hall. Then it was all a blur. I was hit several times by weapons and went down on to the floor, still being beaten. Then there was a loud boom and the hallway lit up like someone had taken a photo with a flash-bulb. I was feeling no pain at all. I managed to get to my knees and I was aware of bodies running down the hall and two people struggling right in front of me. There was another loud boom, and this time screams as the shotgun was fired again. I just couldn't get to my feet, the combination of drink, drugs and blows to the head was taking its toll on me.

The next thing I knew, I was being dragged out of the house by my collar and across the street to where Colin was revving the Porsche impatiently. The German bundled me unceremoniously into the back seat. Windows were going up and lights coming on the whole length of the small street. Colin put his foot down and we were gone. I was in a bad way, my head was pouring blood, I had two shotgun pellets embedded in my right hand, and I knew from the sharp pain every time I breathed that one of my ribs must be broken. But the German was worse. He had fired off his first shot, then hit one of my assailants across the head with the shotgun, bending the barrels in the process, so that when he pulled the trigger for the second shot, the gun had blown up in his hand. He was missing most of his right index-finger and a chunk of flesh from his palm. The blood was spraying out all over the dashboard and the inside of the windscreen of the car. Colin was driving like a maniac to get away from the scene of the crime, alternately praying and sobbing in fear. Me and the German were so anaesthetized by drink and drugs that we could hardly feel our injuries. The German wrapped his T-shirt around his hand to stop the blood and looked over the seat at me.

'Well, we fucked that one up,' he said. 'But do you think Peter got the message?'

I still don't remember many of the details of that night and had to rely on others to fill me in on what happened. But Colin claims that me and the German laughed most of the way home, as though it had all been one big joke that backfired on us. Which I suppose it was.

It wasn't so funny when I woke up to the pain the next morning and had to assess the cost of that night's work. My Porsche was gone; the interior was so blood-soaked that when Colin left it parked up on the street and looked back at it, he said it looked like a slaughterhouse on wheels. I had lost my .32 pistol somewhere in the dark. The shotgun was gone, exploded into pieces of shrapnel. I definitely had a broken rib and a split skull, and Jenny had to pick shotgun pellets from my flesh with a pair of tweezers. The German came close to losing his hand because he wouldn't risk going to the hospital with such a wound. Instead he went to Dublin for a few months and got treated over there. I was still lying in bed at mid-day counting the cost when there was a ring on the doorbell. Jenny showed Julie into the bedroom. She had a small bag with her and poured out four shell-casings from the shots I had fired outside the pub. She had been on her hands and knees looking for them in the dark, in case the police should find them and get my fingerprints from them. I thanked her. She also had news. One of Peter's mates had taken twenty pellets in the face but was not in danger of dying. Peter had also given a statement to the police naming me and the German. He is supposed to have said, 'If those two lunatics had the front to come unmasked, then they were coming to kill me and leave no witnesses.' He later withdrew his statement.

I now had no gun and my money was running short. In order to stay one step ahead of the police I needed money, and to get money I needed a gun. The German put me on to a bloke who had a pub in Battersea and was also one of a gang of villainous brothers who were well-known in south London. He told me to come down to his boozer and he might be able to get me something. Along with Jenny, I went down to see him. He thought he had a line on a couple of revolvers that were for sale, and I told him I would also need a shotgun. He said that if I was desperate I could borrow his own personal shotgun, which he held legally for clay-pigeon shooting. The only trouble was, it was a full-length 12-bore, nearly five feet long. I told him that I couldn't use it unless I could cut it down. It would be hard work trying to rob a bank with a fucking elephant-gun: I could hardly conceal it beneath my coat. But he had no intention of letting me saw-off his prize gun.

I had a bit of work lined up for the next day, and despite repeated phone calls to the pub-man, it seemed there were just no guns available in London that week. I would have used a replica, as I had done in the past on occasions, but I couldn't even get hold of one of those at short notice. At the last minute I accepted the pub-man's personal shotgun. I didn't tell him, but I fully intended to cut it down and face the consequences later. I collected it, and on the way home I stopped off to buy a junior-hacksaw.

The gun was a beaut, with lots of fancy engraving on the stock. I guessed it had cost him a nice few quid. It was almost a sin to take the hacksaw to it, but needs must. I sawed off the barrels until they were an inch shy of the breech, and the butt at the point where the wood curved into the shoulder-rest. A five-foot gun was reduced to eighteen inches. No good for clay pigeons, but great for bank-robbery.

I robbed the Midland Bank on Dingwall Road in Croydon of just under £10,000 in cash, and got clean away. After the first couple of robberies I had committed whilst on the run, I stopped wearing the suit for work. There had been a piece in the *South London Press* describing me as 'The City Gent Robber', so I took to wearing a flat-cap and long overcoat instead. The cap was my only attempt at disguise. I phoned the pub-man and told him I was ready to return his gun. He told me to bring it down to the pub.

I walked into his pub with a shoebox under my arm, which I placed on the bar. After a bit of small talk and a couple of drinks I asked the bloke how much he had paid for the gun. 'Fifteen hundred' I was told.

'By the way, where is it?' he whispered.

I pushed the shoebox across the bar. 'Take a look,' I said.

He wasn't too happy about what I had done to his lovely shooter, but the two grand I had slipped into the box did a lot to temper his bad humour. He took out the money and then pushed the box containing the remnants of his firearm back across the bar to me. 'You've bought it,' he said.

For a while after I escaped, everyone welcomed me back, but now my wild antics were bringing a lot of heat and police attention down on people who could ill afford to have their movements scrutinized. The police were hunting me, and hardly a week went by when there wasn't a report in the local papers about my activities. I was never mentioned by name, but everyone recognized the deeds. People started to fear me, and with fear comes resentment. I could empty some pubs just by walking through the door. A mate of the German's took over a notorious drug-dealers' pub in west Croydon. Formerly known as the Mailcoach, the John B. Keane was reopened under new management and hoping to attract a better class of clientele. Unfortunately, it was located exactly opposite a council estate where most of the wide-boys and drug-dealers lived, and they classed the pub as their territory, no matter who was running it or what the name had been changed to. The new governor asked the German to come in now and again and keep an eye on the place.

We were in there one morning, coming off a two-day drink-and-drug bender, me, the German and Barry, and three girls. The pub was fairly empty and quiet and just the place to wind down. We had been in about twenty minutes when four tough guys from the local estate came in and started to get a bit cheeky to the bar staff. The German went over to their table and politely asked them to mind their manners, and they said they were sorry. A few minutes later I went across to put some money in the jukebox, and as I was returning, one of the lads made an insulting comment about my choice of music. He was a big fat half-caste lad in his early twenties, and when I looked in his direction, he sneered at me. I said nothing and went back to my seat. The lads were drinking pints, so I knew I wouldn't have to wait for long, and sure enough, a few minutes later the fella walked past our table and into the toilets. I gave him a minute, then followed.

I had a six-inch lock-knife on me, but I didn't think I'd need it. As I came into the toilets he was standing at one of the urinals. I walked straight up and smashed his face against the tiles with a two-handed blow to the back of his head. He bounced off the wall and turned to face me with his dick still in his hand and leaking piss down his legs, and I gave him a very unhealthy head-butt in the nose. He slid down the wall covered in piss, blood and snot, and I gave him a hard kick in the groin that finished him. I then marched out of the toilets and up to his three pals. One of them had his back to me and, without breaking stride, I gave him a huge slap round the ear that knocked him off his stool. I stamped hard on his head and leant over the table to confront the other two, who were now looking scared. 'You ever come in this pub again and I'll fucking kill you and anyone else you care to bring with you. Understand?' I said. The two lads nodded. I told them to get their pal out of the toilets and fuck off. The bar staff were delighted, as these boys had been in before trying to put the frighteners on them. We got free drinks all round. But two days later the lads swarmed off the estate in the middle of the night and put all the windows through in the pub. Of course, when that happened, everyone said it was my fault for fronting them. I couldn't win for losing.

As usual my love life was in bits. I was living with Jenny but secretly meeting with Denise. Not satisfied with those two, I was also having the odd one-night stand with any woman who offered, and there were a few. I tried to have as much contact with my kids as possible, but it wasn't easy. Dean and Joe didn't really know me that well, and Lianne barely knew who I was. I had failed in my relationship with my kids just like I had failed in almost every relationship I'd had. It was like I was on a different planet to everyone else. I didn't want to grow up and fully accept my responsibilities, and by running wild and leaving my fate in the hands of other bodies like the police and the courts, I could dodge them. I was great when it came to hate and violence, but I was unable to articulate my love to the people who mattered most, my children.

By mid-January 1993 the writing was on the wall for me. I had shot, stabbed and robbed my way through seventy-nine days unlawfully at large. It was only a matter of time before someone made the phone call that put me back behind bars.

I was sitting in traffic at Streatham Common during rush-hour, having been out all day casing banks I wanted to rob in the future. I was unarmed and stone-cold sober for a change, and on my way back to Jenny's flat. I'd had a creepy feeling all day that I was being watched and followed, but my paranoia was something I'd learned to live with and I just put it down to that. I was driving a brand-new Golf GTi, and I had the driver's window wound down and the stereo blaring. I was waiting for the traffic lights to change and humming along with an Elvis tape when I heard a screech of tyres. Just that one sound was enough. I almost knew what was going to happen before it started. I looked in my wing-mirror and saw a dark-coloured BMW zooming up the road behind me, bypassing the stalled traffic by driving on the wrong side of the road. I looked in front of me and saw a black Volvo turn swiftly against the traffic stream and head for my car. Both cars screamed to a halt right next to mine and began to disgorge armed police officers in flak-jackets and chequered high-visibility caps.

'Armed police, don't fucking move!' was the shout from several hyped-up cozzers. I took it all in in a split second: the gun-barrels pointed in my direction, the shooter's stance of the copper pointing a Heckler & Koch machine-gun at my windscreen and the terrified eyes of the guy in the car in front of me as he stared into his rearview mirror at me.

At that first screech of tyres I had automatically put my car in gear, and before all the occupants were out of the Flying Squad vehicles I had made my mind up to run. I ignored the shouts of 'Armed police!' and stamped on the accelerator. With a loud crunch I rammed straight into the car in front of me and knocked the poor bastard out into the flowing traffic to try and create a gap I could get through. There was now a pistol right at my temple, so close I could smell the gun-oil, and a grim-faced copper holding it.

'Take the keys from the ignition and . . .' he shouted into my face.

I ignored him and spun my steering wheel full to the left and stomped the accelerator again. The powerful engine roared and I shot on to the pavement, just missing the copper with the machine-pistol. I floored the pedal and sped along the pavement, through an empty bus-shelter and out into the main traffic. I almost lost control as I fishtailed around the corner and out into the main road, but I got it straightened up and threw the gears into second, and I was off. I glanced in my rearview mirror and saw the coppers scrambling back into their cars. The chase was on.

If they had not chosen the rush-hour to spring their ambush I really believe I would have got away, but the traffic was too heavy to allow me a clear run. I span around a corner, hoping to make better time on the backstreets, but the BMW was right up with me. I sped down the road at 95 mph, and the BMW pulled effortlessly alongside me and kept pace. A copper leant from the open passenger-window of the BMW and pointed a pistol at me.

'Pull over!' he shouted.

From instinct I began winding my window up. As if that was going to stop a bullet! I was carrying a pocketful of false ID, which had Jenny's address on it. I didn't know how much they might know about me, but there was no point handing them the address on a plate, so I wound the window down again, and as I left them slightly behind at the next corner, I dropped the paperwork out of the window.

It was almost fully dark now but suddenly the inside of my car and the road around me lit up as bright as day. Then I realized it was the spotlight from a police helicopter that was tracking the chase. They were leaving nothing to chance. I knew it was all over now. I began to slow down, and when I turned the next corner I saw the road blocked by police vehicles. I turned off the engine, rolled to a stop and waited.

I was dragged from the car at gunpoint and laid flat on the ground to be searched. The plasti-cuffs were snapped on to my wrists and I was hoisted on to my feet and bent face down over the bonnet of my own car. The metal was warm with the heat from the engine. Suddenly the pile of identity papers I had thrown from the car was slapped down in front of my face.

'You dropped these,' said a voice near my ear.

It had been worth a try.

One of the coppers put his mouth near my ear and began to speak. 'Noel Stephen Smith, I am arresting you for armed robbery and being a prison escapee. You do not have to say anything, but anything you do say will be taken down and may be used against you in evidence. Have you anything to say?'

I had nothing to say. I was too sick to speak. Once again I could hear the sound of cell doors slamming shut and the cry of 'One on, sir'.

When they loaded me into the police Volvo, I noticed the crowds of people who had watched my arrest. It had been a good bit of excitement for them and had probably made their day. I fervently wished I was one of them.

23. Back on Tour

I spent a long weekend in Croydon police station being questioned by the Flying Squad about various robberies. They had known all about me staying at Jenny's flat and seemed to be very well-informed about my movements since I had escaped. They searched the flat and found my shotgun and cartridges, as well as a case full of fake driver's licences, passports and birth certificates which Jenny had been storing for someone. They told me they were going to nick Jenny for harbouring an escaped criminal and having instruments to defraud. I had a long chat with my solicitor, Ian Ryan, and asked him what would be the consequences of me sticking my hands up to everything they had. Ian is one of the smartest briefs I've ever known and I trusted him implicitly. He told me that on a guilty plea I would be looking at at least another fifteen years on top of the sentence I was already serving. I had to think about it.

Pleading guilty to anything had been anathema to me since I first appeared at the Old Bailey in 1977 and got fucked over on a guilty plea, but I was in a no-win situation. I hadn't worn a mask on the robberies, and some of the photographs they had from security cameras were red-hot. I had taken my last fling and enjoyed almost every minute of it, but now was the time to pay the price. If I pleaded not guilty and embarked on an unwinnable trial, I would easily get up to twenty-five years at the end of it. I was thirty-two years old and might see the street again by the time I was fifty, if I was lucky. On the other hand, anything under a fifteen-year sentence would at least leave me a spark of light at the end of an otherwise long, dark tunnel. I decided to stick my hands up.

The copper in charge of my interrogation, DC Greenwood, was more than surprised when I said I wanted to make a deal.

My deal was simple: I would admit to fourteen charges of bank robbery and various related firearms charges, and in return the police would forget about nicking Jenny. I would make a statement detailing my part in all the robberies, but I would not talk about anyone else who might have been involved, driving for me or supplying guns or getaway cars. The Flying Squad leapt at the deal. It would be a nice result for them with little effort on their part. I made my statement. I was charged with bank robbery, possession of a firearm with intent and illegally shortening the barrels of a shotgun. Ian Ryan said he would get my favourite barrister, James Sturman, to represent me at the crown court, and we would work on some mitigation to throw in front of the sentencing judge. I was also charged with being a prison escapee, but I would represent myself on that one.

On Monday morning I was taken under police escort to Croydon magistrates court for a formal hearing. I was designated a high-risk Category A prisoner and remanded in custody. I waited in the court cells until around six in the evening before the police came to collect me. Though I had made a statement coughing to my crimes, that didn't mean I was any friendlier with the police. In fact, I refused to speak to any of them outside of making my statement. I was grateful that they had not shot me when they had the chance during the chase, but they were still the enemy. I was picked up from the court by eight Flying Squad officers. I was handcuffed, led out to a high-speed BMW and put in the back seat between two hulking Squad officers. In front was a Flying Squad driver and another armed Squad-man in the passenger seat. The other four piled into a car behind us. It was dark. Just before the car pulled out of the court-compound, the copper in the passenger seat looked back at me.

'Try anything iffy with us, and I'll put a bullet right in your canister,' he said.

I recognized him as the copper with the machine-gun I had almost run over during the ambush. I said nothing.

I knew they must be taking me to prison but I couldn't figure out which one. We were heading to Banstead, and as far as I

knew there were no prisons out that way except the Category
C jail, Downview, and there was no way they were going to try
and put me in a low-security prison. The atmosphere inside the
car seemed tense and expectant, and nobody was saying much.
As we turned on to a dark, countryish road, I began to get
worried. The thought came into my head that they were taking
me out into the sticks to execute me. The more I thought about
it, the more sense it made. I had been a thorn in their sides for
years, and what better way to remove me once and for all? A
quiet piece of woodland at night, a swift bullet in the head, and
all done. They could say I had tried to escape; I had previous for
it after all. I began to sweat. When we pulled up a particularly
quiet road, I was on the verge of asking them where exactly they
were taking me, but as we rounded a bend in the road I saw the
spotlights of what was obviously a prison. I don't think I've ever
been so glad to see a top-security prison in my life.

HMP Highdown was the newest top-security prison in the
country. It would not be officially opened until the summer of
1993, but it had started taking prisoners in late '92. Until I reached
its gates I had never heard of it. The police checked their guns
in at the gatehouse and then drove me into the prison proper
and handed me over to the screws at reception. They knew I
was coming. I was only the third Category A prisoner they had
dealt with and they seemed slightly in awe of me. Most of the
screws at Highdown were brand-new and just out of training. I
was treated politely and well. After I had been through the usual
reception procedure, I was taken out on to the enclosed internal
walkways by six screws. We stopped outside a gate marked
'Segregation Unit', which is modern prison-speak for the punishment block. I was puzzled. 'Why are you putting me in the
block?' I asked. The screws wouldn't look at my face. 'Governor's
orders,' said one. 'But it's just for tonight.'

Inside the clean, new punishment block I was met by a reception committee led by a short, fat man in a suit, who was obviously a governor. I halted in front of them and waited. The fat
man cleared his throat.

'Noel Stephen Smith,' he began, 'I am the deputy governor. You have been remanded into our custody by the courts for some very serious charges. I have been appraised of your previous prison behaviour and I sincerely hope that we will have no trouble from you. If you treat my staff with respect, they will treat you with respect. Have you any questions?'

I nodded. 'Yeah, why am I in the punishment block?'

'Frankly,' he said, 'it's because after speaking to the police, we weren't sure what to expect from you. It's merely a safety precaution. You will be moved to a houseblock tomorrow.'

'OK then,' I said. 'Show me to my cell.'

True to his word, I was moved on to Houseblock 1 first thing next morning. I had spent my first night back in prison in the familiar surroundings of solitary confinement, and with the exception of the politeness of the screws, it was almost like I'd never been gone.

On the houseblock I met up with a few familiar faces. Rooky Lee and Gus the Jock were the other two Category A men in the prison. I had heard a lot about Rooky over the years. He was an Eastender of the old school, a prolific robber and a gentleman. His nickname was '18 for 1', because he had received a sentence of eighteen years for one robbery in the early 1980s. He had made his escape from Maidstone prison, had been recaptured and was now facing another charge of armed robbery. Gus was a Scotsman who was awaiting trial on charges of robbing several travel agencies of vast amounts of money.

I also got to know a couple of fellas who are still close friends of mine to this day. Stevie B., ex-soldier and master butcher, was doing three years for stabbing a copper. He worked in the kitchen at Highdown and kept us supplied with the best of grub and plenty of yeast with which to make our hooch. When he was eventually released, Stevie came all over the country to visit me in different prisons and kept me supplied with music tapes and filthy magazines. And Nicky Wood, a handsome ex-boxer, if that's not too much of an oxymoron, who specialized in the theft of high-performance sports cars and various other wild criminal scams. Together we were the terror of HMP Highdown, but I'm glad to say that both Stevie and Nicky have now settled down on the straight and narrow.

My first confrontation with authority at Highdown came a couple of days after they let me up on Houseblock 1. A pair of screws appeared at my cell door with a set of high-visibility stripes for me. I had been charged with being a prison escapee, but as I was already on the Category A list this should have negated me having to wear stripes. When the screws tried to present me with my new clothing I laughed in their faces, took the stripes from their hands and launched the gear over the landing rail and on to the safety net below. The screws just stood there, not knowing what to do.

'The security governor has ordered that you wear them,' said one.

'Tell the security governor to stick them up his arse,' was my reply.

Later that day I got a visit from more screws, four of them this time, with the order for me to wear the stripes. I decided it was time to make a stand. Once more I threw the stripes over the railing and told them in no uncertain terms what they could do with the security governor. I was then visited by a PO, who tried reasoning with me. He basically told me that they didn't want any trouble, but if I didn't wear the stripes I would not be allowed out of my cell. I took the stripes from him, threw them back over the railings, walked into my cell and slammed the door behind me without a word. If they wanted to keep me in my cell I didn't give a shit. I had my radio, plenty of books and good pals on the houseblock who would slip whatever else I might need under my door. And I could always swing a line to my neighbours for anything that wouldn't fit under the door. I'd had plenty of experience of solitary confinement, and I liked it.

'Swinging a line' is a practice that is used daily in our prisons. If I want to pass an object to someone in another cell when all the doors are locked, I will first make a line. This can be anything from a shoelace to a piece of thread carefully unpicked from a prison blanket. Once my line is of sufficient length to reach the cell I am throwing it to, I will then weight the end with a chunk of prison soap or a battery. Then I will put my arm through the window bars and, holding on to one end of the line, swing the weighted end until it has gathered sufficient momentum, then release it. The man in the cell next door will be waiting with his arm through his own bars to catch the line and pull in whatever I want to give him. In this way the line can be passed along the whole length of a cellblock. It is sometimes time-consuming, but time is what we have an abundance of.

After a couple of days locked up I was approached by the same PO as before. He offered a compromise: if I would wear the stripes whenever I left the spur for exercise or library, then I would be excused wearing them all the time. This was probably the best I was going to get, so I relented. But even when I left the spur, I wouldn't exactly wear the stripes, I just stuffed them in the back-pocket of my jeans and let them hang down my leg so the stripe was visible. I was never approached about them again.

As Highdown began filling up with prisoners, and they saw how easygoing the screws were compared to other nicks, the cons started taking liberties. One fella smuggled in a six-inch lock-knife through visits. This kind of 'proper' weapon was worth its weight in hash, and the bidding for it was fierce. It went to one of the main drug-dealers and was used to consolidate his position as the junk king. It was used in several stabbings over the next few months.

By the time I had been at Highdown for three months there was a pretty hard-core bunch of prisoners there. We smoked cannabis openly, brewed gallons of hooch in the shower rooms and ripped the piss out of the screws at every opportunity. It seemed as though the screws were content to settle for our antics as long as we didn't actually assault any of them, start any riots or attempt to escape. Some of the more personable screws would even come to the cells where parties were going on and have a bit of a laugh with us. They tolerated puff, hooch and even ecstasy, and some of the screws were not averse to supplementing their income by selling drugs to the prisoners themselves. One was stopped for driving erratically when she was off duty. The police searched her car and found a bag of ecstasy tablets and a quantity of powdered cocaine. When they searched her prison service-subsidized flat, they found a set of scales, a lot more drugs and a list of names of prisoners who owed her money for drugs she had supplied to them inside the prison. She was suspended immediately, and set up home with an ex-Highdown con.

In the early 1990s and before, the drug of choice used by a large percentage of the prison population was cannabis. It was cheap and plentiful and the screws tended to turn a blind eye to it. It is a pacifying drug – and better to have a largely violent prison population mellowed out and craving confectionery than taking hostages and ripping the roofs from their cesspit jails. But heroin was different gravy altogether; the gloves came off if anyone was caught doing skag. Heroin was expensive – £10 for a tiny bag – and highly addictive. With big money came big debtors, and where it might not be worth the candle to stab someone for a sixteenth of puff costing £7.50, it was another matter for a sixteenth of heroin, costing £75 on the street, but worth £300 in prison once cut and bagged. Heroin tends to agitate prisoners, not the drug itself but the craving for it. It upsets the equilibrium of a prison. And though violence is the norm in jail, the introduction of heroin tends to increase it five-fold. The screws knew this and cracked down hard on heroin-dealers and users.

On 28 May 1993 I was taken under armed escort to Maidstone crown court to be sentenced for the crimes I had committed whilst on the run. I was represented by James Sturman, who managed to make my pitiable lack of mitigation sound like mitigation itself. He painted such a sad picture of my life and deeds that I was almost tempted to shed a tear myself. The judge must have been moved, because he sentenced me to fifteen years for each count of armed robbery, seven years for each count of possession of a firearm with intent, four years for sawing the barrels off a shotgun and two years for prison escape, but he made all of these sentences concurrent with each other, *and* concurrent with the eleven and a half years I was already serving. In effect, this meant that I started my new fifteen-year sentence on that day. It was the best I could have hoped for.

Back in Highdown, they were now eager to get rid of me. Just before I had gone on the run I had seen an advert in the pages of the prisoners' national newspaper, *Inside-Time*, from a probation officer in Sheffield who was looking for poetry and prose from prisoners for a publication he was starting up. The Sheffield probation officer's name was Julian Broadhead, and the publication he started was called *Prison Writing*. I had sent off a couple of my poems, and an account of the attempted escape from Wandsworth, entitled 'I Am Spartacus . . .', and after I had been in Highdown for a couple of weeks I got a letter, a cheque for £15 and two copies of *Prison Writing* No. 2, in which my work appeared. I was amazed that he had thought my work good enough to publish. I couldn't get over it for a while, and I was very proud to see my name in print. The letter from Julian was very encouraging, and I immediately wrote back with one of my short stories. This appeared in the next issue of *Prison Writing*, and I began to suspect that I might just be a little bit warm at this old writing game.

With this new-found confidence in my ability to string coherent sentences together on a page, I set about trying to subvert the prison system in a different way. I began to write seditious 'pamphlets' about the staff and governors at Highdown and distribute them amongst the prisoners. Using the pen-name 'the Outlaw', I would handwrite my diatribes, including short poems of the not-very-complimentary variety, mentioning certain screws by name, and pass them on to a mate of mine who was allowed access to the computer workshop. He would then type them up and make plenty of copies for the prisoners. I classed it all as a big jape, but the management didn't see the funny side. The

Outlaw called for all prisoners to unite and rise up against their captors, to rip the roof from their prison and burn it to the ground, to assault staff and sex offenders and to take governors hostage. It was strong stuff, and soon the whole prison was buzzing with rumours about the Outlaw.

The screws were going mad trying to find out who the Outlaw was. As I had always been assessed by the prison system as 'below average intelligence', I wasn't even in the frame. To the system, I was just a 'violent thug', so their suspicions bypassed me and fell on the more intellectual prisoners, such as the fraud merchants and other white-collar criminals in the prison. In the meantime I had a letter from Julian telling me that the *Independent* newspaper wanted to use one of my poems, 'Old Lags', as their Poem of the Day. This was a big shock. It was one thing to be published by someone who specifically wanted prison-writers, but a national newspaper, and a broadsheet to boot – that boosted my confidence no end. It became harder to get the Outlaw's stuff copied and distributed around the prison, as the screws were really cracking down. Anything that went in or out of the computer workshop was scrutinized, and many cells were raided in the search for suspicious-looking paperwork.

But nothing inside a prison can be kept a secret for long, and it was only a matter of time before my name was put up by some slimy grass looking for a few brownie points. I was called to see the PO.

He dismissed the screws who escorted me into the office and told them to wait outside. His opening words to me were, 'So you like to write poetry, do you, Smith?'

I thought he was referring to my recent poem in the *Independent*. 'Helps to pass the time, guv,' I replied.

He held up one of my Outlaw pamphlets. 'Somebody tells me that you are also involved in this rubbish.'

I put on my best look of puzzled innocence. 'What's that then, guv?'

'I'm not going to play games with you, Smith,' he said. 'I'm just going to give you one warning. If you are involved, and it continues, I will send you to a prison that is so far north you will think you are leaving the country. And I will personally supervise your leaving party. Do I make myself clear?'

I knew he couldn't have had any firm evidence of my involvement, or I would have been on the van right now, nursing a few bruises and heading for the M1. I had to be careful in my response.

'If I was involved, guv, I'd certainly take your warning on board.'

He nodded, satisfied.

I decided to put the Outlaw into hibernation. The report on the Strangeways and related prison riots had come out, there was lots of media attention on the prison system once again, and I wanted to see if I could contribute to it. I had a yearning to get the voice of a prisoner heard by the outside world. I had discovered a love of writing and I had plenty to say. I wanted the country to know why prisoners had felt the need to take such a dangerous step as rioting. The POA and the Home Office had plenty of spokesmen putting their side across, but no one was really asking prisoners what was wrong with the system. We were, and still are, the most disenfranchised minority in this country, and our views on the system generally go unheard or are discounted. I wanted to somehow change this and bring certain aspects of prison life out into the open. And *Prison Writing* gave me that opportunity.

The first annual *Prison Writing* competition offered cash prizes in the categories of fiction, non-fiction and poetry by a prisoner. I wrote a piece for the non-fiction category called 'A Voice from the Yards', explaining the truth about prison, as compared to the many tabloid-newspaper reports about 'holiday-camp jails'. As an afterthought I also entered a short story about prison suicide in the fiction category. I was buzzing when I took first prize in both categories. *Prison Writing* had Lord Longford as its patron, and the likes of John McVicar, Jimmy Boyle and Trevor Hercules on the editorial board. Copies were distributed to all the quality newspapers and other interested bodies, even as far afield as South

Africa and America. I was offered the chance to write a short story with the theme of vengeance for an international writers' journal called *Passport*, and I wrote 'No Tears for Eddie', about a young prisoner who gets caught up in a major prison riot in which a screw is killed. The story is about the aftermath of the riot and how the screws and the system wreak their vengeance on one of the prisoners involved. I used some of my own personal experiences in the story.

Julian was very encouraging about my writing and did his best to pass my stuff on to as many influential people as possible. Through this, I was offered the chance to write for the *New Law Journal*, a bi-monthly magazine for those in the legal profession. The *New Law Journal* was edited by James Morton, the ex-barrister and writer who wrote Frankie Fraser's biography *Mad Frank*, among other things. I had a regular slot in the *New Law Journal* for some years, and this allowed me to write about some of the things that were right and wrong in the prison system. I received letters from judges and barristers commenting on my articles and encouraging me to keep writing.

All of this happened in that all-too-brief honeymoon period that existed in the prison system between the Strangeways riots and the ascension of Michael Howard to the helm of the Home Office. After Strangeways, and with the building of the new jails like Highdown, Woodhill and Blakenhurst, it really seemed as though change was coming to the prison system, and change for the better. Men had died and millions of pounds' worth of damage had been done in the riots. Lord Woolf's report into the causes uncovered working practices and jails that had not changed since Queen Victoria was on the throne. He discovered that the majority of prisoners were crammed three to a cell in cells built for one, living in filth and squalor and having to perform their ablutions in plastic buckets and pots. Work and education for prisoners were very low priority, and even getting a weekly shower and kit change for men who were kept locked in their cells for twenty-three hours of every day was a problem. Not even lip-service was being paid to the concept of rehabilitation in our prisons. The men who rioted at Strangeways and other jails, risking the obligatory beating from the screws and plenty of time added on to their sentences, did not do it for a laugh. They did it because they were absolutely sick and tired of being treated like cattle by the prison system. Lord Woolf understood this, and made many recommendations that would improve the system.

Unfortunately for everyone concerned, Michael Howard became Home Secretary. Howard's preposterous rhetoric and knee-jerk policies were lapped up by the hang-'em-and-flog-'em brigade. He got standing ovations when he shouted that 'Prison works!', and when he informed the party faithful how he intended to make prison regimes 'harsh, but fair', they loved him all the more. He started by eliminating home leave, the process by which long-term prisoners coming to the end of their sentences might be partly reintegrated into the outside world. To understand the impact of this on long-term prisoners, you have to realize that for most of them, their home-leave date represented a considerable milestone in their sentences. If, for example, you were serving a sentence of fifteen years, you could expect to be released, with good behaviour, at the ten-year mark. This was known as your EDR (Earliest Date of Release). But, in theory, you were also eligible to be released on parole at the five-year mark. If you were a model prisoner you would be given parole at the nine years and three months' mark. So, after serving one-third of your fifteen-year sentence, you reached your PED (Parole Eligibility Date) and, if you had been on good behaviour and downgraded to Category C, then you could apply for a seven-day home leave as soon as your refusal for first parole came through.

Long-term prisoners looked forward to their home-leave date almost as much as their EDR, not only because they were allowed to go out for seven days, but also because it meant that the worst part of their sentence was over. Return from a home leave successfully and you would be granted a further home leave in six months' time. Return from that and you would be made a

Category D and sent to an open prison. Home leave was the one thing that all long-termers looked forward to, and without so much as breaking sweat Michael Howard took it away. And that was only the start. The prisons' education budget, which had been increased after Woolf's recommendations, was slashed by 89 per cent under Howard. Mandatory drug-testing of all prisoners was introduced. And all resettlement projects for long-term prisoners were shelved.

But Howard didn't have it all his own way. In 1994 there was a highly embarrassing escape from the Special Secure Unit at HMP Whitemoor by five IRA prisoners and a London robber. The SSU at Whitemoor was a state-of-the-art, electronically controlled fortress within the confines of what was considered to be the most secure prison in Europe. Yet the six prisoners managed not only to break out of the SSU but also the prison proper, shooting two screws in the process. All six prisoners were quickly recaptured outside the prison. But one of them, Andy Russell, had already made headlines when he hijacked the helicopter that was forced to land on the exercise field in HMP Gartree and take off with Johnny Kendall and Sid Draper in 1987. Andy Russell's involvement was completely missed by the press at the time, as they concentrated on the five IRA men involved, but it was the second time Andy had left the Home Office with egg all over its face. And his place in prison history is assured. I was on the same wing as Andy in Albany, and though I found him a bit flash, he was entitled to be. After the escape from the SSU, all the escapees were seriously beaten by the screws. In 2001 the Home Office was ordered to pay the prisoners thousands of pounds in compensation for the injuries they received when the prison system took its revenge.

As if an escape from an SSU wasn't enough to turn Howard's face red, it was followed the next year by the escape of three long-term prisoners from Parkhurst top-security dispersal prison on the Isle of Wight. The repercussions of these two escapes almost led to Howard losing his job. But he didn't have the honour to resign and instead weathered the very public humiliation and castigation like the brass-necked bastard he was, by blaming the whole thing on the Director General of the prison service and the governor of Parkhurst. Derek Lewis and John Marriot were forced to resign their posts, and Howard was given the third-degree about it all on BBC's *Newsnight*, when he foolishly agreed to be interviewed by the bullish Jeremy Paxman. Even his deputy, Ann Widdecombe, who was no shrinking violet when it came to turning the screws on prisoners, described Howard as having 'something of the night' about his personality.

Howard's reign at the Home Office is worth mentioning because of the serious effect it had on the prison system and is still having today. In the aftermath of the Whitemoor and Parkhurst escapes, Howard appointed a couple of hardline ex-military men to take a look at the security in our prisons. The Woodcock and Learmont report gave Howard the ammunition he needed to crack down even harder on prisoners. He introduced a system called 'Volumetric Control', which meant that no prisoner was allowed to possess more personal property than could fit into two cardboard boxes of a standard size. Men and women serving massive sentences, and in some cases natural life, would now only be allowed to have the minimum amount of comforts. If it did not fit in the boxes, it was confiscated. And as if that wasn't bad enough, any prisoner could be called on at any time to strip their cell and fit everything into the boxes. Then they would unpack the boxes and put everything back in its place, only to be ordered to do it all again a few days later. Some prisons use Volumetric Control to keep prisoners unsettled. It has become a psychological weapon. Give the screws any lip and you will find yourself constantly packing and unpacking your property.

As well as The Gestapo-like Dedicated Search Teams, Howard also introduced something called the IEPS (Incentive and Earned Privileges Scheme), which in effect created a three-tier class system among prisoners. IEPS lays out three levels for prisoners, the top level being 'Enhanced', the middle level being 'Standard' and the bottom level being 'Basic'. On entering prison every prisoner is designated standard status. If the screws don't like your attitude, or if you misbehave in any way, from not keeping your cell tidy to punching a screw in the mouth, you can be placed on the basic regime on top of any other punishment you may receive. If you are on basic, you will have no access to association, have to wear prison clothes, have only thirty-minute social visits, and be allowed to spend a maximum of £2.50 a week at the canteen. If you are standard, you get association, longer visits, can wear your own clothes and can spend up to £10 a week at the canteen. If you achieve enhanced status, you get still more association and visits and the chance to spend £15 a week at the canteen. I should just make clear that the money you can spend at the canteen is not money given to you by the prison system, but your own money that you can have sent in through the post. The result of IEPS is to divide prisoners still further, as the system firmly believes in the old adage 'divide and conquer'.

Another Howard innovation, MDT (Mandatory Drug-Testing), is almost entirely responsible for the heroin problem that has swept our prisons in the last few years. Howard's attempt to deal with the 'drug problem' in prisons, which until his intervention consisted of cannabis-smoking and the occasional heroin user, was another ill-thought-out idea that was to have serious long-term consequences on the prison system and society as a whole. When prisoners realized they could lose up to twenty-one days a time for giving a positive urine test for cannabis, they soon switched to heroin, since cannabis can be detected in urine up to fifty-eight days after being smoked, whereas heroin is flushed through the body in between forty-eight and seventy-two hours. The result was plain to see when, in 2000, the Home Office reported that a huge percentage of crime in this country was being committed by a small percentage of heroin addicts in order to fund their habits. Our prisons are awash with heroin, and it would be reasonable to assume that at least some addicts get their habit when they go to jail for the first time. I have lost count of the number of friends and acquaintances I have witnessed having their first taste of heroin in prison. And it is a fact that

the most prolific killer of newly released prisoners is heroin over-
dose. People get on it in jail, and when they get out they immediately want more, but they're not used to the potency of street
heroin as compared to the cut-to-shit heroin they have been
getting in prison.

Personally, I have never bothered with heroin. It never appealed
to me after I witnessed a mate of mine spewing his ring up in
a cell in Wandsworth after smoking it. I wasn't interested in any
drug that was going to make me sick before I could get high. I
also saw what the cravings could do to the people who fucked
around with it. I have seen heroin ruin a lot of good men over
the years in prison. Major criminals who you would never in a
million years expect to be touching it are secret 'booters' who
kid themselves that they are only 'dabbling' and that they will
never touch it on the out. Just like there is no such thing as
being 'prison bent', there is also no such thing as being a prison
junkie.

My own drug of choice had now become the written word.
Once I discovered that people in the outside world were actually interested in reading what I had to say, there was no stopping me. I began to write every day, sometimes articles for
prison-based magazines or for magazines outside, and sometimes
complaint forms for myself and other prisoners. I delighted in
crafting a coherent petition I knew would cause uproar. I was
always polite in my written complaints and I made sure that what
I was complaining about was a valid and genuine grievance. I
did not make groundless complaints. Prisoners began to seek me
out when they had a problem with the system, and I gained a
reputation as a cell-block lawyer. I began to study the law, and
in particular the prison rules and standing orders that govern the
day-to-day running of the prison system. I had discovered a way
to attack the system without having to take a physical beating
for it. I was just coming at it from a new angle.

A couple of months after being sentenced at Maidstone crown
court, I was on the move again, this time to Swaleside on the
Isle of Sheppey, but I couldn't settle. I had made myself too high

profile with my complaints and petitions and they couldn't resist trying to dig me out. I ended up in the punishment block at Swaleside for threatening a screw, and I was put on GOAD for a couple of months. In the punishment block I once again bumped into an old pal of mine from the borstal days. Steve Hostetler had made his mark with his escape from Wandsworth, but had been recaptured less than a year later.

Steve was a bit older and a bit wiser but still mad to make an escape in any way he could. We spent hours at our cell windows talking over the old days and slagging off the system. Steve had a tame screw on reception who he would speak to whenever he left the block to go for a visit in the visiting hall, and one day he came back and told me that the screw had informed him that we were both to be moved the next day on the same van. As usual, Steve had an escape plan. He had managed to smuggle a needle and hypodermic syringe into the punishment block, and he had nicked a red biro that one of the block screws had left lying around. His plan was to break open the biro and pour the red ink into the syringe so that it looked like blood. Then he would smuggle it on to the van and, once we were underway, we would grab one of the screws and hold the syringe up to his throat and tell the escort it contained AIDS-infected blood, forcing them to unlock our chains and allowing us to effect an escape. I was game for it. I had never lost my desire for freedom.

The next morning at six my door was thrown open and I was officially told I was on the move. When I got down to reception I was put into a holding cell with Steve. He showed me that he had the needle in his mouth and he had the syringe bottled. We decided we would wait for a stretch of motorway before making our move, let the screws relax and then strike. I was the first to be pulled in for the search. I was taken into a small room with mirrors all over the walls and on the floor and told to strip. The mirrors were to check me from all angles in case I was concealing something. After I had been searched I was given a set of sterile prison-clothing and taken to another holding room. Twenty minutes later Steve was shown into the same room, having passed his strip search without the screws finding anything.

With a couple of high-profile prison veterans like me and Steve, the screws were not taking any chances, as we were soon to find out. We were taken from the holding-room and wanded with hand-held metal detectors, including the soles of our feet. They missed the needle in Steve's mouth because it was so small it didn't register. Then we were double-cuffed. Double-cuffing is now pretty standard in the prison system, but at one time it was reserved for only the most dangerous and escape-minded prisoners. First they put on a normal set of prison handcuffs linking both the prisoner's wrists together, then they attach a heavy manganese-steel cuff to the prisoner's right wrist above the bracelet of the first cuff and attach the empty cuff to the left wrist of a screw, so not only are the prisoner's hand movements restricted, but he is also on a short leash. Any movement by the prisoner will be immediately detected by the screw who is cuffed to him.

Double-cuffed, we were led out to the prison van past a gauntlet of grim-faced screws. It turned out that we were to have seven screws and an SO on the escort with us, not including the driver. We were jam-packed into the small van, and the SO closed the door and told the screws outside to lock it and hand the keys to the driver, who was in a cab closed off from us. The SO then pulled a mobile phone from his pocket, the first time I had ever seen one within a prison, and held it up.

'With this,' he said, 'I am constantly in touch with both the police and prison system. If either of you makes any move to try and escape from this escort, I can have help here in minutes. Do not make any sudden movements, because we are authorized to use reasonable force on you. And that includes batons. Understand?'

Steve sighed. 'So I suppose there's no chance we'll be stopping off at McDonald's for a bit of lunch on the way then?'

The SO tapped the partition to signal to the driver it was time to leave.

There was now no chance that we would make it off the van,

so we spent the journey taking the piss out of the screws. We noticed that every time one of us so much as shifted in our seats, the SO would bring the mobile phone to his lips and watch us expectantly, so we did a lot of shifting just for the fun of it. We had the screws making us roll-ups and holding them up to our mouths so we could smoke them, because we weren't allowed to lift our hands above chest height. When we pulled into the ferry port at Portsmouth, we knew we were headed for the Isle of Wight. Steve went to Parkhurst, and I ended up back in Albany.

In Albany I met up with Andy, who I had last seen at the Verne just before my escape, and Tony Hogan. I had known Tony and his family almost all my life, and his brother Tommy had ended up married to my sister Samantha. Tony is well-known all over the prison system for his mad antics. He can be a charming and personable man and generous enough to give you his last roll-up, but he has a darker side which regularly comes to the fore, and he'll stab you in the eye with a scissor blade for some perceived slight. There is no doubt that Tony can be a funny man and very entertaining, but you must always keep one eye open when you are laughing along with him, and watch his hands.

By now I was more into fighting the system with the written word than throwing digs at screws. But if pushed hard enough, I was still game for the latter. I had bought myself a portable typewriter, an Olivetti Lettera 25, with the prize money I had got from coming runner-up in the *Raconteur* short-story competition, and I spent most of my lock-up time writing on it. I worked in the furniture workshop, putting prison lockers together by day, and during the evening association period I knocked about with Andy, Tony, Andy Pippin and Bobby White, who was into the twenty-second year of his life sentence. We played kaluki or pool, smoked some dope, drank some hooch and discussed prison politics. But as soon as I was locked in for the night at eight o'clock, I was straight on the typewriter for a couple of hours.

One day, outside the furniture shop, I noticed a rubbish skip, where they were throwing broken furniture. There was a swivel-chair in there that had come from the instructor's office. The seat was ripped, and it was in a decrepit state of repair, but it took my fancy. I asked the duty screw if I could take it back to my cell to sit on while I was typing. The screw shrugged. 'Take it if you want it,' was his reply. I took the chair back to the wing and spent a couple of evenings fixing it up. I re-covered the seat with material from the soft-toy class, and at the end of it I had a fairly decent bit of cell furniture. Strictly speaking, the chair was an 'unauthorized article', but I had it in my cell for months and no one said a word.

The DST at Albany were typical of the breed, all leather gloves and chewing gum, most of them under five foot six and trying to make up for their lack of height by standing on the rule book. At one time prison officers had to be at least five foot eight and of a certain fitness to do the job. This attracted a lot of ex-Forces men into the prison service, big, hard men who were used to physical violence and were not afraid of a tear-up. But in the early 1990s it all changed, when the prison service had to allow women officers the same rights as their male colleagues, including working at the sharp end, on the wings. Until 1992 I had never seen a female prison officer opening cell doors on a wing (they were usually only allowed to supervise counts to and from the workshops and other work that didn't really bring them into close contact with prisoners), but when they lifted the discrimination against women they also had to drop the height restrictions. This meant that all sorts of people could become screws: there were tiny ones who looked as though they might blow away in a strong breeze, big fat ones who could barely move out of their chairs, divvy ones who could barely string two words together and would fluff every count, and mean snidy ones who couldn't disguise the fact that they had joined up to work out the frustration of their own inadequacies on a captive population. The flotsam and jetsam of straight society flocks to the prison service, like they did to the priesthood in the Dark Ages. I had a bit of respect for the old-style screws, grudging though it may have been, but the new breed are beyond contempt. You can keep a bit of dignity when being ordered to 'get behind your door' by a six-foot ex-Para, but the same order coming from a spotty-faced lesbian midget of eighteen sticks in my craw.

Anyway, back to my chair. One morning I was taken from work to my cell for a random spin (cell search) by four diddy members of the DST. After searching every inch of me and my cell and finding nothing, one of them, the shortest, decided that he was confiscating my swivel-chair. I tried to reason with him, but it was like talking to a plank of wood. Eventually I lost my temper. I snatched the chair from his hands.

'All right,' I said. 'You want this fucking chair, you can have it.'

I lifted the chair above my head and marched down the landing to where the screws were gathered in the wing office. The DST screws followed me as fast as their little legs could carry them, vainly ordering me to put the chair down. There was a big window in the wing-office, and I threw the chair straight through it.

'Take the fucking chair!' I roared.

I had just happened to wake up in a bad mood that morning and the chair was the last straw.

I stood there, fists clenched, rage sizzling through my body, and glared at the DST. The chair had gone clean through the window of the office and bounced across a desk before smashing into a computer monitor. There was glass everywhere and a couple of screws who were inside the office were staring, open-mouthed, through the shattered window.

'Happy now, you little prick?' I asked the DST screw.

He puffed himself up to his full height. 'You're fucking nicked!' he shouted.

I took a couple of steps towards him. I was really in the mood for a good tear-up. He panicked and pressed the general-alarm bell on his personal radio. The bell sounded loud and clear throughout the prison. On the spur of the moment I thought, Fuck it, might as well give them something to be alarmed about.

I ran back to my cell as fast as I could go, only just beating the crowd of screws that swarmed on to the wing from all directions in response to the alarm bell. I slid into my cell and picked up the heavy end of my two-piece snooker cue. I came out of my cell just as the mob of screws reached my door. I screamed at the top of my voice, like a demented caveman spotting a brontosaurus nibbling his vegetable patch, and swung the cue like a club. My first swing hit the diminutive DST man in the head and knocked him bandy. Then I was into them, swinging and screaming and scattering them in all directions. I had the element of surprise and I made it tell. The corridor was narrow, with locked cells on each side and nowhere to hide, and within seconds I had cleared a space around myself. The screws backed off, unable to get near me without taking a clump from my weapon. I was laughing like a maniac now.

'Come on, you mugs! Who wants it, then?'

There was a momentary stand-off, then a voice from the crowd shouted, 'Draw batons!'

I was fully willing and able to fight until they dropped me through sheer weight of numbers. I felt good, strong and completely in control of my rage.

I waved them on with my free hand.

'Come on then, you fucking slags. Let's have it!'

Some of the screws had drawn their batons, but nobody was brave or foolish enough to be first. Then there was movement in the crowd and the wing PO pushed his way to the front. He was young for a Principal Officer, and he had a reputation amongst the cons as a fair man. His name was Monkton. He stepped out of the mob and slowly put his hands in the pockets of his trousers, and stood there, calm as you like, rocking backwards and forwards on his heels and toes.

'OK, Razor,' he said quietly, 'you've got our attention. So what seems to be the problem?'

I hefted my weapon. 'No problem,' I said. 'I'm just going to smash the granny out of the first screw who tries to lay a hand on me.'

Monkton nodded as if this was a quite reasonable declaration. 'You know you're going to have to go to the block, don't you? I mean, we can't stand here all day, we've got a prison to run. The thing is, if you put down your weapon, I give you my word that you won't be assaulted by any member of my staff.'

My rage was dying down anyway. I had made my point, and I liked Monkton. Putting down my weapon would give him a bit of kudos with the staff. I dropped it on the floor and put my hands on top of my head. The screws immediately rushed me and I felt a few sly digs before Monkton roared for order.

As I was being marched to the block, the general alarm sounded again and several of the screws who were escorting me ran off to deal with this new crisis. I heard from one of the screws' radios that the latest disturbance was on the gardens party working near the greenhouses. I was strip-searched and locked into a block cell. Five minutes later I heard a huge commotion coming from the entrance to the block. I got up to my door and pressed my eye against the thin gap between the door and jamb. I saw three prisoners in a fierce struggle with the screws as they were dragged into the block. One of the prisoners was a mate of mine from the wing, named Danny Leahy. Danny was a typical Bermondsey boy, louder than a bullhorn and as game as a hungry boxer. I kicked my door as hard and as often as I could in the age-old ritual that showed solidarity with other prisoners who were being manhandled by the screws in the block. After about five minutes things went quiet as the boys were put into separate cells.

Danny was put in the cell next door to mine, so I laid down at the heating pipe at the back of the cell and spoke to him through the gap between the pipe and wall.

'Danny, what's the apple?'

He was surprised to hear me. 'Is that you, Raze? What are you doing down here?'

I explained what had happened up on A-wing, and he began to laugh loud and long.

'What the fuck is so funny?' I asked.

And then he explained how he and the others ended up in the block. They had been working on the gardens party, clearing weeds, when the alarm went off to signal my actions with the chair. The screw who was supervising the work got on his radio and asked what was going on, and the panicked reply came back, 'We've lost control of A-wing!' Hearing this come over the radio, Danny and the boys immediately assumed that a riot had started. Danny hit the work-screw with his hoe, knocking him out, and they went on a rampage of destruction, smashing every pane of glass in the greenhouses and setting fire to the lawnmower shed. While I was on my way to the block, Danny and his confederates were having a pitched battle with the screws who went to quell their mini-riot. I had to laugh.

Once more I faced months in solitary confinement. We had a hard-core bunch of prisoners in the block, and we were soon joined by Tony Hogan and an Eastender named Sharky, who were both under investigation for stabbing incidents on the wing. We passed the long hours by talking shit out of the windows and thinking up ways to fuck the block-screws up. Pepe Davis, a lifer who was seventeen years into his sentence, was also on GOAD. Pepe, a half-caste East End boxer, was well-known throughout the prison system. He was used to punishment blocks, having spent the majority of his sentence punching the shit out of screws. He was a very funny man and would have us all in stitches with his nightly observations of the world in general and the prison system in particular.

Exercise in the block was done in cages. There were two cages, and they would hold one prisoner at a time in each one for the daily exercise period. One morning I was in one cage and Pepe was in the next one. Pepe had a habit of stripping naked as soon as he got in the cage, telling the screws, 'You can put a lion in a cage, but don't expect him to dress up for it.' On this day Pepe was naked and lying on the ground sunbathing, when the governor and his entourage came round doing the daily rounds. They stopped at my cage, where I was walking in circles.

'Morning, Smith,' said the governor. 'Everything all right?'

I gave him my standard reply in such situations: 'Go and fuck yourself'; and he quickly moved on to Pepe's cage.

He glanced at the naked Pepe, who was lying on the ground with his head propped up on his prison uniform, and his face went red in embarrassment. He quickly looked up at the clear blue sky.

'Morning, Davis,' he muttered. Then, for something to say, he nodded at the sky. 'It's certainly a nice one.'

Pepe shot to his feet and came up to the bars of the cage. He grabbed his dick in one hand and gave it a little shake in the governor's direction. 'Well, thanks very much, governor,' he grinned. 'I've never had any complaints about it.'

Within a couple of months, Tony, Sharky and Pepe were shipped across to Parkhurst. Danny went to Dartmoor. I hoped I would be on the move soon. Sure enough, one morning my door was thrown open and I was taken to reception. After the usual routine I was double-cuffed and loaded on to a van. My journey to Dartmoor took two days and hit six different prisons along the way. My first stop was HMP Winchester, where I stayed over-night. The next day, the van headed north to HMP Onley in Warwickshire, which was a staging post for the National Draft, which is what they called the weekly prison transfers. After changing vans at Onley, we stopped at HMP Bristol to pick someone up, then HMP Dorchester, then HMP Channings Wood. That evening we pulled into HMP Exeter for an overnight stay. The next morning we were loaded back on to the van and finally reached Dartmoor at midday.

HMP Dartmoor is notorious for its brutality and remoteness. One of the oldest prisons in England, it sits 1,900 feet above sea-level in the centre of desolate moorlands. Constructed from grey granite, it has a permanent air of gloom hanging over its moss-covered walls and buildings. Classed as the 'end of the line' for adult prisoners, it had become a dumping ground for the mad, bad and dangerous of the prison system. For the majority of prisoners in the system, just the threat of a transfer to Dartmoor was enough to bring them out in a cold sweat and make them start toeing the line. As the van pulled up a steep mountainside and out on to a plateau, the prison could be seen in the distance, squatting there in the rain like the calcified carcass of a scabrous grey rat.

The nearest town of any size was twenty miles away, but outside the prison walls was a town of sorts. Princetown, unofficially known as Screw Town, was mostly inhabited by screws and their families and others who had some connection to the jail. Some of the families had lived there for generations and had a long line of ancestors who had worked as screws in the prison. I kept expecting to hear the sound of 'Duelling Banjos'.

Reception was as cold and dank as the rest of the jail but, apart from some screws with fairly interesting facial deformities, it was the same routine as any other jail. I was given a pillow-case stuffed with prison kit and a donkey-jacket. I threw the donkey-jacket on the ground. 'I'm here on a punishment move,' I stated. 'So if you expect me to work you better think again.'

The screws just smiled at each other. One of the prisoners who had been in Dartmoor before pulled me aside.

'Take the donkey-jacket, mate,' he said. 'You'll need it to wear in bed at night, this gaff is freezing.'

So I took it. And he was right. I was grateful for it in the weeks to come.

The first familiar face I came across on the wing was Danny Leahy. He had already been there for a couple of months and he had bad news for me. It seemed there were only eight Londoners in a prison of 700 prisoners, and the Welsh were in the majority and running everything worth touching. The Welsh hated the English, but they had a particular hatred for Londoners, whom they classed as flash cockneys. The hardcore of the Welsh at Dartmoor were from Cardiff, where it seems they spent most of their time injecting steroids and nicking cars. Known as 'The Taffia', the Cardiff boys were mainly big, dopey bodybuilders with budgie syndrome who strutted about playing at being gangsters, but the sheer weight of their numbers meant that they had the run of the jail.

There were very few metal detectors at Dartmoor, and the main work was in the metalwork factory, making gates and prison beds. Of course the factory also did a thriving black-market trade in weapons, and I have never seen better blades than those turned out at Dartmoor. Most people favoured the double-edged eight-inch dagger, but I also saw cutlasses and short swords as long as my arm. Danny told me that trouble had been brewing between the Cardiff and Swansea boys, and that he and his cousin Glen and a couple of other Londoners had allied themselves with the Swansea mob.

'It's going off tonight on association,' he told me. 'And I know you'll want to be involved. Here.'

He pulled a heavy eight-inch dagger from his waistband and slipped it to me. It was made from a bed-spar, and both edges were sharpened like a razor. It weighed a good two pounds. I had only been in the prison for four hours and already I was involved in a war. I couldn't let Danny down, and I would also be fighting for London pride. I took the dagger and slipped it into my jeans.

'OK,' I said. 'See you on association.'

The cell doors were opened for association at six o'clock, and over a hundred prisoners streamed out of their cells. There was a TV in the centre of the wing on the ground floor, and most people brought their cell-chairs and sat in front of it. Watching from the first-floor landing, I noticed the gangsters pushing their way through to claim the first two rows of chairs. Everyone just moved out of the way for them and allowed them to claim the best seats. There were some very big men among them, and they seemed to favour the vest as their lounging apparel, all the better to show off their muscles. Danny sidled up to me at the railing.

'See 'em?' he asked. I nodded. 'Right, give it five minutes and then make your way downstairs. Just stay at the back of the rows with Glen. A few of the Swansea boys and me will be going down the front to have it with them. If any leg it up your way, cut 'em.'

'What about the screws?' I asked. Danny smiled. 'Fuck the screws,' he said. 'If they want some they can have it as well.'

The attack on the Cardiff boys was all about showing who was in charge of the lucrative hooch and drug business on the wing. Swansea and Cardiff hated each other almost as much as they hated the English, but there weren't so many of the Swansea, so they were willing to forge any alliance that would add to their fighting ranks. I nodded to Glen, who was still nursing a nasty stab-wound in the stomach he'd received from one of the Cardiff mob a few days earlier. He had been treating the wound himself, with disinfectant, rather than report to the hospital and end up in the block for fighting. He didn't look too well. Just as *Top of the Pops* was starting on the telly and the Cardiff boys were settled down and passing joints to each other, I saw Danny and a mob of Swansea boys begin to make their way through the rows of chairs to the front. As they reached the front two rows, the tools came out of waistbands and jackets. One of the Cardiff mob was a bit more on the ball than the rest and sensed movement behind, which was just enough to save his life. He turned and saw a two-foot cutlass cleaving the air on the way to his head and jumped forward just in time.

The attack on the Cardiff crew was swift and bloody. Danny swung his cutlass and lopped off the ear of the main man, and there was mayhem and uproar to a soundtrack of the latest hits on *Top of the Pops*. Chairs were tipped over and panicked punches thrown, but the Cardiff mob had been caught off guard and suffered for it. Two of them broke away from the main group and ran up the landing towards me and Glen. I tried to plunge my dagger into the lower body of the one nearest me, but he dodged me and got past unhurt. Glen caught his one by the vest, but was struggling with him and unable to bring his blade into play. I rushed over behind the Cardiff boy and ran my dagger across his arse. The blade bit through his jeans and flesh and he gave a terrified squeal and tried to back away from Glen. But Glen now had the space he needed and he began slashing at his opponent's face and chest. I turned back to the main battle and it was all over bar the bleeding. The Cardiff boys were bunched in a corner of the wing, beaten and very bloodied, and the Swansea mob, along with Danny, were scattering away to get rid of any incriminating evidence such as weapons and blood-stained clothing.

The screws on the wing had done the sensible thing. When the knives came out, they legged it. Now the alarm bell was ringing, but it was too late. A bunch of screws came running on to the wing and started shouting for everyone to get back to their cells. I didn't need telling twice. I slammed my cell door and threw my dagger out of the window. I thought I was fairly safe, as I was brand-new on the wing and unknown to the screws, and I was right. During the three-day lock-down that followed the fight I was searched by the screws, but it was just routine. Glen was caught in the act and taken to the block, but he collapsed from his own wound and ended up in the hospital for a couple of weeks. A lot of the Cardiff boys were treated for stab wounds, and they had lost their place as top dogs, at least until they made their inevitable comeback attack. Just another slice of the rich tapestry that goes to make up prison life.

Dartmoor was a violent prison, but I was used to living on the edge. I could have done without having to live around so many Welshmen and carrot-crunchers, but I could adapt. An old mate of mine from Albany turned up, Gary 'the Growler' Andrews from the class of 1991, and soon joined our firm. The Growler was a Portsmouth football hooligan, but we made him an honorary Londoner, because he was game as a drunken rugby team. We managed to get by and hold our own against the Welsh, and things weren't too bad.

I couldn't get any visits in Dartmoor, it was just too far to expect anyone to travel; so I made an application for Accumulated Visits to Highdown. Accumulated Visits are usually granted to any long-term prisoner who is being held in a prison that is over fifty miles from his home. You save up six months' worth of visiting orders and you can be transferred to your local prison for a maximum of twenty-eight days to allow you to have your visits. I was surprised when my application for visits was granted straight away. I was on my way back to Highdown the very next day.

24. Parole!

I arrived back at Highdown in 1995 and found the prison more settled than it had been during my previous stay. The screws now had a bit of experience under their belts and were not so willing to take a back seat when it came to enforcing discipline. A lot of the screws recognized me and seemed very friendly, despite the trouble I had caused them in the past. There was a good atmosphere in the prison, and I put this down to the hands-on leadership of the number-one governor, Stephen Pryor. Pryor was a progressive liberal who believed in treating prisoners as adults and trying to give them as much responsibility as was feasible in the day-to-day minutiae of prison life. It was his professed aim to have as little lock-up time as possible and instead to have prisoners out of their cells, working or being educated. As a result, there were fewer assaults on staff and prisoners, and few major incidents of the kind that typified other top-security prisons.

Since my first moderate success in the writing field I had stuck at it and had a couple of articles published in the *Guardian* newspaper and *Inside-Time*. The appearance of my poem 'Old Lags' in the *Independent* had led to my being interviewed for a BBC Radio 4 programme on poetry called 'Stanza', which, unbeknown to me, had been heard by Stephen Pryor. So I was surprised when, after a couple of days at Highdown, I had a visit from the number-one governor himself. He started by telling me that my prison record was so bad that he had hesitated to accept me at his prison even for twenty-eight days, but when he heard me speak so eloquently about poetry on Radio 4, he guessed that my record was not telling the full story. I was flattered. He then told me that Highdown was his first prison, and some of his aims for seriously tackling the rehabilitation of prisoners, and I found him to be a reasonable and enlightened man. He offered me a deal: I could stay in Highdown and not go back to Dartmoor on condition that I would cause no trouble for his staff and I would agree to start up an in-house magazine. I would be given free rein, and be in charge of everything from hiring my own staff to deciding the contents. He wanted only the final say on each edition with regard to the possible security implications of any of the contents. We shook hands on it.

For the very first time inside a prison I was being treated as a responsible adult and being allowed to create something worthwhile. I was buzzing with enthusiasm for the magazine project and I got to work straight away. I was granted access to almost every part of the prison and given the use of four state-of-the-art computers and printers. My budget was £400 per issue, not including the wages of a small editorial team and myself. I recruited Alex Begg as my deputy editor, as he had just started writing some very good short stories, one of which had appeared in *Prison Writing*. Alex and I set about starting a magazine from scratch. It was hard work, and as we had no experience, we learned through trial and error. We bullied and harried other prisoners to write letters we could use, and no prison graffiti-merchant or cartoonist was safe from our harassment. We spent a long time finding out how the computers worked, sometimes losing a day's work when we forgot to use the 'save' button. But we were enjoying ourselves and really getting into the creative swing. We had regular meetings with Eileen Jackman, the head of education, to discuss ideas and logistics, and we spent hours choosing a name for the magazine.

Unlike my previous years in prison, I was now looking forward to each day, and I would be up before the cell door even opened planning the day's work. We decided to call the magazine *Sorted*, as it was the stock prison phrase for being satisfied with something. And three months after we switched on the first computer, issue one of *Sorted* was ready to be distributed. We printed up enough copies for every single prisoner to get one, and a couple of dozen extras to send out to other jails and to stock in the Visitors' Centre outside the gate for prison visitors. The first issue contained a history of the ground upon which Highdown prison was built, a short story by Alex Begg, an article on Broadmoor written by Charly Bronson, the story of the Wembley Bank Robbers, poetry by a female lifer called Clare Barstow, a cover by Johnny Samson, plus letters, jokes, puzzles and crosswords from various prisoners and staff. It was a hit. In the first two weeks after it had been distributed, we were inundated with letters and comments from prisoners, and the majority were positive.

It is a great feeling to have created something from nothing and then hear so many people talking about it. Plenty of prisons have their own magazines, but most of them are just propaganda sheets run by the system to get the official message across. *Sorted* was created solely by prisoners, and it contained the things that prisoners wanted to read. It became a huge success, and by issue four we had won the Koestler Award for prison publications, beating some prison magazines that had been established for years. Governor Pryor rewarded us by purchasing a proper printing press.

Eileen Jackman spoke to me one day and said she had noticed that I had never taken any educational exams and had no qualifications. She said that the education department was willing to fund me if I wanted to rectify that. I chose an A Level in law, and a feature-writing diploma course with the London School of Journalism. I passed both, gaining one of only two Honours diplomas handed out that year for the journalism course. I felt I had turned some sort of corner in my life. I was now more known for my writing than I was for clumping screws and causing mayhem. The screws, or most of them, had a more positive attitude towards me, and some of them would even go out of their way to chat to me about the magazine.

My life had changed almost completely by now, and though it felt good to attract so much praise for my achievements, there was still a small part of me that felt I had sold out to the system. The first time I found myself passing the time of day with a screw, part of me was burning with shame for associating with 'the enemy'. I had spent decades fighting the system, and now I felt as though I was being emasculated by it without putting up a fight. These feelings increased when I was offered the coveted position of library orderly. I had always classed orderlies, screws' tea-boys and those kinds of prisoners, as mugs and grovellers, traitors to the real prisoners who were being beaten and tortured in punishment blocks all over the prison system every day. But I was sick of prison, sick of the macho bullshit and tired of prison politics. I wanted to get out, and I knew that accepting a job as a library orderly was a major step towards being trusted by the system. I took it.

I had decided on a compromise I could be comfortable with. I ran the prison magazine and did the library orderly's job, but at the same time I made it very clear that I was no one's puppet. A good percentage of the stuff I wrote for *Sorted* was anti-system. If I thought the system was taking liberties, I would say so, in no uncertain terms. I also increased the amount of complaints, petitions and appeals I was writing for illiterate prisoners. I didn't clump any screws, but I became very vocal and had plenty of loud arguments with them if I thought they were out of line. I maintained a fine balance between being a subversive and vocal opponent of the system who my fellow prisoners could respect, and being just on the right side of good behaviour to keep the system happy. I like to believe that the cons looked on me as one of their own who was semi-retired from the real bad stuff but still sticking it to the screws at every opportunity. And I know that the system viewed me as one they had tamed. So everyone was happy.

I had bumped into Charly Bronson a few times over the years since I had first seen him in Wandsworth jail. Charly was forever being moved around the system and was rarely allowed out of the punishment blocks, so when I heard he was in the block at Highdown I demanded to be taken down to see him. Me and Charly had been exchanging letters and views on the prison system for some time, and I found him an articulate and very amusing writer. I told the governor that I needed to see Charly in order to recruit him to write for *Sorted*. Unfortunately, in the middle of negotiations, Charly punched a governor named Knight over the landing in the block, and as a result his security status was increased to a one-in-twelve-unlock, which meant that before they could open his cell door for any reason there had to be at least one PO and twelve screws in attendance.

Instead I sent a letter to Charly asking him to write for the magazine. He agreed, and I gave him a regular column in the first six issues. This was before Charly had had any of his books published. He also contributed a few of his cartoons, which were strange, but interesting nonetheless. Charly's had a lot of bad press over the years, but he's never killed anyone and has served more hard time than most child-killers. I can identify with Charly, as I know from experience that there are no limits to which the system will not go to drive you mad once you show a bit of spirit. But he's a fine writer and a good man.

I was still writing for Julian Broadhead's *Prison Writing*, *Inside-Time*, *AMBoV Quarterly*, the BoV's national magazine, the *Prison Reform Trust News*, the *New Law Journal* and the occasional piece for the *Guardian*. I was also having some success with my short stories, winning two £250 runner-up prizes in short-story competitions. I was also shortlisted in the annual London Writers Competition. I interviewed ex-middleweight-boxing world champion Alan Minter when he came to Highdown for a sports-day prize-giving, and I met Ann Widdecombe when she came for an inspection. I was told by my personal case-officer, Wendy MacFarland, that I was to be put in front of the board for Category C status. Wendy was hopeful that I would be downgraded, but my previous record was always going to be a big obstacle.

The SO in charge of the classification board was a dour-faced Scotsman who had worked on D-wing in Wandsworth when I was there. There was no love lost between us. He made it quite clear that he thought I was a born-bad bastard who was trying a new angle to pull the wool over the system's eyes. I was refused Category C. I didn't really mind, as I had plenty of years left to do. I was eight years into my overall sentence of fifteen, with the exception of the seventy-nine days I was on the run. In the previous decade I had spent only ten months on the street, and then I was being hunted by the police. I had put in a lot of time proving what a bad man I was, so I had to be philosophical when the system didn't exactly rush to give me the keys to my prison.

Things were going badly on the personal-relationship front. Jenny had dumped me soon after I was nicked, and Denise, naturally feeling betrayed by my moving in with Jenny, was sticking the knife into me at every opportunity. Whenever I tried to talk to her on the phone, she would either hang up or put it down and walk away, leaving me frustrated and angry. In Albany, after she had hung up on me for the fourth time in a row, I ripped the phone from the wall and kicked it up and down the landing in five minutes of wild rage. I was nicked for damaging property and lost six weeks' phone privileges. The worst of it was that my head had now cleared and I realized that I loved Denise and the kids more than anything else in my life. But I just couldn't get through to her. She had made up her mind that she'd had enough and we were finished. My mum would bring the kids up on visits. Lianne was now ten years old and as pretty as a picture. She was very shy with me, having rarely seen me outside of prison. My heart broke every time I saw my children in a visiting hall. To think I had given them up for nothing, just to be one of the Chaps and get the respect of people who were, on the whole, as inadequate as I was. It wasn't a fair exchange. I had missed out on seeing my children grow up, and now it was too late. It was very hard coming to terms with this.

It was while I was at Highdown that I found out that my old friend 'Scotch' Andy Philipson, veteran of countless gunfights and robberies, had died. He had been diagnosed with cancer when coming to the end of his sentence at Parkhurst and had died a couple of weeks after his release. I was gutted. Andy had been a staunch man who would never let his friends down. The only consolation was that he had not died in prison.

Stephen Pryor got a posting to the Home Office, and the new governor who took over in his place was a hard-liner who had worked at Wandsworth. This was bad news for me. The regime quickly changed and suddenly the good atmosphere disappeared. The charity workshops were closed down, education was cut and association became haphazard. It was the first time I really realized how much a prison relies on the attitude of the number-one governor for its regime. The new governor was not interested in getting prisoners out of their cells for meaningful activities, he was more into security gadgets for the cowboys on his staff and showing everyone how tough he was. I knew my days at Highdown were numbered.

Issue ten of *Sorted* had just come out, when the new governor decided to close it down and use the budget for something more useful, like extra rubber-gloves for the DST. The end came for me when the DST descended on my cell and carried out a four-hour search. They found a phone card without my name on it and a one-inch pencil-sharpener. I was nicked, again. Phone-cards had the buyer's name marked on them at the point of purchase from the canteen, and it was against prison rules to be in possession of a phone-card that didn't have your name on it. Phone-cards were gambling currency on the pool table and at cards, so men would clean their name off using prison tooth-powder and use them to pay debts. Nobody had ever been nicked for it before, so I hadn't bothered putting my name on the card, but the new governor was ordering nickings for any breach of the rules, no matter how trifling.

I was on adjudication the next morning. I pleaded guilty to the phone-card, but I drew the line when the charge sheet described the pencil-sharpener as a 'knife'. The new governor listened to my plea of not guilty and asked to see this knife. It was presented to him in an evidence bag, and I knew I was on a loser when he reached into the bag to remove it and pulled his hand away as though he'd been slashed. He put on a big show of sucking his plainly uninjured finger, then smiled at me.

'It seems very much like a knife to me, Smith. In fact it nearly had my finger off.'

We all knew he was play-acting and I'd had more than enough of this bollocks.

'Governor,' I said. 'If you think that's a knife, then you've obviously led a very sheltered life, and God help you if you ever find yourself in a knife-fight and pull something like that. Let's cut the cackle and get on with it, shall we?'

He found me guilty of possession of a knife.

'Smith,' he began. 'I have reviewed your record and come to the conclusion that you are far too dangerous to be held in this prison. Your possession of a knife is only one of a long line of charges that have been proved against you. You will be held in the punishment block pending transfer to a prison on the Isle of Wight. That's all.'

He had got what he wanted. Once again I was on the move.

The peaceful and productive months at Highdown had mellowed and changed me in a lot of ways. I had cooperated with the system as far as I could stand, but in the end they had fucked me for it, and I was back where I had started. But I was no longer the angry young man, willing to throw punches first and ask questions later. I had matured considerably and some of my attitudes had changed, but there was still a spark of serious violence and rage within me. I still classed myself as a criminal, but my writing gave me another string to my bow. I was just better at thinking things through than I had been.

Albany had changed a lot since I had first set foot there in 1990. After the much-publicized escapes of the 90s, both Albany and its neighbour, Parkhurst, had been removed from the dispersal system. They were both now Category B training prisons. As such, they now accepted a different class of prisoner. Fuck-ups, mad-men and hobbits inhabited the cells where once the cream of the British criminal classes partied and plotted. Of the sixty-odd prisoners I now found on A-wing, two thirds would not have lasted five minutes in the old Albany. There were wannabe gangsters from the sticks, strutting about as though they had arrived, and whinging mugs who did nothing but cry and moan about their pathetically short sentences and how hard-done-by they had been. The junky quotient was very high, and fights broke out regularly over £10 debts and who had stolen whose foil. Grasses and nonces were slipped on to the wing and walked around like they were normal people. I decided that if I was going to be forced to live here, I would have to revert to my old self, at least for a while.

There were still a few good men at Albany. Greg Crabtree, the Houdini of the prison system, was finishing off his sentence there, and Mickey Keane, a lifer and well-known prison rebel, Andy Pippin, Johnny Tremarco, the notorious Liverpool hard-man, as well as a smattering of London robbers. I started my reign by burning out the cells of two suspected nonces. This got everyone nervous, and three more suspects went quietly to the wing office and requested a move to the protection wings before they got the same. Me, Mickey Keane, Greg Crabtree, Andy Pippin and a little Irish lifer named Willie Miskimmon got together and founded a secret organization called DAAGAN (Direct Action Against Grasses And Nonces), whose aim was to rid A and B wings of all undesirables. We made a list of suspects and, after getting confirmation from various sources, we either burned them out or got masked up and physically attacked them.

Within three months the message that we would not tolerate kiddy-fiddlers and informers living among us had got through. The screws started putting the undesirables straight on to the protection wings, unless they specifically refused protection, and a few did. The class of prisoner got better.

By summer 1997 I had served just over nine years of my sentence and had already been refused parole three times, but a case in the High Court in November 1996, Regina *v* Governor of Brockhill Prison *ex-parte*, ruled that prisoners who had been sentenced to concurrent terms of imprisonment were entitled to have their remand time counted as part of their sentence. This brought my next parole date forward by nearly a year. I made my application, and at the same time another, to be downgraded to Category C. In July I was informed that I was considered 'far too dangerous' to be given the lower security status.

One month after being refused Category C, I was playing kaluki on the wing with Mickey Keane and Andy Pippin. It was hotter than hell and I had a winning hand, when I was called over the wing tannoy system to report to the office. I didn't want to lose the pot of sixteen Mars bars, so I ignored it and carried on playing. But the call became persistent, so I gathered up my winnings and strolled down to the office. I had never been summoned to the office for anything good, so I wondered what they were trying to pin on me now.

When I walked in and saw so many grim-faced screws standing there, I immediately thought I was going to be ghosted. My heart sank. The PO was sitting behind his desk, mopping sweat from his face with a large red hankie. It went very quiet for a moment, and I could hear the tick-tick of the large electric clock on the wall behind the desk. None of the screws would look me in the eye. I felt sure that some grass had put my name up for a recent stabbing that had occurred at the end of my spur, and that I was about to be taken on the next van to Parkhurst.

The PO picked up a piece of fax paper and cleared his throat. 'Prisoner PJ2679, Smith,' he began. 'I have here notification from the Home Office that you have been granted a parole licence. You will be released from this prison on parole on Tuesday morning.'

I just looked at him, trying to take it in. I tried to speak, but my mouth had gone dry. If this was some sort of joke I was going to kill someone.

'What do you mean?' I finally managed to ask.

The PO flicked the paper across the desk to me. 'Here, read it yourself. You walk on Tuesday morning.'

I picked up the fax, noting the Home Office seal, and read the words.

'Tuesday,' I thought. 'Today is Thursday. I'm out in five days!' It sunk in and I let out a huge roar. 'YES!'

The screws were unhappy about it and that made it doubly sweet.

'See that C Cat that you wouldn't give me?' I said. 'Well, you can keep it. I'm off.'

I legged it out of the office, still in a daze, and went to tell the lads. I had never expected it, not in a million years. I thought

I had at least another three years left to serve. I managed to compose myself before telling anyone, mindful that many of the men I was leaving behind had decades left to serve. Steve Hostetler had just arrived from Parkhurst, and his response to my news was, 'Raze, if you can get parole after all the shit you've caused the system, then there's hope for all of us. Good luck, mate.'

I found out later that a lot of the men who had been sentenced to imprisonment before the 1992 Criminal Justice Act were being granted parole in order to clear the system out. Anyone sentenced before 1992 would be released on their EDR with no legal requirement for supervision within the community. Anyone sentenced after the 1992 Act was automatically on close supervision till the end of their entire sentence. My original sentence had come in 1989, and my re-sentence in 1993 had just been concurrent to the original sentence.

I followed the ritual of giving away all of my possessions to friends I was leaving behind. Mickey Keane got my stereo and I gave my Olivetti typewriter to a blagger and poet from Camden Town named Terry Crockett. My small hidden collection of weapons and coffee jars full of petrol, for burn-outs, was left to DAAGAN.

On 5 August 1997, I walked out through the gates of Albany prison. I had a discharge grant of £48.50 and a travel warrant back to London. I had a vague idea of going straight and maybe trying to earn a living from writing, but no firm plans. It had all happened so fast. As the screws went to close the gate behind me I suddenly had a thought.

'Oi,' I said. 'Where the fuck am I, and how do I get to the ferry?'

The screw shrugged. 'You're in Newport. And there's a bus stop across the road. The buses come every hour.'

And that was that. They slammed the gate and left me standing there with two holdalls full of paperwork, letters and photographs.

Though it was still early in the morning, the sun was beating down unmercifully as I waited at the bus stop in the middle of the Isle of Wight. A car pulled up next to me and the window was wound down. Some bloke in a suit looked out. He looked familiar.

'Just out?' he asked, cheerfully.

I nodded.

'Well, you've got a long wait there. Hop in and I'll drop you off at the ferry.'

Then I realized it was John Marriot, the ex-governor of Parkhurst who had lost his job over the escape. I jumped in, and he drove me to the ferry.

I had seen Mr Marriot on a couple of occasions when I had been shipped from Albany block to Parkhurst block for lay-downs. I had never heard a bad word about him from any of the prisoners who had served under his reign, and, like Stephen Pryor at Highdown, he had the prisoners' respect. On the way to the ferry he told me that he was now working for a mental health charity on the island, and that he was in the process of writing a book that would finally tell the truth about the prison system of this country. When it came time to say goodbye, Mr Marriot slipped me a £20 note.

'Have a celebratory drink on me,' he grinned.

I shook hands with him and we wished each other luck.

It was the first time I had made the ferry crossing above-deck and unchained. In Portsmouth I was met by my brother Mick and my brother-in-law Tommy Hogan. On the drive back to London I sipped a can of beer and smoked a huge joint that Tommy had brought for me. I was truly free at last.

25. The Laughing Bank-Robbers

The conditions of my parole were that I live in my parents' flat on the Stockwell Park estate and report to my parole officer every week. My mum and dad lived alone in the three-bedroom flat, so they were happy to have me back home again. My mum is a great cook and I was soon being plied with good food and plenty of it. In my first month out I gained over a stone in weight. It was great to go for a Saturday afternoon drink with my dad and my brother, and just do the ordinary things you miss in prison, like walking down to the shop for a newspaper and actually paying for things with money instead of signing for them. Getting letters that hadn't already been opened and read and talking on the phone without someone recording and listening to my conversation were also novelties I enjoyed. Not so enjoyable was having to sign on the dole and jump through hoops for a pittance. I always got the same question: 'Well, where have you been for the past decade, Mr Smith?' When I answered with the truth, they would quickly pass me on to someone else. I had to get a job.

My parole officer was OK, but not very helpful in any practical way. He could advise me to get a job, but he couldn't tell me where, or as what. I really fancied making a go of the writing game, but everyone warned me that it would be very difficult to make a living from it.

'By all means write,' said my parole officer, 'but also get a job on a building site if you want to eat as well.'

I got a phone call from Julian Broadhead, who told me that John McVicar was interested in doing a piece about me for *Punch* magazine. I phoned John up and arranged to meet him in a pub in Stockwell for the interview.

John McVicar is a legend among prisoners, not only for his

escape from the Durham unit in 1968, the first one from an SSU, but mainly because of the film that was made of his book, *McVicar By Himself*. I have yet to meet a prisoner who cannot quote sections of dialogue from the film, and it has achieved cult status among prisoners as the only film about British prisons that is realistic enough to satisfy the most critical audience in captivity. So meeting McVicar himself was a slightly surreal experience. I expected him to look like Roger Daltrey, who played him in the film, but he looked more like a fitter version of Elmer Fudd. Over a couple of pints I gave John the lowdown on the modern prison system, and he took a couple of photos to use with the piece.

I also had a meeting with Duncan Campbell of the *Guardian*, who showed me around the offices and gave me a very nice expense-account lunch in a nearby Italian restaurant. He said there might be some work for me at the paper, but as a freelance. I wrote a piece on the heroin problem in jail, which they used in their Society supplement.

Through John I also got to meet the novelist Will Self, who had shown an interest in one of my unpublished short stories. I was invited to dinner at Will's house but felt way out of my depth surrounded by 'real writers' who spoke eloquently about political and economic situations around the world. I felt like a fraud. These people had been to college and had earned the right to have intellectual opinions through hard work and study. And though I was made to feel very welcome, I felt like a tramp in an art gallery.

I was still doing a bit for the *New Law Journal*, but money was becoming a problem. In prison, where my total outlay was £10 a week, a cheque in the post was money in the bank: £200 for a magazine article would keep me in snout and phone cards for five months. But on the out a cheque in the post was spent before it touched down on the doormat. I had to abandon writing and get a real job.

Both my dad and my brother worked for Lambeth Council, so through them I was able to get a job sweeping the roads on council estates. I worked on the estates off Dorset Road in Clapham. For a take-home pay of £109 a week, I pulled a barrow around the estates in all weathers, sweeping the roads and pathways and mopping the vomit and piss from the stairwells. Some mornings I was ankle-deep in empty crack-vials and syringes, but at least I wasn't in prison. I borrowed the deposit for a bedsit. I could have stayed at my parents' flat for as long as I wanted, but I was thirty-seven years old and had been independent since I was fourteen. Besides, there is something a bit creepy about a man of my age still living with his mum. I was in a series of casual sexual relationships with the local good-time girls, and I could hardly bring them to my parents' house.

I now had a fairly friendly relationship with Denise, but there was still a lot of underlying bitterness and rancour we didn't talk about. I drove to her house every weekend in Mick's van and took my daughter out. We sometimes went bowling, or to the cinema, where I slept through such classics as *Spice Girls, The Movie* and *Godzilla*. I was getting to know Lianne, and I loved her more than ever. Dean and Joe were friendly towards me, but they were living their own lives with their own friends. I was just someone who might be passing through again. Joe suffered from asthma and had Crohn's disease, which made him lose a lot of weight. Dean was a happy, outgoing kid who took everything in his stride, but Joe was very quiet and withdrawn, due, I think, to his illness. I tried my hardest to get to know my children and be a father to them, but it was difficult because I had been away for so long, and because they sensed the unresolved problems between me and their mother. I was the stranger here.

I swept roads for four months, scrimping and scraping to get by and reporting to my parole officer every week. The bedsit I was paying £50 a week for looked just like a prison cell, and having no money depressed me. I was starting to think nostalgically about prison, and that was a very bad sign. I had thought that going straight would be easy, but it was hard work. Around the end of November I heard the siren-song of crime insistently calling me. It was subtle at first. I found myself staring into every bank I passed on the streets and stopping to watch security guards making their deliveries. I convinced myself that what I was doing was merely checking the hypothetical. I wasn't going to do anything; it was just the idle interest of an ex-bankrobber. But in reality I was like a recovering heroin-addict standing around outside a dealer's house watching people come and go with the goodies. Sitting in my cold, damp bedsit watching my rented portable telly in the evenings, I would think about the things I would be able to buy if I were to hit just one more bank. Just one. To ease my financial situation. Surely I couldn't get nicked for one?

In early December things were particularly hard. My first Christmas out of prison in years was approaching. I wanted to be able to buy presents for my kids who had missed out on so much. The rent was also due, and I barely had enough money to feed my voracious electricity meter. It was a freezing cold and frosty morning and the chill wind was cutting through my clothes as I swept the road on one of the estates. There was a brand-new BMW parked up in one of the bays. It had all the extras and looked the business. A half-caste bloke, well-dressed and with more gold jewellery hanging off him than the German, walked up to the car and began to unlock it. I leant on my broom and thought what a lucky bastard he was. He reached into the car and took out one of the ashtrays and emptied it on the road I had just swept. I felt my rage bubbling up.

'Oi, mate,' I called. 'I've just fucking swept that.'

He turned and looked me up and down as though I was nothing more than a minor irritant. 'So sweep it again. It's what you get paid for, ain't it?'

That was it. That was the naked flame to the blue touchpaper. The hammer striking the ignition plate. All of my frustration and dissatisfaction with my situation was on its way up the tube to the surface. Here I was, sweeping roads in the cold and being verbally abused by some two-bob muppet who probably hadn't had to raise his hands in defence since the school playground. I dropped my broom and hit him hard with three punches. He went to the ground and I stamped on his face. He was still squealing, so I kicked him in the bollocks. I picked up my broom and dropped it on his chest.

'Here,' I said. 'Sweep up after yourself.'

And that was the end of my career as a road-sweeper.

Walking away from the job I felt free and good. I have great admiration for straight-goers who can struggle on for years in low-paid, shit-end-of-the-stick jobs, surviving day to day and having to swallow the bile of bitterness and disappointment, with nothing to look forward to except a couple of pints at the weekend and eventual retirement. These are the real heroes of the world. I was too greedy, too lazy and too impatient for that kind of life. I wanted everything, and I wanted it now. I never gave another thought to the geezer I had just beaten up. He may have been a drug-dealer or he may have been a stockbroker, but given the fact that he was living on a rough council-estate and driving a pimp-mobile, I'd say the former was the more likely. Whatever his occupation, he had the kind of arrogance that I have often found in straight people. They don't seem to realize that there are people in this world who won't just stare at the ground and mumble apologies when given a bit of lip, and it never ceases to amaze me how surprised they look when the punches start hitting them. Two lessons I learned the hard way from my life are: treat everyone with caution; and if you insult a man be ready to fight.

On my way back to my bedsit I stopped off at a phone-box and made a call to one of my old prison pals. Andy had finished his ten-year sentence and been out for a couple of years. He was one of my best mates in prison, and it was he who had dropped back into the Verne prison when the rope was unable to hold me during our escape attempt. I had seen him once since getting out; we'd had a drink and a smoke and we talked over old times. I knew he was earning a fair living by robbing drug-dealers, and he had given me a nine-bar (nine ounces) of good hash as a coming-out present. But robbing drug-dealers is a dangerous game which can get you tortured, killed and quietly buried on a railway embankment. I told Andy I was coming to see him to discuss some business.

Andy had a nice studio flat in west Croydon, and when I got there his crime partner, Tommy the wheelman, was also there. Tommy had never been a robber. He was more a drug-man and knew everything about the cultivation of skunk-weed, for which he had already served a six-year prison sentence. Andy had met him in Coldingley prison when they were both finishing off their sentences, and they had been working together since getting out. Tommy knew a lot of mid-level dealers and, armed with this information, they pulled a lot of rip-offs. There was now a bounty on both their heads, and pickings were slim as the dealers had wised up. Over a few beers I told the boys that I wanted to put together a robbery team and nick some real money. They were both up for it, and Andy suggested we get in touch with Danny, a staunch guy we knew from jail who was now also out and scratching about for a living.

Andy knew a couple of burglars who had a gun for sale, so we got on the blower straight away and arranged to take it. It was a 9mm Walther pistol with twenty-five rounds of ammunition. I took the gun over to the woods on Tooting Bec Common and test-fired it, just to make sure it was safe and wasn't going to go off at an inappropriate moment. We sold some of Andy's stolen hash to pay for the gun and a second-hand Ford Sierra to use as a getaway motor. We couldn't get through to Danny as he'd changed his mobile number, so we decided to crack on without him. Our first target was the Midland Bank on the corner of Bedford Hill and Balham High Road, which I had already robbed when I was on the run in 1992. We needed ready cash and it would save a lot of time to hit a familiar target where I already knew a tried and tested getaway route. Tommy was the driver, and me and Andy would go inside and do the business. Andy was an experienced robber and knew the routine as well as I did.

It was already dark when we left Tommy in the getaway car, parked in a sidestreet around the corner from the bank. We did a walk-past to check what was going on in the bank. There were about six customers, but it looked sweet. I took a deep breath.

As we reached the doors, we rolled down our ski-masks, and I pulled the gun from my pocket. There was no turning back now. As we burst in, there was a customer walking towards the door with his head down. He was stuffing money in his inside pocket, when me and Andy blocked his way. He was shocked when he looked up and saw us. I waved the gun at him.

'Back into the bank. Get back,' I said.

For some reason he tried to get past us. Andy raised the fearsome-looking fireman's axe.

'Back!' he shouted.

The man took a step backwards and then pulled the money from his pocket and held it out to us. He obviously didn't understand what was going on. By now the other people inside the bank were looking over towards the door to see what all the commotion was about. I grabbed the man by the arm and marched him into the banking hall.

'Everybody, go to the back wall and face it! This is a raid!' I shouted.

There were a few gasps, but the customers quickly complied. I stepped up to the jump and showed the gun.

'Quickly now!' I shouted at the cashiers. 'Let's be having it. Lively!'

We had brought a bag to put the money in, but unfortunately I had left it in the car. As the wads of notes were put on the counter, I began stuffing them in my pockets. But I was wearing gloves and holding the gun in one hand, and the second lot of notes, about £2,000, fell and scattered all over the carpet. Andy began scooping the cash from the counter as well. In about ninety seconds we had cleared all the till money and it was time to go. I have since studied the security photographs of this robbery, and I was surprised to note that at one stage I actually put my gun down on the counter to get more money into my pockets. I was a bit rusty after so many years in jail.

Walking briskly back to the getaway car, I was buzzing. I still say there is nothing like an armed robbery for getting absolutely high. We dumped the Sierra a couple of miles away and got back to Andy's flat in Tommy's own motor. We cleared just under ten grand, and it was a further buzz to see all those lovely banknotes scattered across Andy's front room. I had the bug now. This is what I loved to do.

Within a week the money was spent and we were planning the next one. Danny, when we finally managed to get in touch with him, added an extra dimension to the team. Both me and Andy were do-ers, up-front men who enjoyed being in the thick of it, actually taking part in the robberies. Tommy was very easy-going and perfectly suited to be a driver, but Danny was a strategy man. He didn't rush into anything, and though he didn't mind coming inside the banks and taking part, his real buzz came in the planning stages. Danny insisted on walking or driving the getaway routes the day before a job and on sending Tommy into the banks to have a look around an hour before we hit them, to note the location of the security cameras and gather any other information that might be useful. He also pioneered our use of hands-free mobile phones on the job, so that Tommy could listen in from outside and be ready to pull up the moment we were leaving.

We purchased a radio scanner, an essential piece of kit which allowed us to monitor the police wavebands before, during and after a robbery so the police couldn't sneak up on us, and we also collected information about various banking routines, which is how we came on the idea of robbing the reserve just after it was delivered. There was already a north London firm doing the reserve, Billy Harding and Dave Adams, but they were actually robbing the security guards while they were still inside the bank. This led to them being convicted not only for armed robbery but also for shooting one of the guards in the leg when he wouldn't hand over. They both got life sentences. Our idea was to wait for the guards to leave and then rob the same money from the cashiers, who would put up less of a fight. Adapt and survive is what being a criminal is all about.

Our next job was the Midland Bank on Clapham High Street, which had once been robbed by a young Charlie Wilson, some years before he gained notoriety as a leading light of the Great Train Robbery. We hit this bank on Christmas Eve, my birthday, and wore Santa hats over our ski-masks, wishing staff and customers a merry Christmas on our way out.

We were doing what we enjoyed and earning a nice wage whilst doing it, so we could afford to be a bit whimsical. Though we took our work very seriously, as anyone who was risking death or decades in prison would, we also had a kind of gallows humour that earned us the sobriquet of 'The Laughing Bank-Robbers'. We didn't set out to kill or injure anyone, and I know this for a fact because I was always the man holding the firearm. Our aim was to nick a nice few quid and have a bit of a laugh along the way. Looking back now, I realize that what might have seemed funny and whimsical to us must have been terrifying for both staff and customers of the places we robbed. They had no clue what sort of men we were, all they saw were masked faces and weapons; and I can only imagine the trauma that our victims must have suffered. But we couldn't grasp this, and if any of us could, we quickly dismissed it from our minds, because we all knew, hand on heart, that no one was going to be injured. We were experienced enough not to let anyone get close enough to think about tackling us. And our whirlwind entry to banks was designed to disorient people and get them to comply with our orders without the chance to think. From entry to exit of a bank was never more than four minutes, and sometimes a lot less than that.

We had a very good Christmas and New Year. I was now settled in a nice flat in Croydon. I had a decent car and money in my pocket, and a good wardrobe of clothes. I did the occasional bits of straight work, more as a cover so that my family wouldn't guess that I was back 'at it'. I worked as a painter for my cousin Ronnie's painting and decorating firm, and got some dee-jaying from an old mate of mine from the teddy-boy days. Kris was one of the original teds and still playing rock 'n' roll gigs at small clubs around Camden Town and Holloway Road with his 'Big Beat' sound system.

I was still in love with Denise, and tried to get down and see her and the kids at least once a week. Denise had never taken another man into her life, as far as I know. Maybe I had put her off men for life, but as long as she wasn't with anyone else, I always had hope of a reconciliation. It hasn't happened yet, but I'm still hoping.

In the meantime I met and started a relationship with a beautiful twenty-three-year-old named Lindsey. She was the sister of my brother Mick's wife, Julie, and we had some great times together. Our relationship got a bit serious, but I backed off, not wanting to really commit to anyone while there was still a chance with Denise. Lindsey is a diamond of a woman and she was perfectly suited to the life I was leading at the time. She had a private-school education and worked in the City, but she was completely at ease around my villainous pals and the rockabilly crowd of Camden Town. She didn't bat an eye when she pulled out a bag containing £10,000 in cash from the fridge while cooking me a meal at my place, and she could match anyone drink for drink. Lindsey made sure I wanted for nothing when I was eventually jailed again, and I have nothing but love and respect for her.

By January of 1998, the time of the London Road robbery, our team was hitting an average of two banks a month, and working like clockwork. Croydon, Clapham, Hendon, Cricklewood and Sutton banks all received visits from us. No shots were fired on any of the robberies and no one was physically assaulted. In the Allied Irish Bank on Cricklewood Broadway, we all spoke in northern Irish accents and informed the staff that we were only 'Collecting for the Boys'. I used the proceeds of that robbery to fund a holiday to Dublin with my dad and Mick.

We also took to following post-office security vans on their routes, for future reference. As a team we could have taken on anything and anybody. But after the London Road robbery, cracks began to appear in the structure of the team.

Danny was too smart to want to carry on robbing until we were caught, and I too was starting to have doubts after my moment of clarity at London Road. Andy and Tommy were hitting the cocaine badly and had started using heroin. Though I loved them both like brothers, I was worried about their drug use and how it might affect the team. I had never committed a robbery while under the influence of drink or drugs, and I refused to work with anyone who would. With so much money available, the boys soon developed massive drug habits. I spoke to Danny, who had the same attitude that I had to drugs – that they are OK for recreational use – and he told me that he was getting out after the next big score. He was going to Mexico, to live like a king on the money he had saved. It sounded like a good idea, and I seriously considered going with him. But first we had plans to rob the main post office on Clapham High Street, a job that would give us enough cash to retire on.

The post office had one vital flaw in its security system. We had noticed that at closing time one of the cashiers would come out from behind the jump and lock the main doors while there were still a few customers left inside. Then they would have to keep unlocking the doors to let the customers out one at a time as they finished their transactions. There were three public phone-boxes right outside the post office with a good view of the main doors, and if someone were to keep watch from there, they could see the moment when the door was to be opened for the last customer and give the signal to the team. Then we'd hit the door, march the cashier back in at gunpoint and get his colleagues to let us behind the counter where the safes were being loaded. Simple.

But things went wrong right from the start. When we met up on the afternoon of the job, I suspected that Andy and Tommy had been over-indulging. I wasn't happy and I wanted to leave the job for another day. But we had come unstuck on our last robbery, the Midland Bank at Hendon Central. We had chosen it specifically because it was so close to the Metropolitan Police Training College, and it would be a laugh to strike in their own backyard in broad daylight, but, owing to the bravery of the bank staff, we had only managed to get away with a bag containing

£300 in coins. It was no big deal; as I've said before, it happens sometimes and, short of shooting up the gaff, there is nothing you can do but wipe your mouth and move on to the next job. Unfortunately, it had left us all short of ready cash, so we needed this post-office job. I reluctantly agreed to go.

It was already full-dark when we arrived in Clapham in two separate vehicles. The post office shut at 5.30, and we were geared up and ready to go into action at 5.20. Tommy took up his position in one of the phone boxes, and the rest of us walked about the high street, never straying too far from the post office. I crossed the road and leant against some railings outside the now closed Barclays Bank, the post office in full view and Tommy breathing through the earpiece of my hands-free set. Andy was pretending to examine some carpets in a shop window, and Danny stood near a bus stop. It was a bitterly cold evening and our woolly hats and bulky clothing attracted no attention. We waited.

Tommy's voice crackled in my earpiece. 'Doors being locked now. Four bodies still to come out. We go on the fourth. Stand by.'

I glanced at my watch. It was 5.30 on the dot.

Tommy would inform us as each customer was coming out, and we would go on his signal as the last one was let out. Once we were inside, Tommy would then make his way to the first getaway car and drive round to pick us up on our exit. As usual, Tommy would not be coming inside.

'First body coming out.' I made my way slowly towards the crossing and walked over to the target.

'Two coming out together. Last one left inside. Stand by.'

I could see both Andy and Danny converging on the entrance, ready to rush into action at the signal.

'Last body approaching the door. On my signal.'

All three of us picked up speed on the paths that would take us to within a couple of steps of the post office. I would be first in, and it was my job to secure the cashier and make the rest of the staff open the door that would let us behind the jump. I was ready. I could see the door now and the white-shirted cashier reaching up to undo a lock above his head to let the customer out, and I realized that we were going to have to take the customer back inside with us or she might raise the alarm. I cursed myself for not having thought of it sooner. Still, it wasn't beyond me, I could do it. In my pocket I gripped the gun, and I girded myself for the sudden rush.

'ABORT! ABORT!' Tommy's panicked voice screamed in my ear. I had already changed direction towards the door and it was a physical effort to stop myself from carrying on, but I managed to do it and walk on past the door. I quickly scanned the area to see what Tommy had seen, and there it was, a police patrol-car pulling up on the opposite side of the street.

I walked straight past Andy and Danny without even glancing in their direction and carried on down the high street, my heart pounding and my knees rubbery with the tension. When I thought I was far enough away, I looked back, casually. The patrol car had pulled up outside Woolworth's and as I watched, the two coppers made their way into the shop. I let out a deep breath. I heard Tommy's relieved voice through my earpiece.

'It's not for us. Probably some kid nicking the pick 'n' mix in Woollies.'

I pressed my speak button. 'Meet back at the car asap,' I said.

The car was parked up in a sidestreet not too far from the post office. In five minutes we were all sitting in it, an air of disappointment over us. Andy and Tommy wanted to do something.

'Like what?' I asked. 'All the banks and building societies are closed, and I'll be fucked if I'll lower myself to robbing a poxy off-licence!'

There we were, hyped up and ready to go, but with no specific target. It was a recipe for getting nicked if ever there was one. We considered a small cinema just off the high street and then quickly discounted it. Then there was a late-night supermarket. We decided on the supermarket, but when we went to have a look, it was absolutely packed with staff and customers and not the sort of job we'd want to risk pulling without any planning. It was now nearly six o'clock, so we had to either rob something or get out of the area. Suddenly Andy nodded towards a camera shop. 'Let's do that,' he said. 'It's bound to have a couple of grand in the safe.' I wasn't happy, but we were running out of options. The owner was just locking up for the night and switching off the lights. I decided that some money for our effort would be better than going away empty-handed. 'All right,' I said.

Danny quickly laid out a makeshift plan. We would let the owner lock up his shop and walk away, then we would follow him and hold him up at gunpoint and force him to go back and unlock the safe. It was a bit risky taking him back through the crowds of late-night shoppers, but we were desperate now. The owner locked up and walked across the road behind Clapham Common tube station. There is a short pathway behind the station, with a bit of greenery and a few benches for the winos to hang out on, which leads through to a row of bus stops. Andy called the man when he was half-way up the path, allowing me and Danny to get past him and take up a position on his blind side.

'Excuse me, mate,' called Andy. 'I think you've dropped something here.'

The man didn't take any notice of me and Danny as we passed him. He stopped and walked back towards Andy. Before he knew what was happening, we were all closed around him.

'Listen very carefully,' I told him. 'We know who you are, and we know you have money in the safe in the shop. You are going to take my friend back into the shop, open the safe and give him the money. If you do all this, then you will not be harmed.'

He looked at our faces and knew we meant business. There were plenty of people passing by on the path but no one took any notice of us.

'If,' I continued, 'you decide that you want to be a hero, I personally will put a bullet in your foot and leave you here.'

I held open my leather jacket so he could see the gun in my waistband. He just nodded.

Andy took him back to the shop, and me and Danny walked a short distance behind. When they went inside, I spoke to Danny.

'I don't like this,' I said. 'It's a muggy turnout. We came to nick a right parcel, and end up mugging the owner of a fucking camera shop. We look like right fucking amateurs.'

Danny nodded. 'And I bet there's no more than a monkey in that safe,' he said.

Andy was supposed to clear the safe, leave the owner cuffed up, rip out the phone and lock the shop on the way out. As it turned out, he grabbed the money and just legged it, not even stopping to lock the shop. We hadn't got twenty yards before the bloke was on the blower to the police. The getaway car, which had been parked in a good position for the post-office job, was over a quarter of a mile away from the camera shop. Within three minutes we heard the sirens racing into the area.

There were police cars and vans all over the place, sirens wailing and lights flashing as they raced into the high street. We all split up and ducked down different sidestreets. I found myself on Stonehouse Street, walking at a brisk pace away from the robbery, when a patrol car shot across the junction of the road ahead of me. I knew it would only be seconds before our descriptions went out over the police radio. I took off my leather coat and rolled it up. In the pockets were my gun, a ski mask and a pair of leather fingerless gloves. If I was stopped with these items I would be a million for a nicking. I launched my rolled-up coat over the nearest garden wall and carried on walking.

We all managed to get away and met up at the lock-up later that night. Danny had also had to dump his jacket, containing his ski mask, a pair of surgical gloves and the fireman's axe. The money from the shop's safe amounted to £480. Not even a monkey, just as Danny had predicted. I was depressed. I had always prided myself on my professionalism, and here we were, probably the best robbery team in London, reduced to a bungling shop-robbery that earned us a oner apiece and exes. I had come full circle from my first ever robbery back in '76. Maybe it was time to get out. The next day I flew to Dublin for a holiday.

Andy and Tommy kept on robbing, and eventually they both ended up with long prison sentences. Danny disappeared, maybe to Mexico. And I gave up on crime and joined my cousin's painting and decorating firm full-time. I was approaching middle age and I felt I had taken my last shot at the big time, and it was time to get out while I still had my life and liberty. I had saved a nice few quid from the robberies I had got away with, I had a one-bedroom flat in a respectable part of Croydon, a decent motor, a gorgeous young girlfriend and a regular job that paid a fair wage. I was happy, and the next five months was the best time of my life. I took my daughter out every Sunday and really got to know what a great kid she is. The boys were still a bit distant with me, but as they saw I was staying around this time, they started to open up to me more. I even had a friendly relationship with Denise. I decided that maybe it was time to settle down and write the book I had been talking about writing since I'd been released. John McVicar and Julian Broadhead both put the odd bit of media work my way. John got me a gig on the Edwina Currie show on BBC Radio 5 Live, talking about the brutality that had been exposed in HMP Wormwood Scrubs. Twenty-seven screws had been suspended for beating and torturing prisoners in the punishment block. And Julian got me on local radio talking about literacy in our prisons.

Things were going well until July 1998, and then I had a moment of complete madness that was to send me back to prison for life. There was a bit of a slump in the painting and decorating business, and work was becoming scarce. I had spent all the money I had saved, and once again found myself in dire financial straits. With my pattern of learned behaviour it wasn't long before I found myself looking at banks again as a way of solving my problems. There was a branch of the TSB on Streatham High Road that I had always fancied robbing. I had looked at it several times in the past but never got around to raiding it. In fact, I had been about to rob it when I was on the run in 1993, but I was nicked the day before. Now I began to look at it more closely.

The TSB was a small branch, just perfect for a one-man job. I thought about it for a couple of days, hoping that I wouldn't have to rob it, hoping I would get a phone call from Ronnie telling me that we were going back to work. For the first time in my criminal career I got frightened when I thought about actually going into the bank. I didn't want to do it, but there was an insistent voice in my head that was talking me into it. If I got away with it, I would be set financially for a few months, until the painting work picked up, as it was bound to, in the autumn. I could just do this one last job and all my money worries would be over. What could go wrong? I had done this hundreds of times, hadn't I? Just walk in, demand the money, walk out, job done.

I drove down to Streatham in my own car. I had a ski mask, a pair of gloves and a cigarette lighter in the shape of a .22 pistol. I hadn't bothered getting a real gun because I had convinced myself that this was not going to be a real robbery. It was a one-off. I just wanted a bit of ready cash to tide me over. I had retired from robbery, and after this I would never go back to it again. I parked on a sidestreet and rolled the ski mask up and wore it on my head like a hat. The gun looked like a toy, but I was relying on my experience of intimidation more than the gun. I was absolutely shitting myself, and this was when I knew that I was finally finished at the robbery game. In the past I would have been buzzing and eager to get on with it. But now I hesitated and ended up walking almost the length of the high street before I could screw up enough courage to go in. I had the 'gun' in my hand and was half-way through my opening speech when I realized I had forgotten to pull my mask down over my face. It was too late now, the customers were already scattering to the back of the bank and the cashiers were loading the cash on to the counter. If I pulled the mask down now, it would obscure my vision for a moment and I couldn't allow that when working alone, so I just tried to keep my head down and my face averted from the cameras. As I bagged the cash, one of the cashiers held up a thick bundle of £50 notes.

'Do you want these as well?' she asked.

Does a lifer want parole?

'Stick them in the bag,' I said.

The whole raid took ninety seconds, and I was out of the door with the bag stashed inside my jacket. I ran across the main road, almost getting hit by a couple of speeding cars, and legged it down a sidestreet to where I had parked my car. As I ran I felt a lot of heat coming from inside my jacket, but I dismissed it as nothing more than the sweat and heat of my exertion. But suddenly the money bag burst into flames that began to lick my face. I came to a stop and opened my jacket, letting the bag drop to the pavement. A huge cloud of noxious red smoke shot out of the bag and enveloped me. I should never have taken the wad of fifties. I should have known straight away that it was an exploding dye-pack. It was the kind of basic mistake that I would have expected a novice blagger to make. That was just more proof that I was no longer cut out for this game. The money was on fire and so was my jacket. I quickly ripped my flaming jacket off and rolled it up to kill the fire, and I stamped on the money bag, which burst and scattered burning and dyed banknotes all over the pavement.

Passers-by were stopping to watch this spectacle, and I knew I had to make a pretty lively exit before the police got there. I scooped up a double handful of banknotes that burned my fingers, and stuffed them into my jacket. Then I legged it, leaving the bulk of the money burning on the pavement. I got into my car and took a few backstreets away from the scene of the crime. My heart didn't slow down until I was well out of the area. I relaxed once I thought I was safe, but as I stopped my car to let two women cross the road in front of me, I got some funny looks from them. I glanced into my rearview mirror and realized why. One half of my face and hair was bright red from the explosion of the dye-pack. I looked like a villainous harlequin.

When I got back to my flat, I found I had managed to salvage less than £300 of the cash. I had to scrub my face and hands with a mixture of white spirit and washing-powder, which took off the dye but also a layer of skin. The money I left to soak in a sink full of the same mixture, then I washed it with just washing-powder and hung the notes on a radiator to dry. Most of the dye came off but there was nothing I could do about the singed edges of the notes. After this was done I relaxed with a joint. I decided then and there that my days as a robber were over. I had fallen for the oldest trick in the book by accepting the baited £50 notes and, worst of all, I no longer got the buzz. I didn't enjoy robbery any more. It was no longer a game.

The next day I went into Croydon shopping centre and changed up the damaged notes in various shops. I had risked my liberty for £270, but at least it meant I would eat for a couple of weeks and put a bit of petrol in the car. The next day Ronnie phoned me. He had just been given a big contract and I could start back to work on Monday. I had done it all for nothing. Sometimes fate plays cruel tricks on the unwary.

By 17 August I had forgotten all about the fiasco at the TSB. I had regular work that looked as though it was going to last well into the next year, and life was good again. I got up at 6 a.m. and got ready for work. I was going with Ronnie to price up a job in north London, so I wore a tweed 1950s-style sports jacket instead of my overalls. When I left the house and walked the short distance to the car, my mind was on the day's work. I didn't notice anything out of place, and even my old criminal radar didn't give a tingle. It was a lovely morning, with clear skies and the sun shining down with the promise of another scorcher. I unlocked my car and got inside. I took out a cigarette and put it in my mouth and reached inside my jacket for a lighter. I heard a screech of tyres and looked up in time to see a large black late-model Volvo swinging across the road, broadside, to block the front of my car. Even before it came to a shuddering halt I knew what was happening. Another large dark saloon-car screeched in behind me. In a split second I was surrounded by armed coppers in flak-jackets and high-visibility caps.

For a second everything seemed to go into slow motion. One of the coppers who was standing directly in front of my car pointing a 9mm Glock pistol at my face through the windscreen was shouting, and I saw a bit of saliva fly from his mouth. I looked to the side and saw more contorted and shouting mouths and more gun-barrels. It was unreal, like I was watching a film scene from far away and not actually involved. Then the car windows burst in around me, spraying my face with chunks of glass, and I heard their voices.

'Show your fucking hands! Put your hands up or I will shoot you! Armed police! Armed police!'

And with the voices, time snapped back to normal speed. I didn't move. I didn't give a fuck if they shot me or not because even then I had the feeling that my life was effectively over anyway. I left my hand in my pocket, clutching the lighter, and mentally dared them to shoot me. Suddenly the door was flung open and I was dragged roughly from the car and thrown face down on the pavement.

I was searched and my hands were cuffed behind my back before I was lifted to my feet and pushed against a chain-link fence. I could hardly credit how many coppers there were. They were everywhere and they were all armed. I still had the cigarette in my mouth, but it had crumpled when my face hit the pavement. I spat it out. Then the ritual began again.

'Noel Stephen Smith, I am arresting you as a person suspected of being involved in armed robbery. You do not have to say anything . . .'

I didn't bother listening to the rest. Instead I took a good look at their faces. Some of them looked relieved, others looked smug. So, this is how it ends, I thought. With a score of armed police officers on a quiet residential street in Croydon.

'Have you anything to say?' the DS finished.

'Yeah,' I said. 'Fuck you.'

It wasn't bravado, or rage, or even anger. I said it because that was what was expected of me. A couple of the coppers even nodded when I said it. I was no longer the man I had been but, like an actor forced to play a part that bores the life out of him, I said my line right on cue.

My flat was searched in my presence. I was photographed. And then I was taken in convoy to Croydon police station. On the way I watched the crowds of passers-by in their summer attire happily going about their business. I could have been one of them, I thought, but I chose to be something else. I wondered if I'd ever get the chance to choose again. Probably not. Then I remembered the code: if you can't do the time, then don't do the crime! I smiled at one of the coppers who was sitting beside me.

'Wake me up when we get to the station,' I said, and closed my eyes.

I was charged with eight counts of armed robbery, including the
TSB, the camera shop, and the Midland Bank at London Road,
and eight counts of having a firearm or imitation firearm at the
time of the robberies. I waited for my solicitor, Ian Ryan, to
reach the station, and then I gave a no-comment interview. This
time there would be no deals or confessions. Due to my previous
convictions, I fell under the auspices of the Crimes and Sentencing
Act 1997, commonly known as the 'Two Strikes Act'. If I was
convicted on even one of the charges, I would receive an automatic life sentence. And with my record, and at my age, life could
very well mean life. I was not going to give up without a fight.

I was remanded to Belmarsh prison, the most secure remand
prison in London. Belmarsh was a shithole of the highest order.
Most of the screws were dogs, and it was almost as bad as being
back at Wandsworth. The only good thing about it was that I
met some good people there, like Leroy Skeete, an Eastender on
remand for murder, and Floyd Modeste, an armed robber from
west London who had been nicked for a robbery on a factory
specializing in computer chips. There was a lot of bang-up at
Belmarsh, but I enrolled on the education classes and did a
computer-literacy course. I spent my association time playing
kaluki with Billy Little, the Glasgow murderer who was later
such a big hit with jailed peer Jeffrey Archer that he devoted
plenty of space to him in his *Prison Diary*.

Ian Ryan came, and I laid out my defence for him. I knew
that the Flying Squad had the clothing and weapons that were
dumped after the camera-shop robbery, and they were saying that
they had got my DNA from 'a minute speck of blood found on
the inside of one of the gloves'. As these clothes matched the kit
in the security photographs of the Laughing Bank-Robbers jobs,

they felt it was enough to tie me to these robberies. They also had some good photographs of my face from the TSB robbery. I was going to admit that I had committed the TSB robbery, but my defence was one of 'duress'. In law a defence of duress can be used as a defence for armed robbery if the defendant can prove that he committed the crime because he feared for his life or the life of a member of his family. In order to prove duress, I sought advice from two of my old pals who really had been put under duress and forced to commit a robbery.

Alan Ward and Tony Baker, a couple of south London puff-dealers, were nicked for holding up a Halfords superstore in Croydon whilst posing as policemen. They had got in OK and secured the money, but made the classic mistake of allowing the shop manager to get within arm's reach of the gun. He was some sort of karate expert and managed to knock the gun from Tony's hand. A fight ensued that found the robbers outnumbered by shop staff and taking a terrible beating. The boys fought well and at one stage Tony managed to fight his way out of the shop to freedom, but realizing Alan was still inside being beaten by the staff, he ran back in to help his partner. The police arrived while the fight was still raging, and both the robbers were nicked.

I was good mates with Alan and Tony, and I had been up to visit them on several occasions while they were on remand at Highdown, so I was intimate with the details of their defence. They had bought £10,000 worth of cannabis on credit from a particularly violent dealer, and then had been ripped off themselves, leaving them with a ten-grand debt. The dealer and his gang paid the boys a visit that ended in Tony being beaten with baseball bats and having to be admitted to hospital. When he got out, the dealer paid them another visit, and this time he threatened to kill their families. So they had committed the Halfords robbery under duress.

At their first trial, which I attended, they were found guilty of robbery. Alan received a life sentence under the Two Strikes Act, because he had previously served a ten-year sentence for armed robbery, and Tony got a straight nine years, because he had no previous for violence and did not fall under Two Strikes. But soon after I was arrested the boys' convictions were quashed by the Appeal Court because the trial judge had not given the jury proper instructions on their duress defence. When I was nicked, they were back on remand awaiting a retrial, and it looked as though they might win.

I got in touch with them and asked them if they'd mind me tagging my duress defence on to theirs. I wanted to say that I had been a 'sleeping partner' in the original cannabis deal, and when they had been nicked, the dealer had then sought me out for payment, which is why I had been forced to commit the bungling robbery on the TSB. The boys agreed to give evidence in my defence if necessary. And what can you say about men like them? The old cliché, usually spouted by police officers in their memoirs, that there is 'no honour among thieves', is wrong. Some of the most generous and honourable men I have ever met are thieves and robbers.

My defence of duress only applied to the TSB robbery, where my face had been on show. The other seven robberies in the Laughing Bank-Robbers series showed only pictures of a gang of masked men and were obviously in a different league. I was denying these robberies completely, and there was little evidence to tie me to them. The Flying Squad knew I had done them, but proving it would be difficult. I should just mention that using the defence of duress does not mean you have to actually name the person who has put you under duress. In fact, it is more desirable to tell the jury that you are too much in fear for your family's safety to mention any names. Grassing someone, even someone who has put you under duress, is not acceptable under the criminal code.

In November 1998 I was committed for trial at the Old Bailey. I received a visit from Ian Ryan and the man who was to be my QC at the trial, Owen Davies. I told them that I wanted to come clean with the jury right from the start and tell them about my previous convictions. I wanted them to know that if they convicted me of these charges, I would be going to prison for life. The general public, of whom juries are made up, are constantly fed stories through the media about people who commit horrendous crimes only to receive slap-on-the-wrist sentences from feeble-minded judges. I wanted my jury to be sure of what was going to happen to me if they voted for conviction. I didn't want them to approach their deliberations with the thought that a finding of guilt would only result in a minor inconvenience for me. Nobody had been physically hurt on any of the robberies, and I was gambling on the jury seeing beyond the rhetoric of the prosecution and looking at the basics of the crime: nicking a few quid at the point of a gun. Does that really deserve a life sentence when people who abuse children and commit far worse crimes are given a lot less? I wanted the jury to ponder this before they gave the judge the nod to take what was left of my life.

Owen was not in favour of my plan, and said so. He seemed like a nice bloke, and he must have been good at his job or he would never have risen to QC, but I would have preferred Jim Sturman to be in charge of this case. Jim had been my barrister on previous cases, and he was sharper than a barber's razor and knew his game inside out. But the seriousness of the case warranted a QC, so Jim took a back seat as the junior on the job.

When I received my copy of the defence bundle, all the photographs and depositions that were to be used against me, I became aware of the extent of the police operation to nick me. I found out that I had been the subject of two separate police operations involving three of the four Flying Squad teams in London. Operation Roseman dealt with the Laughing Bank-Robbers case, and Operation Rene dealt with the TSB and my arrest. The names for police operations have nothing to do with the subject and are thrown up at random by a computer. From my copy of the Armed Operation Record I see that there were no less than five aborted armed operations against me, the earliest being on 23 March 1998, one month after I had left the Laughing Bank-Robbers. I don't know why the Flying Squad got tooled up on five occasions and then decided not to pounce. Maybe it was because I showed up with my daughter, or my girlfriend, or one of their informers. It remains classified information, and I don't suppose I'll ever know. I do know that my phone was tapped, because they used a tape of one of my phone calls in court and I was supplied with a transcript of a conversation between me and Alan Ward.

The strategy outlined in the Armed Operation Record by a Flying Squad Detective Chief Inspector named Buckell is to 'ambush' me in the commission of a robbery 'without endangering bank staff, public, police'. The tactics outlined are: 'To mount an Observation Post on suspect's home address. To support the operation with SOII surveillance. To have 3 gunships in a 6 shots attack convoy for the arrest. To use Cougar radio sets, and issue body-armour and high-visibility caps, and be aware that suspect has access to firearms, stolen cars, and radio-scanners.' Authorization was given for fifteen firearms to be used on the operation. There then follow guidelines on the use of minimum force.

The copy of the Briefing, which I have in my possession, states: 'Intelligence suggests that the target of this operation, Noel "Razor" Smith, is engaged in the commission of armed-robbery offences and currently has access to a stolen vehicle and firearms.' Then it has a description of me, along with details of all my known haunts, associates and addresses I have visited while under surveillance. There is also a surveillance photo of me getting into a car, and maps of the area where I was living.

These documents showed me that the Flying Squad had not just come to nick me on the off-chance. They had been watching and listening to me for a long time, and they didn't put this much work in for no result. They were going to be desperate for a conviction in this case. But I was equally, if not more, desperate for a not guilty.

Life went on at what passed for normal in Belmarsh. In January of 1999 I was informed that my parole licence from my previous sentence had been revoked and I was now convicted and serving the remainder of my fifteen years as well as on remand for the present charges. This made not a jot of difference to me, except that I was moved on to a convicted spur. In June 1999 ex-cabinet minister Jonathan Aitken was convicted of perjury at the Old Bailey, and sentenced to eighteen months' imprisonment. He was sent to Belmarsh, and ended up in a cell two doors away from me.

Jonathan's main problem at Belmarsh was not that he was an ex-Conservative minister so much as that he was a friend of ex-Home Secretary Michael Howard. Howard was so detested by prisoners that some of them still spat every time they said his name. As I've explained before, Howard is responsible for the hardships that prisoners still labour under today. I considered Aitken's position. If he didn't get stabbed or coshed by one of the publicity-hungry young bucks who knew they could gain instant celebrity status by such an act, he was in danger of a smack in the mouth by one of the older cons who knew of his friendship with Howard. I watched him for a while to see how he was going to handle himself in our world.

Aitken surprised me. He seemed to settle in very quickly and comported himself with bravery and dignity. He didn't ask for any favours and had shown a lot of courage by not asking to be put on the protection wing. I approached him and introduced myself.

'Do you know Michael Howard?' I asked.

He looked slightly puzzled at the question, then answered, 'Yes, I do, why do you ask?'

I gave him the old slow burn. 'He's a fucking dog,' I said. 'He's put back the cause of prisoners' rights by fifty years, and if he was standing there instead of you, I would already have slashed his face. Tell him that, next time you see him.'

Aitken looked taken aback. He smiled nervously. 'Actually,' he said, 'Michael is a very dear man, and I'm sure he does not deserve the response you mention.'

'Bollocks,' I growled. 'Even his underling [Ann Widdecombe], accused him of being the anti-Christ.'

He grinned reluctantly at this. Then he shrugged. 'Everyone is entitled to their opinion,' he said.

Despite myself I was warming to Aitken. Here he was, fresh

into a very hostile and unfamiliar environment, confronted by a sixteen-stone, tattooed monster, and yet I sensed very little fear in the man. It would have been easy for him to curry favour by agreeing with my comments about Howard, but he didn't. He was game, and he had shown loyalty to his friend, two qualities that are highly prized in prison. And that made him all right by me.

I put the word out that Aitken was to be left alone. And he was. I heard that a couple of mugs were planning to steal his letters from his cell in order to sell them to the newspapers, so I paid them a visit, along with a pal of mine from Essex, called Mickey the Fridge, and warned them off. Mickey was not called the Fridge because of his size, but because he was doing three years for nicking a fridge. But he was a game fella just the same.

In the next couple of weeks I spent a lot of time with Jonathan Aitken and got to know him about as well as you can know anyone in such a short time. I told him that I was a born-again atheist and a liberal communist, at which he chuckled. I also told him that I was a writer and aspiring journalist and asked him if he minded me writing about him. He said he didn't, and he would give me an exclusive interview, as long as I didn't sell it to the *Guardian*.

I sent my first three-thousand-word piece about Jonathan Aitken to Julian Broadhead in Sheffield, and asked him to punt about and see if there was any interest. Julian sent it to John McVicar, who almost broke his finger in his rush to snatch it. He phoned Belmarsh and left a message asking me to phone him as it was a 'family emergency'. When I got through to John he was proper buzzing. He wanted my piece for *Punch,* and he was willing to offer me £800 in cash and a three-page spread under my photograph and byline. I was delighted. I told him that Aitken had also agreed to an interview, and John said that *Punch* would also take that for a similar deal. This was real journalism.

My first piece on Aitken appeared in the 3 July issue, and was quickly pounced on by most of the national newspapers. I got a mention in *The Times*, the *Independent*, the *Daily Mirror* and the *Daily Mail.* The *Guardian*, for whom I had worked in the past, 'thugged' me off in their Diary column, saying in effect that I was

a mug for not slagging Aitken off enough. My interview with
Aitken made the front cover of *Punch* and even led to me being
mentioned in the Nigel Dempster column of the *Daily Mail*, being
slagged off by William Hague's aunt. I laughed all the way to the
bank!

In my opinion, Johnny Aitken is a good geezer who got in
over his head and suffered the consequences. All my life I have
been surrounded by violent men who would open you up like
a tin of beans on the slightest excuse, by rapists, granny-bashers,
child-killers and the scum of the earth. Compared to them, Aitken
is a geezer who told a few lies and got sussed out for it. I don't
agree with his politics, but as a man, he's OK by me. I am still
in regular contact with Johnny Aitken, and I'm pleased to say
that he has put the bad times behind him and found a genuine
peace with God. Good luck to him.

My trial at the Old Bailey came up in June 1999. The place
hadn't changed much since my first visit in 1977. The cells were
still filthy and covered in graffiti, with dried food and other things
stuck to the walls and ceilings. Instead of the old Brixton screws,
the court was now run by Securicor, or 'plastic screws' as they
were known to the prisoners. I was in Court 12, one of the
newly refurbished courts, in front of Judge Goldstein. Goldstein
was known to be fair in his summing-up but harsh in his
sentencing, but I was hoping never to witness him in a sentencing
mood. The prosecutor was John Kelsey-Fry, rumoured to be the
most effective prosecutor at the Bailey.

I was fairly happy with the jury, as there seemed to be a lot
of young people on it, and it's well known that young people
are less likely to convict. The trial lasted three weeks, of which
I spent four days in the box being cross-examined by Kelsey-
Fry. His opening question was about the glasses I was wearing.

'Mr Smith, I notice that you are sporting a pair of spectacles.
Yet in none of the surveillance photographs are you wearing
them. Isn't this just a ploy to distance yourself from descriptions
and incriminating photographs? Hm?'

He was so predictable. Ian Ryan had arranged for me to have

an eye test in Belmarsh, and we had my prescription on hand. I also had photographs of me wearing glasses in 1986, which proved they were not just an affectation for the jury. He was left red-faced.

His next question was equally embarrassing for him:

'Mr Smith, it is correct, is it not, that you have been described as a leading member of the London underworld?'

I leant forward and cupped my ear as though I had misheard him. 'The London Underground, sir? No, I have never worked for them, but I do have an uncle who worked for British Rail.' The jury showed a few grins.

Despite the shaky start, Kelsey-Fry proved to be a formidable opponent and by the end of the fourth day I was glad to leave the box.

Giving evidence for me were my father, my brother Mick, my now brother-in-law Tommy Hogan, and my cousin Michael Regan. On the prosecution side were a score of police officers and over one hundred bank staff and customers. It was a good job that they decided not to call them all or the trial might still be going on today. One thing that has always turned my stomach at trials is how big, hard coppers who are full of piss and vinegar on the streets and in police cells when giving me stick suddenly turn into sycophantic schoolboys when faced with a few geezers in wigs. The way the police grovel in court is a truly sickening phenomenon. I do not change my personality in the box, I just cut down on the fucks a bit.

The trial had some strange moments, including my cousin Michael's run-in with Kelsey-Fry over the English seasons. Michael, in his Dublin accent, gave evidence that he had seen me in a pub in Clapham at the hour I was accused of robbing a bank in Cricklewood. The exchange went something like this:

KELSEY-FRY: So, Mr Regan, you claim that you remember seeing Smith on this date? How can you be sure that it was 4 February?

MICHAEL: I remember the day because it was the winter, and I only seen him once that winter.

K-F: But how can you be so sure that it was that day in particular?

M: Because it was fucking freezing!

K-F: Yes, yes. But how do you know it was 4 February?

M: Well, I don't know about youse Brits, but in Ireland we have our winter in February. Maybe February is summer to youse, but in Ireland it's definitely winter.

K-F: (*showing signs of frustration*) Right. But how can you be sure it was 4 February?

M: (*casually*) It was me birthday, and Razor came to the pub for me party.

John McVicar offered to give evidence for me as a character witness, but Owen thought it might do more harm than good to have a former Public Enemy Number One saying what a nice guy I was. And in the end we decided against calling Alan and Tony, who were just about to start their new trial for the Halfords robbery. After three weeks of evidence, Judge Goldstein summed up in a fair and impartial manner, and the jury retired to consider their verdict.

When the jury had been out for three days without reaching a verdict, the buzz around the Old Bailey was that I was going to walk. The police witnesses had been less than impressive in the box, and one in particular had been proved to be lying on oath. The waiting was terrible, but a general rule of thumb about juries is that the longer they stay out, the more likely they are to acquit.

On the afternoon of the second day Judge Goldstein had called the jury back in and told them that if they couldn't reach unanimous verdicts, he would accept majority verdicts. At the end of the fourth day the jury were called back into court. The clerk asked them if they had reached a majority verdict on any of the sixteen counts on the indictment.

The foreman of the jury answered, 'No.'

Judge Goldstein then turned to the foreman and said, 'Just answer this question "yes" or "no". If I were to give you another day of deliberations, do you think you would be able to reach any sort of verdict on any of the sixteen counts?'

The foreman smiled. 'Not if we sat here till Christmas,' he replied.

Goldstein also smiled. 'A simple "yes" or "no" would have sufficed,' he said. 'But I take your point.'

Goldstein had no choice but to dismiss the jury and order a retrial.

A retrial was not as good as a not guilty, but it was the next best thing. It meant that all I needed in the next trial was three jurors to hold out and believe my story, and the charges would be dropped and I would walk! In effect the first trial had been fought to a draw, and this was further underlined when my sister Samantha spoke to one of the jurors outside the court and asked her what the score had been in the jury room. 'Six–six,' she was told.

I now had a choice to make. My defence team had other cases lined up, so they told me that if I were to agree to have the retrial straight away, then I would have the same team. If on the other hand I wanted to wait, it might be six months before we could get another date. I was feeling lucky. I agreed to go on again straight away. The first jury were discharged on Thursday evening, and my new trial began on the following Monday morning.

Almost from the start of the new trial I knew I had made the wrong decision. I should have waited and given the dust time to settle. It seemed as though the system, outraged at how close I had come to acquittal in the first trial, was now pulling out all the stops. My case was moved from the modern, bright and airy Court 12 to the old-fashioned, dusty gloom of Court 2, the very court where I had been weighed off with my detention sentence in 1977. Courts 1 and 2 are normally reserved for high-profile murder and terrorism cases, and the air of gravitas there could only work in favour of the Crown.

My new trial judge was Walter Aylen QC, a Recorder, and my new jury was made up almost exclusively of women over the age of fifty. There were two men: one was about sixty with an RAF-type moustache who looked as though he might live in Tunbridge Wells and spend all his spare time writing letters to the *Daily Mail* bemoaning the lack of discipline in society since National Service and hanging were abolished; the other man was in his forties and seemed very nervous around so many old women. He spent most of the trial with his head on his chest, refusing to look above shoulder-height.

The right for the defendant in criminal trials to object to certain jurors has long gone. I was stuck with this jury, and from the looks they were giving me before the opening speeches had even been heard, a life sentence would be too good for the likes of me. Judge Aylen was a fat man, and whoever decreed that all fat people are supposed to be jolly could not have had him in mind. He did make the occasional quip, only to spoil the effect by repeating it *ad nauseam* until even the grovelling Flying Squad officers found it hard to keep a polite smile on their faces. And the kind of looks Judge Aylen gave me at certain moments during the trial would have led to violence between us had he given me those same looks anywhere but from the bench.

Kelsey-Fry was prosecuting once again, and he had learned from his mistakes in the first trial. The police officer who had caused the prosecution so much damage by lying under oath in the first trial was dropped completely. There was nothing we could do about it as he was a prosecution witness. Once again I gave a virtuoso performance in the box, but my wit and intelligence were wasted on this jury!

The jury went out for deliberations at 4.30 on the afternoon of 27 July. They were back with unanimous verdicts by 11.30 the next morning. Bearing in mind that they were sent home at 5.30, and back in court at 10 a.m. to continue, it took them two and a half hours to reach unanimous verdicts on sixteen counts, when the previous jury were still split after four days! It was almost as though they had been hand-picked for the job.

I knew that if I was found guilty on even one of the counts, I would get an automatic life sentence. So when the forewoman announced 'Guilty' to count one, the rest of the guiltys became academic. I lost my temper.

'You fucking useless mongs!' I shouted at the jury. 'Thank you very much for giving me a life sentence. I hope all your kids have bald heads and walk sideways!'

I just said the first thing that came into my head. The Securicor guards who were in the dock with me made a move to grab me. I shook them off.

'Touch me again, and I'll break your fucking jaw,' I warned them.

One of them pressed his panic alarm and guards came charging up the stairs into the dock and we had a bit of a struggle.

All through this mayhem in the dock, the clerk was still reading out the counts and asking for verdicts. The jury looked horrified and at the same time totally vindicated. Judge Aylen looked smug. The Flying Squad team were all smiles and patting each other on the back. Up in the public gallery, I could hear Samantha and Lindsey sobbing.

After a brief scuffle, I gave up and stood there, surrounded by Securicor staff. The last verdict of guilty had been read, and it was now time for me to face my sentence. Jim Sturman got up to try a bit of mitigation before the judge unloaded on me. Owen Davies had left the case before the closing speeches because an old 'school chum' of his, Lord Melchett, had been nicked up north for damaging a field of GM crops.

I have in front of me a copy of Judge Walter Aylen's sentencing remarks. He said, 'You are a man of intelligence and wit. However, you used those skills to persuade the Parole Board to release you on parole, and returned to a life of crime very quickly. Armed robbery is dangerous and vicious and terrifies cashiers and customers. You have humiliated decent people and herded customers like cattle. In view of your previous convictions and the circumstances of these offences I would have had to consider a life sentence in any case. You are a danger to society. Despite these considerations I would not have imposed a life sentence but would have sentenced you to a period of eighteen years' imprisonment, which I would have reduced by one year for the time you have spent in custody. Bearing in mind that I have the power to set a tariff greater than half the determinate sentence that I would have imposed, I hereby sentence you to a life sentence on each of the eight counts of robbery. And a period of ten years' imprisonment on each of the eight counts of possession of a firearm with intent. I set your minimum tariff at eleven years, before which you should not be considered for parole. Take him down.'

And that was that. Eight life sentences. If I had killed a customer on each robbery I still couldn't have received a longer sentence. But after my initial outburst in the dock, I took it calmly. Nobody had forced me to rob banks. I did it because I was greedy and lazy and I liked it. And there was no point screaming and crying now that I had to pay for my actions. The code says, 'Be a man in the face of adversity.' No drama, as we say in jail.

The reality of my sentence is this. It was later cut to a minimum tariff of nine years at the Court of Appeal. After I have served nine years, I become eligible for parole. But no lifer is ever granted first parole, and the minimum 'knockback', the period you must wait before applying again, is two years. A high-profile, long-tariff 'danger to the public' like me can expect at least three two-year knockbacks, so I can reasonably expect to serve a minimum of fifteen years before I am released, perhaps longer, depending on my behaviour. I will be fifty-three years old the next time I see the streets.

27. Some Regrets

For the first year after being sentenced I was held at Belmarsh as a Category A prisoner. I spent most of my time writing complaints and petitions for myself and other prisoners. I was still writing for the *New Law Journal, Prison Writing* and *Inside-Time*, and I was Prisons correspondent for *Punch*. I also started to write a book about the exploits of the Balham Wildkatz. I had many years to serve, and I was determined to spend a lot of them improving my writing. I wrote a letter to Will Self, and asked him to have a look at my attempt at a book and see if he had any advice. Will wrote back and seemed interested, so we exchanged a few more letters.

I was still in touch with Denise and the kids by phone and letter. Our relationship was friendly. My youngest son, Joe, had started getting into trouble with the police through drunkenness and violence. I thought it was just a phase he was going through on his way to adulthood, but Denise thought he was taking after me. I couldn't help wondering if my absence had anything to do with it. I had come back into his life with promises to stay, and then I had gone again.

We arranged for Joe to visit me with his probation officer in Belmarsh. We had a good visit, but our conversation was slightly stilted by the fact that his probation officer was present throughout. I tried to explain to Joe that crime was not the answer and that he should put it all behind him and settle down. I felt like a proper hypocrite, sitting there preaching to my son about going straight from the inside of a prison. But we had a good laugh together as well, and when it was time to go we embraced awkwardly. It was on the tip of my tongue to tell him I loved him, but with the distance between us and the probation officer looking on, I just patted him on the shoulder instead. That was the last time I saw Joe alive.

Belmarsh, like all of the local prisons, was packed out with lifers due to the Two Strikes Act. We were being told that most of us would be held in Belmarsh for a minimum of two more years. Belmarsh has nothing to offer by way of amenities to men serving long sentences, so I decided that the time for action was now. In July 2000, I organized a sit-down on the exercise yard for the lifers. We were protesting about the lack of facilities and hoping for quicker transfers. In the end only nineteen of us, from a lifer population of fifty, stayed on the yard and refused to come in.

We stayed there until a senior officer came to listen to our grievances. Then, surrounded by screws with snarling Alsatian dogs, we took a slow amble around the yard before going in. We wanted to show the screws that they couldn't intimidate us.

The next morning, 4 July 2000, my door was flung open and I was on the move. Also on the move were the other two organizers of the sit-down, Johnny 'Little Socks' and Douggie. Johnny went to Wormwood Scrubs, Douggie went to Swaleside, and I was on my way to the most secure dispersal prison in the country, Whitemoor.

The principal officer of Houseblock 1 was waiting in reception to see me off.

'I'll be glad to see the back of you, Smith,' he said. 'Perhaps now I'll have time for other things instead of your fucking complaints.'

'Fuck you,' was my parting shot. But I was glad to be leaving Belmarsh.

Belmarsh was the only prison that ever tried to censor my writing. I was even threatened with solitary if I persisted in writing about prison for magazines like *Punch* and the *Big Issue*. All of my outgoing mail was scrutinized by the security department for articles, so I took to dictating my copy over the phone during association periods. They still listened in and taped all my phone calls, but there was little they could do except deliberately cut me off – which they did frequently. They also managed to convey their displeasure in other ways. I was often subject to strip- and cell-searches, far more often than most Category A prisoners expect. During one search by the DST, after *Punch* had published one of my particularly uncomplimentary articles about them, I returned to my cell to find not only the standard wreckage, but that one of the spiteful bastards had bent my radio aerial into a U-shape. I just carried on writing complaints and articles about them. The war between me and the system was far from over, but it was now more of a cold war.

I arrived in HMP Whitemoor in the afternoon. Whitemoor had a pretty bad reputation for violence. It had only been open for nine years but had suffered several riots and periods of unrest, including one riot in the first two weeks of its existence. There had been the much-publicized escape from the SSU, and the deaths in separate incidents, of two prison officers, who had been on their way to give evidence in the trial of the escapers. There had also been the murder, by other prisoners, of an infamous nonce the press had nicknamed 'Catweazle'. Plenty of screws had been stabbed, and two had been seriously attacked and retired by a prisoner armed with a pot full of boiling oil. Tony Hogan had almost lost an eye there when he was attacked by several prisoners over a £30 drug debt. Whitemoor was not for the faint-hearted.

To me, Whitemoor was like coming home. I was put on 'Beirut', Red Spur on A-wing, which was full of bad boys. There are three spurs on each wing, Red, Blue and Green, and each holds fifty prisoners. The average sentence at Whitemoor is twenty years, but there are plenty of men serving sentences of thirty years and above. Red Spur was a retirement-home for the subversive prison faces of the 1980s and 90s, a scrap-yard full of slightly rusty and obsolete war-machines that were still capable of inflicting devastating damage if you were to press the right button. I settled in fine.

I no longer had the urge to try and escape. My sense of freedom was still strong and the desire to be free is something that can never quite be extinguished, but I am resigned to serving my sentence. Once I reached the age of forty, the thought of life on the run and all the bollocks it entails kind of lost its allure for me. I've shot my bolt as far as trying to escape is concerned.

I quickly fell into a routine at Whitemoor and the time seemed to pass very fast. Prisoners are allowed to cook their own food, so there is a small kitchen at the end of each spur. Prisoners form themselves into 'food-boats', clubbing together in small groups to purchase food, cook and eat together. On my food-boat was Greg 'Houdini' Crabtree, Gary Staggs, who left eight screws bloody and battered in the wake of his own spectacular escape from a prison van, and John 'Shotgun' Shelley, an East End post-office robber and gunman serving fifteen years for blasting a drug-dealer in the head with a sawn-off 16-gauge shotgun. Another face we broke bread with was Bill 'Mr Angry' James, from Bermondsey, who, when not turning into the Incredible Hulk, made a mean spaghetti bolognaise.

The premier food-boat on Red Spur was known as 'The Bears', due to its members' huge size and the gargantuan meals they ate. The Bears consisted of Big Mitch, a six-foot-three, sixteen-stone Essex face with previous for armed robbery but now serving fifteen years for a cocaine conspiracy, plus the last two surviving members of a gang of robbers who were known as 'The Wild Bunch' in their heyday, Frannie P. and Charlie T. Charlie and Frannie are serving thirty years apiece for armed robbery and shooting a security guard. The head of the Flying Squad, speaking to reporters after the lads were weighed off, called them the 'two most dangerous robbers in the country'. Both ex-boxers and tipping the scales at seventeen stone, Charlie and Frannie are true Bears. Also on the Bears boat were three others who more than made up for their lack of bulk with their heavyweight reputations in the criminal world. Johnny Kendall, serving thirty-four years for armed robbery and escaping from Gartree prison in a helicopter; Billy C., serving eighteen years for organizing and leading the Dome robbery, in which he attempted to steal the Millennium Diamond using a JCB and little Tony Ward who, with one eye, one lung and weighing ten stone, had been a thorn in the side of the Flying Squad since the 1970s.

With this calibre of prisoners all on one spur, it's no wonder the screws tend to talk softly and keep their big sticks well hidden. My food-boat and the Bears' food-boat often teamed up together on special occasions, like Christmas dinner and bank holidays, and we would put all the tables together and sit down for a decent meal. And the talk at the dinner table is not always about crime; sometimes we discuss classical music (like who recorded 'Roll Over, Beethoven') or politics ('Yeah, I'd rump Edwina Currie, but I draw the line at Maggie Thatcher') or medicine ('I'm sure I've caught Vietnamese foot-rot from that fucking shower-room'). And with good food, good company and such conversations, we while away the long years.

I get up at 7.45 in the morning, have a cup of tea, a smoke and a shower. At 9.00 I collect my cleaning equipment and begin my job of cleaning the one's-landing and shower room, for which I am paid the princely sum of £8 per week. I finish work at 10.00 and get in an hour at the typewriter before exercise at 11.00. Lunch is served at 11.45, and at 12.15 we are all locked away in our cells until 1.45, then it's back to work until 4.15. At 4.45 we are again locked in our cells until 5.45. Dinner is served at 6.00, and then we are allowed to associate until 7.45. By 8.00 we are all once again locked in for the night. And I go through this routine every day. except weekends, when we are locked up for the night at 4.45. The routine is occasionally changed when there is a major stabbing. or a fire or a tool goes missing from one of the workshops. Then we stay locked in our cells for several days while searching and police investigations take their course.

On the whole, the screws at Whitemoor are a pretty decent bunch, with one or two exceptions among the SOs, and they fully realize that they are dealing with men who have little or nothing to lose. The atmosphere on the spurs is relaxed, and time seems to pass quickly. But we are not really living; we are existing in a vacuum, marking time until someone gives us the order to 'march on' to the next phase of our imprisonment. But outside the prison walls life goes on for our families and loved ones, and though we usually know little about it except what we are able to hear on the phone, during visits and through letters, all of which are monitored and scrutinized by the system, sometimes we are wrenched from our prison-induced torpor and forced to face the consequences of our actions.

My son Joe was getting into a lot of serious trouble. He was nicked for GBH and affray and was put on remand at Feltham young offenders prison. I wrote to him to let him know how disappointed I was that he seemed to be following in my footsteps. It is terrible for any parent to think of one of their children locked up in prison, but when that parent has already experienced the full horror of imprisonment and knows exactly what the child is going through, it is doubly gut-wrenching. We all want better than we had for our children, and for me, Joe being in prison brought home just what a failure I had been as a father. I felt responsible for my son being locked up, because I had not been there for him. Despite the bravado of his crimes, Joe was not a strong kid. He suffered terribly with Crohn's disease, and at one stage his weight had dropped to eight stone, and I worried how he was faring in the violent arena of one of the worst young-offender prisons in this country.

We exchanged many letters over the next few months, and through these I thought I gained an insight into my son's mind. He seemed to be getting along OK and had got a job in the kitchens and enrolled on a computer-study class. He wrote to me that he realized that he didn't want to spend his life in prison, and that he was ready to start a new life when he got out. As the months went by and we exchanged more letters I began to worry less about Joe. He was a good-hearted, intelligent kid who had made a few mistakes, but he was not a hard-core criminal like me. He seemed to be handling his time inside well and was looking forward to getting out. Denise, Lianne and Dean, along with Dean's girlfriend, Danielle, went up to see him in Feltham every week. But I breathed a sigh of relief when, after several months, the charges against Joe were dropped, and he was released.

I spoke to Joe on the phone a couple of times after he got out, and life seemed to be going well for him. He was working with Denise's dad, doing a bit of building work. I was really pleased that Joe had come through his experience of prison and was now ready to settle down. I remember telling Denise on the phone that it had only been a phase he had been going through and there was now nothing to worry about. On 22 October 2001 I spoke to Joe on the phone. He was very cheerful, and he told me all about his job, and we discussed how Chelsea were doing in the Premiership. Before my units ran out I asked him to put his mum on the phone, and we spoke about how pleased we both were that Joe was doing so well.

The most heart-stopping sight for any prisoner is the sight of the vicar wanting to see him. Vicars in prison never deliver good news, and even the sight of one striding down a landing is enough to quicken the pulse of the hardest men in the jail and make them whisper a silent prayer that it will not be their cell door he will be stopping at. A vicar at your door means tragedy and death amongst those you love on the outside.

On 24 October 2001, at 6.05, I walked back from the central hotplate on A-wing with my evening meal. I was talking to a big Geordie named Bud when I noticed a look of fear flit across his face. I followed his gaze and saw the vicar waiting outside my cell. The vicar had a sad look on his face, and I knew straight away that someone I loved was dead. I didn't want to hear it. I walked straight past him and into my cell and put my plate down.

'Are you Noel Smith?' he asked me.

'Fuck off,' I said. 'Get away from my door. You've got the wrong cell.'

He apologized and walked away, but I knew he would soon be back when he checked with the screws.

I sat on my bed and began to shake uncontrollably. I couldn't stop shaking. I looked at the door, willing the vicar to keep away and not come back. As long as I didn't know what he was trying to tell me, it couldn't have happened. There was a light knock on the door and the vicar pushed it open and stepped inside.

'Go away,' I said again, but there was no strength in my voice.

'I'm afraid it's your son, Joseph.'

'No,' I said.

The vicar continued. 'There's no other way of saying this. I'm sorry to have to tell you, he's dead.'

Of all the names that ran through my mind the moment I saw the vicar, Joe's was not one of them. He was only nineteen. I had only spoken to him two days before. How could he be dead?

'No,' I said. 'You've made a mistake. It's not my Joe. I spoke to him a couple of days ago.'

The vicar read from a scrap of paper. 'You're supposed to phone your wife, er, Denise?'

And that's when I knew it was true. I ignored the vicar and walked over to the phone on the one's-landing. My hands were shaking so much I had to dial the number twice before I got it right. Denise picked up the phone on the first ring.

'It's not true, is it?' I asked.

And when she started sobbing my last shred of hope was ripped away. I went back to my cell and cried like a baby in the darkness.

The next few days are a blur. My mates rallied round, and most of the screws were brilliant. The vicar was also a big help. But at times like that the only people you really want to see are your close family. I got the story of what had happened over the phone from Denise. Apparently Joe had been getting along great and was happier than he had been for ages. He had met up with my daughter, Lianne, and a few friends at Morden station and, after having a chat, he told Lianne he was going to the toilet and would be back in five minutes. He never came back. The next day the police, called to a completely unconnected incident, found him hanging from a staircase in an alley. The coroner found no drugs in his system and recorded an open verdict. The immediate area was covered by CCTV, but, to this day the police have refused to hand over the tapes. No one will tell us how Joe died, or why.

I assumed that because I was now a Category B prisoner I would be allowed to go to Joe's funeral. I didn't expect to be allowed out on my own, even though I would have handed myself back in if I had been. There was no way I would dishonour the memory of my son by using his funeral as an excuse to escape.

High-risk Category A prisoners had been allowed escorted visits to family funerals, so I really thought I would have no trouble. But like I've said before, the prison system has a long memory.

I made my application to attend the funeral and was called in front of the security governor. He said he was not prepared to 'risk the safety' of his officers by allowing me even an escorted visit. I did everything but get down on my knees and beg, but he assured me it wasn't going to happen. I left the office bitter and angry. I had spent most of my life proving to the prison system what a dangerous man I was, teaching them never to turn their backs on me for fear of being attacked. And now it had all backfired on me. The one time I needed them to trust me, they threw my previous record back in my face.

If they wouldn't allow me to go to my son's funeral, I decided I was going to stage something spectacular to mark his passing. I wanted to lash out and hurt someone, preferably representatives of the system. Luckily, wiser heads prevailed on me to 'hold it down'. Kevin Lane, a lifer who had lost his wife while in jail, and Steve Montgomery and Greg Crabtree spent hours talking to me and trying to calm me down. It was Kevin who told me that even if I couldn't go to the funeral I was legally entitled to visit the Chapel of Rest. I was about to apply for this when I was called to the office and told that I was being taken to the Chapel of Rest at that very moment.

I wasn't allowed to get on the phone and let anyone know I was coming, and they took me straight from the office to reception. My dad had sent in a set of suitable clothes for me to wear to the funeral, and I now changed into them to visit the Chapel of Rest.

The journey to Sutton took nearly three hours. I was double-cuffed and escorted by three screws and a driver. There was very little conversation in the van. I didn't feel like talking, and the screws were afraid of saying the wrong thing. I hardly even bothered looking through the window at the outside world, I kept my head down and thought of Joe. At least I would get to see him one more time.

It was around lunchtime when the van pulled into the alley behind the funeral parlour. There was no back way into the place, so I was marched along the busy shopping parade and in through the front door. By sheer coincidence, Denise and Lianne had to visit the funeral parlour to organize some flowers, and they had got there ten minutes before I arrived. The receptionist had received a phone call from the escort telling her I was on my way, and she had told Denise. Dean was working nearby, so Denise phoned him and told him to come as well. So when I got there my family were waiting for me. It was the first time in years that the family were all under the same roof at the same time. Joe had brought us all together.

Trying to comfort my family whilst double-cuffed to a screw was uncomfortable and humiliating. When I went in to see my son lying in his coffin, I was very aware of the uniformed stranger attached to my side. As I bent down to kiss my son the hand-cuffs made it so awkward that both me and the screw almost toppled on to the coffin. I felt ashamed that I was seeing Joe for the last time like this.

I got to spend a short time with Denise, Dean and Lianne. We were devastated and heartbroken, but I was proud of the way they were struggling to face up to everything. All too soon it was time for me to be taken back to prison. My whole life I had prided myself on being a man and doing the 'right thing', and now I had to leave my grieving family to cope on their own. As I was driven away and saw them huddled there on the pavement I felt like a rat.

On the day of Joe's funeral I was allowed to visit the prison chapel alone for fifteen minutes, to say my goodbyes. The funeral was attended by nearly sixty youngsters who were friends of Joe's and wanted to pay their last respects, and I received letters and cards from a lot of his friends. I was proud that my son had inspired such loyalty in so many people during his short life. And I wish I had got to know him better while he was still here.

Joe's death had a profound effect on me. In the weeks and months after his funeral I did a lot of thinking, and I was forced to face up to the frightening fact that choices I had made in my life had not only affected me but had consequences for many other people, including my children. I had been strutting about in a dreamworld, full of myself and too busy with macho posturing to notice other people. What was I? I wasn't some heroic Robin Hood figure. Yes, I stole from the rich, but I didn't give the money to the poor. So what if I had morals about the crimes I committed? Did that make me any less a thief and a thug? Joe dying so young made me realize just how I had squandered my own life. And for what? So that other criminals could say, 'There goes Razor Smith, he's a diamond geezer. One of our own.' Did I really give a shit how I was perceived by others of my ilk? We classed straight-goers as mugs and told each other stories of how we had outsmarted straight society while sitting in top-security prisons with real life passing us by. Who were the real mugs, I now wondered.

I had chosen this life. And though, once my choice had been made, no serious effort had ever been made to show me any other path, it was my own stubbornness and stupidity that led me to where I am today. In some ways I was a 'product of the system', but I had entered that system with my eyes wide open and of my own free will. I have to admit it, I liked committing crimes, I liked my status as one of the Chaps and I loved fighting the system. As John McVicar once said, 'Being a criminal is a great life. The only trouble is they put you in prison for it.'

I am now forty-two years old and, including periods of remand and numerous short sentences throughout the 1980s, I have spent nearly twenty-one years in prison. And it's not over yet. I am sick and tired of both crime and prison, and writing this book has been an emotional journey for me. I have had to go back to times and places that would have been best left in darkness and unvisited. But by shining a light on these places I can now see exactly where I went wrong. And that is a major step on the road to self-rehabilitation. In order to change, you must first want to change; and then you must review the mistakes you have already made and make the conscious decision not to make them again.

I recently made an application for a referral to HMP Grendon,

which is one of the few prisons in this country that is totally geared
up to rehabilitate prisoners. It is a therapeutic community and the
emphasis is on group-work. HMP Grendon has the lowest reconviction rate in the whole prison estate, which just goes to show
that if the prison system was really interested in rehabilitating prisoners, then it could be done. Grendon is voluntary, but the prisoner
must pass an IQ test and have several reports compiled on him by
prison staff before being accepted. I am hoping that Grendon will
consolidate the work on myself that I have already started.

But in the meantime I remain at Whitemoor. Another old pal
arrived the other day, Dave Croke, who I used to walk the yards
with back in Albany in 1990. Dave was convicted of being a
hitman for millionaire Nicholas van Hoogstraten and received a
life sentence at the end of that much-publicized case. He's sixty
years old, and unless he wins his appeal he is sure to die in prison.
Another ex-Albany boy, Kenny Noye, is also here and facing the
same fate. And still we come back for more.

Some people may wonder at my extraordinary memory of
events, some of which occurred more than a quarter of a century
ago. Part of it is that prison is so boring that we have little to do
except to remember and relive events that have been important
to us. Prison is mostly routine interspersed with periods of violent
excitement, and we remember anything that smashes the same-
ness of the long prison days. I still meet people in prison who say,
'Oh, yeah, you bashed the night-watchman in Rochester in '77!'
The world of prison is a small and insular one. But another reason
for my amazing recall is that I recently applied for copies of my
prison records under the provisions of the Data Protection Act.

I was supplied with 1,500 pages of history, dating back to 1977,
and at least that many pages were missing. There are certain documents that the system is not obliged to supply, particularly those
relating to Security Information Reports (SIRs) about the prisoner. I was not surprised to see that my medical records from
1977 to 1979 were missing. I still do not know the exact drugs
they forced on me. But some of the documents were pretty
revealing.

Report after report describes me as 'below average intelligence', and one document, written by a prison probation officer, states, 'At Send Detention Centre Smith was assessed as one of a circuit of boys destined to remain in penal institutions for most of their lives.' The fact that they were proved right is not what now bothers me, but rather that they had been willing to write me off at the age of fifteen, and how reports like this affected the way in which I was handled by the system. At that early stage in my criminal career I was still malleable enough to be pushed in a different direction. I don't say it would have made much difference if someone in authority had taken the time to give me a good talking-to instead of consigning my life to the penal dustbins, but it might have.

All of the documents I have been supplied tell only one side of the story and, as per prison-service procedure, all of the names of the people who made these reports have been removed. Its almost as though they are now ashamed of what they have written. And you have to bear in mind the fact that when these reports were written, there was no Data Protection Act and the writers never dreamed that I would one day be able to read them. No names, but their titles remain.

According to these reports, I am 'neurotic', an 'emotionally flat individual' of 'somewhat unstable temperament' who is 'prone to bouts of irrational violence'. One memorandum from the governor of Rochester borstal to the Regional Director of Prisons concerning my attempted escape and assault on the night-watchman is very interesting, as it states that I assaulted him with 'a broom handle', when I know I used a bucket. It also states that the Prison Officers' Association had informed the governor that its members feel 'unable to work on C-wing with the kind of trainees we have at this establishment'. The governor states that he had to ship out several prisoners and agree to an extra night-patrol officer in order to placate the POA. It is no wonder the system held me in such 'high regard' when my actions were causing them such trouble.

There is no mention in any of this documentation about the

violence I suffered at the hands of prison staff, and I wouldn't expect there to be. The POA, backed by the Home Office, will always vehemently deny that they assault, torture and ill-treat prisoners, even when their members are convicted and jailed for it. But you would expect that, it's all part of the game. I will say this though: the prison system of today is a lot different from how it was in the 1970s, 80s and 90s. I still hear of prisoners being assaulted by screws in places like the Close Control Unit at HMP Woodhill, and in some of the local jails like Highdown and Belmarsh, but, on the whole, there is a lot less of it going on than there used to be.

In telling my story I have used false names, nicknames or just first names for most of the people who have been involved in crime. I have used full names only in cases where I have the permission of those people to mention them. I have also used the full names of Peter 'Pete the Nut' Mayne, 'Scotch' Andy Philipson and Mark O'Brien, because these men are now dead and far beyond the reach of the police. No other persons have ever been arrested or convicted for the crimes of 'The Laughing Bank-Robbers'. The names I have used for other members of the team are all false.

I have lived my life abiding by a strange criminal code of honour. And, despite the many vicious and heinous crimes I have committed, the code allows me to face my reflection in any mirror and not suffer too much shame. I did what I felt I had to do at the time, and I do not have the power to change any of it. I have hurt many people, and not only physically. But my biggest regret is the pain I have caused my family. My children were forced to grow up without a father. And my son, Joseph, died alone.

I sometimes wish I could have my time all over again, as we all do, and perhaps I would settle down and become a bus driver or a brick-layer. I would never have to smell the blood I have spilled, or sleep with a gun under my pillow, or examine every new face I met for bad intent. I'd live a quiet life, eating my dinner in front of the telly every evening and going to bed early to be up for work in the morning. But even in the depth of these idle daydreams there is always a small voice coming from some part of me that will for ever contain a residue of adrenaline addiction mixed with molten rage that whispers, 'Who are you trying to kid?'

This is the story of my life. And in the end it was not imprisonment that sowed the seeds of rehabilitation in my mind. It took the death of my son, and the discovery that I had a talent for something other than crime. I no longer feel the need to affirm my own existence by putting a blade across someone's face, or by taking a sawn-off shotgun into a bank. I have found a more acceptable way of expressing myself. I write. Unfortunately for all concerned, it has come a little too late. I already owe the greater part of what's left of my life to HMP. And there will be those in society, particularly the victims of my many crimes, who may think that it will not be nearly enough to cover my debts. Sometimes sorry just isn't enough.

Like the ghost of Jacob Marley, I have spent my life carefully fashioning the chains that now bind me, link by link. And in mitigation I offer only this: I never slashed a face that wasn't looking at me, and I never robbed a bank that wasn't insured.

He just wanted a decent book to read ...

Not too much to ask, is it? It was in 1935 when Allen Lane, Managing Director of Bodley Head Publishers, stood on a platform at Exeter railway station looking for something good to read on his journey back to London. His choice was limited to popular magazines and poor-quality paperbacks – the same choice faced every day by the vast majority of readers, few of whom could afford hardbacks. Lane's disappointment and subsequent anger at the range of books generally available led him to found a company – and change the world.

'We believed in the existence in this country of a vast reading public for intelligent books at a low price, and staked everything on it'
Sir Allen Lane, 1902–1970, founder of Penguin Books

The quality paperback had arrived – and not just in bookshops. Lane was adamant that his Penguins should appear in chain stores and tobacconists, and should cost no more than a packet of cigarettes.

Reading habits (and cigarette prices) have changed since 1935, but Penguin still believes in publishing the best books for everybody to enjoy. We still believe that good design costs no more than bad design, and we still believe that quality books published passionately and responsibly make the world a better place.

So wherever you see the little bird – whether it's on a piece of prize-winning literary fiction or a celebrity autobiography, political tour de force or historical masterpiece, a serial-killer thriller, reference book, world classic or a piece of pure escapism – you can bet that it represents the very best that the genre has to offer.

Whatever you like to read – trust Penguin.